RAMALA

A School on Earth
teaching
The Truth of The Heavens

THE VISION
of
RAMALA

SAFFRON WALDEN
THE C. W. DANIEL COMPANY LIMITED

First published in Great Britain in 1991 by
The C. W. Daniel Company Limited
1 Church Path, Saffron Walden
Essex, England

ISBN 85207 231 7

Set in 10pt Times
by MS Typesetting, Castle Camps, Cambridge
and printed by Hillman Printers (Frome) Ltd, Frome, Somerset

'The purpose of any book, of any vision, is simply to stimulate your own knowingness, to bring forth your own aspect of trust.'

The Ramala Source

DEDICATION

We dedicate this book to the Source of all Wisdom and to all those who serve that Source.

ACKNOWLEDGEMENT

We would like to express our gratitude to all those who have given so generously of themselves in order to make this book possible. Its production has truly been a combined effort, with many individuals contributing in thought, word and deed. To all of them we would like to say a heartfelt 'Thank you'.

CONTENTS

INTRODUCTION

This is the third and last book in the trilogy of teachings published by
The Ramala Centre. It brings to an end a process that began over twenty
years ago, for it was in 1970, soon after David and Ann, the channels
for the teachings, had married that the Ramala Teachers first made
contact. Twenty one years have sped by and during that period
hundreds of talks have been recorded on almost every topic of human
endeavour and enquiry. Thousands of words have been transcribed and
just a small percentage of these have been disseminated in the form of
three books. In 1978 The Revelation of Ramala was first published and
has now been reprinted four times. In 1986 The Wisdom of Ramala was
first published and has now been reprinted once. Both of these books
have also been published in foreign languages. Now, in 1991, we have
The Vision of Ramala and the original prophecy of the Ramala
Teachers has been completely fulfilled. For right from the very
beginning they had said that one day we would create a spiritual school,
a School on Earth teaching the Truth of the Heavens, based on their
teachings, and that we would publish three books which would circulate
all over the globe. Little did we believe them, then, and yet today The
Ramala Centre flourishes in Glastonbury and the three books are a
living reality!

As with the first two books, so this book too is published
anonymously. This is not done out of a sense of false modesty or from a
desire to avoid contact with the general public, but simply to make it
clear that neither of the instruments for the channellings are the source
of the teachings. As the Ramala Teachers are so often saying, when you
listen to a radio, what is important is not the radio but the programme
on the radio. Of course the quality of the radio determines the clarity
with which you receive the programme and in this respect David and
Ann do affect the teachings, but the understandings of life expressed,
the soul consciousness manifested, is not theirs. They, just like the
reader, are struggling to come to terms with the reality of the world in

which they live. They, just like the reader, are trying to discover the presence of The Divine both in themselves and in Humanity all around them.

In this book the Ramala Teachers make a wonderful analogy. They say that what is important is not the channel, who simply acts as a funnel, but is the energy that flows through the channel. When you are faced with the need to pour water from a large container into a small bottle you use a funnel, but what you are concerned about is not the funnel but is the pouring of the water into the bottle without spilling or wasting a single drop. When the water is safely in the bottle, then the funnel can be discarded, for it has served its purpose. In a similar fashion, therefore, you should discard both the instrument and the Ramala Teachers, for what is important is not the actual means of communication but is the energy that is imparted to you through the teachings. Indeed, we would go further and would say that what is important is not even the teachings, but is the response that they generate in you. So do not regard this book as an authority, as a bible, as a book of religious dogma to be freely quoted from in order to sustain a fixed point of view, but see it, rather, as a mirror, created to awaken in the reader his or her own spiritual knowingness.

The Ramala Teachers have always maintained that their purpose in sharing their wisdom and knowledge with us has been to lead us into a greater understanding of ourselves and of our own divine relationship with God. They have always tried to show us that what is important in life is not the world but is God, that the world is but a manifestation of God, a drama enacted for us, so that we can discover the reality of ourselves and the reality of God. So many people in our world today have been seduced into a belief in the reality of the physical world and the unreality of God! They devote their precious lives and time to the pursuit of pleasure, to the accumulation of wealth and material possessions, often at the expense of their fellow human beings and of the fragile environment in which they live. Humanity has forgotten its divine origins. It has become, for the most part, ungodly, and you have only to look at the state of the world today to see the reality of such behaviour. We are heading towards a sociological and an ecological disaster.

This book, therefore, serves both as a warning and as an invitation to change. We can see only too clearly what we are doing both to each other and to the planet. So we must become more holistic, more holy, in our attitudes and behaviour. We must recognise the oneness of all life if we are to survive both as a Race and as a planet. Humanity must face up to one important fact, namely, that no outside force, no benevolent God, no Messiah, is suddenly going to appear and save Humanity from the consequences of its own actions. Great beings have, and will, incarnate on the Earth to show the way, but it is Humanity alone that must save itself. Humanity must begin to take responsibility for its actions. Humanity must seek a new aspect of God, now that the old religious God is falling away. Humanity must discover the God within itself rather than an external God and, through prayer and meditation, must develop its inner link with the Source of all Life. Every individual must attune to their own spiritual knowingness and should act according to it.

The Ramala Teachers have always been reluctant to prophesy, except in very general terms, yet what few prophecies they have made have already proved to be correct. They say that the next twenty five years are years of great change, years when the world will change beyond our comprehension. For not only is the Zodiacal Age changing from Pisces to Aquarius but the planet and Humanity on it is moving onto a new spiral of cosmic evolution. That period of human experience sometimes known as The Golden Age, and which is foretold in many esoteric traditions, will soon be upon us. Only a small percentage of Humanity will be privileged to incarnate in this Age. So it is our actions now in thought, word and deed that will determine our right to participate in this Age. Very little time is left before earth-shattering events will occur which will change the very nature of our planet, when the world as we know it will change completely. Old values, old institutions, old beliefs, will disappear and only the soul that is open to transformation will survive.

So in this book the Ramala Teachers are offering us a blueprint for human transformation. The last channelling in the book, which was received on June 11th 1989, can be said to encapsulate the essence of the Ramala teachings. It took many people, including ourselves, by surprise, but it had the desired effect of making us realise how often in the past we had ignored the exhortations of the Ramala Teachers, believing that time was on our side. No matter what happens now, we cannot say that we did not know, that we had not been warned! The Ramala Teachers have placed our lives in perspective with the Age in which we live and have offered us their vision of the future. It is now up to us to decide on the reality and correctness of that vision and whether or not we wish to heed it. If we do, then we must concern ourselves urgently with the transformation of our own beings. Human transformation will then lead to planetary transformation. If we are going to bring about human transformation, then we must consider wherein lies the power to bring about that change. It lies not in the outer physical world. It lies deep within us all. There is no-one that can bring about that change but ourselves. If we will but only surrender our little ego-wills and attune to the greater Will of our Creator, then we will inherit our divine birthright and, truly, will create Heaven on Earth.

The teachings in this book were all received between 1986 and 1989 and are presented in the chronological order in which they were received. They have been selected from the many teachings recorded, on a purely subjective basis. Some have been edited and condensed but always with strict regard to their original meaning. Inevitably, the personality and the soul-consciousness of the instrument is imprinted on the teachings, for in this form of communication the Spiritual Hierarchy has to work through the mind of the instrument concerned. Nevertheless, over the many years of communication, as trust has been established, so it has become possible for the Ramala Teachers to express concepts of life with which the instrument does not agree or else has not yet grown to understand. We, therefore, humbly offer the Ramala teachings to you, the reader, in the spirit of love with which they were given to us. Our earnest desire is that they will act as the spark which will ignite the flames of your own intuition and so will help you to develop your own personal and unique link to your Creator.

How are the teachings received? Usually a small group of people meet in the Ramala sanctuary. After a short period of meditation, when the energy has built up between David and Ann, the husband and wife team who form the channel and who always sit facing each other, one of the Ramala Teachers overshadows David and speaks through him to give the talk. At all times David is fully conscious of what is being said. He likens the experience to standing behind someone who is giving a talk and yet being able to hear the words before they are actually spoken. The subject matter of the teaching is nearly always a response to some question that has arisen in the Ramala community in recent days or because someone in the meditation group is in need of counselling on some problem that they are facing. The talk normally lasts for around thirty minutes and then the Teacher withdraws and David's personal guide appears to answer any questions that may have arisen from the talk.

If the Ramala Teachers, who choose to remain anonymous, saying only that they are part of a spiritual hierarchy known as The White Brotherhood, sometimes appear to be remote and impersonal, then David's guide, Zen Tao, is the very opposite of that. He has a wonderful and distinctive personality with a delightful sense of humour. Over the twenty years he has been talking to us he has endeared himself to literally hundreds of people. In the question and answer sessions that follow the talks ZT is the abbreviation for Zen Tao. Because he is very close to his instrument and has himself experienced several recent incarnations on the Earth he is well qualified to link the incarnate with the discarnate world. He is often able to translate the spiritual concepts expressed by the Ramala Teachers into a more practical and human standpoint. He is aware, only too well, of our human weaknesses and failings and of the limitations imposed on us by the physical bodies in which we dwell. At all times, though, he takes great care to ensure that he is not regarded as an authority figure and that he does not become a crutch on which we lean. He is always saying that his purpose is not to answer our questions but to get *us* to answer our own questions.

Even through such a restricted medium as channelling, one cannot fail to be impressed by Zen Tao's open-mindedness and tolerance, by his love and his humility, and if this book does nothing else than to introduce him to a wider audience of spiritual seekers then it will have served its purpose well. No matter what the plane of existence from which he speaks, he is, surely, giving us unimpeachable proof of the reality of human existence after 'death'. He is, in one sense, a living demonstration of the concepts expressed by the Ramala Teachers. Time and time again he reminds us that we are not our physical, mortal bodies but are, rather, spiritual, immortal beings. Rather like the astronaut who views the Earth from the depths of space and is touched by the feeling of divinity and oneness of the planet, so Zen Tao views the Human Race from afar and tries to convey to us the divinity and oneness of the Human Race. His final words speak for themselves – 'Remember that you are God-beings, imbued with God-spirit, empowered by God-love, in a God-centred world. Anything or anybody which denies that reality is itself not real.'

For David and Ann the past twenty years of channelling have been a wonderful learning experience. For them it has proved to be a period of schooling but, as we all know, there comes a time when you have to leave school and go out into the world and stand for what you know to be true. So the ending of the channelling marks the beginning of another phase in their lives. What will unfold in this phase, only their Creator knows, but they look forward with eagerness to the challenge. For those who mourn the ending of the channellings we can only reiterate the words of the Master who gave the last Ramala channelling, namely, that for as long as there is a duality of identity, namely the channel and the listener, then there is separation between us and our Creator. For as long as we need a teacher, be it a Master on the higher levels of life or a priest on the physical level of life, then we are creating an intermediary between us and our Creator. What we all need at this time is a direct and strong union with our Creator. This is what we have to work on. This is what we have to establish.

Finally, let us all remember the warnings of the Ramala Teachers. Physical time is running out both for us and for our planet. There is not much time left before great changes will be upon us. The time for philosophising and discussing, for putting off until tomorrow the things that we can do today, is long past. Today, above all else, is a time for right thought, right speech and right action, for living and demonstrating the Teachings of Ramala. We have been given the tools to ground and create Heaven on Earth. Now it is for us to do it. So many teachings have been given to us, and so many have been ignored. So many Masters have tried to touch the consciousness of Humanity, and so many have been ignored. The result of this action is that Humanity will now have to reap what it has sown. But we are all eternal souls. We never die, because we are never born. Let us remember the example of the phoenix and firmly believe that out of the ashes of the funeral pyre of the Old Age will come a New Age of Humanity, the Golden Age of Aquarius.

RAMALA
Glastonbury 1991

THE RAMALA CENTRE

at

CHALICE HILL HOUSE
DOD LANE
GLASTONBURY
SOMERSET BA6 8BZ
ENGLAND

It was in the Spring of 1975 that David and Ann, the founders of Ramala (pronounced Rahmahlah), came to live in Glastonbury. How they came to find and purchase Chalice Hill House is a story in itself, but sufficient to say that their inner guidance told them that this old manor house was destined to be the place where Ramala would put down its roots and grow. Over the intervening years many people from all over the world have come and have helped them to renovate the old house and to turn it into a place of beauty and tranquillity. At the same time that all this work was being carried out on an outer, physical level, so on an inner level, too, creation was taking place. Through the channellings and the meditations, through both group and personal experiences, a wonderful energy began to grow. Today the Ramala Centre is a spiritual power point, a place where weary pilgrims can come and find both outer and inner peace, and can recharge their batteries.

The Ramala Centre is able to offer spiritually minded people, both individuals and groups, an opportunity to come and stay at Chalice Hill House either to make contact with the Ramala point of consciousness, through its teachings and day-to-day living, or else to experience the energy of the power centre of Glastonbury, the ancient Avalon. Guests can either stay on a Bed and Breakfast basis, by paying the current tariff, or else can come, by prior arrangement only, as working guests where in return for working in the Centre their accommodation and meals are provided free of charge. Anyone wishing to stay at the

Ramala Centre should write for our free brochure which provides full information on our facilities and current room rates. The essential qualifications for all who stay with us are a willingness to serve, the ability to be flexible and open to the moment, and a respect for the principles and rhythms of the Centre.

The Ramala sanctuary, the Sanctuary of the Holy Grail, a beautiful pine building situated in the grounds of the Centre, reflects the nature of the spirit of Ramala – universality. No matter what your race, colour or creed you will find no conflict here. All are welcome to express their understanding of life and whilst in return we offer the Ramala Teachings there is no imposition in this matter. We have no desire to convert anyone and only speak of our understandings when spoken to. Each year thousands of people pass through Chalice Hill House and therefore reservations or appointments are essential so that visitors can be accommodated without disturbing the rhythms of the Centre.

The Ramala Centre provides a comprehensive guest information service both on the Ramala Teachings and on the legends and traditions of Glastonbury, including an audiovisual presentation entitled 'The Living Legend of Glastonbury' and lectures on audio and video cassettes, together with articles of interest produced by the Centre. The Ramala Centre is happy to host small workshops or conferences given by people outside of the Centre, provided the subject matter has empathy with the fundamental teachings of Ramala.

We hope that, should you feel the need to make a closer contact with Ramala, we will be able to welcome you to the unique atmosphere of Chalice Hill House and that your experience will be a rewarding one both for you, the Centre and the planet.

ARTIST'S NOTES ON THE BOOK COVER

The figure on the front cover, which is repeated on the back, is intended to symbolize an understanding of life rather than an individual person. It represents a level of consciousness, embodied in human form, and is meant to illustrate to those of us, who communicate most easily through our physical senses, the reality of human thought manifesting on the Earth as a physical presence. At this very special time many people are becoming aware of such realities, which are unique to our species, and which are referred to as visions, channellings or, simply, 'inner knowings'. The forms of the manifestation are as infinite and as unique as is the human soul but, like the Ramala Teachings, many are prophesying of cataclysmic events which will lead Humanity into a new level of consciousness.

I would prefer, therefore, to leave the interpretation of the specific symbols in my illustration to you, the reader, and would ask only that you spend a few minutes meditating on them. What is significant, for me, is that the channelling process described in this book has now ended. It is this, and countless other signs as well, which daily impresses on me the need for a closer communication with our God as we pass through these perilous times. Now, above all, is the time for right practice rather than for discussion. We are indeed in the time of Armageddon and the message of this book, therefore, is very pertinent.

David Maclagan
Harrison Hot Springs,
British Columbia,
Canada.

THE NATURE OF HUMAN RELATIONSHIPS

The physical plane of existence on this Earth, of which you are aware through your five bodily senses, has been likened to a school, a school in which the pupils are learning to relate not only to their fellow human beings but also to the three other Kingdoms of Matter. In the very beginning, the hierarchies which you call the Animal, the Vegetable and the Mineral Kingdoms, the creations of the Lord of this planet, dwelt in harmony. Possessing no free choice, being tied to Divine Will, they interacted naturally, according to that Will, and life on this planet was one of harmony and perfection. Then, after the passing of aeons of time, onto this plane of existence was placed the seed of Humanity, a seed that had first been created on a planetary system far removed from this Earth.

The seed of Humanity was placed on the Earth, in this very special school, in order that the Race should learn one basic lesson, the lesson which it had failed to learn in the solar system of its creation, so far away, the lesson of sacrificial service. The Human Race, therefore, descends into physical incarnation on this planet for life after life after life, experiencing a cyclic and zodiacal pattern of evolution, in order to learn that one lesson, the lesson of sacrifice: sacrifice to its fellow human beings, sacrifice to the planet and to all the creatures that dwell upon it and sacrifice to the innumerable beings who dwell on the planes of existence both above and below that of the Earth and who administer the Will of the Lord of this solar system.

Now you must also realise that the Human Race, being gods in the making, has been given a very special divine gift, the gift of free choice. You can choose, therefore, either to create in your own image or in God's image. The three other Kingdoms of Matter are at your command. You have dominion over them. Humanity, for the moment, is the spiritual master of the Earth. Therefore it is you, and you alone, that determines the nature of any relationship, not just with your fellow human beings and their creations in thought, word and deed, but also

1

with the three other Kingdoms of Matter, who are subject to your will in this particular cycle of the evolutionary pattern of the Earth.

As you look at the state of your world today you can see that Humanity is approaching a time of crisis, of crisis not only in the field of human relationships but also in the field of relationships with the planet. On the one hand Humanity is faced with the choice of whether or not to exterminate itself in a great nuclear holocaust, either by accident or by design, a disaster, incidentally, in which only a minute proportion of the Human Race will be involved. Nevertheless, that minute proportion feels that it has the right to play around with the destiny of the planet and of the millions of human beings that dwell upon it without even consulting them! On the other hand Humanity is faced with the imminent destruction of the planet's environment through wrong relationships with the Kingdoms of Matter to the extent that Mother Earth has become so polluted that she now threatens to turn against the Human Race that dwells upon her being.

Humanity, therefore, has yet to learn the lesson of right relationship. Let us consider, for a moment, what lies at the foundations of right relationship. What should be the basis not only of your relationship with your fellow human beings but of the Human Race as a whole with the other Kingdoms of Matter? Do you have a model, a perfect example, of right relationship, upon which you can base your own relationships? The answer to that question is, of course, 'Yes', but only if you yourself have established a right relationship with your Creator. It is through the understanding of that primary link, of your divine spirit with your Creator, that there comes a true understanding of right relationship. Unless you are aware of the true nature of that link and of what is involved in it, and of the energy that pulsates between you and your Creator, then you cannot establish right relationship with any being or any thing on any level. Now the divine energy which links you to your Creator is love, and when I talk of love be aware that I am not talking of human, emotional or psychological love, but of divine love, that energy which links the Cosmos in one great Plan, in one great Design. It is that bond of love, the true nature of which you can only just begin to visualise as you discover and understand your own relationship with God.

Let us consider the reality of that relationship. That Being Who created you has imbued you with Its spirit. It has sacrificed a part of Itself, the most sacred part of Itself, in order to give you individualised life and to enable you to follow your own evolutionary pattern. It has given you mind with which to explore the nature of spirit. It has given you free choice to choose the nature of your evolutionary pattern and, above all, It has surrounded you with Its divine love, a love that does not judge, a love that is always present to uplift you no matter what you do, no matter how you take Its name in vain, a love that forgives without you even having to ask for forgiveness, a love that gives to you continually every second of your life, requiring nothing in return, no matter whether you respond or not. That divine love is always present. It is always there for you to tap into just by closing your eyes and attuning to the Source of all Life which gave you life. Recognise that your Creator has provided this planet for you and the means to enjoy life upon it. It has given you dominion over the three Kingdoms of Matter that dwell on the planet to help you to fulfil your evolutionary pattern. It has given you the angelic beings for guidance and the elemental beings for service. All of this is placed in your hands, together with the freedom to be whatever you wish to be. So the real basis of a divine relationship is the spirit of sacrifice, one which recognises the evolutionary growth of the human spirit as being of supreme importance.

Recognise that you are placed on the Earth imbued with all the qualities of your Creator. Recognise that you, too, are divine. There beats within your heart that spark of spirit which links you eternally to the Creator of all Life, that is indeed a part of your Creator's Spirit, for you are gods in the making. This divine relationship should be the model for your relationships with all your fellow human beings. Recognise that the nature of your evolutionary pattern is decided by how you yourself relate. You do not evolve by living in isolation. The evolutionary process only begins when you relate to your fellow human beings and to the Kingdoms of Matter around you. You discover the nature of your own being through relationship. The way you meet and relate with your fellow human beings, the way you treat the three Kingdoms of Matter, are but mirrors of your own being. They help you to know yourself, to recognise the aspect of God in you, the divine spirit that should direct every aspect of your being and motivate every action.

Right relationship, therefore, as with the Godhead so with the Human Race, is based on love. The energy of this Earth is sacrificial service in love. This is not the human love of attraction, of possession and retention. It is a free love, a love given and offered freely no matter what the cost. It is a love that forgives no matter what is done. This, then, is the role model that you have to compare with your own relationships of man to man, woman to woman, husband to wife, brother to sister, family to family, country to country and so on. This is the model that you have beating within your heart. Be aware that all those souls who have not established a correct relationship with their Creator, who have not sought that higher union, will find it difficult to establish the lesser union with their fellow human beings. But for those who are aware of the divine link within them, there is available a wonderful and infinite opportunity to assess the true nature of their own human relationships.

Remember the great cosmic truth: do unto others as you would have others do unto you, and so relate with others as you would have others relate with you. That is one of the primary Laws of the Cosmos, for how you relate with the world around you determines the nature of your karma, whether it be good or bad. That which you sow with love comes back as goodness. That which you sow with hatred comes back as evil, remembering that 'evil' is just 'live' spelt backwards, or life in reverse. In the Law of Karma there is no punishment, only the return of that which you have sowed. The degree of what you have sowed depends upon your soul consciousness. The greater the soul consciousness, the greater the ability to sow and reap and so the greater the return. Therefore be aware of the nature of your responsibility in this respect.

Remember that it matters not what others do and say to you. It is only what you do and say that is recorded in your account in the great Akashic Record of this Earth. It is only how *you* respond, how *you* think and how *you* behave in any relationship, for which you are accountable to the Lords of Karma. So no matter what is directed against you in any relationship, no matter what emotions, what thoughtforms, what acts of physical violence, always remember that fact. It is how *you* respond that governs your karma. Remember that the lesson of this planet is sacrificial service in love. Remember that it is how you behave that determines the nature of your evolutionary lessons.

All the great Masters who have walked the face of this planet have taught and demonstrated one truth, namely, that dying is but a beginning. If you are threatened, you do not have to threaten back. If someone is trying to kill you, you do not have to kill them first. There is a greater Law that governs all things. There is a greater reward for those who give freely of their divine love in human relationships. Because of the nature of the world in which you live today you have been conditioned to live solely through your five senses. You are, indeed, sensory beings, yet so much of your sensory contact has been lost for you dwell in the so-called civilised world of the West, where much of your physical existence is either mechanised or computerised, a function of automatism, removed from the reality of life. You have lost touch with the reality of the sacrifice necessary to give you life, of the energy that has gone into your physical creation, energy that you take for granted. You have forgotten the true nature of right relationship. Let us take one little example, the relationship between disease and healing today, and you will see the point that I am trying to make.

If you fall ill today most of you will go to see a doctor very quickly. That doctor will probably give you some medicine and you will then sit at home and expect the medicine to cure you. But what of your relationship in that healing process? If you were not living in the Western World, with its easily accessible medical practitioners and drugs, and you became ill, you would have to seek the wisdom and the treatment of a very different kind of healer. You would then have to spend time in relationship with that person. He or she would have to look at your whole character and to assess the soul nature of your illness, the nature of your physical being, how best to help you, and decide on what was the appropriate herb or form of treatment that would bring about healing. All of this would take time and would demand relationship. But all of that has slipped away in your modern world.

Now most people in your world today have lost the art of right relationship. They relate only when they have to or when they think they need to. They relate only when there is something in it for them, when there is some benefit to be gained or when pleasure demands that a relationship should continue. But that is not the reality of human relationships. That is not the meaning behind the parable in the Bible of the Samaritan who stopped to help the man who was robbed, beaten and left for dead on that road to Jericho. You have to learn humility. You have to learn that every human being is part of the same Race, the Human Race, and that you have to sacrifice to the whole Race. You have to learn that every being that dwells on this plane of Earth is worthy of your sacrifice, of your divine love, of your giving. That is why you are on this planet. That is why you are facing this time of crisis. That is why you are here in incarnation on the Earth at this time.

5

For most of you the lesson of right relationship is applied only to a very small number of people, to husband and wife, children and family, parents and friends, but even within those close links of blood and soul, how often do you actually achieve right relationship? How often is there not bitterness and hatred, the angry word, the implied insult, the lack of humility, the hasty judgement, the egotistical opinion? So I would ask you to always remember the nature of your own unique relationship with your Creator, of the love that is given so freely to you, of the help that is offered to you without condition or judgement. Divine Love is always there, no matter what you as an individual may do. No matter what negative thought you may think, no matter what base word you may speak, that Divine Love is always there. The Divine Presence is omnipresent and will always help you if you will but attune to it.

So if you are to transform yourselves you must begin to understand the true nature of human relationships. Above all, you must begin to act with humility. You must begin to realise that in every relationship that you encounter there is a lesson for you. When problems occur, why is it never your fault! Why is it always the fault of the other person in the relationship! You ask yourself why they do not understand how you feel, why they do not act as you wish, why they do not behave as you want, why, in fact, are they not like you?! They are not like you because each and every one of you is a unique individual being. No two human beings are the same. Each one of you was created for a definite and specific purpose. In that multitude of human creation, therefore, there is the greatest opportunity given to you for human evolution, for every human being is a divine mirror. Have you not recognised that everything that exists around you is the creation of your God? Every human being is imbued with Divine Spirit, every aspect of matter around you is created by the Divine Hand. This school of Earth and every atom in it, down to the least molecule, is divine. Everything that you use is the creation of your God. It is God's creativity placed here for your evolution. Deny even the least molecule and you are denying your Creator. You are denying the very Force that gave you life, that gives you love and that offers you hope.

Humanity is divine. Every aspect of it is worthy of respect, love and admiration. Many times have I said that the Sun represents the consciousness of your Creator. That is why you cannot look at the Sun with your physical eyes, for in your physical bodies you are not worthy to do so. But if the brilliance of the Sun is broken down into millions of small aspects of light and placed inside every human being, then you are able to look at the light individually, collectively and racially. It is only from this individual standpoint that you can create the illusion of superiority. Why should this be so? Remember the nature of your physical existence. There is spirit and there is matter. There is a body of spirit and a body of matter. Your body of spirit lives forever, your body of matter dies. Your physical brain, which contains the record of all that has happened to you in this life on the Earth, formulates your ego self. But this record dies at death and with it dies all the conditioning that you have taken in, all the memories that you have stored from your life on this plane of Earth. But your body of spirit with its memory, the soul, dwells eternally. This is the record of the spirit self, the eternal part of you.

Consider, therefore, on what level you relate to your fellow human beings and on what should be the basis of right relationship. Is it to be the divine spirit or the ego self? The ego self is always present, conditioned by the past to seek the comfort and the love that it needs. None of us likes to be shown our weaknesses, none of us likes to be found wanting, none of us likes to be humble, none of us likes to think of the whole before the individual, for the ego self is conscious only of itself, of its needs, its purpose, its place, its design. But what of the divine spirit? The spirit is universal, the spirit embraces all, the spirit is empowered by Divine Love. So the next time you experience conflict in relationship consider what is controlling that relationship. Is it the spirit or is it the ego self? Is it divine creation or your creation? Is the motivation for the relationship to supply your needs, your wants, your ideas of creation, or is it an act of service, to give of your divine love to uplift all in that relationship, to serve the consciousness of Humanity before even the consciousness of the individual?

Be aware that all of you are approaching a time when human relationships, as well as your relationships with the three other Kingdoms of Matter, will be tested to the limit. If you cannot keep the divine example in the forefront of your minds you will become lost. At all times, therefore, when you act in any relationship, close your eyes and say: 'I have chosen to act in this manner, but if my Creator was sitting on my shoulder, looking at this same situation, how would my Creator act?'. If the answer is 'In the same way', then continue, but if it is not, then think again before you act. Consider the whole, consider the race as one, consider that you are all gods in the making, imbued with the same spirit, empowered with the same love, learning the same lesson, and until the very last of you has learned that lesson you will not escape from this school of life called Earth.

QUESTIONS AND ANSWERS

Q: I would like to ask a question about our relationship with the Mineral Kingdom. I think that there are many people who are trying to attune, perhaps not always very successfully, to the Mineral Kingdom, usually by visiting sacred sites and attuning to the energies there. Sometimes they take with them small crystals or stones and they bury them in the ground at these sites, saying that they are trying to heal the planet. Can you tell me if such a course of action is appropriate, because I don't believe that we have either the knowledge or the power to do such a job very effectively? I also find that there is a certain lack of sacredness in these ceremonies.

ZT: We must first look at the nature of the Mineral Kingdom and recognise that before Humanity incarnated on the Earth the Mineral Kingdom operated in perfect balance and harmony without any human intervention. Nevertheless, as with all the other Kingdoms, the Mineral Kingdom is in the service of Humanity. This means that Humanity is the master and that the great Devic Beings or Lords who formerly controlled the Mineral Kingdom have relinquished their authority to Humanity. They can, of course, take back that authority at any time should they so wish but, in the meantime, Humanity has the freedom to use the Mineral Kingdom as it so desires. The Mineral Kingdom is of service to Humanity in many ways, not just in the obvious way of providing oil, coal and the various minerals that can be mined from the ground but also in a hidden way, of empowering all life-forms through its subtle energies. The Mineral Kingdom is happy to serve Humanity in this way as it pursues its evolutionary path and asks only that Humanity's motivation in using the Mineral Kingdom is of the highest. If Humanity creates wrongly and abuses this sacred trust then the great Law of Karma will inevitably create a reaction to rebalance the effects of such abuse. If Humanity pollutes the Earth then the Earth will respond.

Let us now look briefly at Humanity's relationship with the so-called precious stones or jewels. Firstly, let us remember that such stones have great energy in themselves and that when Humanity interacts with the stones and imbues them with its own energy then the result can be quite powerful. Such precious stones, therefore, become transmitters of human energy. For example, if you take a stone and imbue it with your energies and then go and place that stone in some sacred site, then you are forever linked to that site. Whenever you remember that stone and where you placed it, though you be ten thousand miles away, you are attuning to the energies of that site. A stone, therefore, can be likened to an aerial.

Now I know that there are many people who go around placing certain crystals and semi-precious stones in sites that they deem to be important and who feel that they are healing the planet by such methods. Whilst I respect their aims, this is not the case. The healing of the Earth is not achieved by such little means. Yes, the thoughts are helpful. Yes, the actions are helpful. However you should recognise that great cosmic powers are needed to transform the creations of Humanity – all the wrong thoughts, the wrong deeds, the wrong actions. So I regard the visits to sacred sites and the placing of stones as being more of benefit to the individual than to the planet. As always, though, what is important is the motivation for doing it. Any pilgrimage to a sacred site, to a centre of power, if it is performed with consciousness uplifts not just the individuals involved but the whole human race. What Humanity needs to do is to transform itself, to raise its point of consciousness, and then the planet will automatically follow. It is Humanity that needs to be healed. Humanity is the cause of the Earth's dis-ease.

Q: I feel great confusion with respect to my own personal growth over what was said earlier. I feel that I should be as playful, as joyful and as free in my divine potential as is possible, yet you talk about the need for service and of sacrifice to the whole, the surrender of one's ego expression. I feel some conflict here. Should I as an individual strive to become joyful, powerful and free, or should I be thinking of sacrifice and surrender to the whole?

ZT: It depends entirely on what is the source of your playfulness, of your joyfulness, on how it is created and for what purpose. If you are truly serving Humanity, and by serving Humanity I do not necessarily mean in some great design but just in your normal everyday mundane life, and if you are acting with the highest of motivation, with the purity of your soul consciousness, then you are relating correctly to every being that comes into your aura. Now remember that you are a magnetic being and that you attract into your aura everything that is

9

necessary for your evolutionary pattern. So everyone that comes into your aura each day is there for a very special reason and is worthy of your fullest attention, for they are your evolutionary lessons for that day. Now if you enter into right relationship with them, then, automatically, from that relationship will come joy and happiness, will come a lightness of spirit. You will find that you are imbued with and exude divine love.

Now, equally so, there are many today who seek joy, who pursue a quest for happiness and playfulness, but who are not in the least concerned with the concept of service. For them the joy and the play is an end in itself. This, of course, is simply self-gratification and, as such, is never lasting, is never completely satisfying. Moreover, such a quest soon becomes a way of life. At another time I have explained the difference between joy and pleasure. You cannot seek joy, you cannot create joy, for joy is of the moment. Joy comes from union with God. Joy comes from serving your God in whatever form, in whatever aspect, It may manifest. Joy is born out of spiritual insight, out of a recognition of the Divine in physical manifestation, whereas the pleasure that so many people in your world today seek is very much born out of human creation. Humanity creates its own pleasures and from those pleasures derives a certain amount of satisfaction, but such satisfaction is never lasting and merely creates the desire for yet more pleasures. There can be no end, no fulfilment, to the pursuit of pleasure.

So be very sure in your own life as to the source of your happiness. Do not for one moment think that because you serve you cannot be happy, or that because you are making sacrifices you cannot be happy. Indeed, service and sacrifice can be the instigator of a great and lasting happiness. Consider, for a moment, the true nature of sacrifice. Now you, perhaps, regard a sacrifice as the giving up of something that you possess or value, something to which you are still attached. That is not a true sacrifice. A true sacrifice is when you freely give of something because you can see that such a sacrifice is demanded by the very presence of something greater or of more importance than your own self-being. There is no desire to hold onto what you are sacrificing. When a soldier sacrifices his life in the heat of battle he does not even consider what he is actually sacrificing. He gives his life because he wishes to help his friends. He is not conscious of giving up anything, rather he is just responding to the challenge of the moment. This is true of all real sacrifices. If you hold onto something after you have given it,

10

then you have not really given it. The pursuit of happiness for its own ends is really very selfish. Recognise that you can be happy and joyful no matter whether you live in a slum or a palace. God's love is omnipresent and touches all who open their hearts and minds to it. Joy comes from an awareness of that love manifesting in your life. Joy is your divine birthright.

Q: Many people in the western world today believe that they can learn about themselves, about their relationships, about the future, through the medium of things like tarot readings, clairvoyance and clair-audience, fortune telling etc. Is the use of such psychic phenomena born out of a genuine desire for knowledge or is it rather a sign of fear, a lack of trust that our Creator will provide us with what we need? Secondly, are these psychic skills genuine tools of enlightenment?

ZT: The science of what you call the psychic skills is at a very low ebb. What is practised today, no matter in which field you look, astrology, palmistry, fortune telling, the tarot, even channelling, is but a poor imitation of the true reality of those forms of divination. Now, almost inevitably, Humanity is curious about the future, if only because that which is unknown is different to that which is known! Usually, however, people seek the future because they are unhappy with the present. They want the promise of better things to come. But why is it necessary to seek this knowledge in the first place? Because they are not prepared to live in the present. A person who truly lives in the moment has no time for the past or for the future. It is only the person, literally, with time on their hands who seeks the future.

If you are truly living in the moment, if you are truly experiencing life to the highest of your physical and spiritual consciousnesses, if you are truly attuning to the force of God around you in motion, then of what relevance is the past or the future. Those that truly live in the moment, those who consciously attune to their Creator's will for them each day, have no time for past or future. Moreover, if you know, as opposed to believe, that every hair on your head is counted, that the destiny of even the least evolved soul is guided by great beings, then what is there to fear? So it is only those who do not trust their Creator who seek to know the future. Furthermore, have you ever stopped to consider that if you were to know the future, would you be able to handle that knowledge correctly? Would you accept it or try to change it? I would say that it is a brave or foolhardy person that demands to know of their future!

11

Now having said all of that, do not think that I am saying that you should ignore your own intuitive feelings, your own personal visions. Noah had his visions and built his ark of survival on the strength of them. Any feeling, any vision, that comes to you directly from the Godhead is worthy of your highest attention. Such divine messages are designed to keep you upon your destiny path and to help in the transformation of your spiritual being. There is no need to consult the cards, to visit mediums, to seek the advice of people with psychic talents who in all probability are less evolved souls than yourselves. You have nothing to fear in life but yourself, and by that I mean your own weaknesses. Daily attunements to the Godhead, when you consciously seek to align yourself to the force of God in motion, provide the safest and purest form of guidance.

Q: I recently came in contact with a group of people who call themselves 'immortalists'. Their aim in life is to make death avoidable by the transformation of their physical bodies, using various subtle techniques, so that they can live much longer lives. I would like to ask, firstly, is such a thing feasible and, secondly, is it desirable?

ZT: It is a fact that great Masters can restructure their physical bodies at will and can live for as long as they so choose on the plane of Earth. This means that they can decide when they want to die! They possess the knowledge to do this. I can tell you that there are such beings living amongst you right now who have lived on the Earth for over four hundred years. However let us understand that such beings are not 'normal' souls and by this I mean that they are separate from the Earth's evolutionary pattern and that they incarnate on the Earth to fulfil some very high cosmic plan. Both they and the work that they do remain hidden, for the most part, from the public view. But they do appear at moments of crisis in human evolution and influence the course of world events. Very few souls are aware of their presence and even fewer have had the privilege of actually meeting them on the physical level. They are often found in the remote areas of the world, such as the Himalayas.

There is, of course, another way in which physical life can be prolonged and that is by the transference of the spirit from one physical body to another. By this I mean that the spirit leaves a body that is decaying or dying and takes over a younger, more healthy body in order to continue with its work on the Earth. This is only done with the agreement of both the souls on the higher levels of life. So in this case the life of the physical body is not prolonged, the body is simply changed for another one. Only the soul manifestation remains the same. There are many spirits on the Earth at present that have done this in order to carry on work vital to Humanity's evolutionary pattern. Obviously the nature of the spirit that would perform such an act is one who has transcended death, who has evolved beyond the school of life called Earth and their reason for so doing is never for the individual soul and always for the good of the Human Race or of the planet.

It is only an unevolved soul who would seek to prolong life in order to avoid death. After all, where is your true home? Is it on the Earth or on the higher planes of life? Although life on the Earth is a great privilege, for the soul that has evolved beyond the lessons of this school of life to return to the Earth is a great sacrifice! You can never avoid death except by transcending it and by this I mean that you are aware of the cosmic process of death and dying on every level of existence. To put this in more simple terms, it means dying to each moment of your life, dying to the second of time that has just passed, living the present moment in time as the only time. The only reason for prolonging human life is to fulfil the will of your Creator, to sacrifice the self in service to the Whole. Self-preservation or self-will does not enter into it at all.

Finally I would say that for all of you, at your points of soul evolution, death is the greatest gift that your Creator can bestow upon you. You would find living to, shall we say, even one hundred and fifty years of age, a burden too heavy to bear. Life, without the consciousness to live it correctly, can be very painful, as most of the elder people here know. Could you handle the suffering that is going on in the world now for another hundred years? If you did but know it, death is the great release, death is rebirth, death is life, death is the return to your real family, the family of God. Truly, if there was such a place as hell, it would be to condemn an unknowing soul to eternal life on the plane of Earth.

AN EASTER MESSAGE

Over successive years, fulfilling my role as the World Teacher, I have descended into your midst and have explained a little about the true meaning and significance of Easter. I have said that Easter is a cosmic celebration, a celebration which has a far greater meaning and purpose than that which is placed upon it by any one religion today. However, since you live in a Christian country and are familiar with the format of the Christian celebration of Easter, so I have used Christian dogma to explain to you a little of its cosmic meaning. I would like now to return to the Christian story of Easter and to discuss with you what lies at the root of the Easter celebration: Life and Death.

The Christian religion erroneously concentrates on the life and death of one man, the Master Jesus, and not on the message that that man brought to Humanity. Today, therefore, in your Christian Churches all over the world, what is celebrated is not the living message but the death of that man. As was so often the case with the Master Jesus, many of his higher teachings were given in parable form. Not only did he speak in parables but his whole life itself was a parable for Humanity to draw upon, each according to his or her own point of consciousness. Today, because of the nature of the times in which you live, you are vitally concerned with life and death. This particular celebration of Easter, therefore, is the more poignant for that fact. As Christians remember the life and death of Jesus, so their own lives and their own deaths are brought more sharply into focus. The life and death of Jesus reminds them of their own mortality, for they remember and grieve for the death of that Master, and although they celebrate his resurrection three days later, death for them is still associated with a feeling of loss. That was neither the meaning of that Master's death nor, indeed, the purpose that lay behind his resurrection.

How do you define life and death? For many in the world today life can be described as body consciousness – that is the awareness of life through one's five physical senses. Death can be seen as the absence of

14

body consciousness, when one has returned to the spirit world, when one has attained a state of soul consciousness. But you have been told on many occasions by the Ramala Teachers that the primary purpose of life is the attaining of soul consciousness, not body consciousness. So how can the reason for life be death or, to put it the other way around, how can death be the reason for life? If the purpose of the Master Jesus's death was simply to demonstrate life after death, then after his death he would have appeared before as many people as possible and demonstrated the fact of his continuing existence, the fact that there is life after death. Although the Bible does state that he appeared on the physical plane of life and was seen by certain people, the vast majority of Humanity and, indeed, even of his own followers, were not witness to that fact. For most Christians, therefore, the principle of resurrection, of life after death, is a matter of faith. It is something which they hope they will experience if they believe in and follow the teachings of that Master.

Let us consider the fact that the Master Jesus was aware of both the timing and the nature of his own death, for many, many years before he actually died physically on the cross. So in one sense he was working or walking towards his death. You are all, of course, according to your individual destinies, faced with the inevitable loss of your physical bodies. But this Master was consciously walking towards a sacrificial death, a death of example, a death which has a meaning and purpose far beyond that which the Christian religion ascribes to it today. Why was that Master able to walk that path with such certainty, without fear, knowing that his death would have meaning and purpose? Because that Master was living in soul consciousness and not in body consciousness, because that Master was living in death and not in life. We, therefore, have the enigma of life being death and death being life. There is therefore no divide.

How many of you today would willingly sacrifice your physical life, your body consciousness, to save another? How many of you would walk a path similar to the Master Jesus with the certain knowledge that you were required to sacrifice your life? How many of you would surrender your own life rather than take the life of another? How many of you, therefore, are conscious of your body, and when I use that word conscious I do not mean to imply that you should be unconscious of your body, that you should not be responsible for and look after the physical vehicle in which you dwell for your short lifespan, but, rather, that you are totally and exclusively aware of it? How many of you base

15

your decisions in life around your bodies? How many of you allow the needs of your bodies to determine your lifestyles? This, therefore, forms the basis of the demonstration of the Master Jesus, for he showed that when you have soul consciousness, when you are in tune with the oneness of all life, the true source of your being, that there is no place for body consciousness, that the needs of the body, that the desires of the body, fall away. One concentrates solely upon one's soul being and it is in the union with that soul consciousness, that which we call death, that one understands life.

The Master Jesus, therefore, since he was a being of great consciousness, was in tune with the oneness of his soul. For him there was no body consciousness. There was no thought to pursue the needs of the physical body, to fulfil the desires of the physical body, to obtain the satisfaction which so many people deem necessary today on the physical plane of life. That, surely, is the aim of all beings, to have that oneness with the Source of all Life so that the physical side of life falls away. The test of a true Master, one who has achieved mastery of the physical plane of existence, is that they have become soul conscious whilst in the physical body. They have mastered all the tests of the physical plane of life. That is the purpose of your physical incarnation as well. Each of you according to your soul evolution, your point of consciousness, is facing that very test. Each of you has attained varying degrees of soul consciousness and is manifesting it at times upon the physical plane of life. Equally so, many of you have still some way to go to overcome the body consciousness in which you live, to handle the desires of the physical and to sublimate them to the desires of the spiritual.

But why should life and death be so important at this time? Because you live in a world which is approaching a moment of crisis. No matter what your philosophy, no matter what your understanding of the transformation of this Earth in the not too distant future, of the dawning of the New Age, the Cycle of Aquarius, you can see and feel that the times in which you live are very special, are very different to those which your predecessors have experienced. Life and death today are brought sharply into focus, not just because of the deaths of so many hundreds of thousands of human beings, not just because of the mass suffering caused by droughts, earthquakes, floods, by religious persecutions and ideological wars, but because of the threat of nuclear war and the extermination of all life. Humanity is therefore approaching the supreme test of body consciousness and soul

16

consciousness, the supreme test of life and death, of what is life and of what is death, of what is the meaning of life and of what is the meaning of death.

It is therefore important at this time that all of you, each according to your individual consciousnesses, strive for the highest understanding of your soul being, that you strive to ground that energy in your everyday lives and come to terms with your physical reality, for it is the nature of your soul-being that will decide your physical well-being. At this time, when so many pressures exist in the world in which you live, it is difficult to face all the trials and tribulations of life. Without that soul grounding, without that soul consciousness, you will not survive the cataclysmic events which are to come; you will not rise above them, you will be swamped by them. That, above all, is the significance of this year and of this time of the year. For this is the celebration of Easter, the time of rebirth, of growth, the time of light arising to banish the darkness, the time when you must all make the supreme effort to achieve soul consciousness over body consciousness. For it is how you set the pattern in this year, it is the path upon which you set your feet now, it is the way of life which you pursue at this time, that will decide your future destiny.

There are days coming when you will have neither the time nor the opportunity to relax and to meditate, to think and to consider. You will have to act immediately, without thought, without consciousness of the body, purely on soul motivation, and if you do not now establish the pattern of soul consciousness, in years to come it will be too late. If you have not learned to swim it is too late to start learning when you are thrown into the water. You must establish the pattern, you must establish the link, you must become aware of the soul being within you now and attune to it at all times, to ground and sound its note upon the plane of Earth.

These are not ordinary times. This is not an ordinary Easter. This is the Easter before the beginning of Armageddon. This is the Easter that Jesus would have celebrated before his moment of truth, before his moment of decision. In that demonstration you saw not the triumph of life over death, but of soul consciousness over body consciousness. You saw the return not of the bodily teachings of the Christ, but of the soul teachings. If the Christians of today tuned into not the physical Church and the physical Christ manifest, but into the cosmic Christ manifest, into the cosmic body of Christ, then how great would be the reformation of that Church and how meaningful would be its impact on

17

the world. If you can tune into your soul body, if you can make that manifest, if you can make the true nature of your being resonate on the Earth and release your body consciousness, then you, too, will be a light to follow in the darkness that is to come. You, too, will ground upon the plane of Earth an understanding of the Heavens.

Consider, therefore, this Easter, where you stand. Consider which path you are going to walk. Consider the nature of your body consciousness and of all that goes with it, both in your everyday life and in your relationships with all those people around you. Consider the nature of your soul consciousness. Consider how it has formed and shaped your life. Consider the eternal promise that has been made and is always honoured. Consider the link that lies within you, the link to which in your darkest moments you always turn. When you need help, your God is there. But when the Earth needs help, where are you to be found?

QUESTIONS AND ANSWERS

Q: I would like to ask you to share with us concerning the nature of your relationship with us and with God, to place yourself in a correct perspective, so to speak!

ZT: I, like you, am a soul, on a path of self-discovery, on a path to discover the reality of the God in me. I, like you, have a unique relationship with God. I, like you, am simply playing my part in the evolutionary pattern of this Earth, in what is sometimes called the drama of life. I, therefore, am but an instrument. I am an intermediary, not the Source. I belong to one of the many spiritual hierarchies that exist on the higher planes of life. In just the same way that you have spiritual organisations on the Earth, such as the various Churches, so there are spiritual organisations on the higher planes of life too. Both, I would hasten to add, are fallible! Each one of us in these spiritual hierarchies fulfils our part in the divine cycle according to our spiritual understanding, our point of soul consciousness, and the role which we are destined to play. We can only teach you of our understanding of life, according to our point of soul consciousness. We can only prophesy from our observation of the auric pattern of the Earth and of the individual souls for whom we are responsible.

Our purpose in communicating with you in this way is to help you and the soul group of which you are a part to walk your evolutionary path more smoothly and to further the Divine Plan for this Earth. Since we are not encapsulated in sensory bodies, since we are not bound by earthly time, we have a more holistic view of the Earth and of its evolutionary pattern than you. We are permitted to look into parts of the Akashic Record of the Earth and to see what has been and what is to be. We, like you, are the servants of the one God, and we serve that God by serving you just as you, in your turn, serve your God by serving the many people with whom you enter into relationship during your physical lives.

At all times of communication it should be remembered, because we are not the Source, that everything that we say must be carefully considered before being acted upon. You must always use your God-given powers of discrimination. We would insist that nothing that we say is ever taken as the truth, just because it comes from our side of life. In the same way that you would not blindly accept something that the Archbishop of Canterbury or the Pope of Rome was to say, just because of the nature of their office, so you should not accept our understanding of life just because we speak to you from the higher planes of life. We help you to walk your path in life just as you would help us if our roles were reversed. We are all part of the one Race, the Human Race, no matter whether we be incarnate or discarnate.

Q: Most of us are only too aware of how to develop our body consciousness, but what would be your advice to us at this time on how to develop and strengthen our soul consciousness?
ZT: Obviously, as you are all unique individuals, each and every human being will walk a different path but the first, and the universal, step is to be aware of the existence of your soul consciousness and to realise that it is something which is both real and tangible and, indeed, is already a part of you. In essence, though, it is union with the Godhead which brings about union with the soul. You cannot contact the soul unless you have contact with God. It is the desire for God that creates the desire for the soul. There is a difference between spirit and soul. Soul can be described as the memory of spirit and spirit is the universal link that is within each and every human being. Spirit links you to the Godhead. It is, so to speak, your telephone line to God and it is by using that line, by being open to the message that comes down that divine link, that you become aware of your soul consciousness and of its impact upon your life.

At this very special time, the ending of an Age, when so many of you are trying to transmute the karma of previous lives, the patterns or sanskars that are ingrained upon your soul, it is essential that you understand the vital need to use this link to your Creator. For unless you have union with your Creator you will not be able to handle all the tests that are to come. It is rather like saying, 'How will you face the evil that destroyed Atlantis, when it arises again, if you do not have the consciousness to handle it?'. So, yes, it is good to face and transmute your karmic debts, but you must have the tools to do it. Now is the time to develop those tools. This is not just an intellectual process, one of simply gaining spiritual knowledge, it is a learning of life, an awakening of spiritual consciousness.

There is so much that you can transform in your own everyday lives simply by being aware of the consciousness with which you are living your life. At another time I have told you of a practice that I used, when last in incarnation on the Earth. When you have a choice to make – and I mean by that a choice of some importance, rather than one of choosing what you want to eat for breakfast – after you have made your decision, place it on one side and then say, 'Now I have decided how to act in this situation, but if my Creator were sitting on my shoulder, faced with the same situation, how would my Creator have decided?'. If there is a difference, then consider your decision again!

What you all have to do at this time is to bring your God-centredness into the reality of physical life. Let me give you a simple example. You are all aware of the story in the Bible which describes the ending of the last cycle, the story of Noah and the Great Flood. Now do you think that God just simply appeared to Noah and said 'Build an Ark', and that Noah, because God had spoken to him, went off and built the Ark? Because that was not the case! Why did God choose Noah? Why was Noah ready to listen to God? How did Noah have the strength of character to go against the opinions, not only of his own family and relations, but of the community around him? How did he know that God's vision was correct? The answer to all those questions lies in Noah's soul consciousness. Insight comes to those who are open and ready to receive it. You are all potential Noah's! You have to ground and build an ark of consciousness on the Earth.

Q: As one who tries to walk the same path as the Master Jesus, how is it possible to carry the message of the Cosmic Christ into the traditional body of the Church which, I feel, is desperately in need of that

20

message? Many people feel that much of the ritual and dogma of the Christian Church today is quite meaningless. They would like to change the Church from within but do not know how to do it.

ZT: Does the message of the Cosmic Christ need the Church? Does it require any organisation, any dogma, any ritual? Is it possible, or even desirable, that the Church be reformed? These questions need to be considered first. Moreover, I can tell you, that a being will incarnate upon the plane of Earth who will remove the need for all religions at a stroke. People of all religions, of all creeds, will recognise his holiness and will turn to him, recognising him as living divinity. His Truth will be such that all dogma will fall away.

The fault of the Church throughout the ages has been to think that it alone has the right to teach and to disseminate the message of the Christ. This is not so. Undoubtedly the Christian Church, as it exists today, has to change, but I do not think that it is possible that it will change its dogma. All that can be changed, or so I believe, is the Church's attitudes to the world in which it lives today – that is towards nuclear weapons, towards Woman, towards the Animal Kingdom, towards the sanctity of Mother Earth. The Church has created a mould and it will be difficult to break that mould except through divine intervention.

Almost inevitably, those who seek to change or reform the Church are persecuted by it. This has been the case throughout its history. So what is important is not the Church but the Cosmic Teachings which inspire it. Christians do not, or should not, follow a Church. Christians are people who follow the Teachings of the Christ. The Church is an organisation and, as such, is a creation of Man, not of God. The Teachings, on the other hand, where they have not been interfered with or reinterpreted by priests and scholars, are the creation of God. Each one of you, therefore, that truly follows the Teachings of the Christ, that lives and demonstrates a Christian life, can and will help to transform the Christian Church. After all the Church, like any other organisation, is made up of people, and it is people that bring about change. Unfortunately, as you well know, what is happening at present is that people are voting with their feet and are leaving the Church rather than staying and transforming it. They do not see the Church as being worth transforming, as being relevant to the world in which they live today. Nevertheless, if the Christian Church today was to actually live the Teachings on which it was founded, then it could do much to transform the Western World in particular and the planet as a whole.

However the Church today does not live its Teachings. The Church, to put it another way, is not soul conscious but is body conscious. Therefore as I look into the future I do not see the Church being transformed but, rather, transmuted.

Q: When you speak of what is to come, do you really see the future or are you not remembering the past and because the cycle repeats itself, projecting that as the future?

ZT: I would say that the future – and by the future I mean that which you have not yet experienced in your earthly bodies in this life – already exists on another level of being and that those who are not in their earthly bodies, who are not limited by body consciousness, are, each according to their spiritual point of consciousness, able to tap into that level, interpret it and then share it with those who live on the physical plane of Earth. Now if that seems a little complicated, let me give you a simple analogy! Let us suppose that the Akashic Record of Humanity – and by that I mean the total record of human evolution past, present and future – was the Bible. Each of you, as individuals, according to your scholarly and soul ability, would read and interpret the Bible. Now some would read the Bible and would accept its contents as literal truth. Others would see the Bible as a parable, as a means to an end, to a deeper realisation of God. Others would go deeper still and would place it in the context of other 'Bibles', of other Races, of other Galaxies! So each of you would interpret the Akashic Record according to your point of consciousness and it would be your understanding that you would pass on.

Therefore be aware that when I prophesy I am doing just that. I am tapping into the Akashic Record and am passing on my understanding of it to you. I do not and can not see or understand beyond my point of consciousness. The same is as true for you as it is for me. You all tap into the Akashic Record to different degrees, on different levels, and that is why there are so many visions of past, present and future. That is why so many people lead a different life whilst living in the same dimension of time. Every level of consciousness demands a different level of life. No matter what you see in any vision, if your soul is not touched by it then you will not respond, you will not identify with the vision. When I prophesy to you, all that I am seeking to do is to awaken knowledge that is already within you so that you may know it as part of your being and live it.

22

THE GIFT OF DARKNESS

At this particular time in the cycle of human evolution Humanity has been given the divine gift of free choice. The Human Race evolves itself through the nature of its choices. Let me say, at the very beginning, that the Human Race does not have free will. It only has free choice to do the Will of God. Everything that manifests on the physical plane of Earth is the Will of your Creator. Earth, therefore, is simply a school of evolution and you have been given the gift of free choice to help you to evolve yourselves whilst you are in this school. Now it is entirely up to you how you make your choices. You can choose Light or Darkness, Goodness or Evil, Joy or Sorrow, Pleasure or Pain, to create in God's image or in your own image. The choice is always yours, but I want you to recognise that both of the choices are the gifts of your Creator. They are the tools of learning, given to you in order to help you along your evolutionary path. Goodness is no better than evil, pleasure is no better than pain and light is no better than darkness, for they are all the gifts of your Creator. They all play vital and necessary roles in this school of evolution called Earth.

Now it is difficult for many people to understand that Darkness is indeed the creation of their Creator. You may say that Humanity creates its own darkness. This, to a certain extent, is true, just as Humanity creates its own light, but the greater part of Light and Darkness conforms to a cosmic cycle of evolution. Now is not the time to go into the nature or the purpose of this cycle, of the reason for the astrological and divine influences which initiate cycles that are beyond the comprehension of your spiritual consciousness. Let us just accept that these cosmic cycles do occur and that they have a profound influence upon the plane of Earth. As these cosmic forces touch the Earth so they initiate cycles of Light and Darkness, or should I say apparent Light and apparent Darkness, in order to evolve the spirit of Humanity. As you look back at the history of Humanity you can indeed read of the Golden Ages, the Ages of Light which have existed, just as much as you can read of the Dark Ages, the Ages of Darkness that have existed. If you possess certain psychic abilities you may also recall the splendours of Atlantis and Lemuria, the moments of high spirituality, just as you will also recall the destruction of those civilisations brought about by the degraded behaviour of the people of that time. Such cycles are necessary and, indeed, are destined events.

Darkness, therefore, presents Humanity with one great opportunity: to focus on Light, for indeed if there were not Darkness how would you recognise Light? If you enter a room which is in complete darkness and someone lights a candle in that room, then almost inevitably you are drawn to focus your attention on that light, until it becomes the most important thing in your life. On the physical plane of Earth too, it is always in times of great Darkness that a great Light becomes manifest, upon which the Human Race can focus and from which it can draw inspiration. It is in this way that Humanity is led more fully into the Light. So it is the case that prophets, messiahs, great beings of the Cosmic World, do incarnate on the Earth in times of great Darkness to present to Humanity the greatest lesson of its being and to lead Humanity forth into a New Age, into a new cosmic cycle. As a baby comes forth into the light from the darkness of the womb, so recognise that Darkness is a time of creativity. All things grow in the dark and from Darkness comes birth, comes new life, comes Light. Therefore do not be oppressed by Darkness. Recognise it as a necessary tool of human evolution.

Now I know that for you who are undoubtedly living in a time of Darkness, life can become a depressing affair, but only if you are not aware of the Light. If you concentrate only on the Darkness in this world, on the lower aspects of Humanity, on the wrong human relationships, on the physical tragedies, on the wars and the disease, on the greed and the poverty, on the money wasted on armaments and on the development of weapons so hideous that they defile the very face of the sacred Earth upon which you dwell, then you have every right to be concerned. But remember what is the inherent nature of Light, and the fact that Light is always present even in the Darkness. Consider that when you meditate, even though you may be surrounded by Darkness, even though you may be threatened with death, when you close your eyes and go into the stillness of your inner being, is there not a Light there more powerful than you have ever seen with your physical eyes? Is not that source, that light, always open to you? So where is the Darkness and what is the cause of your concern?

Consider, therefore, the true nature of Darkness. It is an outer, physical thing, and is not of the inner planes, for your spirit does not dwell in Darkness. It is only your personality, the little ego self, that recognises and fears the Darkness that is around it. Darkness cannot threaten the spirit. Darkness cannot oppress and mislead the spirit. Darkness is only a possession of the ego self. Now, of course, whilst you are in physical incarnation on the Earth you have to express yourselves through a physical body and a physical personality, but they are not the true you. They are but vehicles of expression, the servants of your spirit. So the purpose of the cycles of Darkness is to help you to focus your attention upon the Light where your spirit self dwells, for in past incarnations all of you have lived in times of Light and have either abused or ignored that great gift.

Within your souls even now is the memory of cycles of Light, of lives when you were divinely inspired, when your actions were always spiritually motivated, when you walked hand in hand with the angels, when higher guidance was always available to you, when you had only to look at a great Master to know the course of action that you should take. In such lives you possessed great spiritual talents. You could travel to the very boundaries of space simply by closing your eyes and going within. You possessed powers, powers even greater than the power of your nuclear technology today. But as that cycle of Light slowly gave way to a cycle of Darkness so you began to use those cosmic powers not for divine creation but for human egocentric creation.

Now that is not to say that, in the beginning, you used those powers wrongly, to create and direct evil against other human beings but, rather, that you used them simply to fulfil the will of the ego self rather than the spiritual self. You used those powers to create pleasure, possessions and wealth for the ego self, and as you created for the self, so, using the divine gift of free choice, you began to create not in God's image but in your own image. You began to fulfil not God's Plan but your plan. Eventually, as the cycle continued further, you began to use those powers against other people, to the detriment of your fellow human beings and the other Kingdoms of Matter. So you began to enter into a period of Darkness, a period when the Light was withdrawn, when Humanity had to struggle to live with its own choices, to make and create its own world, so that those who lived in that period could truly see what was the reality of human creation as opposed to divine creation.

25

It would be true to say that you are now living in an Age of Darkness, but I can tell you that an even greater Darkness is still to come, for you will see unleashed across the face of this Earth the supreme example of Man's egoism: the destruction of life for purely selfish and ideological ends in order to create a world that the vast mass of Humanity neither wants nor needs. When that happens it will indeed be a time of great Darkness, but recognise that it is a time which you have all chosen to experience. No-one is here by chance. Every one of you present on the Earth at this time has chosen this present incarnation with great care. You have chosen to be on the Earth at this time because it offers you a supreme lesson and that supreme lesson is to exercise the divine gift of free choice in these most demanding times with correct spiritual motivation. It is to search for the Light in the Darkness. It is to know that there is nothing to fear in the Darkness provided you focus on the Light and that it is by such a focus, by such a concentration, by such an attunement, that you will set the pattern of your spiritual evolution for many lives to come. The events of this time will create within your soul a deep memory of that choice of Light and what it means to the spirit.

Now it is difficult, I know, at this particular time in which you live to attune to the Light. Each day, many of you consciously seek your God, seek the counsel and the wisdom of the great Masters, yet is it not the case that you often feel that your prayers are not answered, that you are continually faced with major problems in your life, that the pattern of your life does not unfold according to your wishes and your inner desires? Even the great spiritual Masters present on the Earth at this time seem to conflict as they offer differing opinions as to the nature of human evolution and what is the path to salvation. The religions, too, have become irreligious and create conflict not only between each other but also amongst their own followers. It is difficult for you to know what is the path to God and what is the nature of Light in this Age of Darkness. Let me, however, relate a little story to you in order to show you the reality of the presence of the Light.

This instrument through whom I speak was concerned, before he came into this sanctuary tonight, at the imbalanced state of his body, having only just returned from Canada where he had been on holiday for a fortnight. He felt it wise to attune to his Creator before acting as a channel for this talk, because he was uncertain as to the nature of the talk to be given, whether indeed such a talk should be given at all and whether the energy present in his being would support such a talk. So he sat down in this sanctuary in physical darkness, filled with doubts and fears, his own darkness. However, within five minutes of him beginning a process of attunement, there was a Light present within him which not only gave him the title of this talk and a rough outline of its content, but also told him the nature of the people who would be present to listen to it. Such is the response of Light to Darkness! All that was required was a stillness within, a concentration of attention on that inner being, without any preconceptions as to what the answer should be, indeed, without any desire that an answer should come at all and, finally, when the Light came, the humble acceptance that what was to be said was appropriate for those present here this evening.

Now my instrument is no special being and the example that I have given could have happened to any one of you. It is in the stillness of your hearts, in the total open-mindedness, without any preconditions as to what comes to you, and the humble acceptance of it when it does come, that the real nature of divine guidance lies. That is the Light in your Darkness. That is the Light to which you must turn if you are to survive the Darkness, and by survive I do not mean physically but, rather, to overcome the apparent restrictions of the Darkness that is around you. There is a Light within your being that can illuminate any Darkness. So Darkness can be seen as a gift from your Creator to help you to find your Light, and the greater the Darkness the greater is the opportunity, the greater is the need, to search for that Light.

The Light of your being is within you. It is your birthright to walk hand in hand with that Light. It can give you the answer to any question that you might ask, provided you are open to it. You must not judge it, neither must you prejudge it. You have only to listen humbly to it. Of course the ego self desires this and seeks that, wishes to follow a certain course of action and sets conditions on the nature of your being, but that is not the Light. That is the outer surface around the inner Light. Within you all is a Light that can transform you. So be thankful for the Darkness. See it as a gift from your Creator just as valuable as is the gift of Light. There is no need to judge Darkness. There is no need to oppose it, merely to observe it, and from that observation you will be led into the Light.

As evolved souls you are aware of what constitutes Darkness. Darkness is anything that oppresses and misleads the spirit of Humanity. It is an aware soul that can learn the great lessons of life from observing Darkness, that can understand the reason and accept the need for Darkness, for nothing on this Earth happens without reason. The most hideous atrocity, the most degrading disease, the most evil person to walk the face of this Earth, all happen for a reason. If you could go back into the past lives of the souls involved, if you could see what they had done and what they had manifested, then you would understand what they and those who followed them were learning.

All life is a lesson. Many aspects of life may not be your particular karmic lesson but rather a lesson from which you can learn by observation and if you observe with an open heart and an open mind then you will begin to understand the great Cosmic Laws that control this Earth and you upon it. It is only when you break these Laws that you have Darkness. If you truly understand the nature of these Laws then your understanding will be strengthened by the observation of those who break them. You will see demonstrated for you the reason why you must observe, respect and, above all, live by them, for when you live by the great Cosmic Laws then your life will be one of harmony and peace. In the greatest Darkness you will be a being of Light. In the greatest Darkness you will be the candle that can transform the Darkness around you into Light.

Remember the Light of the great Masters and how they have transformed Humanity. One small spirit in a frail human body manifesting right living upon the plane of Earth can transform millions. One small candle in the centre of a darkened room can illuminate that room completely. One small source of light can become a point of focus for many and can inspire them in turn to search for and to bring forth their own light. Be aware, therefore, of the Light within you. Seek it and you will understand that the gift of Light is no greater than the gift of Darkness. They are all one in the eyes of your Creator in Whom you live, move and have your being. So be aware of that great Being, be thankful for Its gifts and have no fear, for every hair on your head is counted, every deed that you perform is recorded and even the smallest act of sacrifice is noted. Above all, remember that the gift of love offered freely to the most evil of people can create a great Light.

QUESTIONS AND ANSWERS

Q: I am not quite sure if I understand that last comment, when the Master said that a gift of love offered freely to an evil person can create a great light. Would you explain that to us?

ZT: Let us consider the example of the Master Jesus. It could be said that by the conscious sacrifice of his life to the Roman and the Jewish authorities that he created a great light, the light of Christianity. He did not try to resist the evil forces ranged against him. He did not meet force with force, accusation with defence or even judgement with pleas for mercy. He forgave those who murdered him, a true act of love. Yet did not that sacrifice create a great light? The same thing can also be said of other martyrs, both religious and political, where the death of one innocent man or woman created a light which many were prepared to follow and even to die for. Why should they behave in this way? What could possibly be their motivation for such a sacrifice?

Have you ever stopped to consider what you would do, how you would behave, when faced with evil, especially if I was to tell you that you can only transmute and transform evil? You can never destroy it. You can never eradicate it. You do not get rid of an evil person simply by killing them, for that soul will incarnate again and will, in all probability, manifest even greater evil. Evil can only be transformed by the person or persons concerned seeing clearly the reality of what they are doing and then consciously turning from the Darkness to the Light, from the ego-self to the God-self. Evil can only be transmuted by individual transformation, by the soul turning from Saul to Paul, by presenting the other side of their being, usually after a moment of great cosmic revelation, as with Saul on that road to Damascus. Such a transformation creates a great light and much cosmic power on the higher levels of life, where such an event is greeted with great rejoicing. Always remember, when faced with evil, that your first thought should be not how best to destroy it but how best to transform it.

Here in England you have the wonderful legend of Saint George and the dragon. Every child is told of how Saint George slew the dragon with his sword. I wonder how many of you are aware of the other side of the coin, of another legend which relates that Saint George did not slay the dragon but, rather, allowed himself to be eaten by the dragon so that he could then become part of the dragon and transform the dragon from within through his greater consciousness. In the more generally recognised legend the dragon is represented as being evil, but that is not the case, for the dragon is a very sacred beast and represents an aspect of Humanity itself. Here again we find the concept expressed of transforming rather than destroying evil. So, as the Master has just said, you do not have to concern yourselves with eradicating Darkness;

29

you simply have to show your Light. It is your example that will transform others. It is your sacrifice that will create an even greater light. So always focus upon the Light, never on the Darkness.

Q: When you are faced with a constant presence of evil which is due to the weakness of the spirit of the person concerned, what can you do about that? What should you do when you shine your light onto them but they are not capable of responding?

ZT: Firstly, you should understand that it is not the spirit that is evil. It is not the spirit that is the cause of evil. It is your personality manifestation and your soul, the memory of spirit, with its record of the events of your past lives, that is the cause of evil behaviour. Your soul can be compared to your physical brain which, as you well know, records every second of your conscious life. So your behaviour today is, to a large extent, governed by your own reactions to the life you have experienced so far, to the conditioning of your parents, your teachers, your friends and the social society in which you have lived. You are, so to speak, always living in memory! In just the same way your behaviour today is also subject to the conditioning of your past lives. Let me give you a very simple example.

If you had suffered a violent and seemingly unjust death in your last life, let us say you were wrongly convicted of murder and were then hanged for something that you did not do, your soul would constantly be making a strong impression on your mind in this life, firstly, to ensure that you did not place yourself in a situation where the same thing could happen to you again and, secondly, to seek redress for all the suffering that you had experienced in that previous life. So you would find that, on an unconscious level anyway, you did not trust people very easily, that you were always creating barriers to protect yourself, that you were quite a violent person when threatened and that you had very strong feelings about crime and punishment. You would also have instinctive feelings of dislike for the souls of the people who had done this thing to you, were you to meet them again in this life!

However, all these responses would be from your soul, not from your spirit, which is a part of Infinite Spirit and, as such, is pure and holy. So it is the soul which 'remembers' and which demands and creates situations or tests in your subsequent lives in order to transmute the karma of such events. Now, to return to your question, I have to say to you that it is not your responsibility to transform any so-called evil person. Any such transformation has to be initiated and carried through

30

by the person themselves. All that you can do is to be a mirror of their need for transformation, to help them to see themselves in the mirror of your love and your right behaviour. Moreover, if you are constantly faced with an evil being, as you imply, then it is because on another level you have asked for this test. It is the magnetic attraction of your being that is drawing this person to you. Now this can either be because you have agreed, on a soul level anyway, to help this person, or because you need to learn the lesson of how to handle evil. Whatever is the case, the situation will continue to test you until you handle it correctly from your point of soul-consciousness.

Q: Whilst I understand what you are saying, I find the concept of sacrificing to evil very difficult to put into action, if only because to me it smacks of giving in to evil.

ZT: Let me give you one other example, then, to illustrate my point. Several centuries ago there was a spiritual Master living in France, whose lifestyle and teachings were pure and holy. He was, however, arrested by the Catholic Inquisition and was tortured most horribly in order to persuade him to renounce his point of consciousness and so disillusion the many people who followed him. This he steadfastly refused to do and so he was sentenced to death by being burned at the stake. Naturally, he was very aware of the priest who had been responsible for his arrest, interrogation, torture and sentence. This man came to watch his death at the stake, and as he died in the flames, being a wise soul, a true Master, he not only forgave that priest for what he had done but he also made a mental resolution, in the form of a prayer to his God, that he would like to come back in another life in order to try to help this lost soul to see more clearly the true nature of God's love. He truly held no feelings of revenge or hostility towards his persecutor, only the desire to help him. His prayer was, of course, answered and in another life that priest came back as the Master's son, and the Master taught him of the true nature of God's love to the highest of his understanding and thus helped to bring about the transformation of that being's soul.

Here, then, we have a great example of how Light can transform Darkness, of how evil was transformed by sacrificing to it rather than by resisting it, by love rather than by might or will. It all depends on your attitude towards evil. If you see it as a malevolent force and are afraid of it, then if it hurts you, you want revenge upon it. If, however, you recognise it for what it really is, namely, an aspect of God manifesting on this Earth, then surely your only wish can be to transform it, not to hurt or destroy it.

Q: But how do ordinary people, people who are not capable of the sacrifice that that Master made, transform evil?
ZT: You transform evil simply by shining your Light, by demonstrating your point of soul consciousness to the highest of your spiritual ability. You do not recognise your own potential. You have all forgotten who you really are and how powerful is the Light of Spirit that dwells within you. You have forgotten your birthright, the fact that you are truly divine with all the powers of the Divine at your command. Why should this be so? Because throughout your lives you have been conditioned, for the most part, to look outwardly rather than inwardly. You have been taught that the answers to all of life's problems and tests lie without rather than within your own being. You have forgotten the great truth that the Kingdom of Heaven lies within you. So if you want to create Heaven on Earth, if you want to create in God's Image and to act in accordance with God's Laws, if you want to forward God's Plan for this Earth, you must go within and attune to the force of spirit within you.

Q: It seems to me that we are on very dangerous ground here! Surely, if you don't resist evil then you are accepting it, even if it is only tacitly. Are we supposed to believe that everything that manifests on the Earth, no matter how evil, no matter how degrading, is God's Will, is part of God's Plan for us and that we must accept it unquestioningly and without any judgments? That seems very hard!
ZT: It all depends on what you mean by acceptance. I can tell you, with absolute certainty, that nothing manifests on the plane of Earth, or anywhere in Creation for that matter, by chance. There is no such thing as blind fate. Everything that manifests in Creation has both reason and purpose, even if that reason and purpose may be hidden from you. The force of destiny is all pervading in this respect. So we must draw a clear distinction between acceptance and giving in. Do you think that the Master Jesus was giving in to the Romans and the Jewish Sanhedrin by accepting their verdicts? I do not think so, but perhaps he was accepting his destiny. In the story that I have just related, do you feel that the Master was giving in to the Inquisition? I do not think so, but perhaps he too was accepting his destiny. That was why they both forgave their persecutors for what they had done.

There is much Darkness present in the world at this time, but because of your spiritual understanding of the process through which this planet is now going, you accept that fact. Does that mean that you are supporting that Darkness? No! Now, obviously, it is much easier to accept evil at a distance, to see it as being part of the great drama of life, if only because you are not involved, you are not suffering, your emotions are not coming into play. For example, you can look at the violence and the bloodshed now going on in Cambodia and, as an independent observer, you can see the rights and wrongs, the lessons being learned from all that suffering, and be quite dispassionate about it, if only because they are not your lessons here in the Western World. You are not personally involved. But when the suffering is taking place in your own country, in fact in your own family, is it not much more difficult to accept? It is truly only the ego-less person who can accept everything that comes into their aura as a gift from God. Now you are all evolved souls but if someone was to come into this room right now and verbally assault you, to attack your understanding of God, what would be your reactions? I use a stupid example, but you see the point that I am trying to make. As evolved souls you would probably refrain from any violent actions, but what of your thoughts!

Finally, do not think that acceptance involves passivity. On the contrary, it involves great activity on many levels. It is not a question of sitting back and saying that God's Will will be done and of regarding yourself as a puppet on a string. It requires great energy and attention to attune to the force of God within you and to constantly hold the vision of your actions bringing the greatest good, or the greatest Light, to all those concerned in any given situation. So learn to accept that everything that comes into your life each day is there because you have drawn it unto yourself. It is your lesson, your learning experience. The only choice that you have is in how you handle it. Recognise that what you meet each day is your destiny, and you have no choice over that, but how you meet it and react to it, now that is your choice!

Q: I was talking to someone recently who had just been on a course to learn how to use the energy created by the sexual act for positive spiritual growth. Is such a form of tantric yoga a genuine evolutionary tool and can the sexual act be used in this way?
ZT: As always, when we examine any such practice, we have to question the real motivation behind the act. Humanity often creates noble motives for what is simply self-gratification! Now it cannot be

denied that the sexual act does create energy on many levels and that that energy can be directed and used for various purposes, but the bottom line still remains that you are using that energy for your own purposes, for your own ends. Now the use of such energy is comparable to and, indeed, is often allied with the use of magic. There are three kinds of magic – white magic, black magic and pure magic. In this sense white and black magic are similar because they represent the use of the power of the Cosmos by some being to achieve something that is held to be either 'good' or 'evil', depending from which standpoint you look. Pure magic, however, is the only true form of magic, which is when the power is invoked for the sake of the principle which it represents. This means that the power is invoked but is not directed to achieve 'good' or 'evil' but is, rather, left to the discretion of the Creator of all Life. It is saying, and accepting, 'May God's will be done with this power in this situation'.

Now it is just the same with the use of sexual energy. Although you may think that you are using the sexual energy positively when you direct it in some tantric exercise as opposed to some vile and unnatural practice, nevertheless, you must recognise that you are using that energy of creation for your own selfish ends. I would suggest to you, therefore, that the correct use of the sexual act, in any form, is that you dedicate both the act and the energy of creation that comes from it to your Creator and offer that energy back to the Source to express itself according to the nature of its being. Finally, please remember that there are no 'short-cuts' to cosmic consciousness, only 'short-cuts' to self destruction. Remember also that it is one thing to create such power and quite another to use it wisely and with responsibility. You do not give a loaded gun to a young child. The karma for the misuse of such power may be with you for many lives to come.

THE SPIRITUAL REALITY OF WORK

You live in an age of darkness, at a time when much of Humanity does not understand the true reality of life. Only a handful of people realise that God's consciousness is present in every atom that exists in the Universe and that the Divine Plan is being fulfilled on this Earth no matter what the little wills of Humanity may demand. In this time of confusion and chaos, therefore, it is difficult even for evolved souls to remain true to their spiritual ideals, to the understanding of life which they have accumulated during the course of many lives of trial and tribulation, of testing and right practice.

Nevertheless, within all of you is a source of spiritual wisdom which can truly transform you if you will but turn to it. But so many of you have been have been misled by the false values of the civilisation into which you have incarnated. Nowhere is this more apparent than in the work ethos of the Western Civilisation, where work has become synonymous with money and money has become synonymous with power, the power to control the lives of those who do not possess money. The result of this practice is that you have a civilisation today which believes that money can provide the answers to all the problems of life, a belief which is soon to be proved wrong.

Have you ever considered what is the root meaning of the word work. It is simply the expenditure of energy. Work is the outward expression of an inner energy. It has nothing to do with money whatsoever. That it is associated with money in your world today is simply because that is the form of energy exchange which this civilisation demands. However there have been civilisations where money was in no way associated with work, where work was given and expected as a free service. Work is simply the release of energy from within which is expressed without. But what is the source of this energy? Remember that nothing is of you. Everything comes from the Source. Therefore work is the energy of God made manifest. You work in God's image, to fulfil God's Will, to bring God's creativity into physical manifestation. So when you refuse to work you are actually preventing the flow of your Creator from manifesting through you. You are, in effect, blocking divine creativity. So when you are not being creative you are not fulfilling Divine Will and it is inevitable that dis-ease and unhappiness will manifest. Work, therefore, is a means of grounding Divine Energy. Work is the expression of God's Plan for this Earth, and every human being has a part to play in that Plan, a part that is unique and vital.

Western society today worships money and greatly respects those people who are wealthy and successful, if only because they occupy a social position which they themselves would like to attain. So it is almost inevitable that some people are seduced into believing that there are forms of work which are either 'more responsible' or 'more wealth creating' than others and that these jobs, being of greater value to society, should attract higher wages. But I would like to point out to you that this is a false assumption, for in God's eyes all work is of equal value, no matter what the point of consciousness of the soul that is behind the work, no matter what the amount of money that a job generates. The factory worker should be paid the same wage as the factory manager and this is indeed the case in some societies. But why should this be so?

Again, I would ask you to remember for whom you are really working. You are not working for yourself, for your firm or for your country. Each of you, according to the nature of your individual talents, is working for your Creator, to fulfil the plan of your Creator. Each of you has a divine potential which you should strive to fulfil to the highest of your spiritual and physical consciousness no matter whether you are paid a large wage, a small wage or no wage at all. You have come on this Earth to ground divine energy and your destiny is to do that no matter what you are paid, no matter what are the opinions of the society in which you live as to the value of that work. You all have unique roles to play in the work drama of this planet. Each of you has something vital to give to the planet. Remember that you are all instruments of service.

If only those of you who do believe in the spirituality of all life, who are aware of the Divine Source within each and every human being, would become living examples of that fact, then you would begin to transform the people who are aimlessly wasting their lives because there is, apparently, no work for them to do. The truth of the matter is, of course, that there is no work available to them for which they will be paid a wage, but that there is an abundance of unpaid work available in society as a whole which they can and should do.

What do you consider should be the reward for your work? Do you think that money is a fair return for the energy that you have expressed? If you do, then you are limiting yourself, for, truly, even though you have been paid a wage for doing a certain job, the true reward for the expression of your energy will be the Universe giving back to you ten fold that which you have put out. That is the Law of Karma. So it does not matter how menial or how humble your job is, how little you are paid financially, if you will but fulfil your task to the highest of your spiritual consciousness and physical ability then the Universe, which is your Creator in manifestation, will always more than amply reward you. Every task that you do is worthy of the highest expression of your creative energy. Be aware that you give that energy not for yourselves but out of respect for the Source that gave it to you, knowing that the part that you have to play is significant in the eyes of your Creator, no matter what the monetary reward.

It is only too obvious that your world today is in a time of great transition, for not only is the gulf widening between those that have money and those that do not, but with the rapid increase in automation the opportunities for work are rapidly diminishing. Both governments and individuals are being forced to re-examine the work ethos. There is an ever growing number of people who will never be in a position to accumulate wealth. Many of them are becoming disaffected with the roles they have to play in society, for they believe that if they cannot work and accumulate wealth, which is held up as the goal of society, then they apparently have no purpose in life. Moreover, most wealthy people are not prepared to share their wealth with the poor because they believe that they have the right to use the money that they have created through their own hard work solely for their own benefit. The concept of wealth being shared amongst the society is foreign to them, for they truly believe that they are entitled to use their God-given skills primarily, if not solely, for personal gain.

What is needed, therefore, at this time is for evolved souls to positively demonstrate the spiritual nature of work, to show that all human energy is a gift from God and that work is simply God's creative energy made manifest. Humanity must realise that it does not work for its boss or for its firm but for its Creator and that it is answerable to that Source alone as to how it uses its divine energy. Every job that you do, no matter how simple or how complicated it may be, should be done to the highest of your ability because your Creator is sitting on your shoulder watching you perform that job, and the degree of consciousness that you put into the job will determine the nature of how the Source of all Life will reward you. Do not think, however, that the motivation for your work should be the reward or that the reward will always come to you in the form of money. In that you serve the Source, then the Source will serve you according to your needs.

Few people in the world today have a true understanding of the role of money. If you are one of the many people who believe that money is the answer to all the problems of life, that money can give you whatever you desire, then I would ask you this question. What do you consider to be the role of your Creator in your life? It is a wise person who recognises that their Creator, being the Source of all Life, knows their needs even before they do and, what is more, can meet those needs in the very twinkling of an eye should it be necessary. There are, of course, many who have chosen to worship money or Mammon rather than God. They have chosen to place aside the reality of God as the Creator and the Sustainer of Life and to put their trust in the illusion of Mammon. For such people the day of reckoning cannot be far away.

Events are soon to come which will force Humanity to choose whether it works for God or Mammon, to decide whether to place its life in the hands of God or Mammon. How many of you are really prepared to place your life in the hands of your Creator and to trust that Source to provide you with all your needs? How many of you truly believe that if you work and dedicate your creative energy to the Source of all Life that the Source of all Life will give back to you ten-fold? How many of you are even prepared to try to follow this path? So the next time you work, invoke the creative energy that flows through you. No matter how small or how insignificant the task, devote your full attention and energy to it. Complete the task to the highest of your point of consciousness and then observe how the Universe feeds back to you. It will change the way that you work for the rest of your life.

Today you live in a world where many people are not working. They are idle either by choice or as a result of economic or industrial policy. They have, therefore, blocked the flow of the creative energy through themselves and nothing flows to them either from the God-head or from Mammon. Not only are they not creating but they have lost the desire to create. Their life has lost purpose. But they still have that divine creativity within them and it needs to be expressed, no matter what the task, no matter whether they are paid or not. If they will but engage themselves in the humblest and simplest task of service, in the giving of their divine energy to all who come into their aura each day, then they will begin to unblock that flow and the creativity of life will return to them. They will find that they will be touched in a wonderful way, beyond their understanding, for the Source of all Life responds to all those who give freely of their energy to the Source.

Now I know that it is a fact of life that in the world today most people can only earn money by working for other people. That cannot be denied, but remember that people are all instruments of God, are all part of the Divine Plan, and that God fulfils Its plan through people. Obviously there are levels and degrees of work, and the greater the degree of soul consciousness the greater the ability to create. Therefore, inevitably, people will find themselves working for other people of greater will and soul consciousness, but in that fact lies no subservience. For the true soul should recognise that all people are equal in the eyes of God and should treat all people as equals, recognising that every human being can only create according to the highest of his or her soul ability and point of consciousness.

Be aware that every time you work and create to the highest of your spiritual consciousness, every time that you manifest God's energy on the planet, you are uplifting the whole human race. Let me give you an example. Suppose that you are on a beach, the tide has gone out and you are building a sand-castle. You put all your energy and your creativity into that sand-castle. You use all your talents and so create a truly magnificent sand-castle which is admired and enjoyed by many. But then the tide comes in and the waves destroy your sand-castle. It has gone for ever. Was there, therefore, any point in building it or was it all a waste of time? I do not have to answer that question, for you know that through using your divine creativity you have grounded the consciousness of your Creator on the Earth. No matter whether the sand-castle survives for a thousand days or a thousand years, what is important is that you built it, that you used and developed your divine creativity and that it was witnessed not just by those around you but by beings on many other levels. Finally, let us also remember that by the very act of your positive creation you have attracted similar energy to yourself in the days that are to come.

For it is by the correct expression of your energy today that you attract the future unto you. It is by what you do today that you create the power of attraction for what is to come to you in the future, not just in your present life but in your lives to come. Some people work very hard all their lives in menial tasks and for apparently little financial reward, but their reward is in heaven and their reward will be in their lives to come. Some people are destined to face the karmic test of working hard all their lives in menial jobs. But every job has a purpose, every job strengthens the armour of the soul, and prepares the soul for what is to come. Until you can perform a menial task with consciousness, how can you expect to be given a greater one? So give everything in life your total attention and creativity. Each day give of your divine energy to everything that your Creator places in your path and, as you work, do not think of how much money you are making, think of what you can give to the world and to your Creator.

Now I know that there are people in the world today who follow Mammon and who are, apparently, becoming more and more wealthy as each day goes by. The rich appear to be getting richer and to be acquiring more and more material assets. They live in luxury and appear to lead a life of great happiness. But let us examine the reality of this situation. What is the point of consciousness of such people? Monetary wealth is not the same as spiritual wealth. Is the purpose of life to accumulate money or spirituality? What do you take with you when you die, your consciousness or your bank balance? It is often, but not always, the case that people are only wealthy because they have accumulated their wealth at the expense of their fellow human beings, or by exploiting the Animal, the Vegetable or the Mineral Kingdoms. They have, in fact, got rich only by using other people's creative energy, by extorting other people's creativity. So they have acquired more energy than they have actually earned and, ultimately, they will have to pay the karmic settlement for such actions.

I can tell you that the time is rapidly approaching when the value of money will literally be destroyed overnight, when those who are millionaires one day will be paupers the next, when those who are regarded as being the pillars of society one day are seen to be totally fallible the next. It is at such a time that the true meaning of work will become apparent, that the correct work ethos will be recognised, and people will turn from wealth consciousness to soul consciousness. True priests will appear who will give moral and spiritual leadership to the people, who will demonstrate that even though they possess nothing, yet they have use of everything. It is at such a time that the true purpose and meaning of work will be understood. People will give thanks to God both for the work that they have to do and for the divine life-force which permits them to do that work, for they will truly recognise that they are creating not in their image, but in the image of their Creator.

Be thankful, therefore, for each day that you can work. Seize it with opportunity. Be aware of the test that is being placed before you. Give of the highest of your divine energy to each and every task that you perform and truly you will be rewarded beyond your wildest dreams. Those that are poor in spirit are poor in wealth. Those that have poverty of the soul will have poverty of wealth, because it is the quality of spirit which attracts abundance. Finally, may I remind you, yet again, that work is God made manifest, so let us always manifest the highest of our being. Let us always be worthy of the divine energy that flows within us and of the Source of that energy within which we live, move and have our being, and then a true understanding of work will return to Humanity. People will work freely and will give of themselves not for financial reward but for the sake of the energy that has been so freely given to them.

QUESTIONS AND ANSWERS

Q: The Master was talking about the choice of either serving God or Mammon. But isn't Mammon part of God as well?

ZT: Yes, everything is part of God. But what is important is the choice that you make and your motivation for making it. You all have to choose whether you wish to serve the light or the darkness. Both the light and the darkness are part of God. They have been created by God to test you. That is the essence of the drama of life. What you have to decide is how you are going to lead your life, how you are going to relate to all the manifold aspects of life around you. It is not for you to judge the way that other people lead their lives. For example, do not think that because a certain person has become very wealthy through extorting his workers and overcharging for his goods that he is an evil man working against God. He is simply a small part of God's Plan and he will learn as much from this situation as the people that he is defrauding, as will the person who stands and watches the whole drama from afar. That is the purpose of life.

Q: It seems to me that you are making this into too much of a black and white situation. Surely the answer is to use the light to transform the darkness. There is nothing wrong with money. It is how we

41

perceive it and use it that counts. There are many wealthy people in this world who do use their money very constructively. They use their money to help bring about human transformation. So I do not see this issue in terms of black and white, of God and Mammon. I see it rather as an issue of transformation.

ZT: Money is neither a good nor a bad thing. Money is simply energy. What is important is how you create that energy and your motivation for using it. It has not been said that people with a great deal of money are evil people! I know that there are many people in the world who have wealth and who use it very wisely. Nevertheless, it must also be recognised that the test of great wealth is a difficult test to face, especially in a world in which money means power and power gives one the ability to exert control over many other people, no matter whether it be in industry, in government or in politics. So what is important is your motivation for working and the way in which you create your wealth. Of course there are people in the world who work with the highest of motivation and who create wealth justly, but equally so there are people who have created their wealth out of the suffering of other people, such as through the sale of drugs and the deliberate pollution of the environment. So recognise that everyone has the choice as to how they use the divine energy that is freely given to them and with what motivation they use that energy. Money is but an energy to be used and, as such, is neither white nor black, good nor evil, God nor Mammon.

Q: I don't disagree with that, but it seemed to me that the Master was implying that money, and especially a lot of money, was not a good thing, that it was not possible to be wealthy and to be spiritual.

ZT: I feel that you have misunderstood what has been said. The Master did not say that wealth was a bar to spirituality. He merely pointed out that money is only an energy and, as such, you should not get so hung up on the energy that you forget about the source of that energy, namely God. If you regard money as the motive force in life, if you place money before the interests of your fellow human beings and the planet, if you worship Mammon instead of God, then you are inviting a life of suffering not just for yourself but for the whole human race.

Q: I have not been able to find work in this area for some time now and so have been collecting unemployment benefit. I have been living

42

off the state. I need this money not just for my food and rent, but to keep me alive. Are you saying that it is wrong for me to accept this money just because I am not working?

ZT: I feel that you have misunderstood what has been said. What the Master said was that there should be a fair exchange of energy. So what is important is that every individual, no matter whether he or she is working or not, should always ensure that any exchange of energy is balanced. You must always give back as much as you take. You must give of your own energy in return for the energy that is given to you. You must give back to the universe what the universe gives to you, and if the universe gives a great deal to you then you must give a great deal back to the universe. If you do not maintain this karmic balance, then you are creating a karmic debt that will have to be repaid. If you just sit around all your life and do nothing, and expect the state to support you, then you are going to create an energy imbalance, a karmic debt, which you will have to repay in your lives to come.

Q: Are you saying that I will owe karma to a country as opposed to an individual?

ZT: Yes.

Q: So are you saying that I would have to come back and give something to this country to repay it for what it gave to me while I was on the dole in this life?

ZT: Yes. Absolutely. You have to give back equally of your energy to redress the karmic balance. You must understand that money is energy. You are spiritual beings and therefore your money is spiritual energy. Therefore what you are taking from other people is not money but spiritual energy, for that money has had to be created by someone. It is spiritual energy stored in the form of money. Someone had to create it before it could be given to you, and if you are being given this energy then, rather like a bank loan, you are duty bound to pay it back.

Q: But if I was to go around in this life doing healing and voluntary work and things like that, would not that be a way of repaying the loan.

ZT: Yes, of course. As long as you give back as much spiritual energy as you are taking.

Q: How does one measure that?

ZT: It is not for you to measure! There is a Divine Force that judges all things.

Q: Can I just say that there are many people in this world who don't necessarily make it obvious that they are working, and so we shouldn't go around judging everyone as to whether they are genuinely earning their money or not! There are some people who work, but not in a very physical way as in a normal job.

ZT: Yes, I would agree with that. There are many ways and many forms of work. Indeed the whole spectrum of Humanity demands a whole spectrum of work on many levels. It would not be appropriate if you all came on this Earth as ditch diggers! Humanity spreads its talents over many fields of endeavour.

Q: Whilst I understand what you are saying and why you are saying it, nevertheless there are some people who, for example, spend many hours of the day in meditation and who claim that they are saving the world by doing this. That is their form of work. Now is this a reality or an illusion? Is this genuine non-physical work? It would seem to me that there are very, very few souls who do actually possess the consciousness to sit in meditation all the time and who can change the cosmology of our world by so doing. Most of us have to do the more simple things in life, like digging ditches, because we don't possess that degree of consciousness.

ZT: It is not for you to judge or to criticise the actions of others. Undoubtedly some people are living in a world of complete illusion, but their Creator will reveal that fact to them in the fullness of time. Nothing can be hidden from our Creator and the great Lords of Karma. No person or no thing can avoid the karmic reaction to their actions. All that you are responsible for is your demonstration, your example, and remember that one good example is worth a thousand words!

Q: I would like to raise the old question again of whether one should charge for what is sometimes called 'spiritual' work? Should one charge for the use of one's spiritual talents, for healing or clairvoyance for example?

ZT: As I have said on many occasions in response to that question, each individual must act according to his or her own consciousness. For some it would be correct to charge, for others it would not. Moreover, how do you define 'spiritual' work? Is not all work spiritual if it is dedicated to the Creator of all Life and performed with the Creator in mind? Nevertheless, it is a fact that the great Masters never had need to charge for their service to Humanity if only because they could manifest their needs in so many other ways. They were the Masters of matter. So there is your example. But for all those who are on the path to Masterhood the lesson will differ according to their point of consciousness. For some the lesson will be simply to make a fair charge, for others it will be to give freely of their talents only when someone cannot afford to pay for them, for others it will be to give freely of their talents at all times and to allow universal feedback, or God's abundance, to provide for them, which, incidentally, is the mark of a professional person.

Are you aware that in the days of old the definition of a professional person was one who would always give of his or her services without expecting a reward, without submitting a bill. So a doctor or a priest would administer to your needs and they would not expect to be paid for their services. If a gift or a donation was offered to them as a reward for their services it was entirely up to them whether or not they accepted it. Such a path of service ensured a pure exchange of energy and served as a constant reminder as to the source of their talents. Now, in a sense, you are all professional people. You all have the choice of offering your services freely or of charging for them. Compare this with the behaviour of the so-called professional people of today. As with so many things in your world, reality has been reversed.

Q: Is it not the case that we are all people with very loving hearts and that if we give out love every day in every way that is all the work that we have to do?
ZT: Giving love is not work. To give love is the natural act of a human being. It is the natural expression of the human soul. What we have been talking about here is the use of the creative energy which flows through you and its expression on the physical plane of Earth, about the work that is needed in order to manifest the Kingdom of Heaven on the plane of Earth.

Q: As I understand it, if I am to use this creative energy correctly, if I am to work with the right attitude, I need to align myself with the Source of all Life. So what is the most simple way of becoming one with the Source?
ZT: A question that gets right to the heart of the matter! The answer is very simple: to consciously attune to the Source of all Life every minute of your waking day. The more that you consciously attune to that Source, the more that you try to work with that Source, the more that

you dedicate even a simple task like washing a dish to that Source, the more you will find that you are being overshadowed by that Source in everything that you do. You will find, almost unconsciously, that you are attuning, invoking, dedicating and creating every time that you work. Of course, it is so easy to work without thought, to blindly go in and do something on impulse, but how much better to pause, to consider, to ask for help, and then to consciously direct your energies to the work in hand. That is the nature of an aware being, a God-centred being.

Have you ever stopped to consider just what is wealth. A millionaire can consider himself poor in respect to others who have more than him, whilst a pauper can consider himself rich if he has just ten pounds in his pocket. Security is not based on the amount of money that you earn or possess. Security is based on your understanding of how your Creator meets your needs, of how your Creator knows those needs even before you do. You are only poor if you think yourself to be poor. You are only rich if you think yourself to be rich.

In conclusion, I would ask you to separate your needs from your greeds and to realise that your Creator will always meet your needs. There is only one obstacle that can prevent your needs from being met. There is only one blockage that can stop the flow of divine manifestation from reaching you and that is your own behaviour in thought, word and deed. If, as the Bible says, every hair on your head is counted, if your Creator does truly provide you with all the material possessions that you need to walk your destiny path, then if your needs are not being met you have to ask yourself this important question – 'Why should this be so? Why is the abundance of the cosmos not flowing to me?'. The answer is usually to be found in the fact that, to use a gardening analogy, you have not sown your seeds correctly. You have not gone forth and given to the cosmos of your own creativity. You have not been working in harmony with God's Laws. You have blocked the flow of God's energy to you. So carefully examine in your hearts the nature of your work and your motivation for doing it. Dedicate your lives and your work to your Creator and humbly ask for your needs to be met. Then, be prepared for a miracle!

Q: As the first Master said, there appears to be an ever-widening gulf between the rich and the poor on all levels of life, from the individual right up to the national level. The standard of living between the First and Third World countries, for example, is increasing not diminishing.

This must lead to conflict and to bitterness, towards division rather than unity in the Human Race. What can be done about this?

ZT: Nothing can be done, basically, until Humanity changes its perceptions of the fruits of the Earth from 'mine' to 'ours', until it truly recognises that no one person or country owns anything, but is simply the steward of the land and that all the benefits of the land should be shared equally amongst all Humanity. For example, just because a large part of the planet's oil resources are to be found under one particular country, that does not mean that that country has the inalienable right to all of that oil and to dispose of it only to those countries that it chooses so as to make the greatest profit for itself. The same thing can be also be said of food and water. Humanity has to recognise that it is one Race, bonded by the planet in a common destiny.

It must also be understood that with wealth goes great responsibility, both on an individual and a collective level, for to whom much is given, much is expected. If your Creator has given you talents and energies which you have translated into wealth, then you should not hoard that wealth for yourself but should share it with those in need, with those not blessed with your talents. So, at the very least, if the rich people and countries of this world cannot recognise the wholeness or holiness of the Human Race, then they can perhaps share wisely with those in need simply out of a generosity of the heart, out of common humanity.

To answer such a question as you have asked, of course, requires that I grossly oversimplify my answer because we all know that many factors are involved in the present situation. However, leaving aside all the politics, all the ideologies, all the religions, all the financial empires, all the racial attitudes enforced by generations of social conditioning, it basically comes down to that great commandment 'Do unto others as you would have others do unto you', if only because one day, one life, the roles may be reversed and you may be that starving tribesman in a far off country either unable or too weak to help yourself.

Finally, having said all of that, it must also be recognised that nothing happens by chance and that everything is part of God's Plan for Humanity. Every country, every individual, has a karmic destiny, a learning experience, to fulfil. No-one suffers by accident. No-one is rich or poor by a quirk of fate. Countries and individuals attract their destinies to them as learning experiences. Why is one child born deformed and another perfect? Why does one race live in peace and prosperity and another suffer continual prejudice and persecution? The answer can only be found in the great Law of Karma, and if it is not, then, your God is not a just and a loving God.

Now what I have just said does not mean that you should sit on your hands and do nothing in the face of suffering, saying that it is the karma of some one or some country to suffer. No! You must strive with all your might to alleviate all suffering. You must be compassionate to all those in need. You must help where you can help, when help is asked for, but at the same time recognise that this physical world will always contain suffering. The important thing is, firstly, to recognise what exactly is suffering, which is only the temporal body and, secondly, to learn from that experience no matter whether you be the participant or the observer. Know the great truth that ignorance of God's Laws is the root cause of all human suffering.

THE TEST OF ATTACHMENT

Your dictionary, I believe, defines attachment as 'joining oneself to or bonding oneself to another person or to another thing'. It is most often used on your plane of life in the sense of bonding yourself to another person, be it husband or wife, boyfriend or girlfriend, mother or father. It is also used in the sense of bonding yourself either to a material object such as a house or a car or else to a concept such as a political, ideological or religious doctrine. It can also, of course, be used to define the relationship between a guru, a teacher, and his or her followers. However, I am going to suggest to you that all such attachments are doomed to failure and will cause heartbreak. They will only lead to suffering because, ultimately, that to which you are attaching yourself is not, and never will be, perfection. Recognise, therefore, that the qualities that you are seeking and hoping for in any relationship, even if they manifest in the short term, will never endure for long.

So I would like to suggest to you that a better definition of the word attachment would be 'the act of establishing a relationship with any person or object as being of greater importance than your relationship with your Creator'. So if you are truly attuned to the Godhead, if you are at one with the force of spirit that flows through you, there are no need for attachments in any form whatsoever. Indeed, the example of a Master, a truly awakened being, is that they do indeed have no sense of attachment either to things physical or to things spiritual. For when one is attuned to the Godhead, when one has established that divine connection, then all else falls into place beneath it. You can place your friends and your family in true perspective, for you realise that they are just souls, like yourself, following their evolutionary paths. They are making the same mistakes as you, exhibiting just the same weaknesses, just the same attachments as you. Indeed, they are but mirrors of yourself. There therefore can be no permanent strength in any such relationship and to attach yourself to something or somebody that is fallible can only lead, in the final analysis, to suffering.

Have you ever considered what it is in you that seeks such a relationship, that seeks such an attachment? Do you attach yourself to something that gives you pain? Do you attach yourself to something that disquiets you, that does not support your way of life or your way of thinking? No! The reason for you forming any attachment is, surely, because it supports your understanding of yourself and of your way of life. How rare it is that you form an attachment, that you join in that bonding process, in order to *give* to another rather than to receive. The very nature of the human ego is that it seeks through the attachment of human relationships the succour that it needs, the support that it needs, in order to walk its path in life and to face its challenges. How rarely is a relationship entered into in the spirit of sacrifice, of the selfless giving of oneself to another person or thing.

Now I am going to suggest to you that there are three levels of attachment, namely, the physical, the soul and the spirit. Each of these levels demands a degree of attachment. The physical level you are aware of only too well. You know of your need to relate to your fellow human beings and of what you want from them, of what you expect them to do for you or to give to you, no matter whether it be love, security or happiness. That is the relationship which causes you so many problems. If you make anyone into God, if you expect anyone to behave as your God, to take the place of your God, then such a relationship must fail. For there is no human being, no guru, no teacher, no Master, that can replace the Source of all Life, the creator of your being, your God.

There can be only one true attachment, there is only one true attachment that you need, and that is your union with your Creator. If that divine relationship is sustained, then everything beneath that level will automatically fall into place. You are only too aware of how, on the physical level, you become attached to material objects, to houses, possessions and money. On the mental level too you become attached to ideological and religious concepts. These help to form the basis of your understanding of life. You become attached to them because they help you to identify with the society in which you live. You see yourself in relationship through these attachments. But do they reflect the true nature of your being? Could it not be said that if you were to release these attachments to race, to country, to creed, to social position, to sexual gender, that a totally different person would emerge?

Let us now look at the nature of soul attraction and attachment. You have all lived many lives and have walked the surface of this Earth in both male and female form. Because of the need for karmic transmutation, almost inevitably you will incarnate amongst souls with whom you have lived in past lives. You will incarnate amongst souls with whom you will have experienced moments of extreme crisis, souls which you will have killed or will have killed you, souls with whom you will have shared great suffering. There is therefore, inevitably, a strong pull of soul attraction, the more so if you have incarnated in this life in order to transmute the karma of past actions and soul patterns.

Anyone that you feel strongly about in your present life you will have encountered in previous lives. You can, therefore, become attached to that person, to the pattern that you have established with them or they with you. How easy it is, if you have been happily married in a previous life to feel that pull once again in this life. No matter whether you are destined to marry again or not, that attraction is still there. That attachment to what you have experienced, to the joy and the suffering that you have shared in past lives, naturally draws you together. Both the soul qualities that you manifest and the soul group to which you belong will sound a note that will draw souls to you and will lead to you forming soul attachments.

So if you rise above the test of physical attachment, you then have to face the test of soul attachment. Finally, you have to understand that above even that level of attachment there is a still greater force which plays its part: the one and only union, spiritual attachment. Spiritual attachment therefore is the aim of your being. It is union with the Source of all Life. It represents the divine energy flowing through you, to enlighten, motivate and direct you as you live on all the planes of your being. Recognise that when that union is present, then everything else falls into place, that if you seek first the things of the spirit, then all else is added unto you.

The aware soul can look around and can recognise the many levels and degrees of human attachment. You can see the pain and the suffering that comes when a marriage breaks apart, when a mother and father lose their child, when a country loses its leader, when a religion loses its teacher. When this separation happens, then there is much sorrow because of the attachments formed. There is much pain and grief caused by a misunderstanding of what is a correct relationship. What you are then witnessing is the ultimate test of attachment. For the stronger you resist true union with your Creator and place human relationships before it, so the greater is the degree of your suffering as you are impelled towards a true understanding of what is the reality of union with the Godhead.

When you are aware of the presence of your Creator in all things, of the Divine Force that guides and motivates you, that counts every hair on your head, that knows of every encounter that you will make, that anticipates and meets your every need without you even having to ask for it, then of what need is there to seek for any other union? Such is the reality of true union, of true spiritual attachment, when you give no matter what the cost, when you give to serve the evolutionary process rather than for individual gain.

You would say to me, 'Yes, I am aware of my attachments. Yes, I know that I love someone too much, in the wrong way. Yes, I am attached to my power, my job, my money, my social position. Yes, I am attached to my religion, to my Master. But how am I to come to terms with this? What steps can I take in order to break this attachment?'. Let us begin by realising that the process of recognising and releasing any attachment is a gradual one. You cannot fight against it. You cannot deny it, for it will simply come back in another form. You cannot cast it out without first understanding it. The only way to defeat attachment is through a true observation of the nature of the attachment, to see what is the cause of the attachment, what it really means. Why are you attached to somebody? Why are you attached to some material object? Why are you attached to your wealth or social position? Truly examine within your own heart the nature of any attachment and, above all, the support or the pleasure that it gives you. Consider why you are attached to a certain person, to a certain religion, to a certain ideology and, above all, ask what that relationship gives to you. For it is at this point that you have a direct comparison with what your Creator gives to you.

Have you ever considered, within the stillness of your heart, what it is that your Creator gives you through that unique bond of love that exists between you? Have you every considered what the presence of the Holy Spirit within you really means? For those who truly recognise their divinity there is no need for any attachments but to the one divine Source of all Life, Which knows all things. In the times in which you live, where there is a great amount of karmic settlement, where people are suffering on all levels, you can witness the painful results of false attachment. It is by seeing clearly the actions that others have taken, the steps that they have made, the suffering that they are experiencing, that you will grow to recognise the nature of your own attachments. See why you have created them, what needs they fulfil for you. Look at any relationship and say 'Am I giving in this relationship or am I taking? Does my father, my brother, my wife, fulfil a need for me or do I fulfil a need for them? Does my money, my property, my position in life, own me or am I the master of them?'. Seek for the spiritual balance in any relationship and through that balance will come an understanding as to how to handle any attachment.

For those who become attached there is always the pain of loss, for if you become attached to something or somebody and then lose them, inevitably, there is a space, a feeling of emptiness, of human mortality and weakness. But you cannot lose your divine link. It will never be withdrawn. By closing your eyes and invoking one word that Divine Presence is always with you. The Godhead is always present. Never demanding, always giving. Never asking, always listening. Never hating, always loving. Never criticising, always forgiving. Never closed to you, always open to the pure love that comes from your being. That is the nature of the divine relationship. If it is available to all, why should you accept second best? Why place an impossible burden on any mortal human being, a burden which they cannot and never will be able to carry?

Recognise the nature of physical life on the Earth. There can never be perfection. Even the greatest Master that walks the face of this Earth is fallible. So recognise the one true link, the one true union, and empowered by that knowledge come forth renewed. Yes, it requires that you be vulnerable. Yes, it requires that you let go of the concepts and the attachments that you have formed of yourself. Yes, it requires that you release some of the things that you hold most dear, that you are prepared to stand naked before your Creator. But from within your being will come a light, a splendour, that will reveal your true birthright. You will be seen for what you truly are – a child of Spirit.

QUESTIONS AND ANSWERS

Q: I can see very clearly that one should not become attached to anything or anybody, but are you saying that we should strive to become detached?

ZT: No. Detachment is not the opposite of attachment. If you become detached, then you become unloving and uncaring. You become indifferent to the world around you. You must learn to be compassionate and supportive in any relationship. Now that does not mean that you identify with another person's suffering or pleasure but that you become the impartial observer of them. Or, to put it another way, it means that although you may walk along the path of life with someone, be it for a short or long time, your eyes remain fixed on your goal, which is union with your Creator. No one relationship can ever be the purpose of life, the reason for your incarnation.

Q: You talk about sacrifice a lot. In my experience, giving based on sacrifice often leads to resentment, and resentment is a negative thought form that tends to undermine all human relationships, including one's relationship with God. In relationships with human beings is it not better to share rather than to give and to receive negative energy from giving with sacrifice?
ZT: You make several assumptions in your question with which I do not agree. Nevertheless, let us consider giving in its purest sense, in the relationship that exists between a mother and her child. Now a mother gives of herself to her child. She gives her time, her energy, her love, in order to nurture and to raise her child. For most mothers this is a sacrifice. It means the giving up of her own way of life, of her own identity, of her own will, for many, many years, in order to offer the nature of her being to her child. The child does not even ask for that sacrifice to be made, but the mother gives freely of her energy anyway, expecting no reward. It is a true example of divine love, of a spiritual attachment.

Now the mother's sacrifice is vital to the growth, on many levels, of her child. If the mother does not give, and when I use the expression mother I of course mean mother and father, for both are equally important, if the parents do not give freely, then that child does not become a complete human being. It will lack certain qualities of character and nature. Now it may be the case that the parents give of their energies but that the child, of its own decision, chooses to reject them. That is the right of the individual, to reject the attachment, to reject the bonding. Look at the example of the lives of all the great Masters and see how often their sacrifices, their free offerings to Humanity, have been rejected. The nature of divine love is that it has to be expressed and how the individual to whom it is directed receives it, is for them to decide. If they choose to reject it, or to misuse it, that is their decision but the energy is still given. The sacrifice that one makes is the sacrifice of one's own being for the evolutionary cycle of Humanity. That is the true nature of sacrifice and, as such, any sacrifice that assists that great cosmic flow is never in vain. I do not know if I have answered your question.

Q: I think I am talking about giving with expectation and you are talking about giving without expectation.
ZT: That is correct. There is no expectation in a sacrifice whatsoever.

Q: But when giving is given with expectation?
ZT: That is not giving. That is manipulation.

Q: Could you please explain the connection between attachment and fear.
ZT: It would be true to say that the more fearful a person is the more attachments they form, no matter in what area of human activity you were to look. So a person who is fearful of losing the love of someone close to them, desperately seeks that love. A person who is fearful about not having enough money to ensure their financial security is constantly trying to acquire more money. Fear, therefore, in the sense that we are talking about it, is a lack of trust in oneself and in one's ability as a child of God to draw down everything that one needs for oneself at any given moment in time.

Attachment, therefore, is born from the false belief that because God cannot, or will not, supply what a person needs, then they must obtain it for themselves in other ways. So they cling to the people and to the material possessions that they think they need in order to provide themselves with a security blanket. This act of apparent possession, be it of people or material objects, gives them self-worth and serves to confirm to them that their lack of faith in their Creator is indeed justified because they believe that they are responsible for all the creations around them. So we can see there is a direct correlation between fear, or lack of faith in one's Creator, and the need to form attachments.

Q: Does this go back then, to the bottom line, which is this feeling of separation from God, which most of us suffer from at one time or another?

ZT: None of you are separated from God. You might choose, either consciously or unconsciously, to create a gap of your own making between yourself and your God, but your Creator is omnipotent, omniscient and omnipresent. There is no separation unless you choose to create it, and that separation can only be created by denying the God in you or by acting in contradiction to God's will for you and for the planet.

Q: If you were to ask most people 'Would you like to do the will of God?', they would say 'Yes'. But how do we know what is God's will for us?
ZT: I think you are being a little generous towards Humanity in that assumption! I feel that although many people would say 'Yes', what they would actually mean was 'Yes, provided God's will coincides with my will'! Only a very few people in the world today are concerned either about discovering God's will or in fulfilling it. They do not want to know about anything that involves sacrifice or service.

Q: But if one is humble enough, if one realises that it is only by doing God's will that the planet and Humanity can be saved from a great disaster, then the question still remains 'How does one discover God's will?'. Most of us receive all sorts of intuitive flashes but how do we know whether they come from our Creator or whether they are the product of our own imagination and conditioning?
ZT: If you consciously attune each day, and especially in times of test and crisis, to God's will for you and for the planet, and if you do this in a humble and ego-less way, as part of your daily routine, rather like brushing your teeth in the morning, then you will find that the whole nature of your life will flow more smoothly because you are more in harmony with the force of God flowing through you. Now that does not mean that your life will be free from conflict, that you will face no tests, that all your personality desires will be met, that you will be given all the material objects that you think you need. No. What I am talking about now is the force of destiny in motion, the path that you have incarnated to walk, the relationships that, on a soul level anyway, you have chosen to experience, in order to transmute past karma and evolve your spiritual being. By attuning to God's will for you, by surrendering to it on an inner level, you will find that the outer form will then take care of itself. It is rather like buttoning up a shirt. If you get the top button right, then all the other buttons automatically fall into place.

56

Moreover, if you are honest with yourselves, you know when you are fighting against God's Will, you know when you are opposing that force of God in motion within you. You know when you are being a Saul as opposed to a Paul.

Q: Many of us do things wrong out of habit, out of fear, out of weakness. We just don't seem to have the strength or the will to change. Where does one get that strength, that will to do what one knows is right in one's life ?

ZT: The strength to do such things can come only from the perception of one's own experiences, of what one has achieved in the past through union with the Source of all Life. If you have truly attuned to your Creator in the past and have sought and tried to follow Its will for you, if only in very little things at first, then you will know that that way of life really works. You will know the reality of a life lived in harmony with the Divine and you will accept, as second nature, the divine synchronicity of life that comes with it. It is from such small beginnings that you gain the confidence to face the bigger challenges in life. When you know in your heart that you have been helped and guided in the past, then the future holds no fear for you. The strength and the will come from the certain knowledge that you are never alone, that your Creator is omnipresent, and that truly every hair on your head is counted. So what have you to fear, because God *is* here.

Q: Would you please clarify the term soul attachment for me?

ZT: Let us suppose that in our last incarnations, around two hundred years ago, you and I were husband and wife, and that we lived during a time of great conflict and crisis, a time of religious and political persecution, the French Revolution. Let us also suppose that one of us made the sacrifice of our life in order to save the life of the other, because of the great love that we bore for each other. Now such an act would create a strong soul attachment or bonding between us. Indeed, there would also be an element of karmic debt as well.

Now if we were to meet again in our next incarnations, say, around two hundred years later, that previous life experience would be imprinted freshly on our souls. Our souls would recall that past experience and, almost inevitably, we would be attracted to each other, on a soul level anyway, no matter what our physical shapes, no matter whether we were man and woman or man and man, no matter what our social class, religious beliefs or race. When we met and saw each other for the first time in this life we would know instantly that a bond exists between us. Now if you are evolved souls and are aware of the reality of past life experiences, then you will recognise that attraction for what it really is. But so many in the world today, because of their point of evolution, because they are not aware of the nature of a soul attraction that has probably existed for many, many lives, turn that relationship into a sexual, an emotional or a marital one. They feel the attraction on a deep inner level, interpret that attraction as an expression of love, and set in motion a whole new relationship. They translate a soul relationship into a physical relationship.

Now you will all meet people with whom you have had a strong bonding in past lives. You will feel deeply attracted to them, but that does not mean that you have to marry them or to have an affair with them, although some people do try to do this! Soul attraction or attachment does not demand the sexual union which so many people in your world seek today. Recognise that all of you have experienced many lives together and that you have probably been married together many times as well. You will have created deep links, both of karma and of soul relationship. These cannot be denied. As the Master has just said, 'Anyone that you feel strongly about in this life you will have encountered in a previous life'. You will have shared deep experiences with them, but that does not mean that they have to be repeated. There is no point in repeating the same lesson.

Some people, of course, will rise above the physical level and will establish a relationship purely on a soul level. They will form an attachment to the soul quality of a certain person, but be aware that such a relationship is just as fraught with distraction, because that is not the relationship that you should be seeking in life. The one and only true union is spiritual union, union with the Source of all Life, which by its very nature is a destined union. So be aware that you will all feel soul attachments for another person, you will all experience deep feelings which you cannot explain, the result of past lives spent together, but it is up to you to handle such relationships correctly. Because many souls are incarnating on the Earth at this time in order to experience the changing of the Ages, the transformation of the planet, many past relationships are being resurrected. All your past wives or husbands, sons or daughters, friends or lovers will be present. You cannot relive every relationship! So you must always re-enter into a relationship only after deep attunement, only after listening to that inner voice, to the God-force flowing within you.

Q: I have to confess, Zen Tao, that I am very attracted to you, but that must be a soul attraction! So I will have to try and raise that relationship to a spiritual level.

ZT: That would be wise, my lady, because, ultimately, if some disaster was to happen to you tomorrow, if you were to find yourself locked up in a prison all alone, if your husband or your child was to die, what is the relationship that you can count upon? It is your union with God. Human relationships are destined to end and that is a fact. Death is inevitable as is the death of all human relationships, all human attachments. So do not become attached to them. Seek the one relationship that never ends.

EARTH CHANGES

I want to talk to you this evening about the evolutionary cycle of the Earth and of the forthcoming transformation of this planet which is sometimes referred to as 'The Earth Changes'. Great confusion abounds on the Earth at this time, for not only is Humanity in a state of crisis but so is the planet. This state of crisis exists on all levels of life, that is on both the physical, the mental and the spiritual, and is caused not just by Humanity's present actions but also by the fact that much karma is being transmuted at this time. All over the world, as you are only too aware when you read your newspapers each day, people are coming into conflict as they are forced to face tests, tests both of an individual and of a collective nature, tests which they have refused to face in previous lives. Why should this be so? Because Humanity is preparing itself for the next great changing of the Earth's evolutionary cycle. What is so special about the changing of the Earth's cycle and of this cycle in particular? I will tell you.

The Earth has experienced many cycles of change, most of which are recorded only in myth and legend, but you are all aware of the last great changing of the Earth's cycle and of the Earth changes that took place around six thousand years ago. This is the event that is referred to in the Bible as the Great Flood and which has become immortalised as the story of Noah's Ark. So why has the changing of the Earth's cycle now become more critical? Simply because six thousand years ago that cycle was initiated by Divine Will. Humanity, at that time, through its thoughts, words and deeds, could only affect the timing and the nature of that event to a very small degree and, in the final analysis, that moment of great cataclysmic change was initiated by Infinite Spirit. However, when we come to consider the changing of the present cycle, the changing that will witness the dawning of the long awaited Age of Aquarius, it must be recognised that the human influence on this event will be much stronger. It will be stronger not only because Humanity is much more numerous on the planet, and the power of its collective thoughtforms will be much stronger as well, but also, because of recent scientific discoveries, Humanity now has the knowledge and the means within its hands to destroy not only itself but also the whole planet. There is, therefore, a strong possibility that Humanity will initiate this cycle of planetary transformation at an earlier time than has been ordained by Infinite Spirit, and that this will cause great suffering both for Humanity and for the planet.

I have said before, and I will say again, that I can assure you that Humanity will not be permitted to destroy either itself or this planet to any great extent. Now that does not mean that there will not be nuclear explosions and that other forces of devastation will not come into play. Such things are determined by human karma. What it does mean is that Humanity has the choice of either accepting the timing of the divine cycle or of creating its own timing. That, above all, is the real nature of the choice which faces Humanity at this time. It can either accept the natural changing of the cycle or, through its own wrong actions, it can initiate the change prematurely, and can cause it to happen before Humanity, either individually or collectively, is ready for it. You would have every right to say to me, 'Why, therefore, is there so much confusion on the Earth concerning this cycle, if it is indeed a natural event? Why do so many people, both from your side of life as well as from ours, predict events and share their visions as to the nature of these changes, and why do these prophecies often conflict and, subsequently, are found to be in error?'. To answer these questions I must go right back to the very beginnings of human manifestation on the Earth.

What is the purpose of human life on the Earth? Why do you live on this planet? The answer is very simple. It is the gaining of consciousness, of that which is sometimes called soul-knowingness, the wisdom of spirit. You incarnate onto this plane of Earth with nothing but consciousness and you depart from it with nothing but consciousness. All that transpires between birth and death is but an evolutionary lesson in a classroom, to be compared to a fleeting dream. Life is but a dream, like a drama on a theatre stage and, as such, is unreal. Of course, to you it is very real, but that simply reflects the nature of the drama. All that concerns the evolved soul, and I speak to you now only because you are all evolved souls, is the gaining of soul consciousness. Therefore recognise that all things that manifest on this Earth are but lessons and tests to evolve that consciousness. It is an aware being who recognises that the only thing that is significant in this world is consciousness. It is consciousness that created and now changes this world. It is a rise in consciousness that will uplift it onto a higher plane of being and it is a lack of consciousness that will destroy it.

At this time, therefore, I can tell you that all beings of consciousness are approaching a moment of supreme test, a test that is governed by the nature of the cycle. You experience many cycles: the cycles of the planet, of day and night, of summer and winter, the cycle of life and death as you live life after life, the cycle of the changing of the Zodiacal Ages, for example, from Pisces to Aquarius, and so on. In addition to this, you experience the cycles set in motion by the great planetary beings who dwell in this planetary body, the solar system in which you now incarnate. You therefore experience many cycles of change, but all of them have but one purpose – to expand your spiritual consciousness, for it is consciousness that creates and governs all things. Some people like to refer to your God as the Supreme Consciousness. However, always remember that there is an even greater God above the God of which you are aware and which you worship, a God that is beyond your human comprehension. Your God, like you, is subject to higher evolutionary forces. Into Its Being come tests and experiences, into Its Being come cycles of change. You are therefore subject to the influence of cycles, within cycles, within cycles, in a complexity of being that could be likened to the interaction of the millions of stars which you see in your sky at night. It is indeed a source of wonderment to you and quite beyond your understanding to know the destiny and the purpose of such an array.

At this time on the Earth you are concerned primarily with one cycle, the changing of the cycle from Pisces to Aquarius. Therefore recognise that most of you are preparing for this change. Now there are, of course, people on the plane of Earth who are not concerned with and who do not believe in this great change. This is probably because they will die and leave their present physical bodies before this great planetary cycle comes into being. Therefore they are simply not interested in or concerned with this great event, if only because they will not be a part of it. There are others who, whilst being aware of the cycle, are not prepared to face it, are not prepared to accept the nature of the cycle or, indeed, of its purpose, for their life is controlled solely by the drama of life, by the physical reality of the world in which they live. They do not recognise the God-consciousness either within themselves, within this planet or within the universe as a whole. It is mainly for them that this great lesson of the changing of the cycle is approaching.

Now, as I said earlier, Humanity possesses the ability, should it so choose, to initiate this cycle through its own destructive energy, through its own ego, through its own thoughtforms. It could explode its nuclear bombs and so bring about great destruction and devastation. If this does indeed take place then, inevitably, there will be much suffering. Indeed, the great planetary 'Earth changes' that will follow will be seen as a great healing, for it will remove the blight of Humanity's negativity from the face of the Earth. But, as I have said so often before, the race of Humanity will not die. After all these 'Earth changes' the race of Humanity will still walk upon the face of the Earth, but not in its present form. So let me now explain the nature of that race of Humanity.

You are all very familiar with the experience of life through your physical senses. You have grown accustomed to the force of Nature as it exists on the plane of Earth today. You are aware, only too well, of the limitations of the physical world in which you briefly incarnate, of the make-up of your atmosphere, of the make-up of your body, of the water which is so essential for your growth and continuing existence. But conditions will not be the same in the New Age. You will not be able to survive the changes that are to come simply by adapting physically, for the physical body that you are seeking to protect will not exist in the New Age. The physical structure of the human beings that will dwell in the New Age will have changed radically. Whereas, now, a large percentage of your body is water, in the New Age it will be air.

So you can see that the race of Humanity that will walk the Earth in the Aquarian Age will differ in many respects from today. The human form will be different and will vibrate to a different note. The physical nature of the Earth will be very different. The angels and the great Masters will actually be present on the Earth, in physical appearance, and will walk and talk with you. The whole structure of matter, the frequency range in which you live, vibrate and have your being will have been altered. Therefore only one thing, only one factor, can guarantee your survival, if that is indeed your concern, in the natural cycle of this change and that is consciousness, your soul consciousness. For it is your soul that will build the body that you require, that will change the atomic structure of your being and so prepare you for the life of the millennium which is to come – the Golden Age of Aquarius.

63

Now many of you, for a variety of reasons, have been picking up feelings that cataclysmic events that will cause great physical destruction are coming. I can confirm that they are indeed coming. The Earth is to change radically. Events are to happen which will indeed demand that groups of people have to band together in order to survive. Now there has been much prognostication as to how to survive these events, as to where to live in order to avoid the worst of the devastation, as to the nature of the communities that must be formed and what has to be done to guarantee their survival. Much advice has been given, from our side of life as well as from yours, on how to achieve this, but I would say to you that many errors have been made and that much of the information that has been given has been misleading. Let us reflect for a minute on why this is so.

On your Earth at this time you do not have to be a prophet to recognise that the financial systems of your world are in a process of collapse. Whether you are a psychic, a mystic, a prophet or, indeed, simply a banker, you know that the time is fast approaching when the present financial institutions of the world will crumble. This you can prophesy with certainty, but what can you say as to the nature of the timing of that event? You can, of course, make an inspired guess, you can give an opinion, but what will be the event that will initiate the final collapse? That event will, of course, be an act of God. An event will happen on this Earth which will then set in motion a chain of events which will lead to the destruction of the financial empires of this world. But does any being know what that trigger will be? I, from my point of consciousness, dwelling on a plane far above that of the Earth, can say – 'I do not know'. Now there are many on my side of life who are prepared to give opinions, but recognise that they too are only voicing opinions, and opinions are not facts. There is only one being that knows the timing of such an event and that is your Creator, and at this time your Creator has not yet released that knowledge, even to the great Lords of Its Spiritual Hierarchy. We do not know the nature or the timing of that event, let alone the precise timing of the changing of the cycle from Pisces to Aquarius, for there are so many variable factors. It depends, above all, on the response of Humanity, on the thoughtforms that Humanity creates, on the deeds that it performs, indeed, on how it responds to the tests that are before it now.

Consider if, at this very moment in time, one country was to accidently fire a nuclear missile, if a military commander in a moment of error was to release such a missile and it was to explode on a country of an opposing ideology or religion, what would be the response of that country, indeed of all the other countries of your world? Would they humbly accept that a mistake had been made? Would they be open and generous, would they recognise that the safety of the planet must come first? Would they demonstrate the spirit of self-sacrifice, a quality which Humanity has shown only on very rare occasions in its evolutionary path in this cycle, or would they demand retribution? Such a challenge may come. How will the major countries of your world respond? How will their leaders respond? That is the nature of the choice which faces Humanity. There are so many questions that Humanity still has to answer. Yes, great events are coming. Yes, I can see the nature of what will touch the Earth, but as to the timing of those events, that is for Humanity to decide.

Now many people have visions, many people see aspects of the future, many people have the gift of prophecy and can describe clearly the nature of events that are to come. That, of course, is Humanity's birthright and cannot be denied, but how are they to establish the timing of those events. There were many people, for example, who saw the events of the Second World War, who even saw specific actions in that War, who actually witnessed the slaughter, the suffering and the physical devastation long before it actually happened. But although such people saw that War on another level of life they did not know the precise timing of that event, they did not know the country where it would start and they did not know what the result of that War would be. For what the prophet or visionary sees is but one or two small parts of the picture and they only see those with a limited vision too. Therefore, above all, you must remember that anything that is released to you, as an individual, is for your own inspiration, is for your own purpose, is for your own destiny. Any vision which comes to you comes as your birthright. So accept it both humbly and gratefully. You may share it with others but that will often lead to confusion and, perhaps, even distrust. Your picture is your vision, is your destiny. The circle of guides and angels that are surrounding you at this time are responsible for your own destiny. They are there to help you, and will help you, but that is a personal, a unique link, which was created before your birth.

Now there are many beings on the higher planes of life who are making statements as to the nature of The Earth Changes. Let us consider, for a moment, the reality of the information that is being released. Why should that information be released? For example, if your father or your mother had but recently died, they would exist on a level of life which you could contact quite easily, but the consciousness that they would display, the advice that they would give you, would only reflect the consciousness that they had possessed when they were alive on Earth. They would be free from the restrictions of physical life and would see with a clearer vision, but their consciousness would be the same. Therefore the advice coming to you from that higher plane of life, whilst it might have more impact, because of the nature of the message, would be no more valid than if it had been given on Earth. Each of you taps into the level of consciousness that is the equal of yours, and there are a thousand million levels of consciousness on the planes of life above the Earth, right up to that of your Creator. The higher your consciousness, the higher the note that you sound, and the higher the note that responds. You determine that which you receive by the purity of your thoughts, by the purity of your speech, by the purity of your acts. Your purity is your radio aerial and the degree to which you raise that aerial controls the nature of the source of knowledge and wisdom into which you will tap.

Now there are many on the higher planes of life who, with the best of intentions, are trying to help Humanity, but let us consider how they can help. Let us suppose, for example, that a being on a higher level of life released the information that someone on the plane of Earth was soon to die. Now such information, in the first place, would only be released by a very young soul, never by an evolved soul, because in truth the only being that knows the time of your physical death is your Creator. Whilst a being on the higher levels of life might see that death is coming, for that is the privilege of all, even those living on the physical plane of life, that being would not know the actual moment of death. Nevertheless, knowing that death was coming, it would recognise that certain events on the Earth first had to take place in order to smooth that soul's transition. Therefore that being would perhaps deliberately exaggerate its message, and would attempt to bring forward events on the Earth in order to cause the individual concerned to act with greater haste. It would try to force the individual's rate of growth and evolution.

Recognise, therefore, that there are spiritual beings, who because of their soul evolution, abuse the powers that they have on the higher levels of life, even though they do so with the best of intentions. They are only acting according to the highest of their consciousness. They are trying to help and be of service to those on the physical plane of life, but their help is limited by their consciousness, for they cannot see that

66

the help that they are giving is misguided. But that is the pattern of their evolution, for you learn on the higher planes of life just as you learn on the lower. Everything that you do on any level serves to raise consciousness. If guidance is given from the higher planes and is blindly followed by those on Earth and, subsequently, leads to failure and disaster, then, the lesson is learned both on the physical and the higher planes of life.

Guidance, therefore, is only as accurate and as appropriate as the level of consciousness of the being that is giving it. There are many young souls on my side of life, as indeed there are on the plane of Earth, who are only too happy to give guidance out of a misguided feeling of self-importance, but be wary of such guidance. There is only one source and that is your Creator. There is only one Being Who knows the plan for your life, for your destiny, for your Earth, and that is your Creator. Each of you has been given a divine link to your Creator, for within your heart beats the divine spirit that links you eternally and universally to your Creator. That is the guidance which you should seek. That is the guidance which you should follow.

Now I, from my plane of life, can look down and can envisage many of the Earth Changes that are to take place. I can envisage them because I have access to the Akashic Record of the Earth, the record of all human activity in thought, word and deed. I can see the conflicts that are to take place both between nations and individuals, because this is a time of karmic resolution, this is a time when the slate of human activity will be wiped clean so that in the beginning of the Golden Age of Aquarius Humanity will have no burdens, will have the freedom to be as it should be. I, therefore, as any evolved being, can see the nature of such conflicts. I can tell you, for example, as I look at the country of Israel, that because that country was founded on the enforced resettlement, on the suffering and loss of thousands of human beings, it must inevitably attract the necessary karmic balance before the ending of this Age. Any being of consciousness who understands the nature of karma, and who has access to the Akashic Record, can foretell these events.

Many beings on the higher planes of life can and, indeed do, release this knowledge, but those of us who are truly aware of the responsibility of guidance, who know that we are responsible until the ending of time for everything that we say, and for everything that you as individuals do because of what we say, are bound to act with consciousness. You gain consciousness through experiencing the drama of life. If I release that drama to you, if I tell you what is to happen on the physical plane of life, then where is the point of the drama? You have to experience these events, to handle them and to learn from them. You have to invoke your own intuitive energy, to ground and to receive the wisdom of your Creator. You are unique beings, you are gods in the making. That is the nature of your potential. You must learn through your own efforts and through your own mistakes.

Now that does not mean that guidance is not your birthright. Guidance is available to all who seek it, but the nature of the guidance is not to answer your questions but is, rather, to get you to answer your own questions. It is for you to realise the true nature of your own consciousness and to be responsible for it. Now, inevitably, over the passage of time, because many of us on the higher planes of life, and this is especially true of your guides and Masters, have been with you in so many lives on the Earth, strong links have been forged. We have been together in all the great human civilisations. We therefore know each other well and are willing to help each other, and if the note that you send out is pure, if your motivation for guidance is always universal and not individual, then you will be helped. You will be aided in reaching the decisions that you have to make, and that guidance will be but the universe responding to you. You, in turn, will respond to that which comes into your physical life. Indeed, your guardian angels will bring into your aura that which you need for your guidance.

At this time, therefore, be aware of the crisis that is present on the Earth. Be aware of the confusion that exists and recognise that that confusion exists not only on the physical plane but also on the higher planes of life as well, for every individual soul, knowing that this great moment of change is coming, is concerned both for the Earth and for Humanity on it. The Earth Changes represent a great upward movement in the evolutionary spiral, not just for Humanity but also for many beings on the higher planes of life as well, for everything in Creation is evolving. There are, therefore, many levels and degrees of consciousness that are concerned about the Earth Changes. There are many levels and degrees of consciousness who are experiencing the drama of physical life at this time. So be aware that these Earth Changes are coming and that they are part of the destiny of Humanity and of the planet. Recognise that you have the guidance to understand and accept these changes. You will be in the right place, at the right time, not through your own endeavours but because of the guidance that comes to you from above. The note which you sound, the purity of your vision, will guarantee that you will fulfil your destiny, the destiny that you chose before you came down into physical incarnation.

Finally, remember that everything that manifests on the plane of Earth has a destiny to fulfil. There are many karmic patterns to be resolved. Recognise that there will be many souls who will fall by the wayside, who will not be prepared to accept these Earth Changes, who will not release the familiar life style of the Old Age for the challenge of the New Age, who will not accept the presence of the Divine within their midst, within their own being. The time of Armageddon will soon be at hand, when brother will fight against brother, sister against sister, father against child, and all the events that are prophesied in the Bible will come to pass. Then will come the time when the sun and the moon will not shine, when darkness will descend across the face of the Earth, when the stars will move in the firmament, but be not afraid, for this will be the birth of a new Heaven and a new Earth, the birth of the New Age.

There is only one father and one mother for all of you and that is your Creator. You must be true, above all, at this time, to the Source, for it is the Source which controls your destiny. Recognise that fact and realise that the consciousness which you gain and ground now is the key to your understanding of this cycle and of the cycle that is to come. It is the key to everything that will manifest on the plane of Earth, for where there is death and destruction, if your consciousness does not invoke it, you will not be touched. Where there is disease and warfare, if your consciousness does not invoke it, you will not be touched. Only those who have to pay their karmic settlement, who have to balance their akashic record, will suffer in the great drama of the 'Earth Changes'. Those that are truly one with the Divinity of all life will experience a rise in consciousness that will pass all understanding.

This is the nature of the change that is to come. It is not a physical change. It is not an Earth change. It is a change of consciousness. It is the birth of a new Humanity, in a new body, in a new Earth. The key to that birth is consciousness. Remember that vital fact and then a new Heaven and a new Earth will truly unfold before your very eyes.

QUESTIONS AND ANSWERS

Q: In last year's Christ-mass channelling a Master said that this year, 1986, was going to be the last year that we could call 'normal'. Does that mean that 1987 is going to see the start of the Earth changes and that we should use this year to get ready for them and to adjust our lifestyle accordingly?

ZT: The changes that will manifest on the Earth in 1987 will be created by the karmic accounts that are being settled now and these will, in turn, be initiated by the behaviour of the races, the nations and the individuals concerned and the planetary activity which controls their destinies. I can tell you, however, that there will only be localised areas of conflict and warfare, there will only be localised areas of disease, there will only be localised areas of drought and earthquake, there will only be localised areas where the social fabric will collapse. As such, there will only be localised areas where new beginnings will be made from this karmic settlement. But all these occurrences should be seen as warning signs of what is to come, as portents of the future.

I would not want you to regard all these crises that are to manifest on the Earth as being accumulative, finally ending up in one big catastrophe. Rather, see them as separate events which, whilst demonstrating the general human condition, will come and go in response to both individual and collective human karma. However, with regard to the natural cycle of the Earth change, I am prepared to say that this event will not come about until around the year 2000. That may be a foolish thing to say, bearing in mind what the Master has just said! Perhaps so, but as I see the karmic relationships of certain nations, of the karmic debts that have to be repaid, I know that that will require a certain amount of Earth time. Finally, however, remember that the deciding factor in all of this is Humanity. It is how Humanity acts that will determine the timing of this great event.

Q: Of course, I agree with what you have said. But I have been given guidance through my own channel which is telling me to leave my own country and to go and build a survival centre in the U.S.A. Are you saying I should ignore this message?

ZT: Let me give you a simple analogy. If your guidance had told you instead to remain in your home country of Switzerland, and if the mountains had crumbled down upon you and had killed you, when you stood before your Creator would you say, 'Well I was only following guidance'! So there would be two beings who would have karmic debts to settle – you and the being who gave you that guidance! In the final analysis you alone are responsible for handling your own destiny. You alone are responsible for deciding your path in life. Now you can receive inspiration, you can receive guidance, you can read prophetic books, but it is you, and you alone, according to your point of consciousness, that has to take action and then be responsible for those actions. If a guide tells you to go and live somewhere, and you blindly follow that guidance, that is not you accepting responsibility for your actions unless you, as an individual, have already recognised that fact within you and are simply regarding the guidance as a form of divine confirmation. There are many in your world today who do base their actions on such guidance, but just as you would not blindly follow the advice of your local priest, so do not blindly follow guidance. Always test the spirits to see if they are of God, and then test them again!

Finally, whenever you take action, remember that the Universe will always respond to your actions, the force that I call universal feedback, which is your Creator responding to your actions, reflecting back to you on the nature of their rightfulness and their appropriateness. So as you contemplate such a big step as emigration, leaving the country of your birth, it would be foolish of you to leap blindly, on an impulse. Rather, take one small step towards this objective and then see how the Universe, your God, responds to that step. If the flow of the Universe is with you, if you encounter no obstacles, then proceed, but if there are obstacles, then consider why they are there, for if you are one with the Divine then all things flow to you, all things flow with you.

Q: I think that all this talk about Earth Changes and cataclysms is very negative and is actually attracting such events to us. It can also make some people very fearful and take purpose away from their lives. I feel that we should be praying to God for the power to transform both ourselves and this planet. So many people today are focussing on the negative aspects of life rather than on the positive.

ZT: I respect your opinion and acknowledge the motivation behind it. It is a fact that you do draw your thoughts unto yourselves. But did you know that some people are actually praying for the cataclysm, and asking that it comes sooner rather than later, since they see it as the only way of saving this world from human predacity and of initiating the Golden Age of Aquarius? So negativity and positivity are human viewpoints, defined by your perceptions of what is good or bad for the planet and Humanity dwelling on it.

My answer must inevitably reflect my point of soul-consciousness and I share it with you on that understanding. If it conflicts with yours, that does not mean that I am right and you are wrong or vice versa! I believe that the destiny of the Earth and of Humanity on it is pre-ordained. Like the drama on the stage, the plot is created by the author. It is only in the way in which the drama is presented and in our reaction to it that we have an element of choice. So great changes are coming and have, indeed, occurred on other levels, how else could prophecy exist? You cannot avoid your destiny on an individual or a planetary level. The only choice that you have is in how you react to the drama. That is what produces spiritual growth and evolution. However, leaving aside the whole question of Humanity's destruction of the environment of the planet, do you honestly feel that in the next one hundred years Humanity's consciousness will change so dramatically as to support the Golden Age of peace and harmony between all living beings? Whilst some individuals are exhibiting a high degree of soul consciousness, the majority are bound up in their physical bodies and sensory desires. It could in fact be said that Humanity is devolving rather than evolving at this particular moment in time! It will need divine intervention or intercession to bring about the birth of the New Age, and for many people that means a cataclysmic moment of planetary and human transformation.

There are those whose sole concern about the cataclysmic changes to come is in knowing how to survive them. Again I must refer to the all pervasive power of destiny. If you are meant to die in a moment of cataclysmic rebirth then you will die, no matter to what 'safe' haven you have retreated. If you are meant to survive, then even in an area of great physical destruction you will survive. What is important is not the cataclysm, but your attitude towards it and, most important of all, your attitude towards its creator, your God. You all have to die somewhere, sometime. Suffering only occurs when your idea of where and when differs from your Creator's!

Q: At another time you have talked about the end of the Piscean Age that we are now experiencing as being the time of Armageddon referred to in the Bible. Is there going to be a war to end all wars with brother fighting against brother and so on?

ZT: Are you trying to draw me into making a prophecy! What I have said is that in the life and death of the Master Jesus, who was the avatar that grounded and birthed the Age of Pisces, you can see the total destiny for that Age. So the fact that Jesus died a violent death on the cross indicates a violent end to the Age. There will indeed be one more great war, but not between the political ideologies that you would imagine, and there will be a limited use of nuclear weapons. There will also be many civil wars, especially in the East and much religious persecution. There will also be several great climatological changes, which will dramatically reshape the great political and financial empires that exist today. There will also be the coming of the Christ and the Anti-Christ to hone Humanity's spiritual perceptions. More than that I am not permitted to say. The drama is there to be experienced.

Q: The people of South Africa are very worried at the moment. Can you tell us anything about the destiny of South Africa and what aware people can do to help that country?

ZT: In any time of, what I will call, extreme conflict, and this was true of the last great World War as well, there are people on both sides of the conflict who demonstrate a high degree of spirituality, of soul consciousness. Such people touch the lives of many of their fellow citizens. Nevertheless it must also be recognised that even if Jesus had been present in physical incarnation in 1939 he would not have been able to prevent that war. When the collective consciousness of a nation creates a situation of conflict, it is very difficult to transmute that energy. Now that is not to say that it could not be transmuted, but that the people or the political parties that have created that situation really have no desire to dissolve it, to act out of a spirit of sacrifice. The conflict has become a way of life for them. Recognise that any being that stands up and demonstrates the principles of Christ-consciousness, who acts as a mirror to their actions, can be seen as a great threat. Such is the path to martyrdom.

Nevertheless, do not forget that the eyes are the windows of the soul and that what people see cannot be denied on an inner level. Any demonstration of truth is noted and leaves its mark on the soul. So, for example, there would have been many Germans at the end of the Second World War who would have looked back and recognised that the example of a few evolved souls, which they saw and denied in the late 1930's, was indeed a right demonstration of truth. There is a great lesson in that for any soul. The purpose of any prophet or teacher

73

standing forth and demonstrating truth is not necessarily to convert or to save a people from walking a wrong path. It is to demonstrate the cosmic principle so that those who deny it cannot say at a later date that they did not know that they were doing wrong. It is to provide a more lasting lesson in consciousness at a later date.

So evolved souls incarnate into areas of great conflict and strife, such as South Africa, not just to test the strength of their own spiritual beings but also to be a living example for their fellow citizens. As the Master has just said, it requires great spiritual perspective and wisdom to stand forth in such times. One has to recognise that what is important is the right demonstration, the grounding of divine consciousness for all to behold, not the short term result of changing the will of some political party. Any demonstration of Truth is not for the individual, is not for the country, it is for the whole stream of human consciousness. Look at the example of the life and the times of the Master Jesus. So no matter in what country you dwell, no matter what the nature of the conflict that is present there, all that is required of you is that you live your life to the highest of your spiritual principles, that you do not judge the roles that others are playing in the drama of life, and that you recognise that all evil and suffering has a purpose. You may not recognise what that purpose is, but you must accept that it is part of God's Plan for Humanity for, truly, nothing manifests on the face of this Earth that is not part of God's Will for Humanity.

LOOK TO THIS DAY

Look to this day!
For it is life, the very life of life.
In its brief course lie all the verities
and realities of your existence –
    The bliss of growth,
    The glory of action,
    The splendour of beauty;
For yesterday is but a dream,
And tomorrow is only a vision;
    But today well lived
Makes every yesterday a dream of happiness,
And every tomorrow a vision of hope.
    Look well, therefore, to this day.

(From the Sanskrit)

This ancient poem, written thousands of years ago, reveals an understanding of life that has been lost by many people in our world today. We have included it by way of an introduction to the next teaching, because it encapsulates in a few lines the whole essence of the teaching. Does it not also pose the question – 'Are we really more evolved than our forebears?'. The consciousness of its author shines forth from every line and illustrates the fact that Truth is timeless.

LOOK TO THIS DAY

If I was to ask each of you individually what you considered to be the most important day in your present incarnation, almost certainly you would go back into your memories and you would select a day from the past, a day which you felt held the greatest meaning for you. However, would it occur to you, firstly, that your memories of that day would be highly subjective and would include only the events that you chose to remember and, secondly, that your feelings now towards that day would be very different from the ones that you actually felt on that day, because they would be governed by your present state of mind?

So I would suggest to you that if you were to select a day on that basis that it would prove to be a fairly pointless exercise, for the most important day in your life is not a day that has passed, is not a day that is to come, but is the day that you are living now. Furthermore, the most important part of that day is the very minute in time that you are living right now. For the reality that you are experiencing right now could so transform your whole being that you would meet the next minute, let alone the next day, with a totally different understanding of life. It is how you experience today that will decide how you are going to greet tomorrow. It is the consciousness that you manifest today that will determine how you are going to live tomorrow.

But are you actually living in this moment in time? Are you actually listening to me and receiving my energies or are you not, even now, drifting off into some world of your own creation? It is vitally important that you focus your whole being on the here and now, that you concentrate all of your senses, both on the higher and the lower frequencies of life, onto the reality of this moment in time. Remember that although you look with your physical eyes you are also looking with your inner, or third eye, as it is sometimes known, and that you are constantly using senses that extend beyond the frequency range of physical life. It is the sum total of all these senses that determines your understanding of each moment in time. How you live this moment really does determine how you will experience the next.

If this is indeed the case, then why do you choose not to live in the present? Why do you choose to live in unreality as opposed to reality? The answer is very simple. It is because you do not want to face reality and all the lessons that you have to learn, all the tests that you have to face. If you think about it, your memories of the past and your visions of the future are rather like selective dreams. You tend to remember only those things or people that you like or dislike, those events in life which arouse your pleasure or displeasure. You are far happier living in a world of your own creation, a world where your judgments and values are upheld, than in the real world! So what is happening is that if you cannot face the reality of the present you escape either into the hopes of the future or into the memories of the past. In fact, what you are doing is creating your own reality in your minds. You are choosing to live either in your selective memories of the past or in your hopes for the future. Both are illusory.

You have only one reality. There is only one moment of truth and that is this moment in time that you are living and experiencing right now. If you are truly open to this moment then you are experiencing exactly what your Creator has created for you in the drama of life. You are experiencing exactly what you need to experience in order to teach you of divine consciousness and to help you to balance your karmic account. If you are truly living in the moment then you are at one with the flow of the Cosmos, with your Creator's Will both for you and for this planet. Now the essence of this Will is the force that I call Intelligence. Intelligence has nothing whatsoever to do with the intellect. Intelligence is the flow of Cosmic Wisdom that touches every level and every aspect of life. Everything and everyone around you is imbued with this energy, which supports your Creator's Plan both for you and for this planet. An intelligent being, therefore, is someone who is attuned to this flow of Cosmic Intelligence. Someone who is leading an intelligent life is someone who is attuning their life each day to this flow of Cosmic Intelligence, who is open to the cosmic impulse of the moment in time that they are living. As sensory beings, receiving on many levels, you can receive this flow of Cosmic Intelligence in many ways.

If you will but consider the reality of each day, if you will but seek its purpose and meaning for you, then you will begin to understand the true nature of your physical existence. So many people today are actually walking through life with their eyes closed, not their physical eyes but their spiritual eyes, although sometimes they choose to close or avert their physical eyes as well! So many people today are walking through life choosing not to use their inner eye, the eye of the soul. They are doing this not just through a lack of practice in using this eye but because they have conditioned themselves into what they want to see. Even if they were to see something new, something which, for them, was quite revelational, they would reject it.

As you go through life, for the most part, you tend to look with the eyes of memory. For example, when you go for a walk in the countryside and look at an oak tree, you recognise and identify that tree as an oak tree, just like any other oak tree, and then pass on to look at something else, but have you really seen that oak tree? Have you truly looked at it and seen what it is manifesting in terms of its shape, its colour, its health and its energy? You see only what you want to see, you see only what you remember of past oak trees. You are not truly seeing and, therefore, you are not truly experiencing the reality of that oak tree in just the same way that you are not truly experiencing the reality of that moment in time. You are not truly experiencing the force of Cosmic Intelligence. You are, therefore, not attuned to your Creator.

Each hour, each day, has a vital lesson to give to you and you should strive to learn that lesson, if only because each hour, each day, is but a preparation for the next. Each hour, each day, represents an invitation to you from your Creator to attune to Its Intelligence and to become one with Its divine flow of energy. Obviously it takes both time and practice to learn once more to live with awareness, but once you have begun to tune in to that divine flow of Intelligence you will begin to grow into an understanding of life which, at present, is simply beyond your comprehension. Walking through life without being in tune with this flow of Intelligence is rather like seeing life through a pair of spectacles which are covered with a film of mist. Most people walk through life with their vision either partly or wholly obscured, but for those who wipe their lenses clean there appears a clearer picture. It is this clearer vision that leads to a clearer understanding of the reality and the purpose of physical life.

Each day, therefore, should be regarded as a precious gift from your Creator, for you do not know if it will be your last. As you go to sleep tonight you do not know, firstly, if you will wake up in the morning and, secondly, what tomorrow holds in store for you, what new aspect of the great cosmic drama you will have to face, what new lessons you will have to master. Therefore never postpone until tomorrow all the lessons and all the karmic settlements that you can make today. Go to bed tonight feeling that if you were to die in your sleep it would not matter, because you could truthfully say that you would have no outstanding karmic duties to perform, no problems in relationship with your family or friends that have not been settled. Always remember that today well lived creates the framework for a better tomorrow.

Each day represents a step on the ladder of your destiny. Each day lived with consciousness and awareness represents another rung climbed on that ladder. So many people do not climb up a rung each year, let alone each day. Some people even take one or two steps downwards and then have to climb back up again. Remember that as you climb that ladder of your destiny that you are never alone. You are all beings of intelligence surrounded by Divine Intelligence. Everything and everybody that you encounter in your walk through life is part of that flow of Intelligence. Therefore recognise that everything and everybody that comes into your day is there for a reason, for a purpose. It is your Creator presenting Itself to you so that you can fulfil your divine destiny. Finally, remember that each day you will meet your destiny. You cannot avoid it. The only choice that you have in life is the degree of self-effort, the amount of self-energy, that you put into meeting it.

In the Bible there is an account of one of the parables that Jesus told concerning a rich man who was going to travel to a far off land and stay there for a long time. So before he departed he gave each of his servants varying sums of money, to look after for him whilst he was away. The servants all used this money in different ways. One buried his share in the ground, seeing this as being the safest way to ensure the return of the money to his master. Another traded with his share and doubled his investment. Yet another traded with his share and trebled his investment. On his return the rich man congratulated the servants who had increased their money but was displeased with the servant who had done nothing. The parable, of course, refers not to physical money or talents but to the spiritual qualities or talents which your Creator has given to you to exercise.

Using the analogy of the parable, it can be said that your Creator is not in physical incarnation on the Earth but has departed for another land, leaving Humanity with some of Its divine qualities or talents. It is up to you to make good use of the qualities and talents that you possess, which have been given to you in a sacred trust by your Creator. When you return to your Creator you will be accountable for how you have used those talents. The use of those talents is, of course, closely linked with the flow of divine Intelligence, which is your Creator's way of giving you guidance from that far off land as to how to use those talents. So, at any time of the day, when you are faced with an important decision or test, be aware that the divine qualities and talents to help you act correctly are only a moment of attunement away.

So many of you live your lives based on your judgments of the past. You are simply reliving past relationships today. Can you not see that if you live in the past, you are condemned to repeat the past today. But there is another path open to you. You can tap into that flow of Divine Intelligence, take fresh inspiration and create afresh, give birth to the new rather than recycle the old. So value each minute of the day as a God-given opportunity for you to exercise your divine talents creatively. Remember that how you live this minute in time decides not only the future but the past. How can this be so? Because the consciousness that you possess now, the inner eye that you look through now, will determine how you view the past.

Is it not a fact that as you grow older, in physical years that is, you can look back on earlier events in your life, events which formerly you regarded as being traumatic, yet which now you recognise were responsible for bringing great benefits to you? Similarly, is there not someone whose actions you have severely criticised in the past, but who now, in the light of your own experiences, you no longer judge so harshly? Finally, is it not the case that there are many events in your own life which although, at the time, you felt were of great significance but which, as the years go by, have now faded into insignificance? Therefore recognise that how you live this moment in time changes both the past and the future, for physical time is not a straight line of progression but is, rather, a circle of infinity. There is no past. There is no future. There is only the present. That is the only reality that you can know.

So how you live this day and, above all, the energy and the effort that you put into it, will decide the nature of your future and your past. You can, by a change of consciousness at this very moment in time, transform both your future and your past. You can truly change from Saul to Paul. Such an act does not take time, does not demand days, months or even years of practice and study. It is an act of the now. It is an act of spiritual intelligence which, as such, is timeless. So when you awaken from your sleep tomorrow measure each minute of the day with awareness and consciousness. Think, speak and act with awareness and consciousness. See in every thing, in every being, that comes into your aura, an opportunity for spiritual growth and understanding, an adventure in cosmic intelligence.

Recognise that how you handle your tests affects not just you but the whole of Humanity, for one being living a life of awareness and understanding, a life of cosmic intelligence, can truly transform a whole planet. There is nothing to stop you reaching the stars but your own limitations. There is nothing to stop you from being at one with the Masters of the planetary and interplanetary planes except your own unwillingness to be at one with them. There is nothing to stop you from seeing the face of your Creator except your own unwillingness to use your eyes. So look to this day, for it is life, the very essence of all life, in its hours lie all the realities of your human existence.

QUESTIONS AND ANSWERS

Q: Would you please say something about the nature of the relationship between human beings and the other life-forms on this Earth?
ZT: The life-forms of this planet had been in existence for aeons of time before Humanity incarnated on its surface in order to face its specific destiny. Now the life-forms of this planet are the creation of that Being which you call the Goddess, or Mother Earth, and the God of this solar system. These lifeforms have no free choice. They are linked to the intelligence of the Goddess. They automatically obey her will and purpose, as do all the servants of her Kingdoms – the elemental, the devic and the angelic beings. However, when Humanity incarnated upon the Earth, it was given the divine gift of free choice and was also given dominion over these Kingdoms. So the Goddess, of her own choice and sacrifice, relinquished her power and authority, for the time being, to the new gods that walked the face of this Earth, the race of Humanity.

So it can be said, with certainty, that you choose the nature of your relationship with the other Kingdoms of this Earth according to your point of consciousness and your understanding of the nature of physical life. Since Humanity is the most evolved life-form, the other Kingdoms look to you as their god. They look to you for their example, for the sustenance of their spiritual being. They therefore become like you. So you create your own world, not only by your thoughts, your words and your deeds, but also by how you influence the world in which you dwell. You are the creator of everything that happens on this plane of Earth, every single incident – every birth and every death, every earthquake and every flood, every drought and every pestilence. As you look at the Kingdoms of this Earth so you are seeing yourself, you are seeing what you have created.

81

Now, remembering, as the Master has just said, that the divine force of Intelligence touches all things, all life-forms, the choice is always yours as to whether you act in harmony with that Intelligence, and become as one with it, or whether you overrule it and ignore it, and so create in your own image, according to your own desires and thought forms. You decide whether to abuse or to uplift anything that comes into your aura. That is the real nature and the responsibility of the divine gift of free choice. That is the process that turns you from a man or a woman into a god. It does not matter what others do, how others treat the Kingdoms of this Earth. All that you are responsible for is your own interaction, your relationship, what you create in thought, word and deed. Recognise that it is your example that uplifts not just the race of Humanity, not just the other Kingdoms of this Earth, but the whole Cosmos, for all is one – One Intelligence, One Life, One God. You are never alone. You never act in isolation. What you do to yourself and to the world around you affects the whole universe.

Q: You have said in the past that the Human Race originally came from the star system of Sirius. Is it possible that we could make contact with the beings of that system or that we could visit that system ourselves, in one of our higher bodies?

ZT: At other times in the cycle of its evolution Humanity has, in its higher bodies, walked the surface of the other planets within this solar system, but it has never ventured beyond the boundaries of this system. Nevertheless, I would like to make it very clear that since Humanity does not originate within this solar system, that since it is a race apart, the many other levels of existence within this solar body are well acquainted with Humanity's origins and destiny and know of its purpose in being here in physical incarnation on the planet. So whilst they are prepared to offer their services to you on many levels of being, to help you along your evolutionary path, they also take great care to keep separate from you, for your destiny is very different from theirs. They learn a great deal from watching your evolutionary experiences, but they also recognise that the destiny of Humanity is not tied to this little solar system. At some stage in the future the Human Race will return to its own solar system, to its own true place of being. I talk now, of course, of many, many cycles in the future and, as such, it should be of no concern to you!

Q: Are young children aware of the truths that we have been talking about even if they are unable to communicate them to us?

ZT: Until the age of twelve, when the soul is fully in the physical body,

82

a child's understanding of physical life is, of necessity, limited. There are, of course, many differing levels of understanding and many differing degrees of expression, nevertheless, because to a large extent children have not been conditioned by the world into which they have incarnated, they are more open to the force of Divine Intelligence and so will express an understanding of life based on that Intelligence. This, almost inevitably, will lead them into conflict either with their parents or with society around them. This, in turn, leads to a conflict of wills and the person that has the greater will, if only by virtue of their position as parent or teacher, tends to suppress the lesser will, that is the will of the child. So very often a child's understanding of life, which could reveal amazing insights into life, is either limited or even suppressed by the world into which it has incarnated.

I would define a child prodigy as someone who has, for the most part, rejected the conditioning and the understanding of the world into which it has incarnated and who relies, instead, on the flow of Divine Intelligence. The same can also be said for an adult prodigy, a person whom you would call a genius, because they are tapping into the flow of Divine Intelligence as opposed to the conditioned thought of the particular field in which they operate, be it science or the arts. They draw their inspiration from a different place, from a different understanding of life. They are not imitators, but initiators.

So the greatest gift that you can give to any child is to encourage it to be an initiator, not an imitator. It is to help them to bring forth from within their own being their own divine flow of intelligence, their own understanding of the Cosmos. At first, as I said, this will be limited, because they will tend to rely heavily upon their parents and their teachers for their understanding of life but, gradually, if their own intelligence is cultivated and nurtured with wisdom and discrimination it will reveal an understanding of life that will transform this world into Heaven on Earth, into the Cosmos on Earth.

Q: Could you give us some practical guidance as to the best way to contact this flow of Intelligence?
ZT: The ability to tap into this flow of Intelligence is part of your divine inheritance. What was a natural function for you as a child becomes a hidden memory for you as an adult. What you have to do, therefore, is to rediscover an old skill. This does not require the reading of books or the incantation of mantras or prayers. The process of rediscovery is initiated by your very openness to the presence of that

flow of energy. It is difficult, at first, to attune to this flow of Cosmic Intelligence in what I will call the everyday events of life. Almost inevitably you will find that it will be in those moments of crisis, when you find yourself being tested to the limits of your spiritual wisdom and knowledge, when the situation in which you find yourself cannot be answered by your own understanding of life, that you will begin to tap into this divine flow. You will find, at such times, that as you open your heart and your mind to the Universe, so you will become aware of a new energy, of a new understanding of life, that is presenting itself to you.

If you consciously try to attune to this divine flow of Intelligence, even in the small events of life, then you will gradually find yourself becoming more and more at one with it. Every time that you are faced with the need to decide upon a course of action, remember that although there is no right or wrong way to act, for everything is a learning experience, that nevertheless, you are always faced with the choice of acting out of your intelligence, which is limited, or out of God's Intelligence, which is infinite. It is by emptying your mind of the content of its consciousness that you create a space into which that impulse of Cosmic Intelligence can come, even though you do not know from whence it comes. Such an impulse will, perhaps, inspire you to act in a completely different way from the way that you had planned. This flow of Intelligence removes the necessity for a choice, because it enables you to see more clearly the reality of what you are doing. You only think that you have a choice when you cannot see God's will for you clearly.

Now, of course, your ego-self, which is based entirely on your worldly understandings, finds it very difficult to trust a hidden impulse because it does not recognise its source or its reliability. So, quite naturally, it will oppose it and raise many objections! It therefore requires great courage, in the first instance, to attune to and to follow the path of Cosmic Intelligence but, gradually, as trust is built up and you become aware that you are one with this flow of energy you will learn to rely on it at all times. Once you have recognised that you really have no choice, that you can only do God's will, then you will have become truly intelligent.

THE NATURAL ORDER

If you were to go outside on a clear night and were to look up at the sky you would see there the order of the known universe. All is apparent perfection. Although some stars are dying, others are being born in the eternal cycle of life. The essence of the relationship between the stars is one of balance and harmony. You, who dwell on the Earth, can look up at the stars and can indeed plot your course around the Earth by them, so fixed is their order and so regular is their cycle. Have you ever considered the nature of the Being that can command such order? Even if you examine the workings of your own small solar system, with its known planets and their respective satellites encircling their Solar Lord, the Sun, you witness this same order.

However, when you come to look at the Earth and, in particular, at the actions of Humanity on its surface, here you witness only disorder. Why should this be so? It is because Humanity has been given the divine gift of free choice and so can create the nature of its own world. Obviously, this must fall within the evolutionary cycle and the destiny of the God or Lord of this solar system, and must be a part of Its will for Humanity on the Earth, but within those broad restrictions Humanity can choose the nature of its evolutionary path.

Why, therefore, does Humanity choose to live in disorder? Why is there such conflict on the planet between the four Kingdoms of Matter? The answer is simple. It is because Humanity does not follow the Natural Laws, the Laws of the Cosmos. These great Laws enforce the balance between all aspects of Creation. Every God, from your own Solar Lord to the highest Lord of all, is subject to these great Natural Laws, which control the evolution of all Creation. What are the names of these Laws? They are, for the most part, beyond human understanding, but I will list a few of them for you, using terminology that you will understand, simply to give you a very basic understanding of their nature:– the Law of Love, the Law of Attraction and Repulsion, the Law of Passivity and Activity, the Law of Productivity and

Receptivity, the Law of Compensation and Retribution, the Law of Polarity and Balance, the Law of Cohesion and Adhesion, the Law of Cycles and Periodicity, the Law of Supply and Demand, the Law of Cause and Effect (this Law is sometimes known as the Law of Karma), and the Law of Growth and Potential, to name but a few.

Now I know that many people in incarnation on the Earth at this time are not consciously aware of these Laws, but that does not matter, for an understanding of the Natural Laws demands a process of intuition rather than one of scientific intellect. You can observe and learn from the order and movement of the stars in the sky, you can feel their impulse, without knowing, on a scientific level anyway, how they function. Yes, it may require a great intellect with a profound knowledge of atomic physics to describe the actual workings and the balance of the Universe, but what is needed to understand their message and their impulse is not intellect but intelligence. It is from looking at the stars, if you did but know it, that you can learn of the destiny of your solar system and, therefore, of the Earth and of Humanity dwelling on it. The true power of prophecy comes from an understanding of the position, the balance and the influence of all the stars, some of which you are aware, some of which you are not. Be aware, therefore, that this natural order controls every aspect of life, from the highest to the lowest point of consciousness.

Many great Masters have incarnated on the plane of Earth and both through their lives and their work have demonstrated their understanding of the Natural Laws. This is reflected in teachings such as 'Do unto others as you would have others do unto you', 'As a man thinks in his heart, so is he' and 'That which you give freely to the Creator of all Life will always be returned to you tenfold'. Through wisdom such as this you can be led into an understanding of what these Natural Laws imply, namely, that as you as individuals create, so you create the nature of the world around you, not just for yourselves but for the many generations to come. Recognise that today you have inherited the world of your forebears. You are having to live with their erroneous creations, no matter whether it be nuclear or chemical pollution of the soil or mental pollution of the ether. Therefore recognise that you are creating the world in which you will have to live in the future, and that you are creating that world through your alignment or non-alignment with the Natural Laws. If you attune to the Natural Laws, then you will live in peace. The state of peace is not the absence of war but is, rather, a state of alignment with the Natural Laws. If you abide by these Laws on any level – individually, nationally or globally – you will be at peace, for you will be living according to the Laws of Infinite Spirit.

Recognise, therefore, that every human being, according to his or her point of spiritual consciousness, will attune both consciously and unconsciously to these Natural Laws. The aware person soon recognises that as they sow, so shall they reap, that as they create in thought, word and deed, so they are creating the world around them. They learn from experience that that which they give in sacrificial service, that that which they give expecting no reward, that that which they create for the good of all rather than just for themselves, will always come back to them tenfold. They discover that that which they create on all levels of life, both externally and internally, is reflected in the nature of their own being. In this way they create their own states of health or ill health, of wealth or poverty, of harmony or disharmony, of happiness or unhappiness. They realise that they are the creators of their world, not just their individual world but the world as a whole and that they are not just a part of the world – they *are* the world. They become aware of the great truth that there really is no division between them and the so-called savage living in the rain forest of South America and that as they think, so they affect him; as he acts, so he affects them. You are all part of one body, the body of Humanity.

So each of you, according to your point of consciousness and soul evolution, will attune to the great Natural Laws of the Cosmos and should lead your life according to those Laws, no matter what the physical or material temptations that are put before you. You will be tested on your observance of the Laws. You will find, for example, that you will be given an opportunity of making money out of the exploitation of your fellow human beings or one of the Kingdoms of Matter. In the 18th century you could have been faced with the choice of whether or not to support slavery. In the 20th century slavery still exists, even here in the Western World, but it is disguised in subtle forms. People are still bought and sold, not physically but on a financial or a psychological level. Today, however, it is mainly the Animal, the Vegetable and the Mineral Kingdoms that are being enslaved and exploited. Humanity feels that it has the right to buy and to sell the many aspects of these Kingdoms. How are you going to respond to this test? It does not matter what all the people around you are doing. You have to make your own choice, based on your own understanding of the Natural Laws. Everything that you do in relationship with the three Kingdoms of Matter should be in attunement with the highest Law, the

Law of the Cosmos, the Law of Harmony and Balance, the Law of Natural Order.

Humanity, at this time, is faced with a vital choice. There are many people in the world today who do not want to live in order, who do indeed thrive on disorder, because that presents them with an opportunity for the advancement of their own plans, their own ideas of creation. It is, therefore, vitally important that all the souls of aged evolution who do comprehend the Natural Order should clearly sound their note in thought, word and deed, for it is how they lead their lives, the consciousness that they ground and exemplify, that will determine the nature of the great changes that are to come. By gathering in groups such as you are doing now, by offering up energies of love and support, both to each other and to the planet, they are helping to bring about a great planetary transformation. It is by their actions in the days and months to come, by the sacrifices that they are prepared to make, by the offering of their soul beings to the greater whole, that they will help to decide the nature and the timing of the great events that are soon to come.

In your own lives you are only too aware that when you live in disorder you can achieve very little and that what you do create only leads to further disorder. You can never create order out of disorder. Order can only come from order. So as you begin to establish balance in your own lives and to base your every action on the Natural Laws of the Cosmos, you will begin to create order in your lives. I would like you to recognise that one demonstration of cosmic order can truly transform a whole nation and that the grounding of such order can change the whole planet. Therefore strive to be aware in your daily living of the presence of this divine order of things, of the Natural Laws that govern everything right down to even the smallest hair on your head. When you truly recognise that order, the fact that you are accountable for every thought that you make, that every word that you speak is noted and that one day you will have to atone for every deed that you have done, then you will have realised that this Natural Order applies to all things, to all people and to all their inter-relationships. Even the smallest sacrifice that you make is recorded and is witnessed by millions of beings on the higher levels of life and is never made in vain. The greater the sacrifice, the greater the effect not only on the physical level but also on the higher levels of life. Search, therefore, for God's Order. Look at the example of the great Masters that have walked the surface of this Earth. Look at the example of their lives and the wisdom of their teachings, and see the order that they have brought to the world. At the same time look at how an understanding of the true nature of life has grown within you, as your soul has opened up to the experience of the Natural Order.

Be aware that great strength comes from this Natural Order. In the temples of ancient Egypt the initiates on their way to the priesthood had to experience great tests on the astral level. Under the direction of their Masters, they used to sleep in special chambers within the pyramids and would stay there for three or four days. In their dream states they would then face their worst physical fears, no matter whether it be facing the threat of death and surviving or else, indeed, being killed. In these altered states of consciousness they would, for example, have to walk through a pit full of venomous snakes and overcome their fear of them. The test was that if they understood truly the nature of their Creator and Its order they could walk through any plane of darkness and not be touched.

Even on the physical plane, if you yourself are living in balance and harmony you can survive any physical challenge. Though you work in a room full of diseased people, you will not be touched by any disease. Though you are shot at by many guns, you will not be hit. Though you are thrown into the sea when a ship sinks and many drown, you will be saved. For those who live in peace, that is obeying God's Natural Order, there is total protection. Those who follow God's Natural Order will find their own lives in order. For those who trust in their Creator, there can be no fear. People who fear do not trust their Creator, do not trust what the Creator has laid out in Its plan for them and for this planet.

Though others may create wrongly, you do not have to be a part of their creations. Though others may think wrongly, you do not have to receive and give energy to their thoughts: for as you think, so you create. Your world is the world that you have created. As you think in your heart, so you are and so is the world around you. You are magnetic beings. You attract unto yourselves according to the nature of your beings. If you are a violent person, then you will attract violence. If you are a corrupt person, then you will attract corruption. If you are a person sick in the mind, then you will attract disease to your body. You create what you are. You cannot blame anyone else but yourself. The world around you is but a mirror of your own being. Remember that that which challenges you, that that which threatens you, is only a reflection of where you are weak, for where you are strong in the knowledge and wisdom of God's Plan, there can be no fear.

At this time, therefore, in your world of great disorder, where not only the fabric of society appears threatened but also the very planet itself, recognise that you will only be able to survive if you are at peace with your Creator and if you accept Its plan for this Earth and the fact that Its Plan is perfect. Know that as the stars revolve in the sky, and have done so for aeons of time, know that as the Earth is held in perfect balance within this solar system, know that as life on this planet is controlled exactly by the energies of great Beings, so everything that manifests on the physical plane is planned and reflects that greater perfection. What you are faced with is the drama of Humanity. What you are faced with is the challenge of physical life. You have to master and come to terms with that reality. As you create, so you are. As you create, so you will be. How you live today will determine the future, not just for yourself but for the whole planet. One aware soul, living in order, can transform a hundred. That is the role of aware souls today. That is why you are here on the planet at this most critical time: to exemplify and to help those who would follow the path of order.

Each day in your meditations, therefore, strive to establish this order in your being. Try to align yourselves to the Natural Law which enfolds and impels all things. Become at one with it, for it touches every aspect of your being. Every molecule in your body vibrates to that divine flow of Cosmic Intelligence. You have but to listen to it, you have but to feel for it, and that Intelligence is there ready to guide and lead you. In every action there is an opportunity, just before you initiate it, to assess, in an instant of time, whether or not it is appropriate for you to act in that way. Just as it is said that at the moment of death a person sees their whole life pass before their eyes so, in that split second before any action, you can weigh a thousand choices in the balance and can decide how and when you will act. It does not require physical time, merely spiritual time. You all have to choose the nature of your lives, where you are prepared to stand, what you are prepared to exemplify, what you are prepared to sacrifice.

Above all, I would ask you to remember one thing, namely, that that which you create now, the order that you give to the world now, even if you have to make great personal sacrifices, will never be in vain, for who is it that will return to this world in a new body, in a new learning experience, but you. You are the creators of the future, not just for tomorrow but for centuries and cycles to come. You are creating the future of your world by your actions now, and if you want this world to be a better place, if you want to live your next cycle in peace and harmony, then sow the seeds for it now by your own right actions. For as you create now, so you determine not just the future of this planet and this solar system, but the future of the whole Cosmos.

QUESTIONS AND ANSWERS

Q: In the talk the Master spoke about 'sacrificing your life', but I have always felt that it is most wrong to give your life away. I just don't understand the need for this form of sacrifice, of giving your life away. Will you please explain?

ZT: The essence of any sacrifice is the motivation that lies behind it. It is obviously wrong to needlessly sacrifice your life. What the Master was talking about was purposefully sacrificing aspects of your life or, indeed, your very life itself. For example, it can be said that the Master Jesus sacrificed his life, because a Master such as he, who could walk on the water, who could multiply the loaves and the fishes, who could raise the dead, could so easily have avoided his crucifixion at Jerusalem if he had chosen to do so. So he deliberately allowed himself to be tried, condemned and crucified, and in that sense his death was a sacrifice, but a sacrifice he made knowingly because he could see the purpose of it. Now there are many levels, or degrees, of sacrifice. A soldier in a battle sacrifices his life for his friends. If you were out on a walk and you came across a child drowning in a river, you would try anything to save that child and would even sacrifice your life, not on a conscious level of giving up your life, but just in trying to help save that child. So there are many levels on which you can be called upon to make a sacrifice, to give up something that you value most dearly for the good of others, for the good of the whole race. If one has an understanding of why one is doing it and of who or what one is doing it for, then great growth can come from that situation.

You can all recall the many sacrifices that you have had to make in your own lives. If you are parents and have young children, then your life is a constant act of sacrifice to those children. Each of you, therefore, is learning and is exploring the limits of your sacrifice, of discovering what you are prepared to sacrifice, what you are prepared to give up, not just for yourselves but for your fellow human beings and for the planet as a whole. You are discovering if you can indeed

91

sacrifice your greeds as opposed to your needs, if you can overcome your desires for more and more material things, especially if you know that those desires are depriving the people of a less-developed country of the basic essentials of life. A more practical example would be if you enjoyed using a product that was made from whales. Now if many whales are being killed in order to provide this product, no matter how much you enjoy the product, surely it behoves you to sacrifice your desire for that product and to allow the whales to live. So there are many levels or degrees of sacrifice, which vary according to the level of the consciousness of the individual concerned.

Q: Many people are not aware at all of the Natural Laws that you talk about and even those of us that are aware, to a small degree, find it difficult to obey them, so does this mean that we are in great danger of destroying our planet?

ZT: You live in dangerous times because, as you well know, Humanity has the capability of destroying this planet. Who, can prevent this from happening? The answer, quite simply, is only you, the people who live upon and who are responsible for the planet. How are you to change people's attitudes towards the planet? You change people not by words, not by books, not by talks, but by example. If you as individuals exemplify and follow the Natural Laws to the highest of your understanding of them, and people witness that demonstration, then you will change those people because the eyes are the windows of the soul and what the eyes see, the soul inside cannot deny. Let me give you a very simple example.

A businessman is walking along a street in a big city, en route to his office, carrying his briefcase. He is not in a very good temper because he is late, he has had a very bad journey on the train and he has indigestion from rushing his breakfast because he awoke too late. He is concerned only with his own problems and with how life is treating him, which is, of course, unfairly! As he rushes along he sees a blind man on the opposite side of the road, who is trying to cross the road but who is experiencing great difficulty in doing so because the rush-hour traffic is heavy. Whilst feeling sorry for the blind man, the business man is in too much of a hurry to do anything about this situation and justifies his actions by thinking that the blind man has no right to be there by himself in the rush hour. Then he notices that a little boy comes up to the side of the blind man, converses with him, takes hold of his hand, waits for a break in the traffic, and safely guides the blind man across the road. After smiling at each other, they part and go their own different ways.

Now those three people have all been participants in a little cosmic drama! Because the business man has seen that demonstration of sacrifice, that act of love, by the little boy, no matter how grumpy he is feeling, he cannot but be touched by that drama because, as I have just said, the eyes are the windows of the soul. Inevitably that demonstration of sacrificial service will modify his own behaviour and attitude. Indeed, he might even smile inwardly and begin to feel that all is right with the world as opposed to thinking that all is wrong, so that when he gets to his office, instead of being bad-tempered towards all of his staff, he will actually smile and be even-tempered towards them.

Now the blind man and the little boy will never know that they have been responsible for changing his attitude and for affecting the working lives of so many people that morning! They have just played their parts in the drama, to the highest of their abilities, and yet their actions were responsible for transforming the lives of many people that day. You, too, never know when you are not being watched by the eyes of another soul. Everything that you do in life from the highest point of your spiritual consciousness, everything that you do in life to uplift Humanity on this plane of Earth, will always have meaning and purpose and will almost inevitably transform the lives of other people. You are always being observed, if not by beings on the physical plane of life then by beings on other planes and, above all, by your Creator Who is both omnipresent, omnipotent and omniscient.

Q: I would like to ask a question about AIDS. How can we best face this challenge and help the unfortunate victims of this terrible disease?
ZT: I have to say to you that the test of AIDS is only in its infancy. This disease is literally a genetic time-bomb. There will soon be hundreds of thousands of people dying from AIDS all over the world. Now the way to avoid AIDS, for the most part, is simply by right living. If you live a life of natural order, if you respect the sexual act and always honour your partner, if you do not have sexual relations outside the bond of marriage, then you will not catch AIDS. If you do catch AIDS then it is because you have attracted that disease to you through your own aura. No one catches a disease by chance. It is not a question of blind fate that one person gets AIDS and another does not. Dis-ease is caused by dis-harmony both on the inner and the outer planes.

AIDS, like cancer, is one of the great transforming diseases of this Age, because either you transform yourself, and heal yourself, or you die. Now just as it is possible to survive cancer, so it is possible to survive AIDS. Only a very few people will do this, however, because only a very few people have either the power or the will to do so. Is it not an amazing thing that someone who has lung cancer will still ask for a cigarette whilst lying in their hospital bed! Such is the power of an addiction that some people are not even prepared to give up the very thing which is causing the disease in their body, because the personality desire is so strong. They do not want to transform themselves. It is just the same for the people who have AIDS. So the choice is either to transform the personality aspect, or the karma, that has attracted that disease to them or else to die because of it and to learn from that death. Either way a great karmic settlement will have taken place.

Now this, of course, does not mean that you should not be compassionate and loving towards those with cancer or AIDS, just because they have failed to transform themselves. Those who have the disease require not just nursing help but also support and companionship and, above all, the need to be loved. So many who die of AIDS and cancer today die alone, feeling like social lepers, isolated by their disease, rejected by the society in which they once lived. There is no worse death than to die alone, feeling unloved and unwanted, isolated from one's friends. When a person dies, what they need the most is human company and physical support, someone to hold their hand and to ease their transition. Of course, there are many people in the medical profession who feel that the sole purpose of healing is simply to restore someone's physical body back to a state of health, but I would like you to recognise that there are many other forms of healing. Healing can also be of the mind and of the soul, and sometimes by just helping the person concerned to come to terms with the disease with which they are suffering, to recognise that they are the cause and not the victim of a disease, can in itself be a great healing process.

Nevertheless, even though AIDS is a great karmic disease and even though many people who are dying of AIDS at this time have chosen to do so, it must also be recognised that the disease is presenting people today with a very clear choice. They must choose the nature and the purity of the relationship into which they wish to enter. They must choose how they are going to behave and how they are going to relate once they have entered into that relationship. In one sense, AIDS is a great challenge to the concepts of sexual freedom expressed in the

94

1960's and the 1970's. It is making the Western World, in particular, more aware of the nature of the sexual act and of human creation and of the responsibility that must go with it. The sexual act should not be regarded as an act of self-centred pleasure, but rather as an act of cosmic creation. It would be true to say that in the New Age it will only be the pure of spirit, the pure of mind and the pure of body that will inherit the Earth.

Q: We are always being told by the Masters that we should serve and nurture others, but it seems to me that all too often we forget to serve and nurture ourselves. Shouldn't this really come first, not in a selfish or self-centred way, but rather to ensure that we ourselves are healthy and balanced in body, mind and spirit before we go out to serve others? This is a question that I find very difficult to answer at this moment in time, especially where healing is involved. There are so many sick people in the world today that one could go on giving healing until one is drained and exhausted.

ZT: I will begin by saying that it is very difficult to help others unless you are a whole and balanced person yourself. If you are not in harmony and balance then the help or the service that you can give, no matter how pure and well-intentioned your actions, will be very limited. Only the whole person can heal, and if you are not whole and you try to heal others, then you will become drained of energy and you will find that it is you yourself that needs the healing. The whole person, by his or her very nature, has become one with the flow of the Cosmos. They are so attuned to their Creator's power that they have become channels for Its energy and, as such, when they heal, little energy is taken from them. However, if a healer is not channelling pure energy but is, rather, using their own psychic energy, then they will soon become drained and this state of being, inevitably, leads to illness and disease.

So it is important that everyone should devote both time and energy to centring themselves, to attuning to the flow of the Cosmos, especially if they are in the healing fields of service. Before you attempt to heal anyone you should spend at least half an hour centring and balancing your own body, establishing your own state of mind, creating your own link with your Creator. You must attune to the healing energies of the Cosmos and offer your body as a channel for those energies before you heal. It is essential, therefore, that you yourself are in perfect balance on all levels of your being before you try to heal anyone, otherwise you will find that in all probability you will damage yourself on many levels of life. Remember also that you are not Superman or Superwoman! You cannot heal every day. You cannot heal every person that comes before you. However the closer and the stronger your link is to the Source of all Life, the greater will be your ability to serve the person that comes before you according to their needs. To achieve this closeness you need to nurture yourself, not in the sense of pandering to your desires, but in the sense of centering yourself more and more with the will of God.

Q: Could you please tell us something about the karma of nations? Being German I am particularly interested to know if it was the karma of Germany to experience two World Wars or were other factors at work?

ZT: It is all too easy to talk in generalisations when talking about karma, especially about national or planetary karma, but ultimately it is a fact that the nation or the planet is the sum total of all the individuals that go to make that whole. So collective individual karma becomes national karma. Souls choose to incarnate into a certain country either because it gives them the opportunity to learn certain cosmic lessons that they wish to learn or else because it presents them with an opportunity to transmute past karma. Having said that, let us also recognise that not everything that happens in life is always due to past karma. Humanity has been given the divine gift of free choice and so each day, as you respond to the tests and challenges of the day, you are creating a karmic reaction.

Furthermore, let us also remember that the population of the world, the number of souls in incarnation on the Earth, is rapidly increasing. This increase is not just caused by old souls reincarnating. There are many new souls incarnating on the Earth who have not incarnated on the Earth for a very long time. Now these new souls, especially if they are very young souls, will inevitably attract the karma appropriate to their actions, for they still have much to learn, lessons which the old souls learned thousands of lives ago. That is why there is so much negative behaviour on the Earth at this time. That is why the consciousness of the relatively few old souls is being swamped by the unconsciousness of the mass of unevolved souls.

I have often used the analogy of a loaf of bread to explain the present situation. It requires only a little yeast, or soul-consciousness, to raise the mass of dough, or soul-unconsciousness, into a perfect loaf. But the proportions must be right or the loaf will fail. What we have in the world today is too much dough and not enough yeast to raise it. That is why you have had two World Wars in the past and why, almost inevitably, there will be even more suffering in the future. For a mass of young souls, some of whom have not incarnated on the Earth for over five thousand years, are working out their karmic patterns. One of the great lessons in this situation for all old souls is not to take on board the karmic lessons of the young, not to take part in their karmic actions, to be in the world but not of the world.

There are, of course, deep karmic patterns that run back through families, through nations and through races. It would seem that certain sects, certain religions, certain countries are always being persecuted or are always involved in strife. One thinks immediately of Israel, of Ireland, of Poland and, of course, of Germany. Group karma is no different to individual karma. Everything that you do in thought, word and deed as an individual creates individual karma, and everything that you do in thought, word and deed with other people creates what I will call group or collective karma. If ten people band together to act negatively against another person, no matter whether it be in thought, word or deed, then they are creating a group karma. It is just the same on a planetary level too. If you are in incarnation on the Earth at this time and are responsible for helping to pollute or to destroy one of the Kingdoms of Matter, then you are creating planetary karma. So your actions can create karma on many levels. Perhaps you can now begin to understand the wisdom behind that well known aphorism – No man is an island!

When you examine the manifestations of national karma over the ages you have to rely, for the most part, on the history books, which are usually biassed and highly subjective. It is very difficult to discern cause and effect. Very often you are left with a chicken and egg situation. Which came first, which action was the cause of a certain reaction? Let us take the example of Israel. The Jewish people have been persecuted on and off throughout history, but it was the extremes of the Nazi holocaust that created the desire in them to build a haven of safety where they could be free from persecution. Nevertheless it must also be recognised that the modern state of Israel was born out of bloodshed and violence and by the deliberate dispossession of thousands of Palestinians from their native land. Almost fifty years later the bitterness caused by this birth still exists and the conflict has grown to include many nations. The Middle East is like a powder keg which could explode at any moment and could engulf the whole world.

One act of violence leads to another, and who is to blame? Which action was the cause of all that reaction? One great truth emerges from all of this, namely, that you cannot build your happiness on someone else's unhappiness. The Natural Order will not permit someone else to suffer so that you can obtain your desires, no matter how pure is your motivation.

You are interested in the karma of modern Germany. Again we have to look back very carefully at the formation of this country, back in the early nineteenth century, and examine the motives and the aims of its founders. We must assess the purity of their thoughts, words and deeds and how they created the modern state of Germany. Were the wars that they fought wars of defence or wars of aggrandisement? Now nothing in life is self evident. It is very easy to say that the Nazis were evil, the Allies were good, and that goodness quite rightly triumphed over evil because God was on the side of goodness. Oh that life was that simple! For many reasons, few people are ever aware of the true facts of any situation, of the real machinations of international politics and finance. Few people are ever aware of the powerful secret interests that control even governments and kings. Have you ever stopped to think how it was possible for Germany, a broken country in 1918, to rise in less than 20 years to become a major power in Europe with a well equipped army? From whence came all the money to make this possible? Who wanted Germany to be strong again?

So nothing is ever quite so straight forward as the history books would have you believe. One fact cannot be denied, namely, that the Germans were seeking revenge for the ignominious defeat of 1918. That was why Hitler signed his peace treaty with France in 1940 in the same railway carriage that was used for the treaty of surrender by Germany in 1918. The moral of this is that you should always be gracious in victory. You should never set out to deliberately humiliate anyone, be it an individual or a country. The native peoples of North America had a wonderful understanding of this fact and in battle would always give the losing side an opportunity to withdraw with dignity and honour should they choose to take it. In all things one must not look just at the short term result. The victor must ask whether he wishes to enjoy a great victory or to live in peace for the next one hundred years. The price of victory can sometimes be greater than the price of defeat. Many of the armed conflicts going on in the world today have been going on for centuries, with the same souls reincarnating and fighting the same battles. For generation after generation they have been reaping the seeds of karma that were sown centuries before. It will require one great act of cosmic consciousness to break the mold and to balance the scales of karma.

Q: When an evil person reincarnates do they become more evil if they do not transmute their karma? It seems to me that there are a lot of evil people in power today all around the world, not just in politics but in business and many other walks of life. These people are manipulating society at an ever increasing rate and it seems that nobody can stop them. The world situation is daily becoming more desperate. Is this all part of our national or planetary karma?

ZT: Humanity is suffering and it is suffering for one reason only – it has lost the awareness of its own spirituality. It has forgotten its divinity, the fact that the Divine dwells within it and that it dwells within the Divine. Many people today are turning away from what I will call organised religion which, although fallible, nevertheless, does provide some form of moral and ethical guidance. But, having rejected this outer discipline, such people are not replacing it with their own inner discipline, their own soul wisdom and knowledge. They have become amoral and unethical. Moreover, as I have just said, there is an ever-increasing number of new souls coming into incarnation on the planet at this time who are not evolved souls and who do not have a great soul wisdom to guide them. Many of these souls are in positions of temporal power and are wielding an influence on life that is totally disproportionate to their point of spiritual consciousness.

In the Bible many stories are to be found which relate how the prophets and sages of old would suddenly appear before a king and his ministers and would warn them that a certain course of action that they had embarked upon would ultimately bring the wrath and punishment of God down upon them. Sometimes they were, of course, persecuted for their warnings but, more often than not, because in those days people valued the opinions of their wise men and women, they were listened to with respect and their warnings were heeded. Thus a painful lesson could be avoided. Now there are many prophets and sages today who are all issuing clear warnings of the consequences of Humanity's present behaviour. Those that have ears to hear will hear and heed these warnings but the vast majority will not, simply because their feelings and instincts have been swamped by the gross materialism that is present in the world today. This situation, of course, simply reflects the nature and the time of the Age in which you are living and, as such, is all part of God's Plan for human evolution.

Humanity must realise one important fact, namely, that no outside force, no benevolent God, no Messiah, is suddenly going to appear and save Humanity from the consequences of its own actions. Humanity alone can save itself. Humanity must take responsibility for its own actions. Humanity must seek a new God now that the old religious God is falling away. Humanity must discover the God within itself and through both prayer and meditation develop its divine link with the Source of all Life. Every individual must learn to attune to their own soul wisdom and to act according to it.

I can tell you that the vibratory rate of the Earth is being quickened and that the transmutation of karma is being accelerated. Literally, you will reap in the afternoon what you have sown in the morning, for this is the ending of the Age, this is the culminating point of a great learning process. This is Humanity's moment of truth, its time of transformation and transfiguration. The events of the next ten years will challenge the 'ungodly' as they have never been challenged before. Those that do not transform will die, no matter whether it be through war, natural disaster or disease. Only the pure in heart, those who follow God's Laws, the Natural Order, will survive to see the dawning of the New Age.

THE ILLUSION OF SEPARATION

I do not want you to think that my talk today is on some dry, intellectual subject and is concerned only with abstractions, for the root cause of the problem of human relationships *is* the illusion of separation. As I talk to you, now, be aware that you are receiving my message on two levels – intellectually, on the level of the mind, and intuitively, on the level of the heart, for behind every spoken word there is an unseen energy. You receive not just the word but the energy that lies behind the word. So as you listen to the concepts that I am about to express to you, feel as well as think. Be open to the impulse that comes with the words and to the feelings that that impulse arouses in you.

Words, of course, are a great source of misunderstanding. They are the cause of much human conflict. So let us therefore be quite clear as to what we mean by the words 'illusion' and 'separation'. Illusion is a deception. It is a delusion. It is something that is not real. Separation is a unit that regards itself as being apart from something else. The basic fault in human relationships today is that Humanity regards itself as an individual unit, as being separate from all the other aspects of life around it. Humanity sees itself as living and evolving in isolation, as having an aspect of understanding and consciousness to maintain and defend in the face of all other aspects of understanding and consciousness.

But is that the true reality of life? Are you, as individuals, really separate from anything that you see or feel with your physical senses? Are you really separate from either the millions of beings that live on the planet or the millions of beings that live beyond the physical plane of Earth? This is a question which you have probably asked yourselves on an intellectual level, but have not, perhaps, gone into too deeply, because in order to answer that question you first have to ask yourself who you really are. The true answer to that question must, inevitably, challenge your very identity and sense of individuality, and many of you are fearful of losing that sense of identity, of losing that aspect of your being which you call the personality self.

Let me give you a simple analogy. We can say that the fingers on your hands can be regarded as being individualised aspects of consciousness and that a finger on one hand would look at a finger on the other hand and would see only separation. It would look curiously at what the other finger was doing in its relationships with the world around it. Now, truly, those fingers do have individualised consciousness and destiny, but you, the divine being of spirit that you are, with a higher consciousness than the fingers, can stand above those two aspects of finger consciousness and can see that they are both part of the one body. You know that they have a common purpose and destiny, namely, that of fulfilling the greater destiny of the human body of which they are a part. Moreover, you also know that the body itself is directed by yet an even higher form of consciousness, the spirit that is incarnating in it. Therefore, although the individual fingers regard themselves as being separate, it is an illusion. It is only a viewpoint that they, as individuals, have created of the world around them.

Similarly, you, as individuals, regard yourselves as being separate. But what part of you is it that is making that judgement of separation? What is it in the finger that is saying 'I am separate from the other finger'? What is it in you that is saying 'I am separate from my brother or my sister, from the millions of other human beings that live on this plane of Earth, from the other Kingdoms of Matter'? Is it not the aspect of personality that you have created of yourself? Is it not the opinion, the collective thought patterns, that you have created of yourself, which define you as to who or what you are as an individual? Is it not your *physical* experience? Is not that the source of the judgement that forms the separation? But you all know that there is another part of you, a higher part of you, that lives on when that personality dies, the aspect of spirit that was with you before birth and will be with you after death. Have you ever considered what is the opinion of your *spiritual* experience?

You, as individuals, therefore, are like those little fingers. You observe the actions of all the other fingers around you and, unless you are a wise enough soul to rise above the personality perspective and to see the force of spirit that links all beings to the Creator of all Life, you will see only the separation between the fingers and, above all, you will relate only to that separation. When someone stands in front of you, no matter what they are doing, do you see the divinity of that person, the aspect of spirit which links them eternally to the Godhead, or do you see only the aspect of them which is separate from their spirit, their personality aspect? If someone is rude to you, do you judge that person simply by their rudeness? Do you harbour resentments because they have been rude to you or do you recognise that it is not their spirit that is being rude to you but only their personality aspect, the aspect of them that is not linked to the Divine and, therefore, that that is of no consequence since it originates in illusion?

You, therefore, have the choice of either responding to that illusion or of recognising that the person being rude to you is a being of spirit like yourself, is truly your brother or sister, and is linked to you in the oneness of all life just as your fingers are linked to the oneness of your body. They are, therefore, in truth, part of your body. You are all part of the one great Spirit. Therefore no matter what that person creates in either thought, word or deed to define their own illusion, that is not the reality of that person. But how many of you are prepared to seek that aspect of spirit? How many of you are prepared to ignore the personality aspect, both the separation and the reason for it, and to seek for that aspect of spirit which unites all Humanity into the one force of the Divine God.

Truly, the Human Race is one Race. You all may be likened to a million, million fingers on the hands of your God. You are, therefore, all part of one Divine Body. If you chop off even one finger of the divine hand you defile that body. If you kill another human being you are, in effect, chopping off a finger of your own body. You are, therefore, hurting yourself! It is as if you were chopping off one of your own fingers. There is no separation between all the fingers of Humanity. Though you all may perform different functions, though you all may represent different aspects of consciousness, though you all have unique roles to fulfil, nevertheless, you are all part of one body – the body of Humanity. Recognise that as the fingers on your own hands combine to create, to heal, to greet, to give and receive, so, too, do the millions of fingers on the cosmic hands of your Creator manifesting as the Human Race.

So when you attack another person in either thought, word or deed you are, in fact, attacking yourself. When you defile another human being you are truly defiling yourself and, of course, when you defile yourself you are defiling the whole Human Race. Is that not the real meaning behind that great cosmic saying 'Do unto others as you would have others do unto you'? Treat others as you would have others treat you and recognise that as you treat others so you are truly treating yourself. How you respect the human beings around you reflects your respect for yourself. You are all one Race – the Human Race. There is no separation between the races, between the different human cultures, between the sexes, between the old and the young. Though the Human Race, as individuals, performs many different functions, as do the individual fingers on your hand, together they form the hand and can unite to act as one. Each finger, or individual aspect of the hand, performing to the highest of its consciousness, creates the power of the hand and strengthens its ability to function as a single unit.

Why, therefore, do you regard yourselves as being separate from all other human beings, from the black man, the red man, the yellow man or the white man, from your husband, your wife or your children? Why do you think that you are separate from the Animal Kingdom or from the earth on which you walk? What is it in you that creates or needs this separation? Have you ever considered whether this separation will still be present after death? When you have left your physical body and have released your earthly conditioning, your personality of this life, you will find that you will have a new and greater perspective on the oneness of all life.

Where Humanity is in such error today is that it has separated itself from its roots, from its Creator, and from the nature of its being. It has forgotten that the Creator of all Life has created all things, has created all the planes of life and all the beings who dwell on those planes. It has created this World on which you live and the three Kingdoms of Matter with whom you share this World and over whom you have temporary dominion. Its divine creativity is present in all the four Kingdoms. It has created the Human Race of which you are a part and has established a permanent link through the force of spirit between the Race and Itself, for the Race of Humanity is Its children.

At all times, therefore, you are linked to your Creator through a beam of white light to the Source of all Light. You are never alone unless you choose to be alone. You are never outside the love of God unless you choose to place yourself outside that love, to create a barrier against that love coming into your being. Every person that you meet on the face of this Earth is a son or daughter of God and is linked through their spirit to the same God to which you yourself are linked. You are all brothers and sisters of the one God. You are all one family. Therefore if you hurt someone, abuse someone, mislead someone, you are hurting, abusing and misleading your own family, the whole body of Humanity. Above all, when you abuse someone, even someone who has abused you, remember that you are abusing your God, your Creator, the Source that gave you life, the Source that is the mother and the father of your being.

Now, of course, any mother or father will tell you that at some stage in its evolution to adulthood a child will, on a personality level, react against its parents and will turn against those who have created and nurtured it. It is all part of the child's process of growing up and of expressing and understanding its individuality. There is a part of the child that wants to be separate. But, equally so, it is a wise parent who knows that it will be through its experience of this separation and, above all, through the loneliness, the fear and the anxiety that comes with it, that the child will be led into a true understanding not just of itself but of its relationship with its family and with the larger family of Humanity. It is difficult, I know, on a human, physical level to relate to all your fellow human beings as brothers and sisters but it is through the act of uniting with the source of your own being, through unity with your Creator, the creator of all life, that there comes an understanding of the roles that all human beings are playing. It is from union with your Creator that there comes true understanding and acceptance both of your role and of the roles of all your fellow brothers and sisters.

There is, therefore, no separation from the Source, unless you choose to create that separation. The link is always there. You are merely separating yourself from the Source for your own reasons. You are choosing to create your own world as opposed to living in your Creator's world. Now I do not want you to think that just because you rightly choose to live in your Creator's world as opposed to your world that everything will be perfection, love, joy and beauty, that there will be no challenges, no tests, no satanic or saturnic influence. You know better than that. There is as much evil as there is goodness on the face of this Earth. So recognise that they are both aspects of your Creator. Recognise that all people are playing roles in this drama of life. Observe the roles with compassion, energy and understanding, but do not judge the actor. When you go to the theatre and watch a play being acted upon the stage you know that the actors are simply playing roles. Even if some of the actors are playing evil roles, you do not judge or condemn them because they are playing those roles. Indeed, you might even applaud them for playing their roles to perfection! That reflects the nature of human life. As Shakespeare said, you are all actors on the stage of life and you are all playing roles for the benefit of the audience of Humanity. A great drama is being enacted for the evolution of human consciousness.

Now being souls of aged evolution you recognise that you are taking part in a great drama. You observe with spiritual consciousness the roles that both you and your fellow brothers and sisters are playing, knowing that the creator of the drama is the Creator of all Life and that every role is significant. You therefore observe the drama, knowing that you have a role to play, knowing that you must be part of the drama, but also knowing that the drama is happening as part of the divine plan for human evolution. You observe but do not become one with, do not identify with, the drama on a physical level. Recognise that you are linked through your spirit to the source of all life and that the only people who are truly suffering in the drama are those who are separated from their Creator, for what is the drama but the actions of those who are separated from their God. The drama, therefore, manifests separation from God as opposed to union with God. The greatest evil in the drama is the greatest separation from God and is, therefore, the greatest deception, the greatest delusion.

As you sit here now, with your eyes closed, do you regard yourselves as being separate from me, from the other people in this circle, from the energy that is being grounded here? No, we are all as one body! We are all sharing the energies present here tonight as one unit, as one being. But, as you open your eyes, as you prepare to return to your individual personality selves, so does not the separation return? Once more the entrenched concepts of belief and dogma, of social position, of race, colour and creed return to impose their illusion of separation.

It is apparent that, no matter where you look in the World today, human conflict is on the increase. Human society is fragmenting into millions and millions of separate individuals. Human beings are conflicting and fighting with each other in almost every sphere of human activity, no matter whether it be religious, financial, political or ideological. But I can tell you that there is an event soon to happen in your World which will bring about great unity in the Human Race. For is it not the case that the inhabitants of any country, when faced with an outside challenge, respond collectively and in the face of that challenge are prepared to sacrifice their own ideas of separation and to become one nation yet again? Was this not the case in the last World War? When a race or nation was challenged, little petty struggles and selfish objectives were placed aside by most people and sacrifices were made on many levels in order to defeat the challenge to their country. From such a challenge came great unity of purpose and it is at such times that one sees clearly what can be achieved by human unity on a higher level.

But those of you who have already come to terms with the illusion of separation, who are attuned to the oneness of all life, will be prepared for this great event that is to come, as Noah was prepared for the Great Flood with his ark, not an ark of cypress wood and pitch but an ark of consciousness. Those of you that have created your own arks of consciousness, that have placed aside the illusion of separation and have seen only the wholeness, the holiness, of all life and its unity with the Creator of all Life, will be prepared for the events that are to come. You will be ready for the supreme challenge. .

In the days to come, therefore, as you enter into a relationship either with one of the Kingdoms of Matter or with another human being, observe yourself closely to see when the actual beginning of separation takes place. Observe that moment when you begin to separate yourself from another human being, when you begin to judge and criticize them, when you begin to treat them as you would not treat yourself. Then, examine the source of that separation, of that action. When you see someone behaving in a manner that you do not like or understand, place that dislike and judgement aside and try to establish contact with the higher aspect of that person, with their spirit. Act from the highest of your spiritual being and become as a mirror to them, to help them to become aware of the spirit in them, the spirit which they are perhaps ignoring or from which they are separating themselves.

Recognise that it is by contacting the spirit of another human being that you can arouse an awareness in them of their own spiritual being. This is the nature of the power that lies behind the transmutation of all karma and the transformation of all physical matter. This is the basis of the powers of all the great Masters and Avatars. You have the ability to tap into the spirit of every being who comes into your aura and to truly communicate with them, if you will but try it, and of course I mean not on the physical speech level but on the level of mind projection. You have the power to create good in another person. You can create right action in them by your thoughts. That surely is the real meaning behind the Christian invocation to turn the other cheek when you have been struck a physical or mental blow. It is to establish a basis for true communication. It is not to oppose force with force and so help to make the separation between people a reality. It is not to support the actions of someone who has separated themselves from their own divinity. It is always to seek for the higher aspect of life that is to be found in all beings.

You are linked, therefore, to every single human being that incarnates on the physical plane of Earth. You are all brothers and sisters of the one great family of Humanity. You are also linked to the millions of spirit beings on the higher planes of life who have incarnated or are about to incarnate on this Earth. You are all part of the great God of this Solar System. Each one of you has a unique purpose and design. Each one of you has a vital and necessary role to play in the human and Earthly evolutionary cycle. Therefore recognise and respect the sanctity of all those beings, just as you should recognise and respect the sanctity of yourself. Just as you should be humble and forgiving of yourself, of your errors, of your transgressions against the Laws of God, just as you should be aware of all your weaknesses, of the evolutionary advances that you have still to make, of the karma that you have to transmute, so you should recognise and respect those same things in others.

Recognise the great truth that all human beings are just like you! Recognise that they too are actors upon this stage of life called Earth. Recognise that you are all portraying a great cosmic drama. You are a microcosm reflecting a macrocosm. You are portraying on this little stage of Earth the drama of the universe. Do not separate yourselves from that fact. Do not withdraw into the illusion of separation, as do so many on the plane of Earth today, but open your hearts and your minds to the oneness of all life, to the one God that is, and always will be, and of which you are a part. For, in truth, if one was to give a purpose to physical life, it would be to come to the recognition that you truly have no individuality, that there is no you, only the one God of which we are all a part.

QUESTIONS AND ANSWERS

Q: The Master talked about shedding the personality aspect of ourselves but many people, and I am one of them, are afraid to do this, because that is our form of identity. There must be a purpose in having a personality. We are all unique, as you so often say. So if we let go of our personality selves what do we become, because surely we still all have our individuality?

ZT: Let us go back to the example of the drama that the Master has just used. Now the actor is the spirit and the role is the personality. You all incarnate with your roles to play. Each time you incarnate on the Earth your spirit, the actor, chooses to play a different role. This can be as a man in some lives, as a woman in others, as a king in one life, as a beggar in another, and so on. You are all exquisite actors and you play your roles to perfection, but what you must always remember is that you are not the role and that if you identify with the role then you are doomed to suffer, if only because one day that role will end in death. Now the nature of your role is decided by many factors including your karmic account, the soul lessons you have to learn and your genetic inheritance. So you cannot deny or put aside your role, your part in the drama of life, but what you can do is to recognise that it is only a role, that it is not the reality of your true being.

Let me give you a simple example. Suppose that you were to incarnate in this life and that you were to lose your right hand in an 'accident'. So one part of your role in this life would be to experience physical life with no right hand. Now you can either be very upset by this fact and compare yourself with all the other people who have right hands and so feel very sorry for yourself, or else you can accept that that is the role that you have chosen in this life, for whatever reasons, and strive to live your life to the fullest, developing other aspects of your being. Remember that your spirit knows why you have lost that hand and will help you to come to terms with your role, especially in the understanding of why there was a need for you to lose that hand. So you will either choose to lead a life full of self-pity and bitterness, complaining at life's unfairness, or else you will rise above the handicap to lead a fulfilling existence.

I would also like to say that the Master did not say that you should shed your personality. What was said was that you should be aware that if you identify too greatly with your personality, with your role in this life, that it can lead to a sense of separation from the reality of spirit, that you tend to view life through the eyes of the personality rather than through the eyes of the spirit. So, to carry on using my example, a person with no right hand could hold negative thoughts and emotions for people with two hands! I know that I am using a very simple analogy, but I think you can see the point that I am trying to make.

So whilst accepting the role that you have to play, and the personality characteristics that are in-built in that role, at the same time you must also recognise that there is a divine part of you, a part that lives in a

109

state of great peace and stillness, that is capable of manifesting both wisdom and a point of consciousness that the personality cannot even begin to comprehend. When you are faced with a problem, you soon know as to how your personality is going to respond, but how often do you seek the response of your eternal spirit? If someone punches you on the nose, are you always going to punch him right back? We know that that is the personality reaction, but what would be your spiritual reaction?

Q: Yes, how often do we say 'I know that I shouldn't be doing this, but I am going to do it anyway!'.
ZT: But that expression comes later, after you have decided what you are going to do.

Q: Can you tell us how we come to choose our personality?
ZT: Because you are all aged souls, you have earned the right to choose your roles and, carrying on with the analogy of the stage drama, before you incarnate or play your role, you have a casting meeting to see which roles you are best suited for! Just as with a Shakespearean play the actors all choose their parts according to their talents, their sex, their physical stature, their feel for the role etc., so before you incarnate you too choose the role you want to play. You choose your genetic heritage, your karmic bloodstream, your country, your parents, your sex, your role in life and, of course, you learn both from the exercise of that choice and from the experience of the life that you have chosen. Now young souls have no such choice. They are sent down to play a certain role by great celestial Beings who are well aware of what the young souls need to learn.

Q: So if we choose our parents and if we choose our time of birth, what happens when medical science interferes, say in the case of a Caesarean section or an induced birth? Does not that affect our personality and our destiny in that life?
ZT: There are many aspects to be considered here. Firstly, it is sometimes the destiny of a soul to be born by Caesarean section. Some souls choose to experience this form of birth, both for their own and for their parents' evolutionary pattern. For the most part, however, because all the individuals who are involved in a birth have free choice and can affect the timing of that birth, so there are indeed many occasions when a child is born at the wrong time for its planned destiny

pattern. As a result of this, it is possible for a soul to be born far removed from its planned destiny time, which is significant because at the moment of birth you are setting the cosmic frequency for your entire life. That is why there are so many lost souls, at this time especially, who feel that they have no purpose in life, no sense of destiny, who are not in harmony with the direction in which their life is taking them.

Now this feeling of a lack of purpose is, of course, a reflection of the personality self. The spirit knows full well what has taken place and understands the reality of the life with which it is faced. The spirit has the ability to change its destiny pattern, to create a new purpose and a new direction, to seek new understandings through its new role. So there are no really hard and fast rules about this. It depends entirely on the individual situation and the destiny and the karma of the souls concerned. Nevertheless, what I can say, with certainty, is that medical science today is interfering far too much with what is, after all, a cosmic as well as a natural process. This is creating many ripples on the pool of karma and is causing imbalance to the flow of human evolution.

Q: So if somebody does incarnate away from their planned time, is not that likely to upset the destiny of other people, for example, the person they are destined to marry?

ZT: That is a good question! In answer, I will say 'Yes' to you, but you must also realise that when we use the analogy of life being like a drama on the stage that that is a very crude analogy. It is an oversimplistic concept of life which is, of course, in reality, highly complex, if only because the force of destiny, as you would call it, embraces *all* human choices. By this I mean that at any given moment in your life, with all the choices that you have before you, that no matter what the choice that you make it will have been built into what I will call the vast human computer of life and will tie in with all the choices that all the other individuals are making at that time! So even if someone does incarnate outside of their destiny time, that too is taken into account in God's Plan. Truly everything that manifests is part of God's Plan.

Q: So do we therefore choose, before we actually incarnate, to experience certain tragedies in our life, like having a young child die in the family? Do we decide on our own tests?

ZT: Yes, you choose all the experiences that you are going to meet in your life. How you respond to them, of course, is entirely up to you and that is your learning experience.

Q: So when we die, if we've failed at something, we can decide to return in another life and face it again?
ZT: It is not quite like that! The wonderful thing about life is that there is no fail or pass situation. Life is just a learning experience. So what you do not learn in one life is simply repeated in subsequent lives, and then it is repeated on a higher level again and again and then on an even higher level again and again.

Q: When you say higher, do you mean harder?
ZT: No, higher, a higher understanding of the cosmic laws that are involved. You are forever learning. It is not harder in the sense of more difficult to pass but harder in the sense that greater understanding and wisdom is needed in order to reach that point of consciousness.

Q: Why do we always have to come back to Earth to learn our lessons? Why can't we learn them on other levels of life?
ZT: As an aged soul you can, of course, choose whether or not you wish to come back to this school of life called Earth, but if the whole purpose of your being is simply to learn your lessons, then there is no point in not returning to school, because otherwise you will not learn the great lessons that life on the Earth can teach you.

Q: Zen Tao, if we can say that the purpose of life is to learn to sacrifice our sense of self-identity back to the whole, do we ever reach that point in time when we have to learn to sacrifice our sense of soul-identity too?
ZT: Well, of course, you are asking me something which I have not yet experienced, otherwise I would not be here! However I am told by the Masters that that is indeed the case. It is a fact that people who fear death do hold onto the aspect of themselves that they know best, their personality-self. They do this because that is their form of self identity. So the same thing must also be true for those who hold onto their soul identity, although obviously it must be much more difficult to release one's sense of soul identity, because whereas the self identity has only existed for three score years and ten, the soul identity has existed for millions of years! Nevertheless, the Masters do say that one day we will

112

all have to face this great test. It is all part of the cosmic understanding that the smaller is always contained within the greater. We all belong to a greater part, or a greater Being, and although we have self-identity and a sense of separation from that Being, nevertheless we are still part of that greater whole. It is by sacrificing our apparent individuality back to that whole that, although we lose our self-identity, we gain that greater whole and, more importantly, become one with the consciousness of that Being.

Q: But I still don't see why we have to come back here. Why can't we learn on the other levels of life and avoid all this human suffering?

ZT: You learn on all the levels of life. You are learning on other levels right now, for you are living in seven bodies at this very moment in time! When you go to sleep, you do not stop learning, for you visit other levels of life. There is no time when you are not learning. But this Earth, as I have said on so many occasions, is a very special place of learning. It presents you with a sharp and vivid drama which evokes a great emotional response from you. Just as when you go to the theatre and witness a great drama on the stage, you get emotionally involved in what is being presented to you and learn from it, so with the stage of life, where the drama is so well acted that you think it is real too. But it is not. It is only a drama, an illusion.

Q: I understand what you are saying on a psychological level, but when I cut my body it bleeds and hurts. Surely you are not saying that that is an illusion too? That illusion hurts!

ZT: Only a few days ago, my lady, you were recounting the story of when you were sitting in meditation and experienced a sharp pain in your leg. You discovered that there was a part of your being that was separate from your body, a part that was observing the pain yet did not feel it. You realised that you were not that pain and that if you chose to ignore it, it went away and became of no importance. You learned that you can choose whether or not to identify with the pain, in fact, whether or not to suffer at all. It is just the same with watching a drama on the stage or with watching the drama of life. You choose whether or not you are going to identify with it and become one with it. Now that does not mean that you can ignore a bleeding body and it will just go away, but it does decide whether or not you are going to suffer.

113

Q: So are you saying that even if I was being crucified right now I would not have to suffer unless I chose to do so, unless I identified with my body?

ZT: Yes, and that was the way that the Master Jesus handled his crucifixion. When you consider his mastery of all the levels of life, there was no need for him to experience the pain of that death, unless he chose to do so.

Q: So is it simply a question of telling your body not to respond to pain, of mind over matter?

ZT: The body will always respond to any violation of its being. That is a natural function. What you must always remember is that you are the master and that the body is the servant. How else is it possible for mystics to pierce their bodies with spears and yet feel no pain and express no blood? How else is it possible for men to walk on hot coals and not to burn their feet? Such people have come to an understanding of the correct relationship between themselves and their bodies and so can handle such situations. Always remember that you are not your bodies. Know this fact, not on an intellectual level, but in your hearts. You were not your bodies before birth, you will not be your bodies after death. Your bodies are but vehicles in which you temporarily reside. They possess consciousness, which should be respected at all times, but they exist to serve you, the greater consciousness. If the servant usurps the role of the master, then, your life will become chaotic, because a lesser consciousness is now controlling your life.

Q: If you are in the position of being able to help someone else raise their point of consciousness, is it best to help them on the physical level, through speech, or on the mental or even the spiritual level?

ZT: I will begin by saying that, unless you are a great Master, you are not in a position to raise anyone's point of consciousness. It is only the individual concerned that can raise his or her point of consciousness. The only thing that you can do is to be a mirror of consciousness for them, as pure a mirror as possible, so that they can see their reflection in you and recognise the true nature of their being. It is by the energy that you send out in thought, word and deed that you either uplift or drag down your fellow human beings and the purest energy that you can send out is that of divine love, the love that expects no return. If you truly want to help someone then your expression of love must be without desire, without expectation, not because you want them to be

114

like you or any one else. You are giving of your divine energy to help them to transform themselves in whatever way they feel is appropriate, so that they can bring forth the highest in themselves. All that you can do is to surround that person with light and love, to hold them in your prayers and to visualise them as a perfect being in every way.

Please remember that you are not responsible for anyone else's evolution, only your own, and that if you will but concentrate on your own transformation, you will not have the time to worry about anyone else's! Obviously, all evolved souls, by virtue of their point of consciousness, have a responsibility towards their less evolved brothers and sisters, at all times, but the responsibility is that of the teacher, of the way-shower. Always remember though that the best teacher is example. One correct deed is worth a thousand correct words. The gaining of consciousness is a slow and painstaking progress. It cannot be handed over to someone like a gift and, if it is, it is rarely appreciated. That is truly casting pearls before time, not swine, as your saying goes, giving knowledge to someone before they are ready to handle it or accept it into their being.

Finally, it is a fact of life that at a certain point on the path to Cosmic Consciousness, all souls go through a stage of proselytisation, that is when they feel a strong desire to convert people to their understanding of life, if only because it has transformed the nature of their being. This, of course, is only natural but, in truth, the desire to convert anyone is born out of fear, out of a lack of trust in God, rather than out of a genuine desire to serve the Source of all Life. There is no need to convert anyone, to 'save' anyone's soul. All will find their path to God at the appointed time, in the appointed way. All that you can do is to hasten the day of that event by the right demonstration of the spirit of Cosmic Consciousness that flows through you.

THE DRAMA OF LIFE

It was William Shakespeare, as I am sure you all know, who wrote in one of his plays –

> All the world's a stage
> and all the men and women merely players:
> they have their exits and their entrances
> and one man in his time plays many parts.

Now even though those words were written four hundred years ago, they are as true today as they were then, for the wisdom of the heavens cannot be dated. They are a living testimony to the soul consciousness of the man who wrote them, for William Shakespeare understood full well that physical life on the Earth can be compared to a play, albeit on a slightly larger scale than his little theatrical masterpieces, and that when your eternal spirits incarnate on the physical plane of Earth they are simply playing parts, empowering roles in the great drama of life. Above all, though, Shakespeare was aware of the significance of the actor as compared to the role that he or she was playing. He knew that the spirit, the actor, played many parts, many roles in their different incarnations, in their different plays, and that whereas the role or the part that the actor played lived and died with the play, the actor himself went on to play many other roles in many other plays.

So the entrances and the exits in any stage play can be compared to the moment of birth and the moment of death in physical life. For those of you who have been privileged to share in a birth or a death, you will be aware of the separate presence of the spirit at such times and of how purposeless the physical body is without the energy of the spirit to empower it. The presence of the spirit is all pervasive. That is why it is almost impossible to look at a baby and not to feel love for that little being, not because it is so weak and helpless, but because as you look into its eyes you see there the pure reflection of its spirit, as yet unsullied by the personality. You see there the nature of its

116

consciousness, its spiritual being and its power, as it descends into its limiting body of physical matter.

Similarly, as that body approaches its moment of death and the spirit within prepares to depart, you are aware on the one hand of the suffering of the physical body, but on the other hand you can witness the beginnings of a state of peace and tranquillity that defies human description. No matter what the psychological or the physical pain that that person has experienced, no matter what the suffering that they have endured, as you look into the eyes of a dying person you are aware of the presence of a very different being, a being of spiritual consciousness that exists in a state of bliss. It is at times like this that you can differentiate very clearly between the actor and the role that has been played, between the body and the spirit.

So if the soul is there so strongly at birth and at death, why is it not so evident during the remainder of your life, especially when you are adult? Why is it that so many people accept and cause so much pain and suffering? Why is it that there is so much intolerance and prejudice between all of the World's races and religions? Why are your spirits apparently incapable of manifesting their divine note? The answer is simple. It is because you choose to identify only with your physical manifestation. You have become so immersed in your physical body of clay that you honestly believe that that is the only reality. You have become convinced that you are your personality, that you are the role that you are playing. In a sense you are like an actor who is playing Macbeth and who not only plays Macbeth when he is on the stage but when he is off it as well! He has lost the sense of what is real and what is unreal. Indeed, often such a person chooses to identify with the role in order to avoid facing the reality of who they truly are. They prefer the illusion to the reality. This, to varying degrees, is what you are all doing. You are choosing to identify with your role in the drama, your physical body of this life, rather than with your eternal spiritual being. That is why so many people fear death, for what is death but the ending of the illusion and the return to a reality which they have denied for so much of their life.

Shakespeare recognised the great cosmic truth that the spirit of every human being is eternal. You are all spiritual beings with unique points of consciousness. You incarnate into this school of life called Earth in order to evolve that point of consciousness. Therefore your life on Earth can indeed be compared to going to the theatre to see a play. It is only for a relatively short period of time that you watch the drama and

117

respond to it. You then leave the theatre and return to your normal life, carrying with you your memories of the event and your reactions to it. It is just the same with physical life. Your physical life is relatively short and you leave the stage of life to return to your normal plane of existence, carrying with you your memories of that life and your reactions to it.

So when you come into physical incarnation you are in fact taking part in a vast cosmic drama on the stage of Earth. You are, therefore, all actors and actresses. The sole purpose of your incarnation is to act, is to play your role, the role that you have chosen, to the highest of your ability. Each one of you, before you incarnate, chooses the role that you are going to play, bearing in mind the nature and the potential of your acting talents. You could choose to be a king, a high priest, a prime minister, a person of wealth and substance or, just as easily, you could choose to be a servant, a monk in some humble order or a pauper. Either way you will choose according to the nature of your point of consciousness and your soul content. You will not choose a role which you are incapable of playing, in just the same way that an actor will not take on a part in a play that is unsuited to their acting talents. So unevolved souls, like inexperienced actors, will not take on roles which they know they cannot play. It requires an experienced actor, one of talent and ability, to play a major role in any play and, similarly, it requires an evolved soul to play a significant role in the greater drama of life. Only after you have had many incarnations in the hard school of acting called life do you feel that you are ready to take on a role which affects the destiny of nations, if not the whole world!

Now when you look at a drama being enacted on the stage of a theatre you are aware that you are watching two people, the actor and the role that he or she is playing. You are most strongly aware, if the actor is a good one, of the role that is being portrayed and as the drama unfolds on the stage so you react emotionally and psychologically to it. You identify with the role that the actor is portraying. You suffer when they suffer. You are happy when they are happy. If you identify too closely with the role, then you and the actor do indeed become one. You cry when they cry. You laugh when they laugh. Nevertheless, you are always aware, deep down within you, that it is only a drama, that the actor is only playing a part, and that even if someone is brutally killed on the stage that they are not really dead and will rise again to play their part in the next performance! You are also aware of the personality of the actor manifesting in the role, of how they interpret and play certain

118

scenes. You can make a valued judgement of the performance of the actor in the role. Even if an actor is playing an evil role in the drama you are happy to applaud them for playing it well.

You are, therefore, always aware of the duality of the drama, of the actor and the role that he or she is portraying. I would like you to understand that this is also true of life. You, in your physical bodies, are a duality, portraying two roles. You, too, are both the actor, the force of spirit which empowers and gives life to the physical form, and the role that you are portraying, which is your personality self disporting itself upon the stage of life. You are two in one, just like that actor on the stage. Inevitably, the question will arise, 'Why am I doing it?'. Why does the actor act? He acts not just to improve his acting talents, not just to give pleasure to his audiences, but because deep down within him there is this creative urge which drives him to do it. He just knows that he has to act, that his whole purpose in life is to act and that if he does not do it then he is wasting his talents and his time. It is the same for all human beings. They incarnate because they know that life will help them to evolve their point of soul consciousness, will help them to become one with the Source from which they have, apparently, become separated, the Source which is the whole centre and purpose of their being.

The next question which arises is – 'What is the purpose of the Drama of Life?', apart from that of evolving the acting abilities of the actor or actress taking part in it? What is the purpose of any drama? A drama is staged for the benefit of those who watch it. People go to the theatre because they identify, for whatever reason, with the drama that is being staged. As such, they learn from the drama. They experience the emotions of the different roles on the stage. They take sides and form viewpoints and so suffer or experience joy as those sides and viewpoints prosper or wither. If there is a moral lesson in the drama then that becomes their lesson too. A drama can be a wonderful tool for demonstrating the Law of Karma in action! It shows very clearly how the characters in a play cannot avoid the fruits of their actions. Now everything that I have said of the stage drama is also true of the greater drama, the Drama of Life. The whole world, literally, is watching you, is watching your role, as you walk across the stage of life. Truly the Earth is a cosmic stage. You are playing to an audience beyond your comprehension, for not only is the whole of Humanity watching your role in life but so are many cosmic beings. Millions upon millions of invisible eyes are watching your every thought, word and deed. Your lessons become their lessons. Your evolution becomes their evolution. God has separated parts of Itself from Itself in order that It may know Itself.

You can learn a great deal about the Drama of Life by observing with awareness any drama performed on the stage. The great cosmic law 'As above, so below' pertains here. As you watch a drama unfolding on the stage, although you may identify with the suffering on the stage, on an inner level you know that it is not real, that any death is not absolute and final. You know that no-one really dies, no matter how much blood and gore appears on the stage. Similarly, in physical life, the soul knows that no matter how much blood and gore is present in any violent death, no-one ever dies permanently, never again to return and play a role in physical incarnation. The soul knows not only that it will return at that very same point in the cycle but also that it will return at other stages in the cycle and will act many roles in many different dramas. So there is, therefore, no such thing as death. There is no such thing as real suffering. There is no such thing as success or failure. Why? Because the physical world is illusory. It is nothing more than a great drama which has been designed to evolve your point of consciousness through the observation of it. But remember that you are both observer and participant in this drama, for as you watch the world around you, so the world around is watching you! You are all mirrors of consciousness.

It is hard to accept that you are not your personality, that you are not your body. Now that statement in no way takes away from the importance of either the body or the personality. They both have vital parts to play in any physical incarnation, but recognise that they are only costumes, to use the analogy of the stage. They still require the actor, the motor, the driving force of spirit, before they can play their roles. It is equally hard to accept that physical life is an illusion, especially when you are living in it but, in reality, life is like a dream! Now when you are dreaming, are your experiences any less meaningful? Do you realise that you are dreaming and that your experiences are not 'real'? No! To you a dream is real and you react to it most strongly, so much so that sometimes you have to 'wake up' in order to avoid it! Well, in truth, life is like a dream. You go to sleep as you are born and you wake up as you die and everything in between is but a passing dream, an illusion. Indeed, for those who have had an unpleasant life, full of suffering, when they die and wake up they are happy that the nightmare is over and that they have returned to 'real' life! So what is reality? What plane of life is real?

120

The Drama of Life, of course, is designed to appear real, otherwise there would be no lesson in it. If you go to the theatre and watch a play that lacks reality it has very little impact upon you. So, as actors on the stage of life, it is important that you believe in your roles and portray them to the highest of your talents. You are all born with the destiny to play certain roles in life, just as actors are hired to play certain roles on the stage. These roles, of course, can be of so-called good or evil people, but you do not hire an evil actor to play an evil part! You hire an actor whose talents are best suited to the part, a good actor. Any good drama needs the conflict of good and evil to make it come alive and be entertaining. How else could goodness be seen to triumph over evil if there was not evil to conquer? It is just the same in life. Behind all the so-called evil forces of the world, the forces that oppress the spirit of Humanity, there is a divine spirit playing its role. Just because an actor is portraying an evil role, you do not consider the actor to be evil as well, do you? Moreover, if an actor plays an evil role well, no matter what vile deeds he performs, you applaud him for it! It should be the same in life. As you differentiate between the actor and the role, so you should differentiate between the spirit and the body it has taken on. Observe the role or the body, but do not condemn the actor or the spirit for portraying it. Remember that inside every actor there is a divine spirit.

Only evolved souls, those who recognise that life is a drama and who remain detached from it, can be true observers of the drama. Only those who do not identify with the drama, who do not take on board all the suffering and emotions generated by it, can rise above it and can be the masters of the drama. No matter whether you go to the theatre or watch a play on television, if you identify with the drama that you see, then you become part of that drama, you become enervated by it, if only because you are taking on someone else's karma, someone else's lessons. So the purpose of life is to play your role, recognising that it is only a role and always being mindful of the actor within, the force of spirit.

Remember, also, that within every human being, no matter what the nature of the role that they are portraying, there is an aspect of spirit. Always look through the role, see beyond the body and the personality, to discover the true nature of a person. Just as you are more than your physical presence, so is every other human being. A true Master of the physical plane of life, whilst accepting and respecting his or her personality expression, always subjugates it to the force of spirit. The personality, with all of its conditioning, with all of its limiting concepts of the reality of human life, is ever present, but it should never be allowed to become the master for how can the mortal and the finite ever know of the immortal and the infinite? How can something which is born and dies even begin to comprehend something that is never born, because it never dies?

As you reach the end of this century so you are witnessing the final act of a great cosmic drama. The stage is set for a grand finale. Many different characters and story lines have been developed by its author, your Creator, in order to produce a great evolutionary ending. The forces of conflict which have been slowly growing over the past seven thousand years are about to meet in one final great battle. Many physical changes will also manifest at this time which will serve to accentuate the great drama. Only those who recognise that it is a drama, that the suffering is neither real nor lasting, will be able to handle and rise above these events. Only those who recognise the eternity of their being, not as an intellectual concept but as a cosmic truth, will be able to comprehend the divine presence behind this great drama.

So remember that you are actors on a stage, albeit a vast stage – the planet Earth. You are acting out a divine drama written by your Creator and, as such, it is a drama that knows no imperfections. It is a drama which embodies all the lessons of the Age, both for the beings acting in it and for the beings who are watching it on many levels of life. It is an aware person who looks for the hand of God behind every human action and who tries to see divine purpose in all human suffering. It is an aware person who remembers the inherent nature of the drama, namely, its temporality. So never identify with the actor or with his or her role. Do not even identify with the spirit that is empowering the role. Look for the author of the play. Look for the Creator of all Life that created both the drama and the actors taking part in it.

Finally, as you approach this grand finale, know that every hair on your head is counted, that every thought, word and deed that you project not only is being recorded, but is also contributing to the nature of the drama as well. In these times of great change, when not only the human cycle and the planetary cycle are changing, but the divine cycle as well, cling to that which is permanent and infinite – your Creator. Remember that you have chosen to be here because it presents a great opportunity for you to evolve your soul consciousness. Strive to establish a right balance in your life between the physical and the spiritual. Most of you are 90% body conscious and only 10% spirit conscious. Try to redress the balance a little and become 50% body conscious and 50% spirit conscious. Above all, please remember that what is important is not the drama but is the consciousness that lies behind it. Look for the consciousness in every situation, in every person, in every aspect of matter. This final act presents you with a unique opportunity for soul growth. Seize it and do not let destiny pass you by, for what you meet in life is destiny, but how you handle it is determined by your self effort.

QUESTIONS AND ANSWERS

Q: The Master mentioned that many millions of souls are watching us from other planes of life. Why do they watch us when they could so easily come down and experience life on the Earth for themselves, or do they learn and evolve more rapidly from observation rather than from participation?

ZT: Well, firstly, the planet does have a physical size and the millions of spiritual beings that would like to take part in this drama simply could not be accommodated on this small stage! But that is not the real reason. The real reason is that the Race of Humanity is in a very special and privileged position. You have been given the divine gift of free choice and the unique dispensation to create in your own image. Now, although the drama of life on the Earth is fixed, nevertheless, you have the freedom to take part in that drama according to your own individual wills and desires. I mean, by this, firstly, that you can decide when you want to act and, secondly, that you can decide how you are going to play any particular role, where you are going to position yourself on the stage, what mannerisms you will adopt, the degree of consciousness that you will put into the role and so on.

Now I have told you on another occasion that there are many beings in the Cosmos who do not have the divine gifts of either free choice or self-reproduction and that the great Interplanetary Lords regard this plane of life called Earth as a cosmic experiment, an experiment to see if a race of beings can truly learn of Creation through the exercise of these divine gifts without destroying either itself or the Solar Body of which it is a part, if such an event was to be permitted. Therefore many great spiritual beings are watching the drama that is unfolding on this little stage of life. They are watching to see if the Race of Humanity can

123

sacrifice itself, both individually and collectively, for the good of the whole. Can a human being truly give up something that it needs because it sees a greater need in another? Can a human being truly turn the other cheek in the face of violence, not out of weakness but rather out of strength? Can a human being truly love someone that hates them, that is trying to do them harm? Can a human being truly sacrifice its own physical existence in order to further the evolution of the whole?

Many, many beings, many spiritual forms, have drawn close to the Earth at this time as we reach the finale of this great drama. They are closely watching human behaviour in thought, word and deed in the face of such a challenge. It is a fact of life, not just at this special time but also at ordinary times of change in the Cosmic Cycle, that there are, perhaps, a thousand beings in the realm of spirit for every one being in physical incarnation on the Earth. Or, to use the analogy of the stage, there are always more people in the audience than on the stage, that is if the drama is at all worth watching! Actors are very special people. So are you!

Q: You said that we should not judge the soul of a being that is playing an evil role, but is not that soul being affected by the very nature of the role that it is playing? Should we not judge, for example, the very fact that it chose to play that role?

ZT: At this stage in Humanity's evolution, where you all possess varying degrees of free choice, not just on the physical but on the higher planes of life as well, it is a fact that the soul makes many choices. It can choose to portray a physical role of either, what you would call, goodness or evil, or what I would call, positivity or negativity. Therefore, one's motivation for playing any such polarised role in physical life is obviously of supreme importance. One has to look very, very carefully at why a soul would choose to play such a role, of why it needed to experience such a role in order to further its evolutionary progression. Of course, for the soul there is the learning experience of having to portray that role, but do not think that it requires an evil spirit to play an evil role. As the Master has just said, you must differentiate between the spirit and the role. Within the heart of the most negative role there lies a great spiritual being. Remember the example of Jesus and Judas. They were both soul equals, but whose role, do you think, was the more difficult to play, the betrayer or the betrayed? Therefore, whilst you might judge a certain role as being negative or evil, and would most definitely not choose to play that role yourself, recognise

124

also the quality of the spiritual being that is empowering the role and do not judge them, learn from them. Judge the role, but not the spirit.

Q: Yes, I agree with that, but what I said was, does not the fact that you are playing a negative role affect the soul also?

ZT: Yes, but you still have the choice of whether or not to identify with your soul murmurings. Remember that the soul is not pure either.

Q: Could you please explain what you mean by that.

ZT: If you are watching a drama on the stage, shall we say a Shakespearean tragedy, in which a mother has to watch her children being killed before her very eyes, you are aware of her suffering not just because of the dramatic talents of the actress but also because it generates emotions in you as to how you would feel if faced with a similar loss. Now you and the audience around you can suffer with that mother if you so choose. You can go through the pain of the loss of your own children. But recognise that whether or not you suffer in this way is your choice. You choose whether or not you are going to identify with that mother's suffering and become one with it. Now that is not to say that you should not feel compassion for her loss, but that you do not let her suffering become your suffering, that you do not let her life's lessons become your life's lessons. One of the qualities of a Master of the physical plane of life is that they do not take on board the suffering and the karma of Humanity. They remain detached from it. They live in the world but are not part of the world and that is how they are best able to help the world. I would like you to understand this point most clearly.

Now, having said all of that, I will return to your question! The soul, which can be likened to your own personal akashic record, receives impressions of the life that it is leading now, just as it has received impressions of all the lives that you have lived in the past. In Sanskrit these impressions are known as samskaras. So, yes, the soul will receive impressions from a negative incarnation just as it would from a positive incarnation, but remember that the soul deliberately chose this role before it came down into physical incarnation. Why? In order to help it to create balance in its akashic record. You will always be experiencing your soul murmurings but, as with the experiences of this life, it is your choice whether or not you identify with them and become them. It is your choice whether or not you remain detached from them and observe them, and so learn from that observation. Only the spirit is pure because it is divine. So always strive to sound your spiritual note rather than your soul note.

Q: I always like to bring your philosophy down to a practical level! Are you saying that if in a marriage one of the partners is going through a negative stage, or is doing something that is considered negative, that it is possible for the other partner to allow this to happen without identifying with it and therefore not being affected by it?
ZT: Yes. Not only is it possible but it is desirable as well!

Q: So in the situation where my husband leaves me and goes off with another woman, are you saying that I should just release this situation and not identify with all the emotions that I am feeling? This seems very difficult, not to react on any level at all.
ZT: There are as many ways of handling such a situation as there are levels of consciousness. Obviously, if your husband leaves you for another woman, then on a physical level there is a sense of loss, a feeling of rejection, which would lead to varying degrees of suffering. On an emotional level, too, you would grieve that a person whom you had trusted, and to whom you had given your love, had betrayed that trust and had just turned his back on a sacred relationship and walked away from it. This would, perhaps, be a greater source of suffering. But the degree to which you suffer is your choice. The length of time that you choose to suffer is your choice as well. Obviously, just as if your husband had died, there is a natural period of grieving for his physical absence, but if this goes on for too long, and I always say here, for more than seven days, then you are enjoying it too much and it is becoming rather like an addiction! You have to go on living. Life does not stand still. You are not a victim. Every test that you have to face in life has purpose and meaning for you.

Slowly a seed will begin to take root in your physical consciousness that perhaps there is a lesson for you in all this drama. You will begin to look back objectively, even dispassionately, on your relationship with your husband and you will perhaps discover that you were living your life through him, that he had become a crutch to prop up all your own weaknesses, that he had even begun to take the place of your Creator. You will then see all your suffering in a different light and will realise that far from being a negative thing it is, in fact, a positive thing, bringing about great changes in your lifestyle and spiritual understandings. Suffering is caused by your own thoughtforms, by your own opinions, by your own expectations, not being met! But is it not the case that you always blame someone else for your suffering, in your case, your errant husband? You forget that he is just playing a role in the great drama of life and that if you hold negative thoughts about him you are affecting not just him but yourself as well. So let go and let God, the great author of the drama, handle the situation for you, for the highest good of all those concerned.

Q: So none of us suffer unless we choose to do so?
ZT: That is correct. Above all, remember what the Master has just said. You are living at the ending of an Age, at a time of great karmic resolution, where there is much apparent suffering all over the World. Be compassionate towards all those who are suffering, but do not become one with their suffering or you will be dragged down by it and so will be unable to help them.

Q: When we are awake we play our role in the drama of life, but what happens to us when we go to sleep? Do we play a role on the higher levels of life? Could you enlighten us on that?
ZT: I will begin by saying that physical time, the hours of the day, plays no part in this. The fact that you sleep for four or eight hours does not determine the nature of your life on the higher levels of life. It is a fact, though, that much of your sleeping time is taken up by your mind in sorting out all the confusion of the day, because only rarely do you see things through to a mental conclusion. Your minds are like busy bees, continually hopping from one flower to another, from one thought to another. So in reality you perhaps only spend one or two earthly hours in what I will call out of the body experiences. Nevertheless, released from Earthly limitations, those two hours could be the equivalent of two thousand years in spiritual time. So the time that you spend out of your body, whilst you are sleeping, permits you to travel anywhere that your consciousness is capable of taking you.

Now, the difference between you and a great Master is that they are fully conscious both awake and asleep. There is no difference for them between being awake and being asleep. They are fully aware of the lives that they are leading on every level of consciousness. They are, in a sense, omnipresent. They can manifest, at will, on any level of consciousness. You, however, cannot do this. You can only be in one place at a time! When you are asleep, a part of your spiritual consciousness does indeed leave your physical body and can travel to other planes of existence. In this state you are no longer subject to the limitations of your physical body and the conditioning of your personality self. You are truly able to experience the freedom of spirit. You can travel to other planets, to other planes of existence, you can communicate with other beings, within the limitations of your consciousness. You can retain and recall everything that you have learnt and experienced on those travels.

So when you come back to your physical body and awaken to the physical world, all the wisdom and knowledge that you have acquired is there. If you have gone and sat at the feet of a great Master in the Halls of Learning and asked for help in the solution of an earthly problem, the advice you were given will be in your sub-conscious mind. All that you have to do is to bring it forth into physical manifestation. You do this in the silence of your meditation, when you attune to your spiritual self, the very centre of your being. How many of you have gone to bed at night with a problem, saying that you will sleep on it, and have woken up in the morning with an answer. This is what has happened. How many of you faced with an apparently insoluble problem on the physical level, after casting your minds around for days along all your usual channels, all to no avail, finally release the problem to the Cosmos and so create the space into which divine inspiration can come. But it is difficult to let go of all your personality conditioning and to receive inspiration from a source beyond your understanding. It is even more difficult to trust that source, especially if it tells you to do something that your personality opposes.

So you can and do dwell on many planes of existence, both whilst you are awake and asleep. For the most part you are unaware of much of this activity. It takes place on an unconscious level. This is for a very good reason. Most human beings can hardly cope with the plane of Earth, let alone the other eleven planes of existence within this Solar Body! So you are protected from them until you have attained the soul consciousness to understand them. You have incarnated into this school of life called Earth. This is your lesson. This is your drama. When you have mastered it, then you may begin to be in the position to understand a greater reality – a cosmic reality which at present is beyond your understanding.

THE ULTIMATE SACRIFICE

As you look around your world today only a very few people would deny the fact that there is an urgent need for change in almost every field of human endeavour. Everywhere you look you can see human suffering, on either the physical, the emotional or the mental levels, and not only is Humanity suffering but the three other Kingdoms of Matter as well. It is, therefore, a time when many people who are aware of this situation are trying to bring about change in the particular aspects of the world with which they come in contact, with which they are particularly interested. They see the suffering, the human degradation, the pollution of the planet, and so they try, apparently with the highest of motivation, to bring about change, to carry out a healing both of Humanity and of the planet. Outwardly this would seem to be a very right and proper thing to do, but have you ever stopped to discover what is their motivation for doing this, what is the real reason behind their actions?

I want to make it very clear to you that you must always look most carefully at the motivation behind any one of your actions. It is your motivation alone that determines the validity of any action and, therefore, of the karmic reaction to it. So if you are one of those people who are trying to bring about change in the world, it is important that you examine your motivation for wanting to bring about that change, that you discover what is impelling you, what is directing you, to bring about that change. Let me give you a simple example in order to illustrate the point that I am trying to make. In a time of war, if another country takes up arms against your country and threatens to invade you, then you will undoubtedly oppose force with force and a bloody war will ensue. If your force proves to be the greater, the more destructive force, then it will prevail and it will be praised for having saved your country from being occupied by what will be called an 'evil' power. Nevertheless, it must also be recognised that you have used violence to oppose violence. You have reacted to the threat on the same level as the threat, if only because that is the way that it has always been done. But, although you will have saved your country, will you have changed the pattern of human behaviour in the future? By winning the war, will you have ended the need for all wars, both now and in the future? Will you have actually changed the point of human consciousness?

Now there are many people in your world today who feel that it is quite justifiable to oppose what they consider to be an evil force with their own force. For example, there are people who call themselves 'animal liberationists', who seek to stop the acts of violence being carried out against animals by scientists in their laboratories. There are people who call themselves 'hunt saboteurs', who try to stop other people from hunting and from killing animals simply for pleasure. Such people truly believe that the end justifies the means and that they are quite justified in using violence in order to help save animals from violence. There are also people who are against the manufacture and the stockpiling of nuclear weapons, and who feel very strongly that they must oppose any government which supports the use of nuclear weapons, by any means that are available, including violence of thought, word and deed. They therefore devote much time, money and energy to opposing the people who do believe in their use. But do all these actions really lead to a change in human awareness, to a rise in human consciousness, not just in the short term but in the long term as well? Indeed, I would go further and ask if human consciousness has evolved at all, even over the period of the last two thousand years? Do you really think that Humanity today is more spiritually evolved than it was at the time of the incarnation of the Master Jesus?

In your world today, where you can see that on a physical, material level so much needs to be changed if Humanity is to live in harmony and peace, not just with itself but with the planet as well, it is only natural that you should direct all of your energies to trying to bring about change in the world. Nevertheless, I would like to point out one important fact, namely, that you can only change the world according to your point of consciousness. You can only change the world according to your spiritual concepts, your understandings of the need for change. It is imperative, therefore, especially at this time, that you ask yourselves whether or not this is the way to bring about a fundamental change in human consciousness and understanding. Are you really going to transform human consciousness simply by opposing the forces that you consider to be 'evil' and by upholding the forces that you consider to be 'good'?

130

It is so easy in the world in which you live today to be totally distracted by that world, to see around you all the things that need to be changed, all the things that need to be healed, and yet to forget to look inwardly. But if you can only change the world according to your point of consciousness, and if Humanity for the most part has been acting in this way for the last two thousand years and the world has not changed, then surely you can see that what is needed is a fundamental shift in human consciousness if the world is going to change. It is important, therefore, that you understand not only that you are the world and that what you do in thought, word and deed affects and changes that world, but also that you change the world by changing the nature of your consciousness.

So the essence of my message to you can really be summed up in these few words – change yourself and the world will then change as a consequence of this. Recognise that it is by the very act of refining and evolving your spiritual point of consciousness that you will bring about lasting change in the world. The way to change this world is not by outer action alone but by inner action as well. The world as a whole will not change until you, as individuals, have changed. Recognise that the fundamental shift in consciousness that has to come about is not a shift in world consciousness, is not a shift in group consciousness, but is, rather, a shift in individual consciousness. It is you, the individual, through the purification of your being in thought, word and deed, that will bring about a fundamental change in human society and be aware that the basis of this fundamental change is sacrifice.

Now a dictionary defines sacrifice as the giving up, the surrender of something to a higher, a more important and more urgent thing than the thing that is being given up. You will recall that I have said, on many occasions, that the lesson of this planet, that the reason why the Human Race incarnates in this school of life called Earth, is to learn the lesson of sacrifice – sacrifice through service. You should regard all forms of service as service to your Creator and in that you serve each other, then, you are serving your Creator. The nature of that sacrifice, therefore, is that willingly, of your own free will, you are prepared to surrender your own will. That is the ultimate sacrifice, that you are prepared to say and to mean 'Not my will, but Thy Will, be done, O Lord' and, what is more, that you are prepared to accept that Will as and when it manifests.

The implication of this, therefore, is that even though you personally would like a sick child to live, that if that child dies, then, you can accept that that is the Will of your Creator. It is to accept that even though thousands of people are dying of starvation in a country devastated by drought, and you would wish it otherwise, that that too is the Will of your Creator. It is to accept that there will be pain and suffering in the world for those souls who are learning the essential lessons of Humanity through the transmutation of karma. It is from that point of understanding and knowingness, from that position of oneness with the Will of your Creator, that you come to recognise and accept the path of all lesser wills.

Recognise, therefore, that most of the events that you see manifesting on the plane of Earth today are the direct creation of human will. It is the sum total of every individual human being acting out their lives according to what they want, to what they desire in thought, word and deed. You create the nature of this plane of Earth. You create both your physical destinies and the nature of your lives. You create the paths upon which you are now set. That is why the world at this moment in time is in such a state of chaos, for you are living in a world created by human will, a world which knows no purpose or design other than that of self-aggrandisement, of obtaining for the self, both on the physical and the mental levels of life, regardless of the cost to all the other Kingdoms with whom you share this plane of existence.

Let us now examine what I mean by the term 'sacrifice of your will'. It is the willing and the conscious surrender of your will to the more important and the more urgent Will of your Creator. Such a sacrifice becomes doubly significant at this critical time in the cosmic cycle of the Earth, as both the planet and Humanity living on it approach a supreme moment of transformation and transmutation. So it is important that you recognise and accept the Will of your Creator both for yourselves and for this planet. There can only be One Will and that greater Will will always triumph. That is a fact of Cosmic Law. Although Humanity is allowed to create in its own image and to exercise its own little will, that is but a brief and transitory thing. Recognise that human beings only incarnate on the Earth for a short time, your three score years and ten, but the Will of your Creator for this planet and for Humanity dwelling upon it is fixed and is eternal and is known to all those who serve that Will.

God's Will will always manifest. That is how the great prophets of old could prophesy with such certainty because, knowing that greater Will, they could see that the lesser will of Humanity would never triumph. No matter how the odds might appear stacked against some individual or nation in a battle, even though they might be faced with vastly superior forces, the prophets knew that if the Will was that those forces should be defeated, then they would be defeated. No matter what the outer strength or will of a country might be, the prophets could see that on an inner level it was weak and fallible and was destined to crumble. Those who are aligned to the Will of God know Its Will for all things, all beings and all people.

How are you to know this Will? How are you to bring about the fundamental transformation in your lives that will help you to change the world according to God's Will and not your will? For what this world needs now, above all else, is God's Will made manifest on Earth or, to put it another way, is Heaven made manifest on Earth – Thy Will be done, O Lord, on Earth as it is in Heaven, in the Cosmos. You have to be prepared to make the ultimate sacrifice, the sacrifice of your own will. Now that does not mean that you become weak and helpless, that you search around aimlessly for some being or some source to tell you what to do or what to believe. It means that you consciously attune to that greater Will in your meditations, in your prayers, not expecting the answer to be a still small voice within telling you what to do, but recognising that just by the act of attuning consciously to that Will throughout the day that you are aligning yourselves with that greater Will. You are, therefore, each according to your unique point of consciousness, creating the thought that you wish to be at one with that Will, not just for yourselves but for the whole Human Race and for this planet on which you live.

Where there is a will, there is a way. If you are in tune with that Will you do not have to find the way, for the way is already there. It is inherent in the Will. You have all faced those moments of crisis in your lives when you wondered 'How on Earth' as opposed to 'How in Heaven' you were going to handle a certain situation. Yet was it not often the case that in those moments of crisis you drew upon an inner strength and through quietly attuning to your Creator you faced the challenge and handled it correctly, for the Will was there? If you face any problem and cannot solve it, it is because you are not in tune with the Will of your Creator. It is because you are following your own will and not your Creator's Will. Problems occur when your will opposes the Will of Creation. The solution to any problem lies in your alignment with that greater Will through the sacrifice of your own will.

The lesson of this planet is sacrificial service through the power of love. Service, therefore, implies service to your God and in that you help your fellow human beings, who are imbued with the spirit of God, you are helping your God. What is the greatest service that you can render to your fellow human beings? What is the greatest service that you can render to bring about change in this world? What has been the demonstration of all the great Masters who have come down on the Earth? It is to set the example, to show Humanity in physical manifestation what is the reality of a human being who has surrendered to the Will of God. What is the true meaning of sacrifice? In the final analysis it is to recognise that even though you may sacrifice aspects of yourself on the physical plane of life, you have really lost nothing but have gained Heaven on Earth. What do you lose by an act of physical surrender to another human being that you will not also lose at your moment of death? What do you lose by an act of physical sacrifice to another human being that you will not regain after death? For that, surely, is the reality of the Law of Karma. Everything which you send out will come back to you, no matter whether it be positive or negative karma. Everything that you sacrifice to the whole, every act of service to the whole, must always return to you, if not in this life then in another.

Truly, you can lose nothing because you own nothing. You may think that you own something. You may think that you own your possessions, that you have wealth, social position and status, but such things, by their very nature, are only a very temporary part of human existence. Moreover, are these possessions subject to your will or to your Creator's Will? Look at the example of the great Masters who have walked the face of this Earth, sharing their wisdom and knowledge with all Humanity, possessing nothing yet having the use of everything. Their real demonstration lies not in the manifestation of their spiritual talents, their knowledge and their wisdom, but in the demonstration of their sacrifice to the Will of their Creator. They have made that ultimate sacrifice of surrendering their will, their desires, their thought-forms, their physical manifestations, to the Will of their Creator and of accepting the greater Will that flows through them.

The human form can be compared to a chalice and if that cup is already full of self-will then there is no room for Divine Will. So you have to empty the cup of self-will, to make it an empty vessel, so that your Creator's Will can come into it and fill it, and when the cup has been filled with Divine Will you must humbly recognise that which has been given to you in a sacred trust. For some people the change from self-will to God's will can be as sudden as Saul becoming Paul on that road to Damascus, whilst for others it can be a slow process of awakening, simply because there is a slow process of releasing self-will. But for those who truly align themselves to the Will of God flowing through them, who each morning in their meditation say, 'O Lord, thy will be done through me this day. Help me to fulfil Thy will both for me and for this planet', a positive act of attunement takes place on the subtle levels of life, an attunement which creates a solution to all the problems of the day.

Now, of course, the fact that you have aligned yourself to the Will of God does not mean that you, as individuals, no longer have to take action. You, as individuals, have free choice as to how you carry out the Will of God, that is the nature of human evolution. So, of course, mistakes will be made. That is the nature of the human evolutionary path. Nevertheless, over a given period of time, depending on your point of soul consciousness, you will ground God's Will so that others may witness, recognise and follow It. The purpose of all the great Masters incarnating on the Earth is not that Humanity should follow them, should make them into gods, but that Humanity should recognise the Divine Will manifesting in and through them and should be led into an understanding of what is possible for all Humanity.

Consider, therefore, as you face the problems of life, whether you are flowing with or against the Will of your Creator. Search for God's Will pulsating within you. Remember that the change that has to come about on this Earth will only come about from the grounding of that Will and not from the repetition of present human patterns. If you continue to oppose force with force, then you are simply emphasising and empowering that pattern of behaviour for the generations of Humanity to come. If you continue to take from the Earth without giving back to Her, then the Goddess will no longer continue to cooperate with you. You must be prepared to make the ultimate sacrifice. You must be prepared, even if you are one in one hundred thousand, even if you are persecuted for it, even if you are killed for it, to stand for the Divine Will that flows through you. Now that does not mean that you have to oppose or denounce others, it means that you have simply to demonstrate and to speak only that which the Will impels you to do.

So, at this most critical time for the planet, if you want to bring about human transformation, if you want to bring about planetary transformation, if you want to change the path of human destiny, consider where lies the power to bring about that change. It lies not in the world. It lies deep within you. There is no-one that can bring about that change but yourself. Above all, recognise that the change that has to come about can only come about through the sacrifice of the thing that you prize the most – your will. Know that to those who have made that sacrifice, to those who walk hand in hand with their Creator, fulfilling Its Will, who have sacrificed their will to that greater Will, there comes the peace that passes all understanding, the peace of God that creates Heaven on Earth.

QUESTIONS AND ANSWERS

Q: I recently overheard a conversation in which someone was talking about their previous incarnations and the various roles they had played. They used the term 'that was one of my more spiritual incarnations'! If we do indeed have incarnations when we manifest a high degree of spirituality, how is it that we apparently lose this knowledge in subsequent incarnations?

ZT: The truth of the matter is that those who do know of their past incarnations rarely talk about them. It is only those who are uncertain of their past incarnations that talk about them! An incarnation can be compared to your private diary. Would you like your diary to be read by someone else? As I have said on so many occasions, the important thing is not what you have been, is not what you are going to be, but is what you are right now. Which part of you is it that wants to know of your past incarnations? It is not your soul, because your soul already has that information. It is your little ego-self that wants to know about past incarnations in order to give itself a greater status, to explain away a lack of status or importance in this life! It is only those who are unhappy with their present lives who seek the solace of past or future lives.

Your soul contains the consciousness of every life that you have lived. You, therefore, have the knowingness that you have accumulated over your many lives with you right now. You have never been any more spiritual than you are right now. Of course, in past lives you may have had a greater spiritual knowledge and, for reasons of karma or human personality, you may have lived a purer and a more spiritual life, but, truly, you have within you now the greatest potential that you have ever known. You can bring forth that potential from within whenever you so choose. The spiritual knowingness that you have obtained through the pain and suffering of many lives, is yours for eternity. You can never lose it. You can choose not to hear it, you can deny its presence, but it is there. As the Master has just said, it is you alone that decides how you will lead your life. You will either listen to your own innate wisdom or you will deny it. You will either feel moved to sacrifice your lesser will so as to flow with Divine Will or you will not. All that any Master can do is to be a mirror. A Master cannot teach you what you yourself have not already learned. A Master can place you on a path of learning, but it is you that has to do the learning.

Q: I think that most aware people want to lead spiritual lives. We want to do the will of God, but the problem seems to be that we are confused about what the will of God really is. It is very difficult for human beings with all their mental faculties to sort out what are their own thoughts and what are the thoughts inspired by God.

ZT: I would agree. In a world where you are trained to develop and exercise your own will, where from the moment you are born you are inculcated with a belief in the importance and the rightness of that will, it is difficult to regain contact with the creative flow of Divine Will which once pulsated within you so strongly. You have, so to speak, lost touch with God. Now I recognise that in the world in which you live today it is difficult to regain that contact, not just because of all the distractions of the outer world, but also because of the distractions of the inner world, the creations of your mind – your desires, your fears, your beliefs. But the contact is always there. It is still possible to hear that inner voice speaking to you, the more so if you are open to it. Very often it is telling you to do something which you don't want to do and that is why you don't want to listen to it. It is telling you to give to someone who has stolen from you, to love someone who hates you, to turn the other cheek to someone who has hit you, all the things you find most difficult to do. It is, in fact, asking you to behave in a way very different to the one that society has taught you!

By establishing this contact, by attuning to Divine Will, you are, so to speak, establishing a point of reference, so that if during your waking day you meet some person or some situation which challenges you, then, at least, you have that aspect to consider besides your own personality conditioning. It is then up to you how you choose to respond and it is your response that creates the learning experience. An aware person soon recognises that it is easier to flow with Divine Will than it is to fight against It. If you were to lose your child or your marriage partner, and if you accepted that loss as being the Will of God and that it had, therefore, happened for a purpose, then your life would not be destroyed by misplaced grief and suffering. If you can accept an illness and come to terms with it, if you can recognise it as karmic settlement, then where is the suffering? It is, therefore, in essence, a question of trusting your own inner wisdom, your point of consciousness, and of knowing that if you have consciously attuned to the Source of all Life then you can only be acting from the highest of your being.

Q: Does this attunement take place during meditation?
ZT: Meditation is one part of it, yes. You need to attune to the Source in both inner and outer silence. Nevertheless, life also gives you many opportunities for attunement. For example, if you were to return home from work and find two members of your family arguing violently, before you intervened, if you were to say 'I attune myself to the Source of all Life and offer myself as an instrument of service to these two people so that the situation can be resolved for the highest good of all concerned', you would be amazed at how good a peacemaker you were! It is the little prayer before you take action, the little invocation before you sacrifice, that helps you to centre yourself in God's Will for you in any given situation. Let me give you another simple example. If you are taking part in a race, you can either say 'O Lord, help me to win this race', which is the human side of you talking, or you can say 'O Lord, let me be an instrument of Thy Will in this race and may my participation be for the highest good of all the people involved in the race', which is the divine side of you talking. Now you may not physically win the race, but the person who passes the tape first is not necessarily also the winner in the greater game of life.

Q: There are so many spiritual teachers in the world today, all promoting their particular understanding of life, their form of meditation, their answers to the problems of life and, here in the West, many of them charge quite large sums of money for the privilege of doing this. How is it possible to differentiate between them all? How do we find out which are the genuine teachers and which are the frauds?
ZT: The answer is simply to use your own God-given powers of discrimination. If you consciously centre yourself in the Will of God before you listen to any spiritual teacher, before you read any spiritual book, before you listen to any tape or watch any video, then it will help you to be more discriminatory towards that which you are about to

experience. All that you can do is to discriminate for yourself and then to keep those opinions in your own heart, because what is right for you may be wrong for another, and vice versa.

Regarding the subject of charging, I maintain that it is wrong to charge for the sharing of Truth, to ask for money before you share something that was freely given to you by your Creator. I do not hold to the point of view that people only value something according to the price that they have paid for it. How can you value a child, for example, which is a gift from God? You can see how, in your world today, spirituality has been seduced by money. Grounding Truth in the world has become a business, not an act of service. It has become a form of monetary exchange rather than a sacrifice. So it is up to you to discriminate according to the soul note that beats within you. You must listen with your soul knowingness, not with your intellectual mind.

Q: But we have a situation locally where someone is charging quite large sums of money under the pretence of giving unwary visitors a channelling! Is it not correct to warn people about this person or should we say nothing and just let them go along and discriminate for themselves?

ZT: I would make the comparison of going to a funfair with your young son, where there is a big dipper. Now you know that if you go on that big dipper you will feel sick, and you assume that it will be the same for your child. So you warn your son of your experience and assure him that he won't like it. But your son can see that other people are going on the big dipper and are, apparently, enjoying themselves and so he wants to go and experience that ride. He will not listen to you because he is attracted by the glamour of the situation. He has to go and experience that big dipper for himself in order to discover what it really feels like. Amazingly, he confounds your worst fears by enjoying the ride and wants to repeat it! The moral of this little tale is that people have to experience something for themselves and that they cannot learn from other people's experiences. Moreover, are you in a position to tell them what is right and what is wrong for them?

Q: But surely you can tell someone of your own experiences?
ZT: Absolutely, provided they are your experiences and not your prejudices. You cannot say that something that is wrong for you is wrong for everyone else in creation. You cannot say that something is wrong just because it does not agree with your philosophy of life.

Q: Given that there are different paths for different people, are you saying that all paths are correct? I know of some so-called spiritual teachers who appear to invoke and promote very negative energies. Are you saying that all teachers are genuine teachers and that spirituality embraces everything?

ZT: In essence, all life is spiritual but, in practice, every aspect of life is contaminated to a degree. Nothing on the Earth is ever perfection. Even a great Master like the Master Jesus would have been imperfect to a degree whilst in physical incarnation. So what you are really doing is deciding what degree of contamination is unacceptable to you, based on your understanding of life! So, for example, you may reject an apple that is brown and bruised and choose a nice shiny red apple instead. But someone else would reject the apple that you had chosen, because they knew that it had been treated with pesticides and chemicals to make it look more appealing. You were not aware of that fact or, if you were, thought it to be unimportant. So each of us chooses the degree of contamination that is acceptable to us. That is also true of our spiritual paths!

Q: For me the key words of the talk were will and trust. One of my problems is that in my work I see people all around me suffering and very often I can see solutions for them, as I can see the origin of things, but they won't listen to me. I can't cope with this situation any more. Is it my will that I want to help people or is it my service?

ZT: Remember what the Master has just said, that you have not come to 'save' the world, you have come to 'save' yourself and that you 'save' the world by 'saving' yourself. It is very difficult for any human being to take on the responsibility for transforming other people, and you have clearly demonstrated why this is so. It is because you are emotionally attached to the result. You are attached to the results of your actions. If people do not accept your advice, you suffer pain. If people do not change, you suffer pain. If the world is not as you would like it, you suffer pain. Therefore, you are not yet of the consciousness, and I say this with all respect, to be a teacher.

Look at the life of the Master Jesus and think of the people that he didn't heal as opposed to the people that he did heal, of the people that he knew he could heal and yet who were not ready to be healed, because the appropriate lesson had not been learned. Think of the suffering that he knew was coming to the Earth because Humanity, for the most part, would not listen to his message, and which he knew could all have been avoided. Think of the Christ Consciousness which could have transformed the world at a stroke and yet which held back from doing so because Humanity had to transform itself. A true teacher sees a learning experience in all suffering. Recognise how, in your own lives, suffering has helped to evolve your point of consciousness. Finally, remember what part of you is doing the suffering. It is not your spiritual essence. It is your human ego that suffers, the aspect of yourself that has separated itself from the Godhead.

Any soul of consciousness can see where others are going wrong. It is so easy to see faults in others, just as they find it easy to see faults in yourself, but it is so difficult to get people to recognise their faults, just as you find it difficult to recognise your own. The way to make people see their faults is not by pointing at them and saying 'You are doing wrong'. People do not learn that way. People learn best from the observation of perfection. If you are a being of peace, happiness and tranquillity, if all of life seems to flow your way, then people will take notice of you. If you are giving out energies of light and love, then people will feel them. One being of peace and harmony, walking into a room of conflict, can affect the energy of that whole room, just by their presence, without saying a word. Such is the power of transformation, but one has to be a realised being to do it. So if you want to change the world, first change yourselves.

THE PURSUIT OF HAPPINESS

On many occasions I have said that life on the Earth can be compared to going to school. The planet Earth is a classroom and you are all learning lessons, lessons both of an individual and of a group nature. These lessons vary according to the race in which you incarnate, the country in which you are born, the society in which you live and, above all, the karma which you have incarnated to transmute. For every individual the permutation of such manifestly critical factors produces a unique learning experience. So it is obvious that the lessons of a tribesman living in Africa in a drought-ridden land, faced daily with the threat of starvation or of attack by opposing tribes, are very different to people such as yourselves, living in a land of plenty, where even if you decide that you don't want to work the state will still look after you. The lessons of the White Race are not of the earth but are of the mind. You have come into incarnation at this particular moment in time in order to come to an understanding of the mind and to learn to control its creations.

Because you live in the Western Civilisation where, for the most part, your physical life is protected from violent death, where there is an abundance of food and water, where society will look after you if you fall ill or are unable to work, there is a great opportunity and freedom to exercise the mind, to be creative with the mind. Now you believe that you are all honest people in terms of your relationships with your fellow human beings, yet in one important relationship you are all very dishonest, and that is in relationship with yourself. You all think that you know yourselves, that you have a good idea of the nature of your character, of your physical and spiritual abilities, but if the truth were to be known, you know very little of your true selves. Moreover, are you aware that by the very fact of saying that you know something, you are ending the learning process?

It is patently obvious, though, to those of us who observe Humanity from the higher planes of life, that you do not know yourselves. If I were to ask you to try to define your true selves, what would actually emerge would be, in part, just a description of your more meaningful experiences in this life and the conditioning imposed upon you by your parents, by your schooling, by your society, by your work, by your relationships with the other Kingdoms of Matter. But would that accurately define the true you? Is it not a fact that when in life you have to face up to a character weakness in yourself, when you have to come to terms with an aspect of your personality that needs correction, that you shy away from doing it? Though you may spend many hours discussing the weaknesses and the faults of those around you, you are not prepared to spend even one tenth of that time examining your own weaknesses and faults in the privacy of your own meditations. Have you ever stopped to consider just how much of your energy and time goes into looking outwards as opposed to looking inwards, just how often you look critically at the people around you rather than at your own personality self? It is so easy to see the faults in others and yet so difficult to see those very same faults in yourself. So if your eyes can see so very clearly outwardly, why can they not do the same inwardly? The answer is very simple. It is because you do not want to.

If a group of your friends were to sit down and to openly enumerate the faults they saw in you, would you feel helped or would you feel threatened? If someone were to come up to you and point out even a small weakness in your character, would you feel love towards them or would you feel anger? When you yourselves are aware of an aspect of your personality that needs to be modified, do you try to face it and to understand it or do you accept it as an unfortunate but immutable aspect of your character? 'Yes, I do lose my temper, but I can't help it'. 'Yes, I'm afraid that I do get terribly jealous, but that's my nature'. The truth of the matter is that you really do not want to know your own faults. So if all of you would just begin to investigate the nature of your ego-self, would quietly begin to meditate on your own faults, you would begin to come to terms with the nature of your own being and would understand the deep-rooted patterns of behaviour that you are continually endorsing. You will discover that you are an incredibly enigmatic being, a complex mixture of soul and personality traits, and that you are responding to patterns of behaviour grounded deep within your psyche.

For most people in the Western World today the purpose of life can be defined as the pursuit of happiness. Because they are not faced with a continual battle for survival, as are so many people in the undeveloped countries of the Third World, people in the Western World have both the time and the energy to seek and to create pleasure, believing that this will make them happy. They therefore spend a great deal of their time pursuing goals which they think will lead to pleasure. But when these goals have been achieved they then discover that the pleasure is very short-lived and that it spawns the need for yet more pleasure. Most people never stop to consider why this should be so and it is the rare person who ponders on what is the source of happiness, on what it is in them that feels happy or unhappy.

For example, do you think that your spirit feels happy or unhappy, either on the physical or on the higher planes of life after death? No! So both happiness and unhappiness are only earthly values. Have you ever considered what is the source of happiness? Is happiness something which is God-given or is it, rather, self-generated? If there are four people looking at a beautiful view, how can it be that all four people do not feel the same emotions? Why, for example, could three of them be happy and one be unhappy? So it is not the outer world which leads to happiness or unhappiness. It is the inner world, the force of mind that creates this search and striving for happiness, and which, if one does not achieve it, then leads to a state of unhappiness.

In the Western World today you have the freedom to create objectives – objectives of mind, objectives of body, objectives of emotions. You have the chance to create a pattern of events and then to follow that pattern, creating in your image the world which you think you want. The response to this pattern of events, when you achieve them, is a state of what could be called pleasure. So you create your pleasures. Pleasure is not something which is given to you as a divine gift from your Creator, as a gift from the Universe around you. You have to work very hard to create and achieve pleasure. So recognise that pleasure is a creation of your own being. When you achieve your pleasures, you are happy. When you fail to achieve the pleasures which you seek from life, then you are unhappy. And what is it in you that is unhappy but that aspect of self that has not achieved its aims, its purpose in life. What, therefore, is the nature of this self, this ego being, which strives to control whilst you are in a physical incarnation on the Earth?

It is the aspect of your self that was created at birth. It is the aspect of your self that is impelled by the stars and the planets. It is the aspect of your self that is formed by the soul characteristics of your previous lives. It is the aspect of your self, above all, that is formed by your own impressions of the world in which you live, by the people with whom you have come in contact, by the material world which you have experienced. If the world around you has taught you that you are not able to walk on water, then you truly believe that you cannot walk on water and you will never begin to understand how those who can indeed walk on water are able to accomplish this feat. You therefore define your self by the limits that you are happy to accept of your self.

Nevertheless, is it not the case that often, even at an advanced age in life, you suddenly achieve some goal which you previously had thought to be impossible? How often have you suddenly found that you have an artistic skill which you never imagined that you possessed before, if only for the simple reason that you had never tried to develop it before? Is it not the case that each day, if you seek diligently, you will discover facts about your self, aspects of your being, that you never recognised before. So recognise that the limitations which you place upon your self are the limitations which you have created, are the limitations which you, in a sense, have sought. Recognise also that the world which you create in your pursuit of happiness, in your desire to achieve pleasure, is the world of those same limitations. You create the world which you want to experience. You create the nature of your own being.

In the past I have often pointed out the difference between pleasure and joy. Such a distinction is not just semantics. Pleasure, as I have just indicated, is something which you are constantly striving to create in your pursuit of happiness. It involves the movement of time, for you work to achieve pleasure at some time in the future, you consciously set in motion a train of events which you hope will lead to pleasure. Joy, on the other hand, does not involve the movement of time. Joy is of the present. Joy is something which you cannot plan or create. Joy is born out of right relationship with the world that you are experiencing. It is the spontaneous response of your inner being to the world around you. It is that moment in time as you silently watch a beautiful sunset. It is that moment in time as you watch your child mastering some new aspect of life. It is that moment in time when you feel a deep soul bonding with someone with whom you are in relationship. Recognise, however, that once that joy has been experienced, it is gone for ever. If you try to recreate that joy then you are once more caught up in the pursuit of pleasure.

So it is your relationship with the world around you that determines your state of mind and, therefore, your degree of happiness or of unhappiness. If you are open to and are truly experiencing the moment in time that you are living, if you are looking without preconditioned

145

thought, without judgement or comparison, at the world around you and at the people that you meet, then you are truly experiencing your Creator's will for you. You are learning the precise lessons of life that you incarnated to learn, you are facing the precise karmic debts that you incarnated to transmute. It is the acceptance of this fact that removes the need for you to try to control or to manipulate your physical life in order to create an illusory state of happiness. It is the acceptance of this fact that gives you the equanimity to handle all of the apparent vagaries of life. However, if you choose not to live in the moment but rather in a world of your own creation, by projecting your mind backwards into your memories of the past or forwards into your expectations of the future, then you are condemning yourself to a life of suffering, a life where the pursuit of happiness has become the one and only purpose of life. Living in the past or living in the future may give you pleasure, but it can never give you joy. It is only by living in the present, in that moment of true union with the Creator of all Life, that you experience your divine birthright, joy.

It is important, therefore, that you begin to understand the nature of your own being and that you come to terms with the relationship of the spirit and the self, of the real world in which you are living and of the illusory world of your desires and dreams. Are you living in God's world or in your own world? Are you living a life motivated by service to the Source of all Life or by the pursuit of happiness? Now that does not mean that you should not be happy. No, far from it! It means that your happiness is a permanent rather than a transient state of being, born of the recognition that you are a divine being, fulfilling the will of the Divine, rather than from the temporary enjoyment of some material pleasure.

Has it ever occurred to you that it could be the case that the people who make you happy are the very people that are blocking your evolutionary progress in life? I mean, by this, that if you are only happy when you are with people who agree with your concepts of life, who bolster your image of yourself, then you will always tend to seek their company and to shy away from those who oppose your concepts of life, who challenge your opinions of yourself. Now I am not saying that you should always be seeking the company of those who conflict with your own understandings of life but that conflict is not necessarily a bad thing, for it is that which creates momentary conflict in your mind that leads to growth and evolution. So always be open to every facet of the world with which you come in contact. Recognise that in your everyday

146

lives you have the choice as to whether you experience God's world or your world. You have the choice of greeting the events of the world either with equanimity or of riding the rollercoaster of unhappiness and happiness, as the world responds or fails to respond to your needs of the moment. Be aware that even when your needs are met you will then create further needs and that often, after only a relatively short passage of time, you will display a cool indifference to something or someone that was once your greatest source of happiness.

In conclusion, therefore, I would ask you to view both happiness and unhappiness with the same perspective. They are similar feelings – neither one is good or bad. They are both equally transient and, therefore, illusory. If you base your life on the pursuit of one and the avoidance of the other then you are doomed to a life of suffering because you are denying the reality of life. The essence of right living is based on union with the Source of all Life and the complete acceptance of the world in which you live. Everything – every person, every animal, every flower, every stone – is a creation of God and, as such, is part of God's plan for you and your continuing evolution. They constitute the lesson which you have come to learn, the aspects of life that you have come to master.

Recognise that life is but a mirror of your own self, that life merely reflects back to you aspects of your self. It is your relationship with life that reveals to you both that which is true and that which is false in your being. If a person with whom you are in a relationship behaves in a negative manner and as a result you become very unhappy, who is really the cause of that unhappiness? Although you would like to blame the other person, in reality it is you that has caused the unhappiness. It is the inner world, not the outer world that creates all those thoughts and feelings. So all of you must begin to be truthful with yourselves. You must begin to face up to the negative aspects of your being and stop turning a blind eye towards them. Now, especially, is the time to go deeply into your being, in the silence of your own meditations, and to carefully consider the aspects of your self which need to be faced, the karmic patterns that need to be transmuted. Realise that the world is your teacher and, what is more, is a very good teacher, because it accurately reflects back to you the very lessons that you have come to learn. The world is continually throwing you back on yourself, forcing you to face all that you have created in thought, word and deed. So you are you own teacher. You are your own guru.

As we approach the ending of the Piscean Age, with all the transmutation of karma that is implied in this ending, many of you are being forced to face aspects of your beings which you have tried to master over many lives. You have deliberately chosen to come back at this very special time in order to clear your karmic account before the present cycle ends. If you are to achieve this break-through then you must be honest with yourselves, you must look clearly into the mirror of life no matter how uncomfortable this may be for you. Recognise that the middle path, the path of total equanimity, which does not side with happiness or unhappiness, pleasure or sorrow, is the path that you must tread, especially if you are to face and handle the dramatic events of the next twenty years, as the Race of Humanity transitions into the Golden Age of Aquarius.

Remember that life is a learning experience and that the lesson only becomes painful if you choose to make it so. The source of all happiness and unhappiness lies within your own being. You cannot attribute it to anyone or to anything else. Finally, be aware that the more perfected your being, the greater is your capacity to be a mirror and to ground and reflect Light. The role of any Master can only be to reflect the Light of Truth onto all Humanity, to lighten the darkness of all those who would blame Life, or God, for all of their suffering. Try to walk through life untouched by either happiness or unhappiness, by goodness or evil, by light or darkness, accepting everything that comes into your aura with complete equanimity. Know that life is but a great drama, designed by your Creator, to teach and to test you so that you may become divine yourself. For you are gods in the making. That is the real nature of your divine heritage.

QUESTIONS AND ANSWERS

Q: Do you think that you can become closer to God and, therefore, have greater peace of mind, through the discipline of fixed periods of meditation, or is it better to live an active day to day life and to let the experiences of life change your attitudes and your way of thinking?
ZT: Life is like Nature or, rather, I should say that life is part of Nature. There is an ebb and a flow, an inbreath and an outbreath, to all things. So what is important in life, in fact, in any human relationship, is the recognition and the acceptance of this ebb and flow, of this giving and taking. Recognise that there is both a time for giving of your energy

through right relationship with your fellow human beings and the three other Kingdoms of Matter, and there is a time for receiving energy back from them. It is this return of energy, coming back to you, which helps you to see clearly the nature of your own being. It is how you relate to life that reveals the true nature of yourself. So it is difficult, if not well nigh impossible, to give whilst one is receiving and, of course, to receive whilst one is giving.

Now the Master did not advocate that you should all become introverted or that you should sit for hour after hour in deep meditation. There must obviously be times of meditation, times when you still your minds and escape from the material world, times when you sit quietly and analyse your response to the events of the day. This is the basis of all spiritual growth and evolution. This is how you discover the true nature of your being. It is life, after all, that challenges and tests you. It is life that teaches you lessons, and what is life but the Force of God in motion. Now some people, of course, deliberately choose to bury themselves in activity because they do not want to stop and look at themselves, others retreat into long hours of meditation because they do not want to experience life. So in all things there must be balance, coupled with a powerful awareness of the rhythms of your being and the rhythms of life, to ensure that you flow with the tide of life rather than swim against it.

Q: The Master said that it was not a good idea either to lose oneself in the past or to contemplate the future too much, but is it not beneficial to review what one has done in the past, to analyse past actions and the motivation behind them, in order to discover one's faults and to save one from repeating them in the future?

ZT: As I have just said, during any period of quietness it is obviously beneficial to review past actions in order to see if one has acted from the highest of one's being, with the purest of motivation. That is an essential part of one's spiritual evolution. However, when doing this, it is important that you be aware of two things. Firstly, that you are dealing with memory, which is very subjective and selective. You remember only those things which you choose to remember and so your memory is not an accurate record of the actual events that took place. Secondly, it is vital, with any incident in which conflict has occurred, that you resolve the conflict in your own mind as soon as possible, that you come to an understanding of what was the cause and the nature of the conflict and what are the lessons to be learnt from it.

If you resolve conflicts as and when they occur, then the matter is finished, you can release them and pass on to other things. If you do not resolve conflicts, then they accumulate in your mind and much time is wasted as you keep going back over them, as you try to resolve them to your own satisfaction. Moreover, the longer you leave them unresolved, the more you will find that you are dealing not with the reality of any given situation but with your frail and subjective memory of it. So it is vital that before you go to sleep each night you spend time meditating on the events of your day and drawing the learning experiences from them. You must look truthfully at yourself and at the motivation behind your actions. You must resolve your conflicts, place them aside and then be free to move on to other experiences, with your mind unburdened.

Now to meditate about the future is a waste of both time and energy, for what is the future but your dreams? The future, as you visualise it, may never come. You do not know what tomorrow will bring. You may die in your sleep tonight and not even see tomorrow! So, as it says in the Bible, do not put off until tomorrow those things which you can do today. Do not go to sleep on any conflict that can be resolved today, on any relationship that can be healed today. Do not postpone making even the least sacrifice, if it will help in the transformation of another human being, if it will aid their walk along their path in life. This is especially true of the times in which you are now living, where the pace of life accelerates daily, where the opportunity for resolution soon passes by. As I have said on so many occasions, live each day as if it was your last. As you go to sleep each night, leave no problem in any relationship unresolved, so that as you close your eyes you can truly say 'If I was to die now, I would be a happy person, because nothing remains to be done which I could have done!'.

Q: I would like to know how we differentiate between our good and bad qualities.
ZT: The terms 'good' and 'bad' are very subjective, for what is the source that is making that judgement? What part of you is it that decides that a certain action is good or bad? Is it your ego, your soul or your spirit? Moreover, what is 'good' for one person can be 'bad' for another. Therefore, it is best not to judge your thoughts, words and deeds. Rather, you should observe them with a critical but non-judgmental eye. In this way the truth of any situation will reveal itself to you. If you are humble and open to the truth, then you will soon

recognise the truth but, of course, that will be the truth for you, not for anyone else. Naturally, there is only one Truth, which is Truth for all Humanity, but Humanity being at different stages of evolution can only recognise and accept differing aspects of that Truth. This is what leads to so many human conflicts. All that you can do is to discover what is truth for you, what is the truth of your own being. The Universe, being the Force of God in motion, will always reflect truthfully back to you. So let the Universe be the judge of your actions.

Let me give you a very simple example. Let us suppose that you were one of those people who had lost their jobs and were unable to find new employment. After a time, because you felt sorry for yourself, every night you would go out to your local bar and get drunk, in order to escape from the reality of your situation. You would then return home late at night and engage in rows with your wife and children which, sometimes, led to violence. Slowly, over many weeks, you would begin to lose control of your life and would threaten to destroy the very people that you loved the most. Now how are you to discover the truth of the situation that you are in? Some people, of course, never will and will continue to walk that path towards self-destruction, because they do not want to know about what they are doing. But others, if they are open to the world around them, if they are really looking at what they are doing and the effects of their actions on the world around them, one day, in a flash of insight, will suddenly become aware of the pain and the suffering that they are causing to the people around them and will want to change. This is best achieved by simply observing what they are doing to themselves and to their family, not in a judgmental or critical way, but in an analytical way. From the observation of their actions will come an understanding that will create both the motive and the energy for change. Such a change will be a permanent rather than a temporary thing.

Q: We are all talking about happiness, but how do we actually know that we are happy? What is a state of happiness? Is it an emotional or a psychological state of being?
ZT: I will answer that question by asking you all to tell me when you feel happy.

Q1: I feel happiest when I am by myself, communicating with the Nature Kingdom, walking along a beach, for instance, or working in my garden.

Q2: I feel happy when I realise my place in the scheme of things, when I recognise the fact that I am improving myself and yet that I have endless scope still for improvement.

Q3: I am happiest when I talk to God at night and know that I have served Him to the highest of my ability during the day. Of course, I don't often feel this!

ZT: So if this is the case, then you must be unhappy for a good deal of the time.

Q3: Yes, I am afraid that's true.

Q4: I feel happy when I have a sense of rightness in what I'm doing, basically because it brings me some peace within and seems to let my creative energies flow.

Q5: I feel happiest when I am living in the moment and am content with being there.

Q6: I feel happy when I know that I am one with my source.

Q7: I was just thinking that my happiest times were when I didn't even realise it. Often I don't recognise that I was happy until after the event!

ZT: You have made the very point that I was intending to make, namely, that true happiness occurs when you are not even aware of the fact that you are happy, when you are too busy just living life to analyse whether you are happy or not! So it is only when you look back in retrospect that you realise how happy you were. The problems occur when you try to create happiness, when you enter into situations or relationships which you think will make you happy, and then they don't. It is very difficult to work at being happy, to create the factors from which happiness will automatically flow. So it can be seen that happiness is a very illusory state of being. Very often it is a self-generated frame of mind. A certain situation exists and you consciously choose whether you want to be happy or unhappy! Many people like to be unhappy . . .

Q: They deliberately choose to be unhappy, why?

ZT: People are very complex beings. Some people operate on a positive energy, some people operate on a negative energy, and I am using positive and negative not in the sense of right and wrong but of human polarity. In just the same way some people enjoy being ill. On a certain level they consciously seek to fall ill because of all the attention and sympathy they will get. However, what I am trying to get you to understand is that happiness and unhappiness are the same. You should be equal-minded in the face of both. Do not strive after one or the other.

Happiness is not the criteria for determining whether or not you are living your life correctly. Do not think that you can create a state of happiness and then say that your life has purpose and meaning. Rather accept each day as it comes, as a gift from your Creator, and respond to that day as you are so inspired and guided. Happiness comes with the acceptance of the day as it is given to you. Unhappiness comes with the desire to be somewhere else, doing something else, experiencing something else! Recognise that by denying the day you are denying your Creator or, more appropriately, the learning experiences that your Creator has chosen for you.

So, in the silence of your meditations, begin to examine your states of happiness and unhappiness, and to see them for what they are. Try to rise above such states and to see a greater force at work. Discover what it is in you that makes you happy and unhappy. Look with your spiritual eye, the eye that does not criticise or judge, and learn of the aspects of your being that have still to be mastered. Finally, remember, that on the plane of Earth, especially at this time in the evolutionary cycle, trial and tribulation are necessary parts of life. Into everyone's life must come a little suffering. What distinguishes the evolved from the less-evolved soul is not their states of happiness or unhappiness, but the equanimity with which they handle the tests of life.

THE ACT OF WORSHIP

At this particular stage in the cycle of evolution Humanity is experiencing and is operating through the lesson of the duality. So not only is there the positive and the negative, the male and the female in physical expression, but there is also present the divine gift of free choice, whereby Humanity can choose between light and darkness, between happiness and sorrow, between God's will and human will. You have all been given the power of free choice so that by your thoughts, words and deeds you create not only the nature of your being but the nature of your world. With the power of your minds you can create whatever you wish. It is you, and you alone, that forms the nature of the world in which you live.

I would like you to recognise that your understanding of the world in which you live is decided, for the most part, by your own conditioned thought, and by this I mean all the intellectual dogma which you have been taught as 'the truth' in this life. It is the way that you have been conditioned by your parents, by your teachers at school, by your religious leaders and by society around you. Nowhere is this more apparent than in the way that you worship God. Why do you feel the need to worship God? Why do the various Churches create and hold their ceremonies of worship? Primarily, of course, it is to acknowledge the presence of God, to bear witness to that Being. But what is the motivation of the people who go to those ceremonies? Do they go to give or to receive? Do they go to offer their whole beings, their bodies, minds and spirits, in an act of holy sacrifice to their Creator, or do they go to take from their Creator, to make their needs, their physical and emotional requirements known to their Creator and to ask for Its blessings on them, as individuals, so that their lives may run more smoothly?

Would it not be true to say that most people in the world today go to a church to worship their God in order to fulfil a need in themselves, a need that is in fact caused by a lack of understanding of the one true

154

God. For if they are not able to discover the God that is in themselves and in every aspect of life around them, then how much easier it is to worship some idol of God which can take the place of the one true God. For some people, then, the act of worship is an act of laziness, it is an act of delusion, for deep within themselves they know that the concept of God that they are worshipping does not really exist and that the religious dogma to which they bow their heads is very suspect.

Nevertheless, let us recognise that any act of worship, performed by any individual, regardless of race, colour or creed, does create a significant energy in the universe, an energy that is characterised by the motivation of the various people involved. But to repeat any prayer, to sing any song of praise, becomes quite meaningless unless the correct motivation is there behind that prayer and that song. If one is simply mouthing the prayers and the songs, then, no matter if one does it for hours, even for days, all that praise and adoration counts for nothing. For unless that act of worship is coming from the heart, unless one's spirit is empowering every word that is said and every note that is sung, then, it is of little value either to the Creator or to the individual concerned.

It is obvious that when many beings are gathered together with pure motivation, in the name of the one God, that great energy can be created and that this energy uplifts not just the individuals involved but the whole planet. The power of two people praying together in purity is greater than the sum of the two individuals concerned. That is why group worship is so significant, but there must also be times, of course, when one worships alone. Indeed, it could perhaps be said that until one has learned to worship as an individual it is of little significance to worship in a group. Until you have established and sounded your own note, your own point of consciousness, until you have discovered and grown to recognise the God in you and those around you, how can you know what God to worship?

So worship, in essence, is an act of sacrifice to the Creator of all Life. It is an act of offering one's whole being, one's energy, one's talents, one's creativity, back to the Source from which they came. Worship is an act of acknowledging the Creator as the Source and Content of all Life. It is, therefore, a misunderstanding of the act to see worship as being only an act of a limited time in a limited place. Worship is not just an act of going to church, an act of going on your knees and praying each morning and evening in your own home, and of then spending the rest of the time separate from God. It can be of no value whatsoever to go to church in the morning to worship your Creator and then to spend the rest of the day breaking God's Laws, defying God's Will and abusing God's Kingdoms. You cannot worship your Creator for one hour of the day and then desecrate that same Creator for the remaining twenty three hours of the day, or, rather, I should say that you can, and many people do, but it is not worship.

So worship is not the ceremony. Whilst the ceremony does have importance, provided the rest of one's life is lived in harmony and balance with the Divine Source, then the very act of living becomes an act of worship in itself. There is no need for the ceremony at all. Worship can be defined as a twenty four hour a day awareness of one's Creator. Every act of one's physical being should be an act of worship. Everything that you as individuals do in thought, word and deed should constitute an act of worship, of the giving back of your spiritual energy, of your consciousness, to the Source that gave you that energy and that consciousness.

Do you realise that the fact that you have all been given individualised consciousness, that you are not part of a group soul, that each one of you is a unique being, unique in the whole universe, that the fact that you have all been given the divine gift of free choice in order to develop that unique consciousness according to your own wills, represents an extraordinary act by your Creator? There are many Solar Lords in the universe who look with amazement on this experiment in creation that is called the Human Race. They find it quite inconceivable that such divine qualities should be given to such uninitiated beings, that Humanity should be given the freedom to deny its very birthright, to defy the Source of Life and to motivate its actions according to its own little wills!

You, therefore, are in a very special school of learning. You have been given life in order that you may learn of life. You have been released from God in order that you may discover the nature of your God. There is, in truth, no separation between you and your God except where you have created it. You are truly one with your God if you will but choose to be so, and it is in that oneness with the Source wherein lies worship. The true act of worship is to be found in the human being that sacrifices its individuality for the good of the whole. It is to be found in the person who says, 'My life, my needs, my wants, my desires, my opinions, my creations, can be of no value unless they are subjugated to the Will of my Creator'. The true act of worship lies in the words of the being who each morning says, 'O Lord, may Thy Will

156

manifest through me in everything that I do this day'. Worship is deeds not words.

Now for many people worship has become an act of slavish adoration because they have not understood the true nature of worship. They worship out of fear of the power and the majesty of their God. This is especially true of unevolved souls, of primitive societies, where sometimes even blood sacrifices are involved in the so-called act of worship. There is the feeling that the Creator of all Life is a vengeful God Who will take firm action against Humanity if He is not propitiated. But the basis of worship is not fear but love. True worship is an act of love. It is an expression of gratitude to the Source for the note that the individual soul is sounding.

I wish you to see very clearly, therefore, that you are worshipping your Creator in every minute of the day, in every task that you perform, as you use the spiritual talents given to you by your Creator. Recognise that even though you have earned those talents they have still been given to you. So as you use those talents you should dedicate the results of their creativity back to the Source. Work, therefore, is a primary form of worship. Your highest creativity is your highest form of worship. You can see this very clearly when you look at the temples of India or at the cathedrals of Europe, where the people who built those edifices built them not for themselves but to the glory of the Creator of all Life. Often they gave of their services without financial reward.

Let it be understood, therefore, that whenever you work you should always dedicate that work to your Creator. Even if you are doing a task which you regard as unpleasant, which you do not want to do, which the personality self within you is resisting, remember that that task is simply a lesson which you have chosen to learn. Moreover, if you were to introduce the element of worship into that task, no matter how unpleasant or how menial you thought it was, you would find that in performing that task to the highest of your physical and spiritual attributes you would achieve a fulfilment beyond your understanding. The most unpleasant task, done as an act of worship, is soon finished and in the finishing comes the release, for that which you have dedicated to your Creator, when completed, automatically releases you to the next stage of your evolutionary path.

I wish you to understand most clearly that as spiritual beings, as magnetic beings, you attract unto yourselves the aspects of the world that are appropriate to the note or the frequency that you send out, for every atom in the world around you dances to the tune of your Creator's

Will. Therefore you will automatically attract into your magnetic aura everything that your Creator has deemed necessary for your evolutionary status. All that you can do is to choose how you will respond to the lessons that your Creator has placed before you. All that you can do is to choose the attitude with which you will face those lessons, whether you will respond in a positive or a negative fashion. Two people standing side by side can both witness and experience the same events and yet the attitude of each of them towards those events can be very different. It is how the individual reacts to any situation that determines the learning experience.

If you humbly dedicate every conscious thought, word and deed to the honour of your Creator, if you align yourselves with the Source of all Life, then to you will flow the energy of the Source of all Life. A task that you dedicate to your Creator, that you do in union with your Creator, is soon done. It can be compared to a person swimming in a river. The swimmer can choose either to swim against the current of the river or to flow with it. Swimming against the current he will make slow progress. He will soon become tired and will have to rest. But by swimming with the current, by being at one with the flow of the river, he can increase his speed and cover a much greater distance at the cost of much less personal exertion.

Recognise, therefore, that every single person that you meet, being an infinitesimal part of your Creator, is worthy of worship. Recognise that every aspect of the three Kingdoms of Nature with which you come in contact each day, being the creation of that Creator, is also worthy of worship. Can you not see the contradiction of going on your knees in some church or temple and of worshipping and singing hymns of praise to your Creator and of then going outside and abusing your fellow human beings, the animals, the trees and the very ground on which you walk. If that is indeed how you worship, then you have not yet begun to understand the meaning and the purpose of the act of worship and the real nature of your Creator.

Worship applies not just to an act performed in a church, it applies to all of life. Worship is not just the hour or two spent in a religious ceremony on one day of the week, it is of eternity. Worship is twenty four hours a day acknowledgement of your Creator. Worship means placing every act of your being on an altar. As you bless and eat the food on your table, as you acknowledge the sacrifice of the Animal and the Vegetable Kingdoms, so you are making your table into an altar, and by so doing you are also acknowledging the gifts of your Creator to you. Have you ever considered the fact that if your Creator did not wish you to have that food, that food would not be there? Have you ever considered the fact that if your Creator did not wish you to have all your many material possessions, those possessions would not be there? Have you not recognised that they can all be removed in the twinkling of an eye, as an act of Divine Will, if your Creator so wills it?

Every atom in your world vibrates to the Will of God. Every atom in your World can only fulfil the Will of God. Your world, therefore, is God in manifestation. So be aware that how you acknowledge and worship that world is a direct reflection of how you acknowledge and worship your God. If you see only disease and unhappiness in the world, then that truly is how you see your God. If you think only of yourself, of fulfilling your own desires regardless of the world around you, then no matter how many times you go down on your knees and pray to your God, you are truly not worshipping that God. So many people pray to God for what they want, for what they want God to give them, and when their prayers go unanswered they begin to lose faith in their God. This is because they have not yet begun to realise the nature of the flow of divine energy in life which is balance, for unless you give of your energy to the universe, the universe will not give back to you. The nature of the energy that you send out determines the nature of what you will attract back to you. But you have to give of yourself first, you have to give of your spiritual and physical being, and then the universe will respond.

It is very often the case that menial work, work which the personality regards as being unpleasant or even degrading, by its very nature and sacrifice can be creating the energy potential that will attract back in perhaps an entirely different field, from perhaps an entirely different source, the very thing that your heart desires. For remember that God's energy being in all things, all things respond to God's Will. Anything that you do as a true act of worship demands a reply. Your Creator cannot and will not deny you anything that you humbly ask for, provided you have earned it by your own giving. But when you ask for something, always state very clearly first, 'Only if it be God's Will for me', for you would not want to attract something into your aura that would distract you from your true purpose in life, your spiritual destiny. So remember that you have to earn God's gifts. God gives you your spiritual consciousness, God gives you your physical body through which you experience life on the Earth, God endows you with certain talents, but then it is up to you to choose how you will exercise

159

those gifts. You have to create the potential that will attract the flow of the universe back to you. You choose the nature of your world. You choose the nature of your worship.

So let us see that worship is not just as an act carried out in a church, as the continual repetition of ancient dogma, especially if that dogma has no meaning today, but rather let us see worship as the adoration of the Creator of all Life. Let us see worship as a continual act of being, not as something that takes place in isolation from the rest of life. Let us recognise that the true worship of God is the worship of the God around us, is the worship of the God within us. Therefore anything that we do to defile our body in thought, word and deed, anything that we do to defile another human being is desecrating that God. You must acknowledge the presence of God in everything and everyone around you, in every action that you perform. That is the true nature of human worship.

It is obvious that there should also be times when you join in, what I will call, formal worship, times of prayer, meditation, concentration, openness, giving and receiving. There should also be times of group worship, times when the energies of many different souls unite to form a powerful beam of light that reaches far out into the universe. But let all times of worship be times of offering not times of demanding. Let the act of worship be a genuine act of surrender to the universe. How often when you pray to your Creator do you offer to do the tasks which the personality does not want to do? How often do you ask your Creator for extra tasks to be imposed upon you in order to speed up Its plan for the evolution of Humanity? How often do you ask that your Creator's Will be done not yours? How often do you truly sacrifice that ego consciousness on the altar of the God that gave it to you?

So look within your hearts now as to the nature of how you worship. Try to understand that worship is a universal not an individual act, that it cannot be done in isolation from the world in which you live. Recognise that every time you inhale a breath of air that that too is an act of worship. Recognise that every thought, word and deed that you create is an act of worship and, moreover, that your Creator knows every breath, every thought, every word, every deed that you create and that they are all recorded for eternity. Therefore let it be said that when you leave your physical body and return to the higher planes of life that truly your life has been an act of worship, an act of true worship to the Creator of all Life and that you have given back to the Creator of all Life just as much as the Creator has given to you.

160

QUESTIONS AND ANSWERS

Q: It would seem to me that there is still a great deal of spirituality left in the Churches. Nevertheless, a lot of people who are deeply spiritual still feel the need to leave the Churches and to come and join groups like this. Is there any way in which the Churches could work with New Age groups, of working with them in parallel, if you see what I mean, rather than opposing or even denouncing them? I know that the Churches are changing, but they don't seem to be changing fast enough.

ZT: The Churches only change according to the dictates of their leaders, who in turn respond according to the feelings of their congregations. However, you must also recognise that if the Churches are exemplifying the Truth, then what is there that needs to be changed, because the Truth does not change. If the Churches' dogma is true, then it is true for eternity. So what the Churches are in fact changing is false dogma, is dogma which is not true and which has been created in the past in order to sustain the Churches and to give them authority over their followers. Now I am not saying that the Churches are wrong and that what they are preaching is misleading people. There is much good in the dogma and the religious practices of every religion. Worship creates energy which can be used by the Higher Forces. No matter even if a religion is a false one, the energy created by it can be used by the Higher Forces. Any form of worship which points the individual towards their Creator and invokes the highest feelings in them is obviously beneficial both for them as individuals and for the planet as a whole.

Nevertheless, in the final analysis, it is the point of consciousness of the individual concerned that will choose the nature of its worship. So the fact that so many people today are changing the nature of their worship is because they are finding the dogma of a particular Church too narrow and too limiting. They have recognised that the picture of life must be greater than the one painted by their religious leaders and so they are leaving the Churches, not in a sense of rejection but rather to discover a greater picture, one that embraces all the Churches, all the religions. I see this very much as a natural process, one that indicates that the consciousness of Humanity is truly awakening. Moreover, it is by people leaving the Churches that the Churches themselves will be compelled to re-examine their dogma and change, or else they will atrophy and die. Finally, I would ask you to remember that you do not

161

have to go to a church, that you do not have to belong to a religion, in order to know and to worship your Creator. Even if there were no Churches you would still feel the need for worship, but would you choose the format that exists today?

Q: I would like some more information about the duality of the soul and the spirit. Until now I had believed that they were the one and the same thing, but from this talk I gather that they are not. Is this correct?
ZT: You should not see the soul and the spirit as being part of the duality of life. They are both part of one body, your spiritual body. The soul can, very simplistically, be described as the memory of spirit and it is for this reason that many people often use either or both of these words to denote the eternal part of their being. Your soul is the cosmic record of all that your divine spark of spirit has experienced on many planes of existence. In one sense the spirit and the soul can be compared to your personality and your physical body. Your personality could not express itself without the brain, or the memory, of your physical body. Likewise, your spirit could not express itself without the manifestation of the soul. They go hand in hand.

When the Master was speaking of the duality of life he was referring to the nature of the evolutionary cycle in which you live and learn today. The purpose of this duality is to present Humanity with the opportunity to exercise its divine gift of free choice. So, every moment of your physical lives, you are faced with the need to exercise a choice – a choice between light or darkness, positive or negative, God's will or human will – and by that choice you establish the very nature of your life and, of course, your karma. I would, however, like to make it clear that this choice is not a question of right and wrong. Just because you choose darkness does not mean that that is wrong. It simply means that that is the learning experience that you have chosen. The very essence of the duality is positive and negative, male and female. How can you say that one is right and the other is wrong! Recognise that both are the creations of your Creator. So what is important is the motivation behind your choice. So why you choose and how you choose is your learning experience. You will learn as much from choosing light as from choosing darkness. That is the nature of the drama of life. That is why you should not judge another human being. Observe, yes, but judge, no.

Q: Am I right in saying that the spirit is pure energy, an aspect of its Creator, indeed, still linked to its Creator, but that the soul, containing the memory and the conditioning of past life experiences, can sometimes be very impure?

ZT: That is correct. The soul is the record of all your past life experiences. The soul records the aspects of life that still have to be transmuted and faced. So the soul is the seat of karma and, as such, is impure.

Q: At this moment in my life I am unsure as to the work I should be doing. I am certainly not getting any satisfaction from the work that I am doing. Can you give me some advice as to how I should handle this? I feel that I really want to do something that is more involved with helping people.

ZT: Firstly, I would ask you to recognise that all work is worship and, even if you are doing work that you don't like, that if you do it properly, that in itself is a great lesson to learn and that from that lesson will come your release. Also, remember that the secret of happiness lies not in doing what you like but rather in liking what you have to do. Secondly, you must also recognise that you all work for many different reasons. You don't work just because society expects you to work, just to earn money in order to buy the essentials of life. An old soul works because it needs to express its creative talents in some field or other and, if it did not, it would become very frustrated. A young soul, on the other hand, works because it needs to learn the discipline of work and because, if it did not, as the expression goes, idle hands would lead to mischief. So be aware that you all need to work because the process of work is, in itself, a form of meditation which reaffirms your union with God and because work forms part of the essential balance of life. As the Christians of old used to say, you need your hands to grow, prepare and eat your daily bread, but you also need those same hands to pray.

Nevertheless, having said that, it is a fact of life that at certain times in your life you are best fitted to do certain kinds of work. It is obvious that the work that you are able, and want to do when you are young will differ from the work that you are able, and want to do when you are older. As a young man of twenty you have a lot more energy and vitality than an old man of seventy. So, to a certain extent, the birth cycle in which you are living determines both the nature of your work and the nature of what you have come to learn. At another time, when we have spoken about the true meaning and significance of birthdays, we have described the seven decades or cycles of physical life, and the lessons that are associated with each of those cycles. As you grow older and enter into a new cycle, say from your fifties into your sixties, so you will often feel within you the need to change the nature of your work. Of course, you must always be sure that it is indeed a genuine need for change and not simply a case of change for change's sake or of changing in order to avoid doing work that you should by now have completed.

Now if you don't like your work because you are in fact doing work which in some way is harming either Humanity or the three other Kingdoms of Matter then, obviously, it is right and proper that you should consider a change, but you should be very careful about changing your work simply because you don't like it. You should always consider whether or not you have learned all the lessons that your work can teach you. You should always consider whether or not you have given all that you can give of your spiritual talents to your work and whether or not your very presence there is serving as an example to all those who work with you. Finally, remember that in the natural cycle of life, when you have truly finished your work, you will always be released from it. When you have completed your work to the highest of your ability, in fact when others judge you to be good at your work, that is often the time when you feel a need for change and when, indeed, change comes as a natural course of events.

Finally, I would advise you to be very careful of what is, for the spiritually minded person, the ultimate temptation, namely, to give up your physical work in order to better serve Humanity and your Creator on the spiritual level. Although on the surface this would seem to be a very noble act, it is the rare soul, an ego-less soul, that is truly capable of making this decision. Even the great Masters perform physical work to some degree. It is essential that you maintain a balance in your life and that even if your head is in the heavens, your feet are firmly placed on the ground. Now this does not mean that you should not be a teacher of your spiritual knowledge, because the teacher will learn as much from teaching as the pupil, but that you cannot renounce the physical world of matter until you are the Master of matter.

Q: I would like to know the difference between the purpose of life and the destiny of life.

ZT: Put simply, the purpose of life is to fulfil your destiny. Your destiny is the role which you have chosen to play in this life and the spiritual lessons that you have chosen to learn. In the case of an evolved soul this role has been selected by the soul itself. In the case of an unevolved soul the role has been chosen for them by great spiritual beings on the higher planes of life and they are inculcated with the need to play this role.

Q: Even though I am a relatively young person, I still feel that I am not fulfilling my destiny and that I am not doing what I should be doing, namely, being of service. Have I strayed from my destiny path?

ZT: With the greatest of respect, my son, what you have just said can be compared to Jesus or Buddha, at the age of sixteen, saying: 'I don't feel that I am fulfilling my destiny'! They would only have said that because the most significant part of their destinies lay ahead of them and because they were still preparing for them! So I would ask you to recognise that most of your life is still ahead of you and that much of what is happening now is but a preparation for the significant events in your life that are yet to come. The early years of any incarnation can be likened to the erection of building stones into a firm foundation so that an edifice of service can be created at a later date. You still have much to learn, much to discover, not only of life but of yourself. It is only the disciplined being that can truly be of service.

I will however say that most of the people who stray from their destiny path are totally unaware, on a conscious level anyway, that they have such a thing as a destiny, let alone of the need to follow it! So to be aware of the force of destiny is a sign of an awakened soul. It is always easy to see the force of destiny at work in your own life when looking back in retrospect, but it is more difficult, is it not, to recognise the force of destiny in the present? All that you can do is to ask your Creator, in your prayers and meditations, to help you to seek out and to follow your destiny path. Then, as each day comes, learn to accept it and try to discover its inner meaning and purpose for you. Slowly, on a deep, intuitive level, you will begin to discern the presence of the divine in everything that you do, impelling you along a path that somehow seems vaguely familiar to you!

Q: My father is dying and I am having to help him face that fact. However, it is difficult for me to face the fact of death myself, let alone help anyone else. Can you give me some advice on how to handle this situation?

ZT: The death of anyone is always a good test of your point of consciousness, if only because it brings out your own attitudes towards death, and in particular your own death, into sharp focus. Now the first thing I want you to understand is that no-one dies except at their appointed time. If a person dies it is because their Creator has decreed it. No-one dies by chance. So if you really believe in life after death, if you really believe that the higher planes of life are where you truly belong, that they are your true home, then your father is simply returning home in order to fulfil his Creator's wish. He is returning to the place from whence he came. He has reached the end of his allotted time on the plane of Earth, he has reached the end of his lessons, his spiritual tests, and now he is leaving for his holidays. What is wrong with going on holiday!

So for your father death will be a pleasant experience. The significance of his death will not be just for your father but for all the people that he will leave behind. So the real lesson is not for your father, it is for you, and both the manner in which you handle his death and the awareness of life that you grasp from this situation will result in a great learning experience for you. If you truly die with your father, if you become one with his moment of transition, then you will witness a moment of great joy and happiness. You will understand the true nature of his release. You will appreciate that death is not the process of suffering that it is commonly held to be. Death can be viewed with as much joy as birth.

Death, like birth, is simply a moment of transition. The pain which is so often associated with death is not physical pain but psychological pain, the pain of having to release the physical aspects of life and, in particular, the physical relationships of life and all the memories that go with them. So your father has to learn to release the physical world and you have to learn to release your father. If your father is genuinely fearful of death then all that you can do is to share your understandings of life with him and to gently point out to him, firstly, that death is inevitable – and it is a waste of time and energy to fear what is inevitable – and, secondly, that he has already died many times in his present life, in fact to every minute of his life, so what is just one more death amongst so many.

Q: A wise person once said that to mourn is to question the wisdom of God. Do you feel this to be correct?

166

ZT: Yes. What is the purpose of grieving for someone who the Lord Himself has recalled. What you are saying, in actual fact, by expressing this grief is that the Lord is wrong to do this and that your understanding of when they should die is correct!

Q: But surely it is not wrong to mourn someone's passing? Is one not entitled to a little grieving?

ZT: There is a natural process of mourning after the death of a loved one, when one grieves for their absence on the physical plane of life, when one remembers, with thanks, all that that soul has been in one's life. But this process should not take more than seven days. If it does, then you are enjoying it too much! Remember that most of you only do the things in life that you like, you rarely do things you don't like. So you only carry on grieving if you have chosen to do so. If you don't like grieving, you won't do it. Some people, of course, like to grieve.

Q: Yes. I know of someone who loves to grieve. She spends all her time visiting cemeteries and having a good cry. But she enjoys doing that.

ZT: In a similar fashion, some people like being ill. They enjoy the attention that they get. Always look at the part of you that is grieving. It is not your soul, the eternal part of your being. It is your ego-self, the mortal part of your being, that grieves, because it does not know of the meaning of eternal life.

THE CYCLE OF LIFE AND DEATH

You meet to celebrate the festival of Easter. Over successive years I have spoken to you about the significance of this festival. I have told you that Easter has been celebrated for thousands of years and that it was a time of divine worship long before the Christian religion even came into existence. So recognise that the Christian celebration of Easter reflects only one small aspect of this festival, which has been honoured by many millions of souls, as far back as the very beginnings of Humanity's walk on the plane of Earth.

Easter, therefore, should be seen as a natural festival, a festival of Nature. Indeed, the priests of old celebrated Easter on the day of the Spring Equinox, for that moment in cosmic time was regarded as the moment when life was renewed on the Earth. The Spring Equinox was seen as the moment when life began to return to the soil, when Nature began to bud and reproduce itself and to show forth its promise for the future. Easter was seen, therefore, as a ceremony both of renewal and promise, the renewal of life on the Earth after the darkness of winter and the promise of the fruits of the summer that was to come. Easter was significant because it was widely regarded as a symbol of the renewal of God's commitment to the Earth and to Humanity who dwelt upon its surface.

So the priests of old celebrated the four great festivals of the Equinoxes and the Solstices, not just because of their physical significance for the Earth but because they reflected the eternal cycle of birth, death and rebirth, not just here on the Earth but in the Cosmos as a whole. The priests would use these natural cycles as opportunities to demonstrate to their followers the true nature of physical life on the Earth, the reality of the continuing cycle of human evolution. So in one sense the celebration of these festivals could be regarded as parables, with the participants taking from them each according to their point of consciousness and spiritual understanding.

168

This is especially true of the Christian celebration of Easter, for with the trial, the crucifixion and the subsequent resurrection of the Master Jesus, you have a wonderful teaching vehicle. In the story of Jesus you have demonstrated the essential ingredients of physical life – birth, sacrifice, death and rebirth. Above all, though, the Easter Story of the Christian religion celebrates the existence of the soul after death, the continuing presence of consciousness after death, of a state of being in which one is not subject to the limitations of the physical plane of life but in which one is still, nevertheless, learning and serving God.

Because of the karmic nature of the events that are at present manifesting on the Earth, I would like to talk to you now about the challenge of Easter in the sense that it symbolises the cycle of life and death. I would like you to examine your own concepts of life and death and, in particular, to ask yourselves when you think you are alive and when you think you are dead. Do not think that you are alive only when in your physical body or that the ending of life in that body means death for, truly, there are people who are living in physical bodies now who are 'dead', just as there are people who are no longer in their physical bodies yet who are 'alive' as I speak to you now. The cycle of life and death is not defined simply by one's ability to manifest in a human physical form. Divine Consciousness is infinite and eternal. It never dies because It is never born. This principle, above all, was taught by the priests of old in their celebrations of the solstices and the equinoxes. Life is a cycle, a circle, rather than a linear progression, and death follows birth just as naturally as birth follows death. All that changes is your awareness of that state of being. In similar fashion winter comes after summer and summer dies into winter. Without the one there could not be the other, without the darkness there could not be the light and, as I have so often said, everything grows in the dark. Life and death, summer and winter, light and darkness, are all irrevocably linked together, the one always foretelling the other. If you did but realise it, in the unending cycle of the seasons you have demonstrated for you a great Natural Law, the Law of Cycles and Periodicity.

Many times I have said to you that you come into this world only with consciousness and that you leave this world only with consciousness. All else is modelling clay in your hands for you to mould according to your motivation and your creativity. That is the nature of your evolutionary process. So being souls of aged evolution, what you are truly seeking, above all else, is the gaining of soul-consciousness because, being aware of the eternal cycle of life and death, you are also aware that the consciousness with which you die is the consciousness with which you will be born in your next life. You enter into life with the total soul-consciousness you have gained in all your previous lives. Be aware that the note that you sounded at the moment of your last physical death was the note of your entrance into this life. Remember also that along with your soul-consciousness you bring your physical attributes as well as your karmic debts, your physical restrictions, for you will always reap that which you have sowed in your previous lives. You can never avoid the all pervading Law of Karma.

Now I know that many people have a vision of God as a benevolent father sitting in the heavens Who either bestows divine benefits upon his children or else lovingly chastises them for their misdemeanours. Nothing could be further from the truth. That is not, and never has been, the role of God. Your Creator released you upon your evolutionary walk in life with the divine gift of free choice so that you alone would be totally responsible for discovering and evolving the divine nature of your being. By the act of bestowing that very gift upon you, your Creator became the observer of His creations. Your God witnesses but does not intervene in human evolution. He, and when I say He I talk not in terms of masculine gender but rather of cosmic positivity, because your God transcends all human sexuality, He does not judge your thoughts, your words or your deeds because He knows that the Law of Karma, the Law to which even He is subject, is all pervading in this respect. The Law of Karma judges you, not your God. The Law of Karma ensures that there is perfect harmony and balance in the Cosmos, not your God.

Remember, therefore, that there is no escape from the Law of Karma. Whether you like it or not, you are subject to its decrees. As you sow, so shall you reap. As you give, so you shall receive. That is the inherent nature of Creation. Therefore recognise that you incarnated in this life with the karma, positive and negative, that you have created. You are now living and facing the karma that you have created in past lives. You are now creating the karma that you will have to face either in this life or in your many lives to come. So recognise that you are a god, a creative being, and that you are the master and creator of your destiny. The very life that you are experiencing right now, with all of its joys and all of its sorrows, is the life that you have created for yourself, is the lesson that you have chosen for yourself, is the karma that you have elected to face and transmute. If you understand this one great cosmic fact, then you understand the true

170

nature of human existence on the Earth, you understand the reality, or should I say the unreality, of the physical world.

Every single aspect of the physical world is both mortal and fallible. Everything comes from the dust and returns to the dust. Only one thing endures, only one thing is constant, and that is consciousness, or the force of spirit in motion. It is consciousness that determines the note of your physical being. It is consciousness that is with you before birth, is with you throughout your life and is with you after death. Your consciousness manifests on all of the twelve planes of existence within this Solar Body. Even now it is manifesting on some of those planes and will continue to do so after your physical body dies. For some people the act of death even passes unnoticed! Only the body knows death, not the consciousness. Only the body is limited by the physical restrictions of the plane of Earth, not the consciousness. The drama of life is played out on a small stage, defined by your sensory organs and the four Kingdoms of Matter. This school of learning is not your true home, for you are divine beings created in the image of your Creator. So if you are alive before birth and if you are alive after death you can never die, only change your classroom!

It is difficult, I know, on some occasions, to accept the need for someone to die, especially if they are young in physical years, with so many skills and talents to give to the world, with so much potential unfulfilled. The death of a young person is nearly always regarded as a tragedy. Let us look at this aspect for a moment and, as I usually do, I will take the example of the life of the Master Jesus. Here was a man who, apparently, if he had but lived for another forty years, would truly have transformed human society at that time, yet he was condemned to an early death by the political and religious leaders of the time. Was this a tragedy? Do you think that his death was an act of blind fate or was it a carefully planned event, an act of conscious sacrifice to demonstrate a great cosmic principle? Do you think that anything can manifest on this Earth which is not God's Will? On the contrary, it is the wise soul who recognises that our Creator's Will is paramount in all things. It is not for us to question that Will, but to observe and learn from it and to try to see the greater picture.

In the case of the Master Jesus we can see that he died to show Humanity that even in death Evil cannot triumph over Goodness and that there is a state of consciousness, of life, after death. Moreover, he showed us that sometimes we have to sacrifice to God's will even though we do not understand it, even though we would like to avoid it.

171

Jesus, as an evolved Master, could have avoided his crucifixion so easily. At any time he could have transported himself from that situation but, instead, he consciously chose to sacrifice his physical being to fulfil the will of his Creator even though, on a physical level, he could not understand or see the purpose of his sacrifice. With the benefit of the passing years we can see what came from that sacrifice, not just in the sense that that Master was released to serve all Humanity from the higher levels of life but that his death was the start of a great birth, the Christian religion, which has touched the hearts of millions of souls. It was necessary to release the old in order to initiate the new. Death, therefore, is not only a great transmutor, it is a great initiator. Death is not an ending, it is a beginning.

It is difficult, I know, to accept the need for death, particularly one's own death, especially if one has become attached to the physical level of life. Herein lies the root cause of all suffering. If you place your trust in the finite and the fallible then you are doomed to suffer, but if you place your trust in the infinite and the infallible, then what is there to fear? Coming to terms with the process of death, therefore, requires trust in your Creator, an understanding that everything that happens to you is His will, even if you do not understand the reason for it. Let me give you a simple, but emotive example. Suppose you were a mother with two young children and you were dying. In your unconscious state, as you floated down that tunnel that lies between life and death, you would see your Creator standing there, in the Light, beckoning you to come towards Him, and at the other end you could see your children, urging you to stay with them. How would you respond? Would you choose the children or would you choose your Creator?

Now that, in essence, is the choice that all of you face at this time. Of course, you all have different choices before you, depending on the nature of your soul being, but I have deliberately used the emotive example of children to make my point more clear. Would you say that you have any choice other than to obey your Creator's will? Would you choose physical life or life on the higher planes? Would you place your children before your Creator? Ultimately, it all comes down to a question of trust. Do you trust your Creator? Do you accept His will for you? If you truly trust your Creator, if you truly know that every hair on your head is counted, if you really understand that your Creator's will for you is that you fulfil your chosen destiny, then every sacrifice that you make to fulfil that will can only result in the highest good for all concerned.

Sometimes, you know, you have to die in what could be called tragic accidents, not only as a lesson to others but also to advance your own consciousness, to overcome a blockage in your own soul being. Sometimes you have to die of your own free choice, you have to make the sacrifice of, shall we say, giving your life in battle to save another, or of diving into a cold sea in order to try to save a young boy who is drowning. The reason for this is that out of such a sacrifice comes great human transformation, not just for those who witnessed your sacrifice but for all those who tap into the energy generated by such an act, for the soul consciousness of the whole Human Race will have been uplifted.

When you are in your physical bodies your soul expression is limited, but when you are released to the higher planes of life, especially after such an act of sacrifice, not only is much human karma transmuted but you are then in a position to touch every single soul on the plane of Earth. Perhaps you can now begin to see the true significance behind the death of the Master Jesus. The power of a risen Master on the higher planes of life is all pervasive. Every physical atom of matter is touched by the consciousness of such a being. But on the physical plane of life even a Master such as Jesus has limitations placed on his being, whereas on the higher planes of life his power becomes unlimited. Moreover, having but recently lived on the plane of Earth, his connection with and understanding of Humanity's evolutionary path is strong.

So I ask all of you to think most carefully of the reality of life and death, not just in your own lives but in Nature all around you. At this time of the year, especially, as the rebirth of spring comes after the death of winter, be conscious of the power of the Cycle of Life and Death and, above all, seek to align yourselves with that Cycle. At the same time, though, be mindful of the death of winter that must inevitably follow. See how this cycle of birth and death is reflected in your own lives and in your own creativity. Recognise that the widely held perception of death as the ending of life was only created by Humanity in order to make physical life more real, more significant. Death is not the ending that most people believe. For an evolved soul death can be likened to going to sleep at night and waking up the next morning on another level of being. The finality of death has been created by Humanity in order to give substance to the illusion of life.

For a true Master there is no difference between life and death, for a true Master dies to the minute that has gone and lives only in the present. The past is death, the present is life. If you hold onto the past then you cannot live life. If you are not prepared to die to each moment of the day, then you are truly not alive, you are not leading life as your Creator intended. The minute that has past has gone for ever, is truly dead, so if you cannot release the past then you are trapped in death. Above all, remember the true nature of matter and the reality of physical life. Whilst you must always respect every aspect of physical matter and handle it with consciousness, remember that it will eventually return to the dust from whence it came. Physical matter is in a constant cycle of generation and degeneration as it is used and moulded by generation after generation of Humanity as they walk their path of life. But you are spiritual beings, imbued with cosmic consciousness. You have come from a planetary system far removed from this solar system. You are only placed in this school of learning for such a short time in order to discover the true nature of your being, which is divine. You are a god. All that you have to do is to realise that fact!

Finally, may I once more remind you of the lesson of this planet, which is sacrificial service. You were born with the destiny to serve Humanity, to serve the planet, and to serve the God which is present in both Humanity and the planet. It is necessary to sacrifice in order for you to obtain cosmic consciousness. It is necessary to give in order to receive. It is necessary to die in order that you can be born again. It is necessary to trust in the God that created both you and this school of life and to know that the Divine Plan is perfect and will be carried out. It is not in the nature of God to fail!

So as you meet at this time, to honour the sacrifice of the Master Jesus, remember also the sacrifice of all the other Masters who over the Ages have incarnated on the plane of Earth in order to ground their point of consciousness and to point the way to human salvation. Many of them, too, chose to sacrifice their physical lives in order to reduce the great karmic burden that holds Humanity down. You, like them, have to sound your note, have to demonstrate your point of spiritual consciousness both for the planet and for the race of Humanity who dwells on it. Remember that no sacrifice is ever made in vain, for the energy of every human endeavour is available to the whole Human Race.

You live in a time of great planetary transformation, a time when many people will die both from human and natural destruction. You must be ready to meet such deaths with spiritual understanding and to

174

give comfort to those who will grieve. Teach the great truth, that nothing of human spirit is ever lost at death. Nothing of spirit ever perishes and that the consciousness you take with you at death will be with you at birth in your next life. Above all, I would ask you to remember that the manner and the consciousness with which you die transforms not just yourselves, not just your family and close friends, but the whole human race, for the note that you sound lasts for eternity. Herein lies the true value of the sacrifice of the Master Jesus.

QUESTIONS AND ANSWERS

Q: What advice can you give to me about gaining spiritual strength? I feel so powerless in the world today.

ZT: The gaining of spiritual strength is not like going to the local gymnasium, where you practise a series of exercises in order to strengthen your physical body. The gaining of spiritual strength comes from the acquisition of cosmic knowledge, sometimes known as Truth. Great strength comes from cosmic knowledge, from union with the Source of all Life. I will illustrate this point with a simple analogy. If you know that a certain lake is frozen, then you are happy to go and skate upon the ice, provided you know the ice is thick enough. But if you do not know how thick the ice is, then you would be very frightened of going onto that lake. It is your knowledge that removes the fear and gives you the strength to act.

It is the same with life. The experience which you have of the reality and presence of God, not the books you have read, not the words that I am speaking now, not the dogma you have been taught by some priest or teacher, but your own unique spiritual experience, this is what gives you the inner strength to face and handle the outer world. Once you know that God is omnipresent, omniscient and omnipotent, then you truly have nothing to fear. It means that you can walk through a place of great Darkness and know that you will not be touched. So it would be true to say that the strongest person on the Earth today is the person that has the strongest union with God.

Q: Is that the same as faith, Zen Tao?

ZT: No. Faith can be a great illusion. For example, to continue with my analogy, you can have faith that the ice on the lake is thick, go onto the ice and then fall through, because it is not. Faith, therefore, is but a substitute for a lack of knowledge. Because you do not know, you have to hope that you are right, and so you walk forward in faith. Now, sometimes, because of your ignorance, you have to rely on faith in order to walk your path in life. Sometimes you have to make choices, relying only on your faith, because you cannot see clearly the path that you should take. However, I should make it clear that only on very rare occasions does your Creator ask you to take big decisions based only on faith. Nearly always you are forced to make a decision because you are not seeing clearly the choices that lie before you. When you see clearly, when you know, there is no choice.

Q: If it is such a limitation to be in a physical body, why must we, or why do we, choose to keep on incarnating in a physical body for life after life after life?

ZT: You must understand that the path of human evolution on the Earth demands many different human experiences and, as such, the denseness of the human physical body varies quite widely, depending on the nature of the cycle. There are times, as I am sure you have heard, such as in the great civilisation of Atlantis, when the human physical body was not so dense and was far less limiting. At such a time human senses were far more extended. Humanity could walk and talk with the angels, could see and communicate with the devic forces, could travel across the vastness of space. Today, of course, because of Humanity's behaviour in thought, word and deed, the human body is very dense. It is indeed most frustrating for a spiritually aware person to be in the human body at this time, but that is a lesson which you all have to accept and learn. That is why those of you who have lived in the glorious Ages of the past find life today so restrictive. That is why although you want to see and hear beyond the human frequency range, which it is your birthright to do, you are unable to do so.

One of the facts of life which you all have to learn is that you reap what you have sowed. Thus, today, although many people talk about protecting the environment and cooperating rather than coercing Nature, that attitude is the exception rather than the rule. For I can see that radio-active material is still being buried in the ground, seas are still being polluted, mineral resources are still being exhausted, and the attitude of 'Well, at least it will be alright in my lifetime' seems to prevail in many quarters. But how can you, in all honesty, hand over a sick planet to your children? What is the point of having children if you

176

do not bequeath them a healthy planet on which to live and rear their children?

Finally, and here is the great irony, who are going to be your children's children but yourselves! Do you realise that? So you will truly reap what you are now sowing, just as you are now reaping what you sowed two hundred years ago. You have created the dense world in which you are now living and if you do not like it, then that is a lesson well learned! You will understand why it is so important to have union with God and to strive with all your might to lead a life of peace and harmony, of goodwill towards all people. Having said all of this, though, do not think that life is all pain and suffering. Joy abounds everywhere if you will but recognise it.

Q: You once said that the moment of death is the most important moment in our lives, because we reunite with our Creator. Do you mean that we actually see our Creator as our right, or do we have to make an effort and direct our minds to achieve this?

ZT: Please do not think of your Creator in the terms of a super human being, who is waiting there to shake your hand and to congratulate you when you pass over to the other side of life! Your Creator is not a being in that sense at all. Understand that your God is the totality of this planetary system in which you now dwell. Your God *is* all the light, love and power, all the wisdom and knowledge, the total Will of this planetary system. How can such a Being be contained by any one form? When you die, as with birth, so you choose the life you want to lead, the plane of existence on which you want to dwell. It is your innermost thoughts, your soul murmurings, that direct you to your 'Heaven'. So, for example, if when you die you are still attached to the Earth and to events in your family and society, then you will stay close to the Earth and be able to observe all the events going on. If you are attracted to the guides and Masters then you will be drawn to them. If you truly desire to merge with your Creator and give up your unique soul identity, then, if you have reached the point of consciousness to do so, that is what you will do.

Q: Why is it that apparently thousands of years ago, in Atlantis and Lemuria, Humanity evolved to a higher level of consciousness than we possess today? Why has Humanity regressed or degenerated? I thought we were evolving.

ZT: Why did the rose in your garden bloom last summer, but then die back with the onset of winter? Why will it bloom again next summer, and will its fragrance be any different? The Human Race, being part of the essence of this planet, grows in cycles. It is subject to the Law of Periodicity, one of the great Cosmic Laws which control everything in the Cosmos. It is subject to planetary and to zodiacal influences. That is why you have the rise and fall of nations and civilisations, of races and religions. Perfection can never be sustained for long on this plane of Earth. Decline or decay must follow growth or development. Unless you die, you cannot be born again, you cannot begin again, you cannot repeat the learning experience again. Until there is an ending, there cannot be a beginning. On the Earth everything returns to the dust from which it came, ashes to ashes, dust to dust.

It is the same with the great civilisations of the past. They are no exception, even though they have risen to far greater spiritual and technological heights than you know today. The nature of the cycle is that every civilisation approaches what can be called a 'moment of truth'. You are approaching yours now. At such a time the civilisation faces a supreme challenge, a challenge necessary for its further growth and evolution. The challenge facing the Race of Humanity today is one of wholeness or holiness. Will Humanity recognise the human race as one race, one people, one family, imbued with the same spirit, part of the same God? Will Humanity recognise its unity and its divinity, or will it descend into tribalism and competition? Will it recognise the God in all Humanity or just the God in itself? It is the answer to such questions that will decide the fate of twentieth century Humanity. No matter what happens, in your lives and cycles to come you will be able to look back and to know why certain events happened.

Q: I find that very hard to accept. Moreover it conflicts with the known evidence of Humanity's evolution. Most people feel that both they and life are evolving and that if they are going through all of life's challenges just to reach a certain point and then go down to the bottom again, then what is the point of struggling to become better and wiser people?
ZT: If you were an aged person, you would look back on the cycles of your present life and would recognise just how your physical body evolved to a point of perfection in your youth and then began to decay. Right now, recognise that all physical matter in the world is degenerating. That is the nature of the physical world in which you live.

178

So why should Humanity be any different? What evidence do you have to show that the Human Race is evolving? Of course, it has evolved technologically, but is it really behaving in a more evolved way than it did, say, even two thousand years ago? If the Master Jesus were to come on the Earth today, do you think he would be treated any differently, except, perhaps, in the nature of his execution? Why do you feel that you are evolving when even your sun is decaying. This Solar System is dying. That is a fact of life, or should I say a fact of the universe.

Now here I would like to make a distinction between physical evolution and spiritual evolution or, what I call, the gaining of consciousness. Physical evolution comes about as a direct response to the environment of the planet. You can see this most clearly in the Animal Kingdom, which adapts, often with great rapidity, to changes in the environment. This is evolution in order to guarantee the survival of the species. Obviously the human body is a part of this process. Spiritual evolution, however, demands a very different procedure. The gaining of spiritual consciousness is a self or, should I say, soul initiated process. It is, therefore, a very, very slow process because the individual soul determines the rate at which it gains consciousness. So the bottom line is that you decide whether you evolve or devolve.

Consider the reality of just one cosmic cycle. A Zodiacal Age lasts for around two thousand of your Earth years. You have to experience all twelve signs of the Zodiac. However the Zodiac also reverses its cycle and you have to experience the twelve signs in reverse, so to speak. So that is about forty eight thousand Earth years in just one cosmic cycle. There are, I believe, one hundred and forty four cosmic cycles, so you all have a lot of living to do, especially if you believe that you incarnate on the Earth about every two hundred years! During this period you are, hopefully, slowly gaining in consciousness, through sacrifice and service, through life and death. You are rather like a gold prospector panning for gold, only you are panning for consciousness. You have to sift through a great deal of rubble to occasionally find a small nugget of consciousness! Finally, I leave you with the thought that if this Solar System is decaying, then why is that not also true of the Universe? Only the Creator of the Universe knows the reason and purpose for Its creations.

THE PURPOSE OF PILGRIMAGE TODAY

You are all aware that there are many levels of life both above and below the level of the physical world in which you live today. I would ask, however, that you do not regard these levels as being separate but, rather, as intertwining, each one linking with the other. You, with your physical senses, are aware only of a certain frequency range. You can only see, hear and feel within the limits of your physical being, and unless you are super sensitive, unless you can sense beyond the normal sensory range, you will not be able to experience or to know of these realms. But they do indeed exist and I would ask you to accept that you dwell upon these levels in your higher bodies, even whilst you are living on the physical plane of life.

Let me use the example of the power of electricity. Even though you cannot see it with your physical eyes, nevertheless, you are aware of its presence and you use it in your everyday lives. So electricity can be identified and measured scientifically, even if it cannot be sensed physically. Likewise, through the use of Kirlean photography, it has been established that food that has been blessed has a greater energy field, a greater aura, than food that has not been blessed, and this too can be measured scientifically. I would therefore ask you to recognise that there are energies both above and below the physical plane of life which play a very significant part in your everyday living and, according to your inner sensitivity and awareness, you will discover their presence and their significance.

I would like you to recognise that a pilgrimage is, in essence, a sacred journey to a source of power, a power that emanates on levels beyond the physical plane. In the days of old and, to a lesser extent, in more recent years, the devout followers of all the great world religions used to go on pilgrimages, and although they usually went either to worship at the shrine of some great teacher or religious martyr, or to visit a place where some significant mystical experience had taken place, that was only the outward manifestation that attracted them. On an inner

180

level they used to go on those pilgrimages in order to place themselves, their bodies, their minds and their spirits in the vortex of cosmic energy that was to be found at those places.

So although the pilgrims had to make an outer journey by physically travelling to whichever centre of power they were attracted, when they reached the place of pilgrimage they had to make an inner journey. They had to open themselves, their hearts, their minds and their souls, to the cosmic energy that pulsated there and allow themselves to be transformed, reborn and re-energised for the spiritual work that they had come to do in that life. A pilgrimage, therefore, if embarked upon with the right motivation, is a time of great spiritual significance. It is not usually undertaken by the young in body or, indeed, by the young in spirit, but rather by those who have matured physically and spiritually, by those who have reached that moment in time when they are prepared to be an instrument of service to the world in which they live, by those who have grown to recognise the presence of God in all things, by those who want to serve that God to the highest of their physical and spiritual abilities.

When you go on a pilgrimage, to place yourself in a vortex of cosmic power, it is obvious that the manner in which you travel becomes of vital importance. If you walk, as did many of the pilgrims of old, humbly, openly, sharing with those you meet along the way, travelling not just expecting to receive but also to give, to give of your energy to the centre of power, then out of that meek and humble attitude can be born an experience of great transformation. However, if you go self-centeredly to the place of pilgrimage, wanting only to receive or to impose your understanding of life on it, then you will severely limit what you will receive. But for those who are truly open there can come a moment of great transformation that can turn a Saul into a Paul. A great exchange of energy will take place as you align your physical and spiritual being with the power emanating from that holy centre, for as you offer up your energy to your Creator, as you offer up your physical and spiritual being to Its service, so there descends from the Heavens above the power of your Creator to purify and energise you, to send you forth renewed and revitalised, as messengers of Its divine light.

Let us recognise, therefore, that a significant exchange of energy takes place when you go on a pilgrimage. At another time I have likened the process of pilgrimage to that of the bees. Although a bee flies from flower to flower seeking pollen for itself, what else is that bee doing? By the very act of going from flower to flower, from centre to centre, it is also pollinating the flowers and promoting the growth of the flower kingdom. In a similar fashion, when you go on a pilgrimage, you too are giving and taking in the eternal process of life. You give of your energy and receive cosmic energy in return. You give of your spiritual being, and receive from the spiritual energy of the centre.

At this time in the world many people are embarking on pilgrimages of great importance. They are important for many reasons. Firstly, because a pilgrimage is a microcosm of the macrocosm, for you are all on pilgrimages and what else is your whole life but a pilgrimage. Your whole life is, in reality, a spiritual journey from birth to death and when you embark on a specific pilgrimage within that life, then, it becomes a point of focus, a moment in time when you become aware of that greater pilgrimage. A pilgrimage, therefore, becomes a journey to a place of peace, to a moment of outer death, a time when you go carefully over the nature of your life so far, just as you go over the nature of your whole life after death.

A pilgrimage is a time for meditating on the struggles and sacrifices that you have made in order to reach that place of pilgrimage, for examining your motivation for going on the pilgrimage, for sharing openly with your fellow pilgrims along the way, for recognising that people from different races, from different countries, from different religions and beliefs, can all unite as one in a common purpose to sacrifice to the one God. It is therefore a great opportunity for understanding the nature and the purpose of Humanity, and in that you share openly and fully with your fellow pilgrims, who of course are with you not by chance, for it is in the nature of the Divine Plan that you have all chosen to be there, to give to each other, so you will understand the nature of your being through receiving the nature of their being. A pilgrimage, therefore, can prove to be a great moment of personal revelation.

Pilgrimage at this time is also significant because there will be days in the not too distant future when it will not be possible to go on pilgrimages to many of the holy sites. It will not be possible, firstly, because there will not be the opportunity for long distance travel, either financially or politically, secondly, because most people, faced with serious problems both in the world and in their own country, will want to stay home and, finally, because in the great Earth changes that are to come many of the holy places to which people go on pilgrimages today will be removed from the surface of the Earth only to reappear, of course, in another Age, in another time.

The significance of you, who have all travelled from countries far removed from Britain, being present here in Glastonbury today, is that you have come in order to tap into the source of cosmic energy that is grounded here on another level. It can be compared to plugging yourselves into a source of electrical power. The result of this is that when you depart from Glastonbury at the end of your pilgrimage you will have forever attuned yourselves to this power, and in your moments of meditation, in your own rooms, in your own homes, in your own countries, when you close your eyes and go deeply into the stillness of your being, you will find that you will have become as one with this source of power, with what it has to give to you, with what you have to give to it. You will have established a communication link that will last for eternity.

Recognise that over the course of your many lives you will have visited many similar places of power and that you will recall the experience of them even now in your soul memories. Many of you are here today because you have been here before, because you have witnessed the significant events that have taken place both here and in other centres of cosmic energy. It is because of the nature of the ending of this Age, with its moment of cataclysmic transformation, with its moment of karmic transmutation, that you return to this centre of power to seek its energy. It represents for you all an act of renewal, an act of commitment. Your pilgrimage here is a statement of your spiritual being, a statement of your purpose and intent.

So this pilgrimage is an opportunity for you to go deeply into the nature of your own being and to share with those who travel with you of your inner feelings and thoughts, of that which you are receiving from this centre of power. Remember, however, even though you are all pilgrims together, that for each one of you the experience will be unique and, probably, quite indescribable. It could be that the understanding of the experience will be something that will come to you perhaps weeks, months or even years after the event. Your pilgrimage can be likened to an acorn seed planted in the ground. You have no concept of the mighty oak that will grow from that little seed.

You live in a world that demands instant performance, instant creation, instant satisfaction. So it can be very illuminating to consider the example of the acorn. Although the acorn is small in size, let us remember the energy, the potential, that is contained within that seed. When planted in the ground that seed will, in time, become a mighty oak tree. So within its being is the total plan, is the total design and purpose of its being. It is the same with you. Within your spirit which is so much smaller than the acorn is a potential that is far greater than the oak tree. Only a few of you have begun to realise the nature of that potential, the potential of your Creator which lies within you all. Recognise that that potential is there waiting to be used and that you are the ones that have to discover it. That is why you feel the need to embark on pilgrimages such as this. You place yourselves on a special journey, on a journey of self-discovery, to discover the truth of your own being and the nature of your own spirit.

A pilgrimage, therefore, is a moment of great significance in your life. For many people it can prove to be a turning point, a change of direction, a change of career, a change of residence, a change of being. It is a time when the old falls away to reveal the new. This is especially true of this great power centre of Glastonbury, whose emblem is the phoenix, the mythical bird which consciously burns itself on a pyre so that it can rise renewed from the ashes. For it is here that you can become aware of the true significance of death, of the fact that the old being, the old form, has to die and fall away before the new, the more majestic, the more spiritual being, can come forth. You can learn that there is great release in this moment of apparent death, for in that you die to your personality selves, in that you release the images that you have created of yourselves, the conditioning of the world in which you live, all that you have been taught as being 'truth' by your parents, by your teachers, by the society in which you live, in that you can release all of that and be open to the new, to the energy of this place, so you will emerge both transfigured and transformed.

At this time, therefore, in this year, in this Age, to go on such a pilgrimage as you are now embarked upon is a great blessing. Recognise that it is a blessing not only that you have sought but also that you have earned. It can prove to be a time of great transformation for those who are open, for those who go beyond their normal senses, for those who listen to their innermost beings, to that part of themselves which they rarely seek or communicate with. A pilgrimage can be a time of great revelation, a time when you can truly be uplifted into the divinity of your own being.

Every pilgrimage, therefore, is a pilgrimage to the Source of all Life, to Infinite Spirit Itself. Every pilgrimage is a time for being open to that Source and, when you receive from It, for being humble and, above all, thankful for that which has been given to you, the blessing of your Creator. It is a time for remembering the sacred promise of your

Creator that you are forever joined to the Godhead, that you are never alone unless you choose to be so, that you never have to search for your God because your God is already within you, that your needs are met before you even think to ask for them. It is in that certain knowledge that you can safely place yourself in the fire of transformation and become a pilgrim.

QUESTIONS AND ANSWERS

Q: Why is Glastonbury a spiritual centre?

ZT: You have to understand the reason behind the creation of, what you would call, a power centre. Power centres are created on the Earth to fulfil Divine Will. What you know as geometry, mathematics, the science of the universe, decides the nature and the position of a centre of power on the Earth and, therefore, its purpose in what could be called the cosmic Grid System. In essence, these centres of cosmic power are transformers of energy, both above and below the human frequency range. They ground and transform cosmic energy for human use. The ancient peoples recognised these centres of power because they, with a greater inner sight than you have today, could see the flows of such energy. They realised that by invocation and prayer at these centres, they could increase, direct and use, either constructively or destructively, the power that emanated from them. So Glastonbury has been the centre of many significant events because it is a centre of power. That is why people are attracted to it on an inner level. Of course, it is only one of many centres of power situated all over the world. It has no pre-eminence over all the other centres of power except in one respect. It is a centre of power which will control the focus of energy for the coming New Age, the Age of Aquarius.

Q: So power centres are to be found all over the world?

ZT: Yes. As you look at your physical body you are aware of the centres of energy which exist within it on a higher level, sometimes known as chakras. They are comparable to the main organs of your physical body, your heart, your lungs etc. Now countries are just like people. They have their organs, their chakras, their places of power, their centres of activity and creativity. Every country has what you

185

would call an etheric grid, a system of power lines which govern the structure of its being. If you look at any country, on an etheric level, you can see a sight comparable to an x-ray photograph of the human body. You can see the inner etheric pattern of the country. So a pilgrimage in any country becomes, in a sense, a journey of self-exploration, of awareness, of your country's higher being. It is also a journey of self-discovery, as the Master has just said, because you are an integral part of your country. Depending on your point of consciousness you will be attracted to an appropriate centre of power in your country. That is why people are attracted to differing places of power within a certain country.

Q: It was mentioned that the forthcoming Earth changes would make some power centres disappear. Could you explain what was meant by that please?

ZT: This planet is approaching a time in its evolutionary cycle when it will change dramatically, rather like a snake throwing off its old skin. Every so many thousands of years, no matter whether Humanity is in incarnation on the Earth or not, this planet goes through a metamorphic change as part of its natural cycle. As your physical body replaces itself every seven years, so does the planet's body. This is essential for the planet in order to preserve the creative, the reproductive nature of its being. So at its appointed time the planet goes through a cycle of transformation. This involves movement of the planet's landmasses, movement of the waters, and the restructuring of the matter of the Earth.

Now, in that Humanity lives on the Earth, it is affected by and, indeed, affects this process. For example, if Humanity were to explode nuclear weapons of a significant size upon the Earth, the surface of the Earth would be dramatically affected. Therefore the need for the soil to be both cleansed and renewed would be accelerated and the planet would respond to this threat to its fertility. Please understand that the Earth is not an insentient, powerless being. The Lord of this planet, that being who you know as Mother Earth, the Goddess, is a great planetary being, possessing profound wisdom and power. By the invocation of a single word she can transform the whole nature of her being. Ultimately, although she has released partial dominion to Humanity, she controls the planet and the nature of what manifests on its surface. Nature is her nature. She allows Humanity to mistreat her being at this time as part of Humanity's evolutionary lesson, but at any time she can take back the authority that she has extended to Humanity, the more so if the very safety of the planet is threatened.

Anyone looking with an aware eye can see that the planet needs to be revitalised, regenerated, made new. If Humanity continues to abuse the environment in the way that it is now doing then the day will soon arrive when it will be difficult, not just for Humanity, but for all lifeforms, to sustain life. So be aware that this moment of rebirth is coming. The timing and the nature of the changes are known only to God. Whilst Humanity can, and will influence these changes, it can not and will not prevent their happening. The test for Humanity lies in its acceptance of the Earth changes as a natural and necessary happening, as an event which it has chosen to experience.

Q: If just one in one hundred people were aware and would direct their energies to the healing of the planet, would this be enough to save the world?
ZT:You must understand that there are two cycles of evolution that are in operation at this time – Humanity and the Earth. The Earth's cycle would take place whether Humanity lived on its surface or not. It is a natural cycle which affects all the planets in our solar system. Humanity's cycle is peculiar to Humanity and is part of an ongoing evolutionary process on many levels of existence, in many Ages, which is designed to lead Humanity back to God consciousness, to merging with the Source of its creation. At this time in history the Earth's and Humanity's destinies interlock.

Now you talk of the concept of a small percentage of Humanity changing and of this changing the world and its destiny. Just one person on the Earth, by uplifting their point of consciousness, their soul note, will change the whole consciousness of Humanity. As you uplift your being, so you uplift the whole Human Race. Every least sacrifice made helps to transform the whole Human Race. But the human cycle is separate from the Earth's cycle. Whilst Humanity's behaviour in thought, word and deed modifies the nature of the Earth's cycle, it cannot prevent it from taking place. You cannot stop a natural process from taking place, unless you are a God, of course! You cannot stop the process of birth and death, and so it is with the Earth. So do not think of the events that are to come in terms of desirable or undesirable, as something that can be invoked or avoided. Rather, just as a woman cannot stop her own menstrual flow, so you cannot stop the menstrual flow of the Earth.

Q: The real problem is, Zen Tao, that the whole concept of a cataclysmic change causes great fear in some people, because they see it as the ending of life. How do you combat that?

ZT: You cannot change human consciousness and how people feel. If you, as an individual, fear death, then you will fear any form of cataclysmic change. If you believe that you are the master of this world, the master of your own destiny, in fact the master of creation, then you will fear any understanding which denies those beliefs. If, however, you have come to an understanding of death, if you see it as a natural event which leads to spiritual transformation and a return to the planes of existence where you truly belong, then what is there to fear? How can you not welcome death as a friend, for death returns you to the Source from whence you came. If you did but know it, death is the greatest gift that your Creator could bestow upon you.

Remember that Earth is a school of life. Just as you go to school on Earth at a certain age and leave at a certain age, so you do the same in the greater school of life called Earth, only you enter and leave at a soul age rather than a physical age. You pass through different classrooms as you grow older, you take your exams and then you leave to face the challenge of adult life. Earth, like school, is designed for people of a certain age. When you have outgrown your school, when you have learned your lessons, then you leave it to pass on to higher things. There is no need to return unless you are going to return as a teacher, to share of your knowledge with the people who are then in the school.

So, disconcerting though it might seem, if you were to return to Earth at exactly the same time in the cycle, only the next time around, life, to all intents and purposes, would be just the same. The school does not change, only the souls who are passing through it in order to learn the lessons of the Earth. So the purpose of entering this school of life called Earth is to learn its lessons. Be thankful for the experience, be grateful to those who provide and run the school, and then go forth with your new-found knowledge to create on other planes of existence. The Masters who incarnate on the plane of Earth are only way-showers. In spite of their great powers they do not transform the Earth. That is not their role. They invite you, by their example, to follow in their footsteps. They might take on some of the karma of the world in order to ease the human burden, but they don't prevent fresh karma from being created.

Q: I don't believe that.

ZT: That is your birthright and it should not be otherwise! You must always exercise your powers of discrimination in all respects.

Q: We are travelling as a group on this pilgrimage. What can we do to share the message that we have received as a group when we return to our own countries as individuals?
ZT: When you return to your own countries you do not consciously have to do or say anything unless you wish to share of your experiences with your friends at home. By placing yourself in the energy of a power centre you have already set in motion a whole process of transformation which will bear fruit at an appropriate time in the future. So do not feel that you have to teach anything. Do not feel that you have to change people. As was the case with the disciples, when they received the grace of God, after the death of Jesus, they were obviously ready to receive it, but it was the power coming down through them at the appropriate time that in turn gave them the power to speak in tongues, to go out and heal the sick, to teach all those who sought their guidance and wisdom. When you are ready, you will be used. Of that I can assure you! There is a great need for true servers on the Earth at this time.

Q: Some people feel that even holding the thought of a cataclysm in one's mind is a negative thing and will draw it down to us. What do you say to this?
ZT: You must realise that no matter what concepts or visions you may have for the future, no matter what dreams you may have experienced, no matter what ideals you hold for Humanity, that none of them will come into being unless Humanity, individually and collectively, changes today. It is the behaviour of the Human Race today, in thought, word and deed, that attracts tomorrow. It is how Humanity treats the planet and the four Kingdoms that dwell upon it that will decide the nature of the Earth's being tomorrow. If you wish to have a new world order tomorrow then you must transform the world of today. It is the seeds that you sow now that will create the fruits of tomorrow. Tomorrow will never come, unless you live today rightly. So begin, today, right now, and begin with yourself. Transform yourselves and you transform the world, for you are the world, and the world is you.

   Finally, as I have said on so many occasions, the destiny of the Earth has been decreed, the drama has been written, and Humanity has no option but to accept it. The only choice that Humanity has in the matter is in how it reacts to the drama, how it receives it. One's attitude towards the great Earth Changes that are to come is determined by one's point of consciousness, one's understanding of the purpose of death and suffering. Many people see the Earth Changes as a positive rather than a negative event and welcome the cataclysm as a cleansing of the Earth and a transmutation of human karma. My advice to you would be to tell you not to worry about it. Just take each day as it comes and live it to the highest of your spiritual consciousness. Do not waste time and energy living in the future, rather, live today with consciousness, for today well-lived will create your vision of the future.

THE CHOICE OF MORTALITY
AND IMMORTALITY

You live in a time of great darkness. Many names, in many different religions and understandings of life, have been given to this period of time, names such as Kali Yuga, Armageddon, the Confluence Age, the Day of Judgement, and so on and so forth. It is a time when human understanding is being pushed to the limits of its boundaries. It is important, therefore, that you understand what is the nature of darkness. You know that when you enter a room that is dark you can experience that darkness, and yet by simply turning on an electric light, the darkness is instantly banished. But where has that darkness gone to? The potential for darkness is still there because if that light were to be turned off, the former darkness would immediately return. So we can see clearly that darkness is only the absence of light. It is not a state of reality. It is a state of illusion, which is there one minute and can be gone the next, and in your own personal lives you are only too aware of how a moment of darkness can be replaced by a moment of light and vice versa.

You must recognise, therefore, that to a large extent it is you, and you alone, that determines your periods of light and your periods of darkness. You have the ability to control your own personal light switch, so to speak, using the analogy of the electric light, and to decide whether you are to live in a state of darkness or in a state of light. Nevertheless, you should understand that the darkness has a great meaning and purpose for you, for it is only when you are in the darkness that you grow to understand and to appreciate the light. If you are one of those people who loves the sunlight, who likes to feel the sun's warmth on your skin and to observe Nature responding to the sun's energy, then if you were forced to live in an underground cave you would yearn for the sunlight. So you can appreciate how the absence of the light brings forth a yearning for it, an appreciation of it, and a desire never to be parted from it again.

The purpose of all darkness, therefore, is to lead you forth into a stronger yearning for the light. Truly, if you will but examine the nature of your own darkness, you will discover that it is illusory, that it is not of God, and by that I mean that it is not of God in the sense that God abolishes all darkness by Its very presence, by Its very Light. So the essence of darkness is that it can only exist where there is no light. At this time, when you are surrounded by so much darkness, it is difficult for you to realise that there is a light switch, so to speak, under your very control, namely your spiritual point of consciousness. You must recognise, of course, that the power of your consciousness, of your light alone, is not sufficient to light up the whole World and to remove all the darkness in that World. Nevertheless, in your own small world, you are the master of your own light switch and by the shining of your light you can illumine the darkness around you.

I would like you to understand clearly that in this struggle between the darkness and the light what you are in fact faced with is a choice between mortality and immortality. For it is that which is eternal or immortal, which knows no limits, which knows no form, that is the light, and it is that which is mortal, which has limits, which can be defined in form, that is the darkness. This darkness, therefore, only exists on what is called the physical plane of life. Beyond this plane of life, after physical death, there is no darkness, only light. It is only on the physical plane of life that you have to face this great test of darkness. It is, therefore, you, and you alone, that decides the nature of your light and the nature of your darkness. It is you, and you alone, that can apply the great test of mortality or immortality to every action in your life and so determine your own light and your own darkness.

I wonder if any of you have really understood the full implication of immortality, if you truly recognise, not as an intellectual concept but as an integral part of your whole being, that you are immortal? If you truly can accept that you were in existence before birth, that you will be in existence after death and that, even now, whilst dwelling on the physical plane of life, you are also dwelling on other planes, then you have recognised the immortality of your spirit. You have understood the promise of your Creator that It will never extinguish your spirit, that you are an eternal being of light. If you have reached that point of consciousness when you know that you will never die, when you know that even if you were to lose your physical body you would still live on other planes of existence, then you must also recognise the illusory nature of everything that exists on the physical plane of life, which is so very mortal. You must also recognise that the material possessions which you covet so greatly are all illusory, that they can never be regarded as permanent, that they will all decay into the matter of the Earth from which they came.

In your brief physical lives you are constantly faced with the choice of having to decide just what it is in life that is important to you, just what really matters to you. Is it the size of your house and the quality of the furnishings in it, how much money you have in the bank, the make and year of your car, the good opinion of your friends, the recognition of your intellectual prowess by your peers, the achievements of your children and so on? Are these the aspects of physical life that are important to you? Are these the qualities of life to which you have become attached? Or is a deeper understanding of life beginning to make its presence felt? Is the feeling beginning to emerge that behind all these physical attachments there exists an eternal being that has quite a different set of values?

On many occasions in the past I have said that you come into this world only with consciousness and that you leave this world only with consciousness. Everything else between birth and death is but modelling clay in your hands, the physical aspects of matter with which you play and learn your lessons in this school of life called Earth. Now whilst, of course, you must respect every aspect of physical matter that is placed in your guardianship, for you are divine beings and have been given dominion over the three Kingdoms of Matter, nevertheless, you should also realise the temporality, the mortality, of those Kingdoms. You should understand the nature of their molecular structure, the nature of their intelligence and the nature of their divine purpose.

Above all, you should realise that you, as human beings, are here on one quest, on one quest alone, and that is the quest for consciousness. For as you die, so you will be born again. Everything and everybody that you have not released in this life will be with you in your next life. All the karma that you have not transmuted in this life will have to be faced again in future lives, whereas all the karma that you have transmuted, released and learned from in this life will be gone forever. Recognise, therefore, that the nature of the consciousness that you take with you at your moment of death is of supreme importance, and that if the remembrance that you take with you is of your physical possessions, your physical achievements, your relationships with those you have loved and hated, the world in which you have lived, then you will surely return to those attachments in your next life.

193

The mark of an evolved soul, therefore, is that they are beginning to grow into an understanding of the necessity for not becoming attached to the material or physical aspects of life. They have reached that point of consciousness when they can begin to see that there is no such thing as perfection in this World and that even the greatest Master, on incarnating into this World, will, to a degree, become tainted by the World and will, to a degree, reflect some imperfection. So it is essential, at this most testing time, that you understand the nature of what is actually manifesting on the Earth, recognise the nature of its imperfection, and do not become attached to the results of that imperfection. You must recognise the immortality of your own being, the eternity of your own nature and the quest upon which you are now set.

In truth, what is this Earth but a questing place for consciousness and anything which distracts you from that quest should be regarded as a temptation. Of course an evolved soul can incarnate onto the physical plane of life and can choose, if it so wishes, to lead a life of wealth and luxury, a life of spiritual isolation. It can draw to itself everything that it needs on the physical plane. That, surely, was one of the great temptations or tests that the Master Jesus had to face. For with the cosmic powers at his command he could have had a vast temporal kingdom, together with all the temporal power, the wealth, the palaces and the servants, that he could have desired, coupled with the blind adoration and obedience of those who served him. Nevertheless, he chose to reject all of that, to give up that temporal path and to follow a path of sacrifice and service, in order that he could ground the Christ Consciousness on the plane of Earth.

Each of you is called upon to handle the physical matter of this Earth which is given to you by your Creator, according to your karmic needs. You should therefore respect every aspect of matter that comes into your aura, but at the same time do not forget that it is only modelling clay! It has simply been placed in your karmic pattern for your karmic needs. Remember that all matter is mortal and, therefore, is illusory. So if you become attached to that which is mortal and illusory, then you are doomed to a life of unhappiness, for you are continually questing for something that is not real. Your life becomes a process of desire after desire after desire. It is a wise person who sees clearly that on the physical, material level they can never be satisfied, that they can never have what they want because, by its inherent nature, it is illusory.

194

For example, you may spend a lot of time and money in order to buy the latest model car which has become the apple of your eye. But once you have acquired it, does not the pleasure that the car gives you begin to decline with the passing of time until, when the next model is produced a year later, along comes another desire and the first car is discarded even though there is no need for a change. But have you thought about the sacrifices of the Mineral and the Vegetable Kingdoms that were needed in order to make that car? Have you thought about what you yourself sacrificed to earn the money to buy that car? Have you ever considered how much of your immortal life you sacrifice for a mortal desire? Do you ever think about your fellow human beings all over the world, of their right to health and happiness, to the essential elements of life, and of how your lifestyle affects them? Do you ever think of the sacrifices that have to be made by other people so that you can achieve your short term desire? How much does the Western World today, with its vast financial and industrial empires, take from the rest of Humanity in order to satisfy its short term desires?

I want you to see very clearly that if you become attached to the desires of physical life, which I have shown to be illusory, then your state of being is doomed to rise and fall with the fulfilment of those desires. So you are basing your life on an illusion! It is the wise soul, therefore, that at this time, above all, can understand and practise the quality of non-attachment and, by that, I mean can differentiate between the immortality of the spirit and the mortality of every aspect of physical life around it. For the non-attached person understands that the physical aspects of life that are around them are mortal and are, therefore, illusory, and that to become attached to them or to the fruits of their actions is to invite suffering. The only attachment one can, and should, have is to God.

If you accept that God's Will manifests in every aspect of life around you, then you must also accept that the physical life that you are now experiencing is the very life that God wants you to face. It is the test that you have drawn to yourself, the understanding of life that you have come to learn. Life is God's Will for you this day. It is in the nature of how you respond to the day, your attitude to the day, that brings growth and evolution. So if you worship anything before your God, and by God I mean God's Will for you and for this planet, then you are doomed to a life of sorrow and grief because, inevitably, God's Will will be done, and if you have not aligned yourself with that Will, if you oppose that Will, then you will suffer. If you place anything – your husband, your

195

wife, your children, your relations, your country – before your God, then you are doomed to sorrow. Let us understand the nature of that sorrow. The sorrow lies in the fact that your desires for your family, for your relations, for your country, for your understanding of life, are not being fulfilled. You are unhappy because your will is not manifesting on the Earth, and yet how can your little will ever manifest on the Earth if it is subject to the greater Will of your Creator? So grow to recognise that it is the little wills of Man and Woman, the foibles of human desire, that create confusion and conflict in the World, and at the same time search for and try to align yourself with the Will of God which controls all things.

Now when I say that you should strive to be non-attached, I do not mean that you should isolate yourself from life, that you do not have compassion for whatever is manifesting around you. Compassion means passion for, passion with, understanding for the paths that others are walking, for their needs, for their spiritual requirements. You can truly look at a person who is suffering and give them your love and your understanding without having to identify with their suffering, without becoming a part of that suffering. You can do this in the knowledge that their lesson is not your lesson and that your support, your love, can help them to learn their lesson. It is not for you to remove that lesson, to block that lesson. It is for you to support the Will of God flowing through that person and that lesson.

If you become attached to your own ideas of creation, to your own ideas of God, to your own concepts of life, then inevitably there will be sorrow. Most people in the World today are totally attached to their mortality, to their thought forms, to their desires. Are you not even now full of physical desires – the desire for material possessions, the desire for happy relationships, the desire for peace on this Earth? Yet those desires are born out of your mortality and not your immortality, for what is the death of even your husband or your wife in the scale of immortality? What is the death of even a country in the eternity of the Divine Plan for human evolution? It is the wise soul, therefore, who knows that death is but a moment of rebirth. I want you to see clearly that out of every death there is a birth. That is the promise of immortality. That is why you are eternal beings. As you die, so you are born again. As you descend into the physical matter of life at birth, so you have the divine promise of life after your physical death. As you enter into this school of life on Earth, so you know that you will have to leave it, one day, when your lessons are learned, to return again to your true form, to your true spiritual home. That is the promise of immortality and if you really understand and live life as an immortal being then you are living a life without fear. Fear, basically, is a lack of faith in your immortality. Fear is a lack of understanding that the nature of life is immortality.

The essence of non-attachment, therefore, lies in the understanding of the quality of immortality. It lies in the recognition that God's will, which is immortal, that God's Plan, which is eternal, manifests on this Earth and that you, as divine beings, are part of that Plan and can therefore never know death. I wish you to see clearly, especially at this time when there is so much violent death and suffering in the World, that truly all this darkness can be removed by the turning on of your own personal 'light switch'. The darkness is still there but the presence of the light has removed it. So grow to recognise the light and the darkness in your own being. See clearly how the presence of light in your own being removes your darkness, which is your fear, your greed, your pride, the darkness of those qualities in your being which you have yet to understand and master.

Above all, do not become attached to the world in which you live. Surely you can see that at this time of great change, where nothing is constant, where nothing is fixed, where the understanding of yesterday is soon replaced by the understanding of today, that to become attached to anything invites sorrow and suffering. If you become attached to your mortality, to that which is of the Earth, then you are doomed to suffer the results of change, for the things which you love, and from which you derive pleasure today, may not be here tomorrow. The past has gone forever and if you choose to live in the past then you are doomed to a life of unhappiness. You can, and must live today to the highest of your spiritual consciousness and as this day too passes, so release it and go forward to face the new day unencumbered by the loss of what has passed.

Great changes are coming. It is only the soul that is free from attachment that will comprehend the nature and the purpose of those changes, that will understand the nature and the purpose of life around it. It is only the soul that is free from attachment that will be capable of recognising the nature of its own immortality, that will be able to die with a true understanding of its being. The purpose of life is the gaining of consciousness and death is but the transfer of that consciousness onto a higher plane of life, on which you will create, yet again, in another form, in another dimension.

You are eternal beings of creation. You are not limited by this Earth or by your physical body. They are the tests which you have to face at this time. You are not of the Earth or of the body, for you are divine, you are gods in the making. Recognise your birthright. Become attached to that which is divine and is eternal, become non-attached to that which is of the Earth and is mortal, and in that you truly do that then you will be able to understand and release, in the twinkling of an eye, all that appears as darkness. The suffering that you perceive is the suffering that Humanity has created. Your God does not create suffering. Humanity suffers through its own ignorance, through its own lack of understanding of the true relationship of the human spirit with the human form. For those who truly recognise the divinity of both the form and the spirit there is Heaven on Earth, which is your birthright.

QUESTIONS AND ANSWERS

Q: I find it very hard to be non-attached to what I call environmental issues, because I feel it threatens human existence on the planet. For example, we know that certain countries are cutting down their rain forests. Should I be non-attached to the plight of the rain forests and not fight to preserve them? It seems to me that non-attachment can be a recipe for inaction.

ZT: Obviously it is a fact that the rain forests are being destroyed by Humanity's ignorance and avarice. Everyone knows that trees are being cut down and that this will affect the environment, but you also have to be aware that in the eternal scheme of things Nature will correct this temporary imbalance. The Goddess will take action to preserve her being and to restore balance to her Kingdoms. Humanity is just scratching the surface in the timescale of the Earth's evolutionary pattern. For example, are you aware of all the destruction caused by the civilisation of Atlantis? No! So recognise that the Earth, like your own physical body, has amazing powers of regeneration. So Humanity's pollution of the environment today is not a fatal disease, simply a passing illness.

Nevertheless, it is important that those of you who feel strongly about right relationship with the planet and about exercising right stewardship should work to the highest of your consciousness and ability to bring about public awareness of this situation and to change governmental attitudes. It is both right and proper that you should care, but you should take care not to become attached to the fruits of your actions. If you fight a long battle and then lose, do not feel that you have failed and become despondent. Do not let it affect other aspects of your life. Recognise that the Divine Plan supersedes your desires, no matter how pure is your motivation. All that you can do is to work from the highest of your being and to always act with probity. Everything that you do is part of your learning experience. That is why you are here. Finally, remember that nothing is ever lost. Every effort that you make, every least sacrifice that you make, uplifts the consciousness of Humanity and goes on your karmic record.

Q: So even if a rain forest is lost, Humanity can still gain in consciousness?
ZT: Yes.

Q: But surely the destruction of the rain forests is not part of God's Plan? Surely it is Humanity that is causing the destruction and God is just the observer of that. God is just allowing Humanity to do it.
ZT: If you accept that you are an aspect of God in physical manifestation, that God's energy impels every molecule of matter around you, that God's Will manifests on the Earth, then you must also accept that within the Divine Plan provision has been made for certain aspects of Nature to be sacrificed in order to further the evolution of human consciousness. Finally, please remember that life is not real. Nothing ever dies. Nothing is ever lost.

Q: So Humanity is allowed to make mistakes so that it can learn both from the mistakes and the consequences of those mistakes?
ZT: Yes, that is correct. It could be said, for example, that God does not want Humanity to fight wars. As each war that Humanity fights becomes more and more horrific, so many people pray to God to stop wars. Now you might suppose that such a prayer, from a sincere person, would be reason enough for God to intervene and stop a war, but God does not. Why should this be so? Firstly, because Humanity would still continue to create the political climate in which war was the only solution and, secondly, because the death and sacrifice of every war provides Humanity with a great learning experience. Remember that no-one really dies in any battle, because the spirit never dies, and that the 'death' experience is a great vehicle for raising human

consciousness, both for those who partake of it and for those who observe it.

Q: Can you tell us when the Christ Consciousness will return to Earth and usher in the New Age of Aquarius?

ZT: When any human being is born there are really only two beings who know of the timing of that birth and they are the soul to be born and its Creator. Now many great beings have a profound knowledge of the plan for human evolution. There can therefore be many understandings, many interpretations, as to the timing of an event as significant as the return of the Christ Energy. However, such an event is not controlled by any earthly clock or calendar. Therefore, truly, no being knows the exact timing of such an event. What I can say, however, is that those of you who are open to the Christ Energy will sense a great shift of energy when that event does indeed occur. It will not be an instantaneous thing. The change will manifest over a period of one or two years, but people will suddenly become aware of a great shift in human emphasis, what I will call a relieving of pressure. It is rather like someone who has been seriously ill for a long time suddenly becoming aware that the healing process has begun and that their body is on the mend. So I believe that most people will not be aware of the Christ Energy until some time after Its birth.

Q: The Master spoke about lightness and darkness and the existence of positive and negative forces. Would you say that by following the light we are creating a positive force and that by following the darkness we are creating a negative force? Or is it the case that darkness is a complete absence of any force?

ZT: When I use terms such as light and darkness I am being allegorical. I use them in the sense of flowing with Divine Will as being light, and flowing against Divine Will as being darkness. The energy of creation is there for all to use. It is how you use that energy that creates, allegorically, light and darkness. Now there are some people who talk about the forces of darkness, about Satan and the Devil, about fallen angels and black magicians, as being forces that God fights against. Let us understand that these forces are all part of God's Plan. They are not outside of God's Love, God's Energy and God's Will. They exist in order to test Humanity, firstly, by presenting you with an alternative path so that you might have a choice to make between 'good' and 'evil' and, secondly, so that you can learn from reacting to them. Do you want to run away from evil or destroy it? Do you want to overpower evil or transmute it? Again, what is important is your reaction to it.

Now there are beings and forces that are called upon to play testing roles. You have all played such roles yourself. There has to be a Judas in order to test a Jesus. Do you think that the soul of Judas, when it was choosing its destiny before birth, was very keen to play that role! So one should never judge evil. One can only shine one's own light in the face of evil, always with the purpose of transforming, never of destroying. Understand that there are beings who use God's energy negatively, that is by opposing God's Will, but that that too is part of God's Will. The saturnic or satanic forces, the testing side of life, are only part of this present cycle. They are not a permanent facet of human evolution. The time will soon come when they will no longer exist.

Q: Will that be in the Golden Age?
ZT: Yes, but they will return again in a later cycle! I wish you to see clearly that in any aspect of life, be it good or bad, what is always being tested is your attitude towards it.

Q: In the East people seem to be taught and prepared for dying, but in the West it is considered a traumatic and a terrible thing. How can we teach people to die and to pass over into the spirit world in a serene way?
ZT: I think it would be true to say that there is just as much fear of death in the East as there is in the West. There may be a different attitude towards death but the fear of death is quite universal. Why should this be so? Because, ultimately, an understanding of death is based entirely on one's point of soul consciousness. Certainly, here in the West, death is regarded as an unfortunate event, rather like an illness, and so one's children and friends are pushed away from it, because it might even be contagious! Death is regarded as being unnatural and so people must be shielded from it. The Master has just said that you only understand the purpose of death if you understand the purpose of life. If you think that this life is your only existence, then you obviously fear its ending. Whereas if you think of death as a beginning, then what is there to fear? You look forward to the event with eager anticipation.

So how you face death, especially your own death, is a very unique and personal thing. All that any individual can do is to be open to the

201

death experience, to see clearly what is the reality of death, to sweep aside all the illusion that surrounds it. After death, some people are made up to look better in death than they did in life! This, surely, negates the whole purpose of death. It must be understood that death is a natural process. Every being, every thing, in physical manifestation, dies. At an early age children should be led gently into an understanding of death, firstly through the Vegetable Kingdom, then through the Animal Kingdom and, finally, with the Human Kingdom. Nature is a great tool of learning and can offer great insight into the process of death.

Ultimately, of course, every one of you has to learn to face death on a daily basis, because if you are not prepared to die today, then you are not prepared for life. You are not living life correctly. If you are not living in the moment, then you are not living in correct relationship with your family, your friends, your country and so on. The essence of life is that one dies to the moment that has passed because one has lived it completely, because one has fulfilled one's spiritual responsibility towards it. So you prepare for death by dying today! For the aware soul the day that you die is just like any other day, for death is not the ending of life, but is a moment of transition, before you become conscious of a new life and a new beginning.

Q: After the Golden Age you said there would be another testing time. Why does Humanity have to start all over again? Will there never be an end?

ZT: You are infinite beings. How can the infinite have an ending? As far as reincarnating on the Earth over and over again goes, that is up to you. Humanity returns to the Earth for three basic reasons. Firstly, to transmute the karma of actions in past lives and to restore the karmic balance. Secondly, to learn of your Creator, and therefore of yourself, through the manifestations and experiences of physical life. Thirdly, to help those who have not progressed to your point of soul consciousness. So if you have learned the lessons of this planet and discharged all your karma, there is no need to return. You can get off the cycle of birth and rebirth. But I have to tell you that for many of you that is still some way off in the future!

Q: It seems to me that one of the major problems in the world today is that people are not fighting evil. Is it not the case that the forces of evil are triumphing because the forces of good are not standing up and fighting?

ZT: You have to understand, as the Master has just said, the nature of goodness and evil, of positive and negative energy. It is not a question of winning and losing, rather, it is a question of what is your Creator's Will for the planet at this time, of what are the spiritual lessons that Humanity has the need to learn. Sometimes the lessons of one group of souls takes precedence over the lessons of another. Sometimes a sacrifice has to be made in order to fulfil a higher purpose. Do not confuse the immediate effects of an action with the long term fruits of that action. Remember the example of the Master Jesus. At the time it would have appeared to the early Christians that evil had triumphed, even to the extent of crucifying the Living Christ, but we who have the benefit of hindsight can see that that was not the case.

So do not think that evil ever triumphs or that goodness ever fails. There is truly no gain or loss situation. Both are simply learning experiences. In the world in which you live today, where there are so many unevolved souls in physical incarnation, it is inevitable that at times the more evolved souls feel swamped. There is this feeling of 'When will Humanity ever learn?', as yet another country goes to war, as yet one more religion persecutes another, as yet more of the environment is irreversibly destroyed. Do not become attached to your point of consciousness. Do not be like the student who has just entered university and who treats the younger children just entering primary school with both scorn and intolerance, forgetting that he, too, was once like them. All that you can do in any situation like this is to act with the highest of motivation from your point of consciousness and to recognise that the destiny of the planet and of the Human Race are in the safe hands of your Creator. God's Will will manifest on Earth as it does in Heaven.

UNDERSTANDING FEAR

I am going to talk to you about something that you have to contend with every minute of the day that you are awake, and that is fear. I wonder if you have ever really considered just how much fear plays a part in your life, indeed, how much of your life is actually governed by fear. Have you ever thought it necessary to investigate what is the cause of fear, whether fear is a necessary or even a desirable emotion? Finally, have you ever spent time on seeking a way to handle your fears, for it is only when you understand the origins of fear that you will be able to lead your life in peace – a peace which is your birthright. I am now going to suggest to you that there are in essence two kinds of fear – physical and psychological. Let us examine this.

Physical fear is that which pertains to the physical body and is closely allied to instinct. Physical fear is concerned only with the present, with what you are actually sensing at any given moment in time. It is, perhaps, best demonstrated by the Animal Kingdom for an animal, whilst being alert to protect itself from danger at all times, does not live in a state of fear. But when that animal is challenged or is frightened in some way then it follows its instincts and either flees or else responds by challenging that which is causing it fear. It can be said that thought or reason plays no part in this action. It is a natural response to the situation in which the animal finds itself. Unlike human beings an animal is not capable of analysing the cause of the fear. It responds instinctively.

Humanity, of course, being in an animalistic body also has its instincts. You can all remember incidents in your own life when you have experienced physical rather than psychological fear. Perhaps you were walking home on a dark night and were startled by something. Perhaps you were travelling in a plane and were suddenly placed in a life threatening situation. In both these cases you were confronted by something which, at first, caused you to respond instinctively, but if you were able to analyse what was causing the fear and to understand its origins and how much of a threat it constituted to you, then the fear soon disappeared. Nevertheless, for a few moments in time you would probably have responded instinctively. Your physical body would also have responded to such a situation by increasing the flow of adrenalin, thus enabling you to do things you would not normally have been able to do, like swim a great distance to avoid drowning or jump a great height into a tree to avoid being attacked by a wild animal. That is the response of the human physical body to such a challenge.

For the most part, however, Humanity has tended to replace instinct by thought. This, after all, is what differentiates the Human Kingdom from the Animal Kingdom. The Animal Kingdom not possessing the ability to think rationally relies solely on instinct, whereas Humanity can analyse and compare, can create mentally and inspirationally, can project itself into both past and future, and can in fact create its own reality. So for the most part Humanity allows thought to over-rule its physical instincts and this characteristic, indeed, is demanded by its evolutionary pattern and cosmic status.

Let us now consider the nature of psychological fear. You all know so well your deep psychological fears: fear that your child may die, fear that a loved one will reject you, fear that a husband or wife will desert you, fear of catching a disease, fear that you will lose your wealth or a possession which you prize above all else. Then there are the fears that are associated with time: will I be able to achieve what I want to achieve in the time that I think is available to me, will the world situation in ten years time be so bad that my financial security will be threatened. Finally, in the world in which you live today, where there is so much personal and national conflict, where everyday the papers are full of reports of gory accidents, of murders, of droughts, famines and earthquakes, where human violence and degradation is daily brought to your attention, there is this fear that perhaps such events will happen to you. The net result of all these fears is that a strong desire is created within you as to how to avoid such events, as to how to protect yourself from the world around you. Instinct as a means of protection is, of course, usually ruled out because instinct is not deemed as being adequate enough in the conditions that prevail in the world today.

So it would probably be true to say that most people are concerned mainly with psychological fear. Now I want you to see very clearly that this is not a fear of the moment in which you are living, because if you were challenged in any way at this very second in time you would respond. You would face that challenge. You would not panic or surrender to your 'animal' instincts, you would use the rational power of thought to face the challenge. So recognise that psychological thought is concerned solely with the past or the future. It is concerned with the past in that if you have done something of which you are ashamed then you fear that it will be discovered, that past inadequacies will be revealed to humiliate you before your friends today. It is concerned with the future in that because the future is unknown you cannot control it. You do not know what lies in store for you and therefore you fear that you will lose something that you prize even above your own soul being, and that something is usually either a material or a psychological possession.

So when we come down to the root cause of fear we realise that the fear which causes the most grief is the fear of the unknown. If you know what is going to happen to you, then you are not fearful. If, for example, you were about to make a plane journey and, for whatever reasons, you were frightened of flying, if you were able to see into the future and to know that you were going to arrive at your destination safely, then there would be very little fear. Similarly, if you were very ill and were concerned about your health and your future lifestyle, if you were able to see into the future and to see yourself living a healthy and active life, then, again, there would be very little fear.

Let me give you another example. If someone was chasing after you and you believed that they were going to attack you, then that situation would be a fearful one. But if you then realised that you had dropped your purse and they were chasing after you to return it to you, then that knowledge immediately removes the fear! So we can see very clearly that knowledge removes fear. What you know, you do not fear. You only fear that which you do not know, the unknown, and what is the unknown but the creations of your mind, your own unique thoughts about what constitutes a threat to you, about what would happen to you *if* certain events were to take place. So, in fact, you create your own fears and you create them not out of a response to reality but out of a response to your concept of the future which, in all probability, is wrong.

If knowledge removes fear, then how are you to obtain that knowledge, how are you to discover the reality either of the past or of the future? Your knowledge of the past is contained within your physical brain cells, your memory, which is both highly subjective and highly selective. Your knowledge of the future is non-existent because your physical brain, having not yet experienced the future, has no understanding of it. So the only knowledge that you have, in this life anyway, is based on your experience of the life that you have lived up to this moment in time. Now if, for example, your life has been one associated with wealth and many possessions, and if this situation has given meaning and purpose to your life, then, obviously, you would be fearful of losing that wealth and those possessions because you believe that they are your security and that you could not live without them. So your life would be controlled on a subconscious level by this overwhelming fear.

When you come to terms with your fears, what is being challenged, therefore, is your understanding of the world in which you live, your earthly knowledge. But there is another source of knowledge within your being that can help you to handle your fears, namely, your spirit. For you are dwelling, even now, within your spiritual body, which links you to the Source of all Life, Which knows all things past, present and future, Which does not even see separation between past, present and future, for time is purely an earthly measurement. Your spirit will lead you into a true understanding of your fears. It will not cause your fears to slip away, for they are part of your psychological being and are very real, but it will sound another understanding of life and will give you a wider perspective of your fears. Your spirit, being linked to the Source of all Life, will bring the Source of all Life into your life. You will grow to recognise the great truth that fear is simply a lack of trust in your Creator. When you are not as one with your Creator then there is room for fear. If you can accept that fact then you can understand and come to terms with your every fear.

Consider the situation or the person that you fear most in all the world. Now what would be your reaction if you had to face it or them right now? Would you really be fearful or would not the fear disappear in the face of that reality and would you not then summon up every ounce of your physical and spiritual being in order to meet that challenge with right action? Have you ever considered what would happen if you had to come to terms with your greatest fear – death? Have you ever asked yourself why you fear this one certainty in your life? For if there is one thing that is certain in your life it is that you are going to die! Why do you fear not just your own death but the death of your loved ones and friends. If, like you, they are all going to die at some time, if, like you, they have to leave this physical plane of life as part of the natural cycle of their being, then why do you fear their going?

You fear their going, basically, because you do not understand the reason for their going. You do not have the knowledge as to why they have decided to die, as to why they have decided to leave this school of Earth. How many of you, if faced with the serious illness of your child, would be fearful if you had the knowledge as to why that child had taken on the illness and why it had decided to die? You can see, therefore, that spiritual knowledge, the knowingness of your Creator, removes fear. You can also see that this knowledge has nothing whatsoever to do with physical memory, that it comes from a very different source. It is not an accumulation of all your physical experiences so far. It is a tapping into the source of Infinite Experience Itself, and what is the source of that Experience but your Creator, that Being Whom, you refer to as God.

So where there is union with Infinite Knowledge, where there is union with God, there can be no fear. That is why fear can be defined as the absence of God or, rather, as the absence of a trust in God, for if you are linked to the Source of all Life there is no place for fear. If you are empowered and motivated by your spirit, by the force of God in motion within you, then you have knowledge of all of God's creations and manifestations. Now, of course, as you face the problems and tests of everyday living you will frequently have to act without this certain knowledge. There will be times when you will have to take a step forward in what you call faith – not blind faith but certain faith. Knowing the force of God in motion as you do, having opened yourself and your intuitive process to the wisdom of Its Being, feeling that this is the correct action to take, you will proceed in faith. After such a step observe very closely to see whether the world around you supports or denies your action, to see whether you are at one with the flow of the Universe.

You should never take action out of fear, for that means that you are not taking action in the moment but rather out of fear for what you think may happen in the future, a future that exists only in your own mind, a future that is based purely on your projection of the present. Be aware that any action that is not grounded in your present reality, that is based on what I call psychological as opposed to real time, is motivated by fear and will indeed only lead to further fear. Recognise that for the person who is linked to the God within and who has true awareness of the moment in time that they are experiencing, who has a spiritual understanding of the life that they are living, there can be no fear.

The most precious thing that you can possess, therefore, is a knowledge of your Creator. For if that knowledge removes fear then just think how much of your time will be released for spiritual growth and learning. Think of how your relationships will change overnight. Think of how you will look afresh at your husband or wife, at your children, at your possessions, at your own needs for material security. Think of how you will look at the world anew. So recognise that the end-purpose of knowledge, therefore, is the abolition of fear, for fear can only function in the unknown. When you know, you no longer fear. When your thoughts, words and deeds are motivated by Divine Will then there is no place for fear. A person that is fearful cannot act with the same power as a person who is at one with the Source of all Life. A person who lives in fear cannot function effectively on any level. When you see a person acting out of spiritual knowledge you see a Master of this plane of life. When you see a person acting as one with God, demonstrating the I AM God presence in the world, you see a being that has abolished fear.

It is the birthright of every human being to live without fear. You are only fearful if you choose to be so. Therefore if you are a fearful person examine the cause of your worst fear. Spend time and energy processing that fear, for in that you acknowledge and come to terms with your worst fear you will establish the understanding and the knowledge to handle all your other fears. So many of you live from fear to fear. As one fear is removed you create another fear and the process multiplies with the diversity of your fears. A person who is fearful is helpless and cannot help another but a person who is fearless can change the world, can influence the course of history, for what is there to fear when you act as one with God?

There are many things in the world at this time which can create fear. There are many karmic situations coming that will create even greater fear. Fear can be likened to a contagious disease that can quickly spread and affect many people. So it is vital that all old souls who possess the knowledge and the wisdom of the Divine should stand forth and demonstrate that fear is not a part of their being. All young souls should try to understand the root cause of fear, namely, a lack of trust in the Creator which created them and in the world in which they live. A Godless person is a fearful person. A God-filled person is a being of joy, a saviour of the world. I can say to you in all honesty that truly you have nothing to fear but yourself.

QUESTIONS AND ANSWERS

Q: On a soul level do we have fears? Is there such a thing as a soul fear?

ZT: The soul, which can be likened to the memory of spirit, is a record of all past life experiences. Now these experiences present themselves to your subconscious mind not as a specific recall of past life events but more as an instinctive feeling. It is this feeling which can be projected into the conscious mind as a physical fear. For example, if in one of your more recent lives you were, shall we say, burnt at the stake as a heretic or as a witch, then you would incarnate with a deep awareness of that death by fire and of the physical conditions that led to your death. These could manifest on the physical level either as a fear of fire or of putting yourself into a position were you could be persecuted for your spiritual beliefs. Moreover, if in this life you were again to meet the very souls who were responsible for your death, you would feel deep concern about them and would exercise great caution in your dealings with them. It is these feelings that can sometimes develop into psychological fear.

Q: So are you saying that it is these instinctive feelings that are the cause of all our fears?

ZT: No. I would like to draw a clear distinction between the instinct and the fear. You can have an instinctive feeling about someone you meet for two reasons. Firstly, there can be what I will call the animal instinct of your physical body which senses that that person threatens danger to you for whatever reasons. Secondly, there is the soul instinct which senses the nature of the person's soul and its capacity to challenge you as it has probably done in previous lives. Both of these instinctive feelings are telling you to exercise caution in your relationship with that person. Now whether or not you are fearful of that person is a different question altogether and it is here that you have to understand the nature of fear, as the Master has just said. For it is you, and you alone, that decides whether or not you are going to translate those instinctive feelings into fear.

If you have confidence in the protective power of Spirit and in your ability to invoke it, then what is there to fear? Moreover, even if that person does represent a threat to you, are you going to be fearful of that threat or are you going to consciously choose how you will handle that threat. To be fearful is not action, it is inaction. Time spent in fear is wasted. So recognise that instinct and fear are separate and that the one does not automatically lead to the other. You always have the choice either of being fearful of a person or a situation or of accepting that if you are truly guided and watched over, then, you are always in the right place, at the right time, to face the challenge that you need. So rather than being fearful, invoke the divine power that flows through you to give you the strength and the wisdom to correctly handle the situation in which you find yourself.

Q: But is it not possible to meet someone in this life and to be genuinely fearful of them because they have caused you great sorrow in a previous life, perhaps even murdered you? Is this not your soul protecting you?

ZT: Your soul holds the record of all your past lives, and of all the experiences that took place in them, both happy and unhappy. You receive these soul memories as impressions that impinge upon your conscious mind. It is often the case that one, two or even three complete incarnations can be devoted solely to transmuting or balancing out the soul memory of a previous life. For example, if in one of your previous lives you had had a very unhappy marriage, resulting in you being killed by your marriage partner, then that soul memory would require quite a lot of transmutation! So, to help balance out that soul memory, in your next life you could experience a marriage in very happy circumstances where, although on an inner level you would feel very wary of marriage and of your marriage partner, you would live to a ripe old age in happiness and contentment. The soul memory of this life would then help to balance out the record already created.

All human beings possess this soul memory but, of course, it manifests in different beings to different degrees. An evolved person, one who is aware both of the existence and the purpose of the soul and of its import on physical life, will constantly be aware of the soul's presence manifesting in their everyday lives. They will have grown to recognise the presence of their soul memory just as they have grown to recognise the presence of their physical memory. They will be aware that the soul memory is not something of this life, but that it comes from an inner part of their being. With this understanding, it is important that both soul memory and physical memory are placed in their correct perspective and that their limitations are realised. Do not look at the present through the eyes of memory but rather allow the present to transmute the memory. To fear what is past is as time consuming and as energy wasting as it is to fear what is to come. It is only by living totally in the moment that you will learn the lessons that you have come to learn, that you will balance the karma of your soul.

Q: But is it not sensible to be fearful of someone who could kill you?
ZT: As I have just said to you, if you are fearful then you are not living in and facing the moment. If you *are* living in the moment then what is there to fear, certainly not death! Have you not yet recognised that if you are frightened of death then you are frightened of life. For what is life but death to every minute of the day.

Q: It seems to me that the greatest human fear is fear of the unknown, and since most of us are living in a perpetual state of unknowingness how can we be anything but fearful?
ZT: You would do well to ask yourself, firstly, what is the unknown and, secondly, why are you so fearful of it? What is the part of your being that is unknowing, that does not know of its reality? For certain it is not your spiritual being which knows its destiny intimately. Moreover, is it intelligent to fear something which you do not know? You should also consider how it is possible for the great Masters who walk this Earth to know all things past, present and future, to know exactly what is going on in every human relationship at any given moment in time. So if everything is known, on one level anyway, even if not by you personally, then what is there to be fearful about.
   It is only the spiritually ignorant person who is truly fearful. Such a person believes that they are pushed hither and thither by the vagaries of blind fate. Life is always seen as an uphill struggle, as being unfair, with no moral justice prevailing, especially where they are concerned! Whereas the mark of a knowing person, a Master, is that they are able to walk the path of life with certainty, knowing that they have the power to face and handle every challenge that comes into their lives. So it can be seen that spiritual knowledge, not intellectual knowledge, leads to the ending of fear.

Q: But did not the Master Jesus say on the cross 'Father, why hast thou forsaken me?'. Was not this a state of unknowing, a state of fear?
ZT: No, it was not. What Jesus, the man, was questioning was why the Christ Energy was leaving him, the Energy that had been over-shadowing him for the past three years, the Energy that had been the source of his teaching, his healing, his prophecy, his mission. When the

Energy withdrew it was as if his very spirit was leaving him and Jesus asked why. The reason why the Christ Energy left was twofold. Firstly, because Jesus's physical body was no longer capable of containing the Energy due to its weakened state and, secondly, because the Master Jesus had his own test to face on that cross. All of us have to face the moment of death alone. That is the final test of our soul being. No-one can face death for us. We die alone, no matter who is holding our hand on the physical level. So even the Master Jesus had to face death alone and that was why the Christ Energy withdrew.

Q: I personally have a great deal of fear of pain, physical pain, but isn't that quite natural? Could you say a little about the relationship of fear and pain?

ZT: Both instinctive fear, as opposed to psychological fear, and pain are bodily not mental experiences. As the Master has just said, they are associated with your physical or your animalistic body. But most of you know that you are not your body and that when you die your spirit rises from your body onto a higher level of life. Your body, on the other hand, decays to dust and returns to the earth from whence it came. So your physical body is mortal but you are not. You are an immortal being. You come from a far higher plane of existence and as such you should be the master of your body. Now a master is not someone who rules by virtue of their position in the hierarchical scale but by virtue of the fact that they have the greater knowledge and wisdom. So you should be the master of your body and recognise that the pain and the fear of the physical body are not in fact your pain and your fear.

The physical body is designed to feel and to respond to pain and its bodily instincts, but you always have the choice of whether or not you are going to identify with that pain and with those instincts. The stories are manifold of people who have been experiencing great pain and have suddenly found themselves leaving their bodies and experiencing no bodily sensations at all. How is it possible that the yogis of India can stick knives into themselves, can sleep on a bed of nails or walk on hot coals and yet experience no pain. How can they die for a week and then return to life. Only because they are the master, not the servant, of their bodies. Their bodies work for them, not against them. They have a common purpose and understanding. So the next time that you experience pain, realise its source, realise that your body is talking to you, but then choose whether you wish to identify with it. Do you want to associate or disassociate yourself with the pain.

213

Q: But is it not true to say that we can learn a lot about ourselves and life from pain?

ZT: What is the purpose of pain, and I am talking to you now not of psychological or emotional pain, but of physical pain? Pain is your body shouting for attention. Pain is a means of getting attention from the rest of the body and from you, the inhabiter of that body, to a state of imbalance, to a need for action. I will use the example of toothache. A tooth has perhaps been decaying in your mouth for weeks if not months, but you have chosen to ignore the warning signs because you are not aware of your body. Even when you do notice a few niggling pains, you still do not take action. So eventually you will experience a full-blooded toothache! This is the body calling for a focus of attention upon the particular aspect that needs to be healed.

The purpose of pain, therefore, is to focus attention and to demand a response, not just to remove the pain but to remove the cause of the pain. In the case of the toothache, it is no good just taking painkillers to hide the pain. You have to look for the cause of it. So you must all learn to establish a dialogue with your body and to listen to its needs. You should always be responsible governors not dictators. Your body is the temple of your soul and you should maintain it in perfect harmony and balance so that it can perform the work of spirit. The purpose of spirit is to uplift and purify the body, and to raise its vibratory note so that it can be a better instrument of service.

Q: Would you advise me about having an abortion? Do we not have the right to decide whether or not to have a child?

ZT: I will begin by saying that I can only give you my opinion, which is but a reflection of my point of consciousness. I can only express my understanding of the purpose of creation. It is not a question of right or wrong. It is a question of what you as an individual are prepared to accept as right or wrong. Even if you were to stand before a great Master who revealed the highest truth to you about abortion, you would still only be able to respond according to your point of consciousness. So all that I can do is to lead you into an understanding of the spiritual reality of this situation and then leave you to make your own decision.

For the most part Humanity does not understand creation, and by that I mean the process of conception and birth. Above all, it does not understand the part that its Creator plays in every aspect of creation. Humanity does not understand that it is an instrument of Infinite Spirit and, as such, that it is always creating in Its name. You cannot create without your Creator's agreement. If you understand this fact then you will also understand that every soul that incarnates into physical matter, no matter whether it be a foetus or a baby, incarnates as an instrument of Infinite Spirit. It is an act of great deliberation. It is not an act of blind chance. Conception does not happen because you are either careful or not careful with your means of contraception. Conception only happens if it is part of the Divine Plan. Therefore the fact that you have life within your womb is for a divine purpose.

It might interest you to know that the only reliable and effective means of contraception is the mind. Truly, creation always takes place on the level of the mind. So if you protect yourself in your mind from the act of conception, then that will work more efficiently than any of your contraceptive devices. Therefore on the level of the mind any woman who has life beating within her womb has invited that life to be there. Conception is not an act of human copulation. It is an act of God. So what the mother and the father are really deciding, and it is a joint decision because the life inside the mother's womb has been created as much by the father as by the mother, is whether or not to accept that gift from God. For that is what every baby is. Now there can be reasons, as you well know, why some people decide not to accept that gift from God and choose to have an abortion. All that I would say is that you should consider very carefully before you reject a gift from your Creator. Remember that your Creator does not give you a gift just to make you happy, just to bring pleasure into your life. The purpose of your incarnation is spiritual growth and evolution, the gaining of consciousness. Therefore every situation is designed as a learning experience, as a test, to bring forth from within you your deepest understanding of God and of the nature of Creation.

One of the main reasons for having an abortion today is to save the mother from having a so-called deformed baby. There is this understanding that if the baby is deformed, if it is not perfect, then you are quite entitled to get rid of it. Of course every mother and father has this choice, that is their birthright, but do they ever stop to consider what that child could teach them? What understanding of life could it lead them into? What karmic lesson could it help them to learn? Remember that the form of the baby is not important. What is important is the force of spirit that beats within it. You know from your own observation in life that even though a deformed baby usually grows up to be a deformed adult, he or she is often capable of expressing great consciousness and love.

In the final analysis, therefore, the choice of whether or not to have an abortion can be regarded as a kind of cosmic test. Of course some people will deny that it does constitute a test and will maintain that it does not matter what they do. Others will feel that they are simply unable to face the test and will decide to postpone it to a later date, perhaps to another life. Others will decide to have an abortion but, at the same time, they will say to their Creator that they will be happy to receive the unborn baby back into their lives at some time in the future when they are better able to handle it. No matter what the decision that is made it is of concern only to the individuals involved and to their Creator. Ultimately it is the point of consciousness of the mother and the father that will determine how they will act and on that there should be no judgement, moral or otherwise. Always remember, though, the inherent nature of the great Law of Karma, and that as you sow, so shall you reap. As you give, so shall you receive.

Q: What happens to the soul of a foetus when it is aborted?
ZT: Only a very small aspect of spirit resides within the foetus during the early months of gestation. Indeed, at the moment of birth only one-seventh of the spirit resides within the physical body. So the total aspect of spirit in the body is very small at first and only increases very slowly with the growth of the foetus. It is still living very much between two worlds. If the foetus is aborted, then obviously the spirit has no vehicle through which to express itself in physical manifestation. It therefore cannot fulfil the destiny it has chosen and so it returns to the spiritual realms to wait for another opportunity for incarnation. Now, in some cases, as I have just mentioned, this can be through the very same parents again, but if this is not possible, for whatever reasons, then it will seek other souls who are willing to accept it. This will, of course, inevitably create a feeling of rejection within the aborted soul which will need karmic transmutation.

Q: What can be the spiritual reasons for a miscarriage?
ZT: A miscarriage happens when the soul which is within the foetus is not happy with the circumstances into which it is incarnating. There can be three reasons for this happening. Firstly, because for whatever reason the body which the soul is forming has become imperfect and so it withdraws because the body cannot support the destiny it has chosen. Secondly, because for whatever reason the soul decides that it no longer wishes to pursue the destiny that it has chosen. So the soul withdraws

from life because it simply cannot face life, perhaps because of the nature of the vibrations that are around it, and waits for another opportunity. Thirdly, because some souls have a destiny only to touch the Earth plane for just a very short time. All they need to experience is being in the aura of the Earth for a few weeks and then they withdraw, having completed their destiny.

THE QUEST FOR CONSCIOUSNESS

On many occasions in the past I have said that you enter this world only with consciousness and that you leave this world only with consciousness. It is this consciousness which forms and builds your physical body and it is this consciousness which leaves that physical body when it is no longer able to operate in it and to be of service through it. I have also said that you enter this world with the soul consciousness with which you last left this world. So any consciousness which you acquire on the physical plane of life is never lost. Even though it may appear that in their present life someone is being unfairly penalised, because they are suffering from a deformed body, or from financial deprivation, or from painful human relationships, be aware that that is not the total reality of the situation. For out of any suffering comes great spiritual growth and awareness and the consciousness which you earn from these experiences will be with you for eternity.

Once you recognise that the physical matter of this world is but modelling clay, to be used and moulded by yourselves, time and time again, for divine purpose and intent, then you can begin to understand the purpose that lies behind all human activity, which is the quest for consciousness. For this Earth is a school of learning and you are pupils in this school, which has been prepared so carefully for you by your Creator, the Lord of this solar system. Your Creator's consciousness is manifest in all of Its creations, if you will but bear witness to it. There is divine meaning and purpose in all of Its creations, in all of the human situations in your world, if you will but become aware of it.

Think back to the incidents in your own lives, to the times of apparent darkness, when you have lost faith in everything, when you have been pushed to the very limits of your spiritual understanding and endurance. Is it not often the case that subsequently you can see that those incidents were responsible for creating a great inner understanding and knowingness of life? For that is what consciousness is, the knowingness of God, the knowingness of the Supreme Intelligence that manifests all things upon the Earth. Moreover, would it not be true to say that no matter what assails you in the physical world, if you are at one with your Creator, then, nothing can touch you? If you can rise above any suffering, any deprivation, and see purpose in all things, then where is the suffering, where is the deprivation?

If you look back at the life of one the great Masters, and I take the life of the Master Jesus simply because most of you are aware of his life, because of your Christian upbringing, you will notice that even after he was overshadowed by the Christ Consciousness, that did not mean that the rest of his life automatically became a life of perfection and harmony. Indeed, to the contrary, you can see that it was the very presence of the Christ Consciousness that created conflict and, eventually, led to his death. You will also remember that as he was losing physical consciousness on the cross he spoke the now famous words 'My God, My God, why hast thou forsaken me?', which indicated that he was aware that the Christ Consciousness was leaving him. The Christ Consciousness could no longer stay in his imperfect body, the body that had been prepared, nourished and purified so specifically for It, and so It was being forced to withdraw since It could no longer operate through that body.

In similar fashion, all of you, to varying degrees, are channels for that Christ Consciousness. The purer the channel, the purer the individual, in thought, word and deed, the more that divine energy can flow through you and become a part of your lives. The purer the channel, the greater the percentage of Christ Consciousness and the smaller the percentage of ego consciousness, the more that body is able to be of service and to fulfil the Will of its Creator. If your body is impure, you block the flow of divine energy, of divine consciousness, and impurity can exist on any level of your being, on the physical, on the mental or on the spiritual. All is not purity even on the spiritual level, for you carry with you in your soul, which is the memory of spirit, the deep impressions of all that you have done in your past lives. So the errors of the past, the karmic debts that need to be transmuted, the lessons that have to be learnt, are with you even today, on every level of your being.

So recognise, therefore, that even though you accept the Christ Consciousness into your being, you will still be tested. Be aware that you will be persecuted and reviled by the world around you for demonstrating that Consciousness. The purpose of attaining a high point of consciousness is not to lead a peaceful life, living in isolation from a world of which you want no part. No, it is to go forth and to sound your note in the world at large. Remember the example of the Master Jesus. No matter what the difficulties, no matter what the personal tests he had to face, he drew his strength from the knowledge that he was fulfilling his Creator's Will, a Will which he accepted without question. The greater your point of divine consciousness, the greater your ability to be of service and the more that is expected of you in every aspect of your being.

So many old souls today are happy to serve and to ground their point of consciousness, but only on their terms. They are only prepared to serve if certain commitments and certain obligations are met. They are only prepared to serve according to their understanding and concept of what constitutes service. They do not recognise that it is that very understanding which limits their service, for who are they to choose how, when and where they will serve, to place their limitations on God's power? It is a wise person who recognises that they are merely a channel for the flow of divine energy, and that it is not for them to choose who that energy will serve. Finally, remember that as channels you all emit two energies. There is the energy of the channel and there is the energy that flows through that channel. They are very different energies in both source and nature and will, of course, attract very different kinds of people.

I would like you all to understand that at this particular time in the evolutionary cycle your quest for consciousness is of supreme importance. You are experiencing darkness in order that you may see the light more clearly. You are experiencing darkness because in past lives, when you lived in a time of light, you chose to ignore it. The purpose of darkness is to help you to focus on the light, and at this time in the world most people are very aware of the need for light, not the light that is capable of transforming Humanity instantly into a realised race, but the light that will help Humanity to understand more clearly the true nature of its own creations in thought, word and deed.

This is the time, above all, when Humanity must watch closely everything that it creates on every level of its existence, for this is the time of supreme test. This is the time of the ending of the Age, of the changing of the Cycle, the time of the transformation of the planet into a world of which you can barely conceive. I can tell you, with certainty, that it is how you handle this darkness, how you pursue your quest for consciousness, that will decide your role in the New Age. Every little sacrifice that you make is noted. Every act of service that you make, no matter how small, is noted. Every step that you make on your quest for consciousness is noted. So you lose nothing by your sacrifice and your service but you gain the world, for the gain in consciousness that you make now will be with you for ever.

This time is also of great significance because you are being presented with a unique opportunity for realising the true nature and purpose of the drama that is being enacted for you. Remember, however, that you, too, are a part of the drama and that it is not for you to judge or to condemn either the other actors in this drama or the roles that they are playing, rather, it is for you to observe them and to grow in wisdom from your observations. As I am always telling you, this Earth is a school of life and at this time you are being presented with one of its supreme moments of learning.

In your world today many people have become disillusioned with God because of what is manifesting in the world. Indeed, some people even blame God for the present state of the world! The familiar cry is often heard, 'How can God permit such things to happen? If our God is a God of love, how can He permit all the human suffering that is now taking place? Why does He not stop it?'. The people who make such statements do not understand the role of God in this great drama, for God is not the intervener, God is the observer. Humanity is simply suffering what Humanity has created by its own actions. God will help *you* to change this world but God will not change this world simply to remove Humanity's suffering. God will help *you* to transform your being but God will not transform your being just because you ask Him to, rather like a wizard waving his magic wand. The whole purpose of this school of life is that you learn from your actions, as you sow, so shall you reap. The great Law of Karma is all pervading in this respect.

As any good teacher will tell you, any learning experience is directly related to the energy, the effort and the sacrifice that is expended by the pupil. It is the same with life. The greater the test, the greater the opportunity to strengthen the character of the soul. Those tests in which you have died in past lives have had a profound effect upon your soul being and have been primarily responsible for moulding your point of consciousness and for establishing your understanding of what is Truth. You are prepared to die and, indeed, have often done so in past lives, for what you know to be the Truth, for there is no greater God than Truth, and what is Truth but God's Will made manifest on the Earth. So in these times of darkness there is a great opportunity for seeing Truth, for discovering God's Will, both for you and for this planet. Every day you are presented with new challenges so that you can hone and evolve your point of consciousness. It is not for you to question and to judge that day, rather it is for you to observe that day with an aware eye, to be open to its every moment. You should be prepared to serve the day rather than expecting the day to serve you. You should be prepared to give of your consciousness no matter what the cost, and as you give, so shall you receive.

I wonder if you all realise how fast time is racing by, how soon your physical lives will be over. No matter how old you are, most people can sense that time is speeding up. Moreover, there is a physical time scale to this present Cycle. Each day, therefore, must be grasped as a heaven-sent opportunity for gaining consciousness, for seeing the conscious-ness of God in every aspect of life around you, for that is the only God that you can ever know whilst you are in physical incarnation. That is one of the limitations of this world of matter in which you live. You have been placed in a dense body of matter, placed in a school of learning, shut off from many of your higher senses, just to witness this very special drama created for you by your Creator. You have been separated from your Creator so that through the drama of life you will find your way back to your Creator, from whence you came.

So as you wake up each morning be aware of your quest for consciousness. Attune consciously to that quest and let it motivate your every thought, word and deed during the day. If you align your being with your quest then your day will have both purpose and meaning. If you awake each morning to the thought of 'How can I serve you this day, O Lord' rather than of 'O Lord, how are You going to serve me this day', you will be establishing the correct balance for the day. If you follow that simple rule, then, as the days go by, you will know the reality of that great cosmic truth, that as you give, so shall you receive. You will know that any sacrifice that you make with pure motivation will be rewarded tenfold, for even if you sacrifice your life, what are you actually losing?

What, in reality, belongs to you? Your physical body belongs to the Earth. The material possessions which you prize so greatly and which you think belong to you, in reality belong to, and are controlled by, the Lord of this Earth and will eventually return to the Earth. The truth of your reality is that you possess only one thing and that is your consciousness or, what I call, the knowingness of God present in your soul being. This is the knowledge which is yours for eternity. This is the knowledge which is the key to the door that leads to a universe of expanded consciousness. You are learning through incarnation on this small planet, in this small solar system, to be gods of the Universe. It may appear to you to be a very hard lesson, but remember that that which is of the greatest value always requires the greatest sacrifice. It is by the greatest sacrifice that you will acquire the greatest consciousness.

Recognise that all of you, being unique aspects of Infinite Spirit are following very individual quests. All of you are sounding differing notes and, as such, are responding even now to my message in differing ways. Such is the individuality of the Human Race and yet in that individuality lies great strength, for when all the individualised aspects of human consciousness have evolved and have grown together they will form a great cosmic being. Nevertheless, at this time in the world, you can only be responsible for the evolution of your own point of consciousness. It is not for you to judge others, to criticise their path, to question the nature of their being. You can only sound your note and walk your path to the highest of your consciousness. You can only follow your quest for consciousness.

So, in conclusion, I would ask you to examine deeply the true nature of your own being. At all times seek to align your being with the universal force of Infinite Spirit. Realise the temporality of this physical world. Value every second of your day as a great opportunity for the gaining of consciousness. Handle all the tests that you have to face with equanimity, in the knowledge that you are never alone unless you choose to be so, and that your Creator is only an invocation away. Consider yourselves as chalice cups waiting to be filled with divine energy. The only thing that prevents your cup from being filled is if it is already full of your own ego-self with all its blockages and limitations. The only difference between you and a great Master is that the cup of a great master has been filled with divine spirit, whilst yours is probably only a quarter full. So remember that you have to empty the cup first before it can be filled. You have to accept the preference of divine will over your will. You have to accept the preference of a divine world over your world.

I know how hard it is for you to surrender, to sacrifice of your being, for you feel that you are surrendering a most precious part of yourself. But have you ever stopped to consider what it is that you are actually surrendering? It is your ego-self, it is the personality opinion that you have formed of yourself, the importance that you have attached to your concepts of who and what you are. That is why you find it so difficult to serve, especially to serve those in need, those who have not yet walked the spiritual path as far as you have. The lesson of this school of life called Earth is sacrificial service. When you deny your birthright by refusing to serve you are denying your very purpose for being here, you are cutting off the flow of the Universe to you, for as you serve others, so others serve you, as you express your divinity, so the Divine expresses Itself to you.

Finally, remember, that as you walk your path in life, the Universe is walking it with you, for you are never alone. Your every thought, word and deed is watched and noted by beings on many different levels of life, who are watching with interest this experiment in human evolution. There are those who say that the experiment will never work, that Humanity will never be prepared to sacrifice itself for the whole, but there are others who believe that such a transformation is possible. Such beings hold the vision that one day a race of Humanity will walk the face of this Earth who will regard the country as being of more importance than the individual, the race as being of more importance than the country, the planet as being of more importance than the race.

Such a race of Humanity will have gained the consciousness to recognise that by sacrificing to the whole they have in reality lost nothing but have gained the Holy Grail – the presence of God in their own beings. They will know that it is that very God-presence in them that will raise them to levels as yet undiscovered, that will enable them to achieve that which they had previously thought to be impossible. Your task, today, is to allow the Holy Grail to fill your cup, and to join that select band of Masters who have evolved beyond the need for physical incarnation, who now stand above the Earth and who serve not just the Human Race, not just this planet and this solar system, but the whole Cosmos.

QUESTIONS AND ANSWERS

Q: The Master spoke about our possessions returning to the Lord of this Earth and, earlier on, he mentioned the Lord of this solar system. Does this mean that there is a hierarchy of Lords or Gods? Could you explain this to me?

ZT: The Lord or God of this Earth, sometimes known as the Goddess, because she is 'feminine' or 'negative' in energy as opposed to the 'masculine' or 'positive' Lord of this solar system, that Being Whom you call God, is responsible for the matter of this Earth. Through her devic and elemental kingdoms she controls all aspects of physical matter. She has, however, temporarily given Humanity dominion over her kingdoms. So Humanity can create with the matter of this Earth as it so wishes. At any time, though, she can restore her control over her servants and impose her own will, her own order.

Now each of the planets in your solar system has a Solar Lord who rules over it. All these Lords can be considered as being 'negative' in energy with respect to the 'positive' energy of the Lord or God of this solar system, that Being Whom you call God. This God is the God which Christianity refers to as 'Our Father in Heaven'. All the Solar Lords pay homage to the Lord of the Solar System, your God, Whose spirit dwells in the sun and Whose body is this solar system in which you dwell and of which you are a part.

In terms of cosmic evolution our God is not particularly high up in the cosmic scale of things! There are many Gods greater in presence and power than Him, for example, the God of Sirius. There are Gods greater than the God of Sirius, and so it goes on and on, beyond our comprehension. Ultimately, or so one is led to believe, one comes to the Source of all Life, Infinite Spirit, the supreme God, to use our terminology, Who is beyond our understanding and consciousness. So when I use the word God, I use it to conform to your understanding of God, but there are many levels of Gods, on levels of being beyond our comprehension. Finally, let us not forget that you are all gods too! All the molecules of consciousness within your physical body look to you as their god. You can impose your will on your body and can do with it as you wish. It is your soul consciousness that determines the consciousness of your body. All the beings in your body look to you for their example. You are 'God' to them. How often do you consider that fact? Be aware that as you purify your body and raise your point of consciousness so you are uplifting all the beings inside you as well! What a divine responsibility!

Q: I made a commitment to service several years ago, but I don't seem to have been used very much. What is the waiting all about? Aren't I needed?

ZT: There are obviously many levels and degrees of service. One can very easily make the commitment to serve but is one ready for service? Be aware that if one tries to serve before one is ready to serve then harm can result. For example, if you try to be a healer before you have properly learned to channel healing energies, then you will most probably deplete your own energies and far from being a healer, you will be the one that needs to be healed. So, firstly, one has to prepare oneself on all levels to be a server and, then, one has to learn how to serve, in what field one is best suited for service. Above all, one has to learn and recognise one's own limitations, to learn when to say 'No'.

Now it is a brave or, perhaps, a foolish person that says 'Lord, I am ready for service. Why are you not using me? Give me more work to do than I am doing now'! Why should I say this? Because the Lord, Who knows full well the murmurings of your heart, will never give you more than you are capable of handling. So the time that you have now is time that has been given to you to prepare yourself inwardly for service, time to resolve aspects of your being that, perhaps, are blocking your capacity to serve. And what is time, after all? The Master Jesus had to prepare himself over many years for his ministry, but was his service any the worse for that? Was it late or inappropriate? All of us are called for service when we are ready and when the time is ripe for our particular form of service. In the meantime, let us wait patiently and prepare for when that day comes.

Q: That surely invites the old excuse 'Oh, I'm not quite ready yet, therefore I can't serve'. Surely we have all got to begin somewhere. We have all got to practise service first.

ZT: That is correct, but I would make a distinction between total service and partial service. The very basis of life is service. Every day you should offer your total being in service to your Creator. Every day you are serving someone, either in the home or at work. A body that is not used for service is no better than a corpse. But there are times in your life which are best suited to total service, times when you can serve to the highest of your spiritual consciousness and potential. A medical student trains for many years to become a doctor. Obviously, he or she is of service during their training, but they cannot really be called healers and be of true service until they are fully qualified. Indeed, much damage would be done if they were to go around trying to heal people before they were qualified, not least to people's confidence in doctors. It is the same with true servers.

Q: These days a lot of chemicals are used in the production of our food, which must decrease the nutritional value of the food, apart from what it does to us healthwise. Is there a special prayer or a special technique which we can use in order to neutralize the effects of chemicals and make the food safer to eat?

ZT: Whenever you bless food, on an etheric level you uplift its vibratory note, its life force, and so its true nutritional value. So one portion of blessed food will be of greater value than a similar portion of unblessed food. However, on the physical level your body will still take in the chemicals, which will accumulate within your body and will lead to illness of the body. Of course, if you are an evolved being, a yogi, you can purify your body through certain spiritual practices, but for the ordinary person in the street it is difficult to purify your body, although fasting and diets of elimination do help in this respect. Unfortunately, some chemicals will be with you for the rest of your life, so it behoves you to eat wisely at all times, trying always to eat natural rather than packaged and processed foods.

Q: You have always advocated a vegetarian diet, presumably out of respect for the sanctity of the Animal Kingdom. But if life is not real, if no one or no animal ever truly dies, then does it matter if we kill the animals for meat? Moreover, are they not uplifted by their sacrifice to us? Do they not find evolution through us, because of their sacrifice?

ZT: That is a good question! I will begin by saying that meat is not a natural food for the human physical body, and it is certainly not for an evolved, a refined body, a body of high vibration, like the body of a Master. The important thing to remember about eating meat is that it densens, it coarsens, it lowers, the vibration of a physical body. Obviously it has a nutritional effect on the body, that cannot be denied, but it lowers the vibrational rate of the body, just like negative thoughts do. So if you want to advance your consciousness, if you want to experience life on a different level of being, you should not eat meat. That is why all the true Masters are vegetarian, without exception. Moreover, the way in which animals are raised and treated today, the way in which they are factory farmed and then transported unthinkingly to slaughter houses, to be processed into meat, densens their vibration considerably. When you eat the meat you are also taking in all those vibrations, all the fear, all the negativity, and you have to transmute that.

227

Now, as you rightly say, any form of sacrifice is a form of service. The animals are being of service to Humanity as they sacrifice themselves for food, and they will attract good karma for that. Their point of consciousness will be uplifted. I hope that all those of you who do eat meat, always remember this sacrifice, acknowledge it and give thanks for it. Be aware that how you behave on the energy provided by that meat, your behaviour in thought, word and deed, either affirms or negates that animal sacrifice. If you do not already have a blessing for your food, may I suggest:–

O Lord, bless this food. May it find evolution through me
and may I use it for a spiritual purpose.   Amen.

Humanity is creating much karma with the Animal Kingdom through wrong relationship, through the abuse of its dominion over that Kingdom. Inappropriate treatment will lead to disease, which will affect Humanity. I do not have to remind you that the AIDS virus originated in the Animal Kingdom.

Finally, of course, life on the plane of Earth is but a drama. No one or no thing ever dies for ever. Like actors on the stage, all will return to play their role in the next performance. But that is not an excuse for killing any one or any thing! What is important is your relationship with them, how you behave in thought, word and deed, what goes into your karmic account. If you are truly questing after consciousness then you will treat everything that comes into your aura as being divine, as worthy of respect because it is divine. So it behoves you to accept any sacrifice that is needed with great consciousness and awareness and to take it only if it is necessary to further your own point of consciousness. Always remember to give thanks for and to acknowledge any sacrifice and so complete the circle of service back to the Creator of all Life, Which offered it to you in the first place.

Q: I would like you to help me to act with consciousness with regard to a situation I find myself in. I have been married for many years now, but I know that my husband has entered into a close relationship with another woman. What should I do?

ZT: Every relationship has great significance and meaning for all the people involved, for both participants and spectators, far beyond the outward appearance of that relationship. So let us begin by recognising that every relationship is a learning and growing experience and that although the lessons might be painful, there is nothing to fear if your primary relationship, your relationship with your Creator, is on a sound footing.

That such a person should appear to form what is often called the eternal triangle, which is as old as is human relationships, is to test two things. Firstly, it is to test the strength of the marriage and the strength of the relationship between you and your husband. Secondly, it is to test the person that is threatening the marriage. For when it says in the marriage service, 'Those whom God has joined together in holy matrimony, let no person pull asunder', it is stating the fact that great karma is caused when someone knowingly breaks up a marriage by seducing away one of the partners. Now it could be said that a marriage could not be broken unless the relationship between the husband and the wife was weak and at fault. This, of course, is true, but, equally so, it must be recognised that if someone intrudes knowingly and with full consciousness into a marriage and causes its destruction by the use of their will, to satisfy their own desires, then they have contributed to the breakdown in no small extent and are destroying something that has been blessed by God. That creates great karmic responsibility.

That such triangles in relationship form is nearly always to produce clarity in a marriage relationship. It is to help both the individuals concerned and other married people to see clearly the nature of their own relationship, to examine why they married, their own motivation and purity, and to establish to what extent they are prepared to sacrifice to that marriage. For remember that in any marriage the sum of the energies of the two individuals is greater than two. The husband and the wife together create a third energy, which I will call the creative energy, no matter whether a child is produced or not, which is the creativity of the marriage. Marriage, like any other social institution, is only as strong as the energy and the will of the people involved. People have to work at a marriage in order to make it successful. It requires both sacrifice and commitment. So often it is easier to walk away from a marriage than it is to remain in it and have to face and solve all the problems of the relationship. Nevertheless, be aware that you cannot walk away from anything, for the Law of Karma will demand that you return to that relationship, perhaps in another life, in order to transmute any karma that has been created and to face the lessons that you formerly refused to learn.

Be aware that at this time in the evolutionary cycle of life all human relationships are being tested to the limit. All of you are being asked to examine what is sacred in your life, what is the true nature of your relationship with God and with all of Its creations. You are having to face many tests. Now to some people a test is seen as a threat, but I would ask you to realise that a relationship built on firm foundations, with correct motivation, which daily invokes the blessing of its Creator upon it, will never fail. Only that which has been created negatively, out of wrong motivation and for selfish reasons, will fail and disintegrate.

All that you can do in your present situation is to be true to yourself and to concentrate on sounding your note clearly and purely. Do not waste your time and energy in making emotional threats and accusations, in sending negative energies to those involved in the relationship. Just lead your life to the highest of your spiritual being, attune to your Creator in the silence of your meditations and accept, however hard it may be, that you cannot control other people, that you cannot be responsible for their actions. Just let the path of destiny run its course and know that if you act from the highest of your consciousness then you can do nothing else.

Finally, to all who are in such an eternal triangle, to all those who are thinking of 'having an affair', I would ask that you remember the wisdom of Tolstoy who, in his great novel 'Anna Karenina', clearly illustrated one of the karmic facts of life, namely, that you cannot build your happiness on someone else's unhappiness. You cannot expect to gain your happiness at the expense of someone else's suffering. The lesson of Anna Karenina is an appropriate lesson for this age in which you live, for as you sow, so shall you reap.

THE ONE AND ONLY GUIDANCE

Among a large majority of people in your world today there is a feeling of helplessness, of powerlessness. There are many who feel quite unable to cope with the pressures and the demands of modern life and who are bewildered by the patterns of human behaviour now manifesting on the planet. They feel unable to come to terms with the present path of scientific advance and are fearful of the apparent threat that Science itself now poses to the very existence of the planet. Above all, though, due to the vast disparities in wealth and standard of living between the so-called developed and non-developed countries of the world, due to the racial and sectarian divisions that are now appearing at an ever increasing rate, due to the many wars and armed struggles between countries, religions and political ideologies, there is a feeling growing that the presence of God no longer walks the face of this Earth. Many people feel that Humanity has, in effect, been abandoned to its fate and that it has lost its divine birthright. How else is it possible to justify all the violence and the bloodshed now manifesting on the Earth? Can it really be said that all of this suffering is part of God's Plan?

In response to this challenge, many new forms of guidance have begun to appear. There are many, of course, who still seek guidance and solace in what I will call the conventional forms of life, in established religion and science, but there is also a growing number of people who are seeking new forms of guidance, who are going back to the traditions of their race, be it east or west. Inevitably, in response to all this human questioning, many gurus and cults have mushroomed. These have tried to present new visions of life in order to give both meaning and purpose to the present human predicament. They have tried to explain, through prophecy and mediumship, what the more orthodox religions have been quite unable to explain. Nevertheless, even amongst this alternative guidance, no matter where the channels come from, there is division and conflict, there is a lack of agreement

231

on the destiny not just of the planet but also of Humanity which dwells upon it.

The reason for this, as I have said on many occasions, is that the accuracy of any prophecy, channelling or teaching is directly proportional to the purity and the soul-consciousness both of the source of the teaching and of the human instrument that is receiving and grounding it. So, almost inevitably, any message, any teaching, coming through a physical instrument is distorted to a degree and will be inaccurate in some respect. Almost inevitably, the soul and the personality consciousness of the physical instrument will influence both the message and the teaching. That is why there are those who say that they have seen the future, who know the timing of the worldshattering events that are to overtake Humanity, who have led their followers to places of 'survival', who have established religious practices designed to 'save' the souls of their followers and yet who, in the short term anyway, have been proved to be very wrong. That is why there is so much conflict amongst the so-called New Age Movement. That is why there are so many 'answers' to the problems now facing Humanity. That is why there are so many gurus appearing all over the planet who are offering conflicting teachings about the path of human salvation.

One fact, however, is indisputable, even to the most unobservant of human minds, namely, that the pace of life on the Earth is rapidly increasing. When you consider how, even over the last seventy years, in just one short human lifespan, transportation by plane has evolved, you will see the point that I am trying to make. For in this short period of time not only has the technology rapidly evolved but the numbers of people using this technology has also increased dramatically, with consequent changes in their lifestyle and expectations. Compare this transformation with the rate of transformation of, shall we say, just five hundred years ago! Whereas the design for a coach or a ship made five hundred years ago would have lasted for, perhaps, one hundred years, the design for a car or a plane made today would be obsolescent after ten. This simple example can be applied to every field of human endeavour. Have you ever stopped to consider where the world of computers will take you in the next ten, let alone the next fifty years? So Humanity is living life at a faster and faster pace, but is Humanity any happier than it was even five hundred years ago? Is Humanity using all this advanced technology wisely, for the benefit of all the Races and for the planet as a whole?

So on the physical, material level the path of human evolution is changing dramatically. Time is speeding up. The vibratory rate of the Earth is being quickened by the actions of great Cosmic Lords in order to balance the denseness of human behaviour which is threatening the very existence of the planet. However, this quickening has increased not only the pace of physical life but also the rate of karmic settlement. This means that Humanity is being compelled to face tests which strain its point of consciousness, its spiritual understanding, to the very limit. Only those who are truly God-centred, who are coming from a point of God consciousness rather than body consciousness, will be able to handle this great cosmic challenge. Again, I will compare this present situation to the problems that have been caused by the advances in speed, size and frequency of public transportation by air. This means that much of Humanity has the freedom to travel all over the planet with the result that many human problems, instead of being rooted in one place or in one country, are now spread all over the world. Local problems have now become planetary problems. Humanity can no longer act in isolation.

Modern technological advances have intensified rather than moderated the physical challenge to Humanity. Here, in the Western World, you are in the forefront of this technological revolution, but has it led to a comparable revolution in human consciousness? Is Humanity really any more evolved, any more aware, any more God conscious, than it was one, two or even three thousand years ago? Recognise that amidst all of this twentieth century technology the basic equation of life, namely, man, woman and human relationships, still remains. Are you any more happy, any more contented, any more wise because of all this technological progress? Yes, you have a higher material standard of living. Yes, you have a plentiful supply of food and water, available to you at very little personal sacrifice. Yes, you have a life where most of the physical dangers have been removed, where disease only rarely threatens. But if this is the case, then why are most people so unhappy with their lives? Why has the suicide rate increased in most western countries? Why are human relationships, and the institution of marriage in particular, disintegrating? Why does Humanity no longer respect the sanctity of all life and pay homage to its Creator?

Humanity has, to a large extent, lost touch with its roots. Living in a world dominated by human technology, it has forgotten whence it came and whither it will go when it dies. Humanity has forgotten exactly what is the motive power of all life, what is the source of the energy

233

which creates, impels and controls all things. Above all, Humanity has forgotten its own divine link, its own divine heritage. It has lost sight of the fact that every human being is either a son or a daughter of God. Inherent in this divine heritage is the guidance that any earthly father would give to his son or daughter and this is especially true of your Divine Father. Your Creator is both omniscient and omnipresent and will always guide you if you will but seek Its guidance with an open heart and an open mind. Moreover, at your very moment of birth you are linked with the celestial beings who will be with you for the whole of your mortal life, your two guardian angels and your doorkeeper, and they have but one purpose in life and that is to serve and to guide you. Finally, remember that there is always available to you the guidance not only of the great Masters but also of the whole Spiritual Hierarchy on the higher planes of life. All that is needed to tap into this source is a few quiet minutes of invocatory attunement.

Now many people in your world today believe that all this advanced technology will, somehow, provide the answers to all the problems of life that Humanity is now facing. They have made Science into a god. Of course, Science is, in reality, the study of God, but it is not, and never will be, God. A closer look will reveal that many of the problems now facing Humanity, especially the environmental ones, are caused by that very same Science! Humanity, as a whole, and Science, in particular, are now becoming aware that it is the effluent from cars, planes, power stations and industry in general that is destroying the delicate environment of the planet just as much as the rapid increase in erroneous thoughts, words and deeds by the human population. However, even though the major causes of pollution have been identified, is Humanity prepared to change its patterns of behaviour? Is Humanity prepared to make the necessary physical sacrifices in order to save the environment of the planet? You must understand that all technology is but a tool in the hand of Humanity, and if the hand that uses that tool is not aware, is not properly guided, is not working with divine intent, then it can be a very dangerous tool.

Does Humanity, however, have either the power or the will to transform this present situation, especially if it has not been able to do so in the face of far lesser challenges over the past five thousand years? Is Humanity capable of suddenly bringing about a change in its consciousness and, as a result of this, a change in its patterns of behaviour? Only if it recognises its divine birthright and seeks divine guidance! It is only the clear mind, the clean intellect, that can see that

Humanity has to find a new form of guidance and by this I mean guidance that is not of this Earth, guidance that is not subject to human conditioning, to the material concepts of life, to the restrictions of time and space, that has not been polluted by the dense vibrations of the physical plane of Earth. Such guidance can only come from that point of stillness within you, from the God-centre within each and every one of you. This, therefore, is the real challenge that faces Humanity at this time. You all have to choose where you want to stand on the wheel of life. Do you want to stand on the periphery of the wheel, being spun round at high speed, in a confused and bewildered state, constantly being ruled by time and matter, or do you want to stand in the centre of the wheel, in a place of peace and stillness, in the innermost part of your being, your divine spirit. It is only from such a centre that you can draw on divine inspiration and take right action.

The one and only guidance is the divine guidance which comes from deep within your soul being, which you receive in those moments of stillness, of silent attunement to the Source of all Life. Such guidance will reveal paths to walk and understandings to follow that are very different to those held and generally accepted by the world today. It therefore requires great courage and faith not just to listen to but also to put into practice such guidance. It is difficult to walk alone, against the stream of life and public acceptance, but you must learn to do it. Do not be afraid of being ahead of your time, of being mocked and even persecuted for heralding the New Age. Your demonstration is your lesson, is your karma, is your passport into the New Age. Grow to recognise that every human being is unique, unique not just in their soul being and soul note, but in the path of life that they have walked and in the balance of their karmic account. So it follows that for every human being divine guidance will be unique, responding to the unique soul note of the individual concerned.

How easy it would be if you could just close your eyes, enter into the stillness of your being and receive this divine guidance, rather like turning on the radio in the morning in order to listen to the news. But, alas, you all know better! Why should this be so? Because, using the analogy of the radio, your radio has very little power and can only receive the guidance very faintly. Your radio is quite serviceable but it needs to be empowered before it can operate efficiently, in just the same way that you have to connect a radio to a power supply before you can receive the radio station. So you have to empower yourselves in order to obtain this guidance. You have to empower yourselves by purifying yourselves in thought, word and deed and by establishing a pattern of stillness and silence, times when you consciously attune and direct your thoughts towards the Creator of all Life and humbly offer your being in service to that Lord with no thought of return or reward.

How many of you actually attune to your Creator on a conscious level during your everyday lives? How many of you actually make the effort to quieten your minds and bodies at fixed intervals throughout the day and try to attune to your Creator and Its Will for you? That is the guidance of which I speak. Now, for most people, guidance does not come as that still small voice within, telling you clearly what to do in any given situation. Guidance, for the most part, comes from the practice of constantly attuning to the Creator of all Life so that you know, almost intuitively, the path of right action without even having to ask. By seeking the counsel and wisdom of your Creator in times of peace you will be able to attune automatically to them in times of crisis. Remember, also, that your every action causes a reaction, that is the Law of Karma, and that how the universe responds to your actions enables you to check on the rightfulness and appropriateness of those actions. I call this process 'universal feedback'. How the universe or the world around you is responding, provides a mirror to your actions. This enables you to check on all your actions.

The world today presents you with a great challenge. It is a time when you must go boldly forth into the unknown. It is a time when you must explore new relationships, both with your fellow human beings and with the three other Kingdoms of Matter, for it is only by so doing that both Humanity and this planet will be saved. It does not need a wise person to see that little has changed in the field of human relationships over the known course of human history. Humanity today behaves in much the same way as it did in ancient India and Sumeria, certainly as it did in ancient Greece or Rome. The only difference between then and now is that the vibratory rate to which Humanity is being subjected is much higher, because the vibratory rate of the Earth is being speeded up. One result of this vibratory increase is a great intensification in human relationships. This not only brings out all the weaknesses of Humanity but also all of its strengths. So it is a time when all people of consciousness should stand forth and be counted, should sound their note. God works through people and the New Age has to be grounded on the Earth by the people who are open to the new, by the people who are attuning to the note of the new rather than of the old.

Those who seek and follow their own divine guidance will discover not just the reality of life on the Earth but the presence and purpose of their Creator in all things. Now is the time to take a quantum leap forward in consciousness, to discover that everything in creation has God-consciousness and responds to Divine Will. It is important, therefore, that you create your moments of attunement, that you try to become still and to contact the I AM presence of God within you, that you truly follow the ancient commandment 'Be still, and know that I am God'. For without these moments of stillness you will follow the path of the vast mass of Humanity and will be swept along like lemmings to destruction. Just because society as a whole follows a certain course of action and adopts certain values, that does not mean that you have to join them. Surely you can see that many, if not all, of the great advances in human understanding have come about only because certain individuals chose to stand against the tide of popular belief, and by stand against I do not mean by consciously opposing but, rather, by simply upholding what they knew to be true. How did they know it to be true? Because of their own inner guidance.

If I use orthodox Christian terminology it will, perhaps, help you to distinguish between the paths that are open to you. As you walk through life you are constantly choosing between what has been called the divine and the satanic paths. The divine path is the path that leads to oneness with the Creator of all Life and, as such, is empowered by the will of your Creator. The satanic path is the path which Humanity creates in response to its own egotistical thought forms, to its own desires to be as god. However, because Humanity cannot accept that it alone creates the satanic path, so it has to place the responsibility for such a creation on some poor individual called the Devil or Satan who has to shoulder the burden of human guilt! But, truly, the satanic path is just the other side of the coin. You all have to make choices, every minute of your conscious lives. Unless you are a living Master, and have become one with the Creator of all Life, then, inevitably, you will err. Do not be ashamed or downhearted. To err is only human and, of course, your Creator has made allowance for that in the Divine Plan. Just realise that it was simply separation from your God, from your guidance, that created that situation of error in the first place and resolve to learn from that experience and never to repeat the same mistake again. Life is a classroom. You are allowed to make mistakes. So recognise that suffering is simply the repetition of the same mistake – separation from God.

I would like you to see clearly that the difference between the divine and the satanic is guidance. It is guidance, or the absence of it, that decides the nature of the path that you walk in life. Do not, however, think that guidance will guarantee you a smooth path in life. Look at the life of the Master Jesus. You all have lessons to learn and karma to transmute. What guidance will do is to ensure that you fulfil your chosen destiny and fulfil it with understanding and commitment. Remember that guidance not only flows through you but that it also flows through other people and that God works through all people. So be aware that everything in life, the people and things that you like as much as the people and things that you dislike, has a message for you, is a learning experience for you, is your guidance as well. So you must always be open to the moment and greet it openly and joyfully, for it truly represents your Creator talking to you, guiding you.

It is an aware person who sees the hand of God manifesting in their daily lives and who acknowledges and gives thanks for that presence. That is true communion. Recognise that you can choose whether to walk your path in life hand in hand with God, or not. Indeed, that is the only path that an evolved soul can walk, for that is the path to the mastery of the physical plane of life. You will only be able to accept the happenings of the next twenty years physically, mentally and spiritually if you are truly walking hand in hand with your God, if you are at one with the Creator of this great drama.

The world today is approaching a time of great testing and, therefore, a time of great evolution. It is a time of the sorting of the wheat from the chaff, a time when many will fall by the wayside and will perish. But it is also a time of great beginnings. It is a time of great happenings on all of the many planes of life. It is, so to speak, the final act of a great drama that began almost seven thousand years ago. You are all privileged to be here to witness these times and to see in your short life span of seventy years the culmination of seven thousand years of human evolution. You are privileged to be here to see the transformation of Humanity into the Golden Age of Aquarius. So face this great challenge with trust in your Creator. Go boldly forth into the new Age, secure in the guidance of the God within you, which is truly the one and only guidance that you have.

QUESTIONS AND ANSWERS

Q: I'm not sure that I understand the difference between divine creation and human creation, which the Master just talked about. Is not human creation, divine creation too?

ZT: Humanity has been given the divine gift of free choice, a gift which so many take for granted. It can choose how it wants to create. It can create either positively, that is according to God's Will, or negatively, that is against God's Will. Furthermore, every human being creates according to his or her own unique point of consciousness. So what would be right creation for one person could be wrong creation for another. Let me give you a simple example. You are all aware of the way in which Humanity uses many aspects of the Animal Kingdom for scientific experimentation, in order to test the effects of new drugs. Now some people would see this as an acceptable use of animals, since proven drugs can save human lives and animals should make the sacrifice for the sake of the higher life form. Other people would argue that the use of animals in such experiments is obscene, and that Humanity has no divine right to do this. What is right or wrong creation? Who is to say? God can be the only judge of all actions.

Ultimately, as far as you are concerned, it comes down to a question of spiritual knowingness and motivation. Scientists should not do something which they know within their hearts to be wrong, no matter that the laws of the land approve of such actions. Nevertheless, God does not stop Humanity from creating in any way that it wishes in thought, word and deed. Humanity can do what it likes with God's creations, but it will have to transmute the karma for whatever it does with them. Above all, though, Humanity must recognise that it is sowing seeds by its own creations and that it will have to witness the flowers of those seeds. So your children and your children's children will inherit the fruits of your actions today. What a divine responsibility! It therefore behoves you to use your divine gifts wisely and to always create for the highest good of all concerned, if only because in all probability you will incarnate as your children's children!

Q: I hear you speak a great deal about transmuting karma, but I don't understand what that means. How exactly do you transmute karma?

ZT: An understanding of the Law of Karma is beyond human comprehension. It is a complex cosmic subject, and so whenever I talk

239

about it I always have to oversimplify my descriptions and use worldly analogies. This is what I am doing now when I say that karma is simply the movement of energy so as to create a state of balance in the universe. For example, if in either this life or one of your past lives you had created a certain amount of energy in a negative way, and by negative I mean against the Will of your Creator, then either in this or in a subsequent life, you would have to balance out that negative energy with an equal amount of positive energy. In this way you would equal out the energy balance, repay your karma, and restore balance in the Universe. The inherent characteristic of the Universe is to restore itself to a state of balance, and so you as an individual, being part of that Universe, would yourself want to restore the balance. So the transmutation of karma is simply the rebalancing of what you have created in other lives, by right action in this life, by aligning yourself with the Will of God. To transmute is to wipe the slate clean, is to pay back all past debts by rebalancing the effect of your actions in past lives.

Q: So are you saying that the Universe will only let us go so far in any course of action and then its inherent tendency to rebalance itself will make us retrace our steps? It will, in fact, stop us from going any further along a certain path?
ZT: The Universe, which is the force of God in motion, will only permit you to go so far. There are limits to the degree that you can draw on your karmic account or, to put it another way, the heavenly bank manager in the sky will only allow you a certain amount of overdraft and when you get to that figure he will take action!

Q: So our free choice is limited to a certain extent?
ZT: Yes.

Q: So it is only free choice with strings attached!
ZT: I would say, with limitations on the extent of your choices. To use a very simple example, it could be said that Humanity has the ability to completely destroy this planet with its nuclear weapons, but if Humanity elected to do so, it would not be allowed to do so. Higher Forces would intervene and would take away Humanity's free choice in this respect.

Q: In recent years the Cold War between Russia and the West has changed dramatically. Now, peaceful overtures are being made by both sides. Is this because the Cold War had got so serious that the Universe would let it go no further and so intervened on an inner level, or is it due to a definite shift of consciousness on the part of both sides?

ZT: You must understand that very few governments, in fact I will say no governments, are altruistic. Neither side has suddenly had a change of heart and has decided to change their policies for the good of the whole world. It is, of course, a fact that the major powers in the world are changing their political postures and their rhetoric, but this is purely out of self interest. Why? Firstly, they recognise that the Arms Race can not be won by either side and that the financial cost of this race is crippling all the countries involved and, secondly, because of various nuclear accidents, some known, some unknown, they now understand that nuclear pollution knows no boundaries, respects no countries or religions. Now this does not mean that either ideology has lost their desire for supremacy but that they are not prepared to shoot themselves in their own foot, as the expression goes, in order to achieve it. The motivation of all governments remains the same – self interest. Until this changes, world relationships will not change, and the world will still be a dangerous place in which to live, a playground for frail human egos.

Q: The Master spoke of our link with our Creator and of this guidance being the only guidance worth having. He said that we had to be pure in thought, word and deed in order to get it. Could you just explain a little more, on a practical level, exactly what pure in thought, word and deed means? It is a nice expression, but what does it mean? What would be a daily programme to achieve purity of thought, word and deed?

ZT: By its very definition, purity means an absence of impurity. Your Creator, being completely pure, presupposes that everything that is impure is not of the divine, but is a creation of Man and Woman. Therefore each day you should check your behaviour in thought, word and deed to see if you have been coming from the highest of your being, if you have been pure, if you have been divine, in your living. It is, so to speak, to monitor your own behaviour and to compare it with the purity of your Creator as the standard. Now this is not a mind game of self-justification for what you have done or not done. It is not an intellectual exercise to justify a certain course of action. Rather, it is a genuine openness, an eye that neither criticises nor judges, but seeks to assess the rightness of your actions against the standard of your Creator. So many of you have lost sight of the existence of, what I call, the God-impulse in your lives. So many of you have lost contact with the source of divinity in your beings.

Q: Can somebody take over the karma of somebody else?
ZT: Yes, that is quite possible, but it is usually only done by a Master who can see clearly that the person concerned has learned their lesson, understands the nature of the actions that created the karma in the first place, and who recognises that to take on the remaining karma will allow that person to walk more quickly along their path of divine evolution.

Q: So it would only be an older soul taking on the karma of a younger soul?
ZT: Yes, that is correct. A younger soul would not knowingly take on the karma of an older soul. The transmutation of karma is only done by Masters, not by ordinary souls, because it is only they who can see into the akashic record of the person concerned and understand the path that their soul is walking.

Q: Do great masters like Jesus also transmute the karma of the world?
ZT: Yes. When great Masters come into physical incarnation they nearly always transmute portions of human karma in order to relieve the pressure of the collective human karmic debt.

Q: So is that what Christians imply when they say that Jesus died to take away the sins of the world?
ZT: Yes, I believe so.

Q: But whatever he took away, Humanity must have more than replaced it in the last two thousand years. So it must be an on-going job, removing the sins of the world!
ZT: Although you jest, would it surprise you to know that there are great beings in existence who do just that?

Q: Do you feel that Sai Baba is one of these? It has been said that he is capable of transmuting individual karma?
ZT: Understand that all great Masters have the power to do this, to transform and transmute another's karma by the energy of their being. Because they are omnipresent and omniscient they are aware of all aspects of life, at all times, on all planes of being. They do this out of

their great love for Humanity, to help it along its evolutionary path. In true service they do this expecting no reward, no thanks, no praise. It is indeed the case that very often the greatest service goes unnoticed, the greatest Master passes unobserved. It is only the aware eye that notices such things.

Q: Did the human race evolve out of animals and do humans incarnate as animals?

ZT: According to my understanding, the Animal Kingdom had been present on the physical plane of Earth, and had been evolving for aeons of time, before it was decided to place the Race of Humanity in this school of life called Earth, so that it could pursue its own unique evolutionary cycle. What then took place was that the spirit of Humanity was placed in the most suitable animal life form for its evolutionary purposes. So it was in that amazing union of Mother Earth and Father Sun, or Spirit, that the Human Race was born. Obviously, a process of physical evolution then took place, as the spiritual beings inside evolved the most suitable life form. The same process takes place when your spirit enters into your mother's womb and begins to form its physical body after conception has occurred. So, over many incarnations, the human physical form developed and evolved from its original animal form. Humanity never evolved from the Animal Kingdom. Humanity, as a species, is both individual and unique, and comes from a solar system far from this planet, whereas the Animal Kingdom belongs to a group soul and is very much a creation of this Earth and is empowered by the Lord of the planet, that being who you call the Goddess, or Mother Earth.

To the second part of your question, do humans incarnate as animals, the answer is yes, but only on very rare occasions. To my understanding, it is only done when a very special lesson needs to be learned. So it should not be seen as a punishment or as a sliding down the evolutionary ladder, a return to whence Humanity came, because, as I have just said, Humanity did not evolve out of the Animals. I know of one such incarnation where the soul of a very selfish being chose to incarnate as a cow for one life in order to appreciate what it is to lead a life of total service, which is the life of a cow. In this way a little balance could be returned to the soul patterns of that being. On another level, as you evolve and grow to become one with your Creator, so you yourself become omnipresent through union with the Creator of all Life. This means that you become aware of the life experiences of all

243

life forms, because you are those life forms. So you are all the animals and see life through their eyes, so to speak.

Q: So if I understand you correctly, what you are saying is that if we seek and follow this divine guidance, which is within us, we will grow to become one with our Creator and that our lives will automatically be aligned with the Will of our Creator, so that we will always create positively and only have positive karma?

ZT: I couldn't have summed it up better myself! If you will all, each day, make the effort, perhaps only for a few minutes throughout the day, to align yourself with the divine guidance that flows through you, you will be amazed at how easy your life will become. Now that is not to say that there will not be tests and problems, that you will not be challenged, because you will, but that the attitude that you will have to the solution of those problems will be radically changed.

Q: The Masters are always saying that the whole purpose of life is service, is to serve Humanity, is to serve the planet. The trouble is, Zen Tao, that I am so busy leading my life and raising my family that I just don't seem to have time for service. Does that mean that my life is being wasted?

ZT: You must recognise that there are many levels and many forms of service. Everyone does not serve in the same way, to the same degree. Not everyone can be teachers, healers, counsellors, rulers and so on, and serve in a formal position. Each one of you is a unique spiritual being and will be called upon to serve according to your soul note and your destiny in life. Remember, though, that one of the greatest forms of service is simply example, is the example of your soul and physical being, is the example of your own personal lifestyle. If you are leading a balanced and harmonious life then the note that you sound, the energy that you exude, will touch everyone that comes into your aura every minute of the day. You can walk into a room of conflict and pour oil on troubled waters just by your very presence. You are aware how the whole energy of a room changes when a true Master walks into it, so it is the same for all powerful souls, souls of aged evolution, only to a lesser degree.

Your thoughts, words and deeds are most powerful and by creating positively and harmoniously on all levels of life you serve not just those people around you but the whole world, for you are in the world and the world is in you. Moreover, you never know who is watching your example and the effect that your demonstration is having on them. If you greet everyone you meet each day with a smile, with a loving thought, with a positive affirmation, then you are being of the highest service. So recognise that service exists not just on the physical but on the mental, the emotional and the spiritual levels as well. There are as many forms of service as there are people. Each day your Creator will present you with innumerable opportunities for service. The only choice that you have is in the degree and the quality of your service, for you are all born to serve. That is the inherent nature of Humanity. Finally, be aware that it is not until you have demonstrated your ability to serve in the small things of life that your Creator will ask you concerning the larger and more important tasks.

THE IMPORTANCE OF CHOOSING
YOUR LIFESTYLE

Throughout the Ages the great Masters and Teachers who have incarnated on the plane of Earth have always taught Humanity that it should live in the World, but should not be of the World. The implication behind this well-known aphorism is that Humanity should ever recognise the true nature both of its being and of its spiritual home. Always remember, therefore, that you are beings of spirit, that you do not belong to this planet, that you incarnate on this plane of existence for but a fleeting second of spiritual time in order to learn the lessons of this school of life called Earth. For the most part you dwell on other levels of existence, beyond the limitations of your physical bodies and egos, beyond time and space, in an environment of constant peace and harmony, where there is no separation from the Godhead, where you are aware of the eternal nature of your beings.

So the whole purpose of your brief incarnation on Earth is to learn, is to gather consciousness. As I have said, on many occasions, you come into this world only with consciousness and you leave this world only with consciousness. The physical matter of the Earth is but modelling clay, for you to mould and play with, in order that you may learn of the divine nature of your beings, in order that you may recognise that you are God, that there is no separation between you and the Source of all Life. So it is vitally important, not just that you lead your physical existence with awareness but that you devote every precious second of that existence to the purpose for which you came. Inherent in this is that you choose your lifestyle with great care.

In the world in which you live today there is a great conflict between the forces that are sometimes referred to in the Bible as God and Mammon, between those who would lead a life based on the accumulation of spiritual consciousness and those who would lead a life based on the accumulation of material possessions. It is only too evident in your world today, especially with the current rapid increase in the human population, that there are many young souls walking the surface of this planet, some of them for their very first time in this cycle. Their point of spiritual consciousness is naturally very low and this manifests in their lifestyle, in their relationships with each other and in the manner in which they lead their lives.

As the numbers of these young souls increase, especially here in the industrialised Western World, so their pursuit of materialistic goals, of gross consumerism, has become identified with the very purpose of life. Those of you who do hold to a higher purpose in life have become swamped by the thoughtforms and the activities of this mass of less evolved souls, with the result that you too have become confused by the state of the world today. For it would appear that those people who earn large sums of money, who have beautiful homes and clothes, who go on expensive holidays, who are regarded by society as being 'successful', are fulfilling the purpose of life whereas those people who are not materially successful are regarded as 'failures', as lesser beings, who should imitate their supposedly 'more successful' brothers and sisters.

Great confusion exists at this time over the difference between what I will call a high standard of living and a high standard of life, between those who seek and demonstrate a high material standard of living and those who seek and demonstrate a high standard of life, one which reflects and respects the divinity of all life. It is essential that you understand the difference between the two and consciously choose which path, which lifestyle, you wish to follow. A high standard of living implies competition with other human beings for the limited material resources that are available on the planet. It means that the purpose of your life is to use your God-given talents to accumulate personal wealth and possessions, that you do not set a ceiling on your desires but, rather, remove the ceiling! It means that you are choosing to enter the consumer rat-race, that you are always seeking to have the latest and greatest 'toys', regardless of how much it costs you, society or the planet. It means that even if you do not have the money to pay for all these new possessions then it is perfectly alright to go into debt and borrow the money, to finance your greed out of the greed of others. Above all, it is to establish financial goals in life which, if you do not achieve, can be the cause of great unhappiness and can lead to the creation of a sense of failure and of feelings of jealousy and envy towards those who do achieve such goals.

On the other hand, however, you can choose to lead a high standard of life, a life that is based on the spiritual laws of the Cosmos. Now this

247

does not mean that you will be without money, that your needs on the physical plane of life will not be met but, rather, that the whole purpose of your life will have spiritual rather than material goals. It means that your whole life will be guided not by the ethos of consumerism but rather by co-operation, that you will always work in harmony with the three other Kingdoms of Matter, taking care not to abuse them in any way whatsoever. Above all, it means that you will always work to serve your fellow human beings rather than to compete with them, that you will wholeheartedly demonstrate the lesson and purpose of this planet – sacrificial service through the power of love.

It is important, therefore, especially at this critical time in the Earth's evolution, that all souls of aged evolution should examine most carefully the nature of their lives and the human values on which they are based. Why should I say this? Because here in the Western World you are fast approaching that moment in time when the bubble of gross consumerism is going to burst, when many young souls will be hurt in the collapse of the great financial credit bubble. I can tell you that, at a stroke, consumerism will disappear and those people who have worshipped the god of Mammon will suffer greatly. It is at such a time that those of you who have chosen to follow the other path, the path of co-operation, will be able to act as a light in the darkness and, above all, will be able to be of service to those who have chosen to follow Mammon. I would like you to recognise that the whole purpose of life on this planet is one of service, service to the family, service to the community, service to the race, service to the planet, and it is only those who serve that will find spiritual fulfilment.

At this time, therefore, when the material world is such a distraction, when it would appear that financial success is the key to happiness, when those who have money appear to control almost every aspect of life, when everyone is being encouraged to create wealth no matter what the degree of exploitation of the three Kingdoms of Matter or, indeed, of the Human Kingdom, it is important that those who are seeking a higher standard of life rather than a higher standard of living hold fast to their vision and ground and demonstrate it in their everyday lives. It does not matter if you stand alone in the crowd. It does not matter if your aims, your way of life, are different to all those around you. What is important is that you choose your lifestyle and hold fast to it, that you ground what you feel is the spiritual reality of life. Do not be diverted from this, do not become distracted by the ever changing world around you. You have come to change the world, not to let the

248

world change you. Your spiritual being is eternal and constant. The physical world is finite and ever changing. So never let the mutable world govern your immutable soul.

If you are to be a fixed point in an ever-changing world, then it is essential that each day you go within, you attune to your spiritual point of consciousness. You must ensure that your roots are firmly planted in the inner world before you venture forth into the outer world. It is the strength that you draw from the divine world that will enable you to handle the tests and challenges of the physical world. It is your inner spiritual being that must choose your lifestyle, that must choose the world in which you are to live, the manner in which you are going to live, the people with whom you are going to live. At this time in the Earth's cycle, especially, hold to that which is permanent, hold to that which is eternal. Do not be seduced by the temptations of the glittering material world. Do not be misled into thinking that money provides the answer to all the problems in the world, that money gives you the right to manipulate people and their relationships. I know that for many people money has replaced God, but that belief is soon to be shattered and for those who have worshipped Mammon as God there will be much pain and suffering. However, for those people who have placed the physical world in a correct perspective, who have recognised that all matter is impermanent and is caught in the cycle of birth and death, of growth and decay, for those people who have based their lives on spiritual principles, there will come the understanding as to how to handle all the challenges of this world.

Remember that it is you, and you alone, that decides how you are going to lead your life. You choose your earthly lessons. That is, perhaps, the most important choice that you ever have to make. You can choose to live your life either in God's image or in Mammon's image. But remember that you are not making that choice just for yourselves. You are not making that choice even for the thousands of people who will watch your demonstration. You are making that choice for the many generations to come, of which, incidentally, one day, you will be a part. By your sacrifice and service now you are sowing the seeds for the future. You are recognising your divine inheritance and the inherent quality of your soul. You are saying: 'I am a being of spirit. I am a spark of God manifest in human form. Though I live in a world of gross materialism, I will not be a part of it. I will live only according to my needs, not my greeds. I will recognise the needs of others before the needs of myself. I will ensure that the poor and needy are fed and clothed before myself, for I know that all my needs will be met by my Creator. If I serve God, in the form of all Its Creations, then God will serve me.'

It is a fact that few people in the world today believe in, let alone trust, the saying in the Bible 'Seek you first the things of the spirit and all else will be added unto you'. The implication behind this saying is that if you serve God, then God will serve you. If you hand over your life to God, then God will look after all your material needs, but note that I say needs, not greeds. Now I know that there are many people today who go out and work hard in the world in order to create a financially secure position in life, believing that only then will they be able to be of service to the world, to share some of their wealth and experience with the world. But often such people have to make great sacrifices in both their family and social relationships, in their own personal lifestyle and in the way in which they relate to the three Kingdoms of Matter, in order to accumulate such wealth. They are constantly beset with financial concerns and worries, for they believe that if they fail then both they and their families are doomed. You can walk this path if you so wish, but recognise that there is another path. If you serve the Creator of all Life and all of Its creations, then all of your needs, financial and otherwise, will automatically be met. Your Creator will take care of you on every level of life, just as a parent looks after its child.

At this time, therefore, I invite all of you to examine your lifestyle most closely, how you lead your life each day, how often you actually say 'Not my will, but Thy will be done, O Lord'. Now, obviously, as you are the person who is judging your lifestyle, it is difficult to remain unbiased because your conditioned mind will tend to support the way of life to which you have become accustomed. It is difficult to overcome the habits of a lifetime, but it can be done. One of the best ways of doing this is to establish the role of what I will call 'the observer' in your mind, an independent eye that simply observes your lifestyle each day. This observer does not judge, does not praise or condemn, but simply observes the effects of your lifestyle, not just on yourself but on all those around you. Gradually you will find that you and that observer become one and that from that truthful observation of your life the need for change will become readily apparent. It is then up to you whether or not you change your lifestyle in your image or in God's image.

If you are to change in God's image, then there must be times set aside when you try to establish union with God, when you try to bring

God into your physical being. If you cannot find the time in the day in order to commune with your Creator, then of what is the purpose of life? If you cannot find the time in the day in order to unite with the Source of all Life, then of what is the purpose of living? You have only to look around the world today to see millions of examples of people who are living their lives in total ignorance of their Creator, people who have cut themselves off from the Divine Source within, people who base their lives on the pursuit of pleasure and who consequently suffer from the heavy burdens of desire, anger, greed, delusion, pride and jealousy. Nevertheless, amongst these millions, there will always be the few who will stand forth by their very demonstration of service to their Creator. They are points of light in a world of darkness.

Remember that the greater the purity of your being in thought, word and deed, the greater your ability to be of service. Remember, also, that the greater the simplicity of your lifestyle, the greater your ability to be of service. Be aware that your possessions can sometimes end up by possessing you. I can tell you that no matter what karmic debts you have created, either in this life or in past lives, all of them can be transmuted by spiritual service at this most critical time in the Earth's evolution. Indeed, this, the ending of the Age, is the supreme moment for the transmutation of karma. That is precisely why so many souls are here in incarnation on the Earth at this time. Recognise that you are the midwives of the New Age, for not only are you giving birth to and educating the children of the New Age but also by your thoughts, words and deeds you are sowing the seeds that will flower into the New Age. Therefore remember that your own demonstration is of paramount importance, for it is the note that you sound, the point of consciousness that you ground, that is influencing all those who are searching around at this chaotic time for meaning and purpose to their lives.

The greatest lesson you can demonstrate at this time is to be in the World but not of the World. It is to show that you can live in the material world and yet not be controlled by that world. It is to reject all the materialistic values of western society today and yet to show that you can still lead a happy and fulfilled life, a life with meaning and purpose. It is to recognise the temporality of all earthly things and the eternal nature of the human soul. It is to recognise the One Divine Source that creates, empowers and controls all things. It is to recognise that a Divine Plan exists for all Creation, a Plan that does not know failure. It is not in the nature of the Divine to fail! So although, to the unevolved, it would appear that you are making a great sacrifice by

251

placing a ceiling on your desires, by abandoning the pursuit of pleasure, by placing the needs of others before yourself, by offering your life in service to your Creator, in reality, by that very sacrifice you are placing yourself in the Divine Flow of all Creation Which will meet all your needs regardless of any little drama that is being played out on the physical plane of life. Whereas those who have placed their trust in money and material possessions will see their 'security' removed at a stroke.

It is the aware soul who recognises that the sacrifice that they are being called upon to make is such a little one. For what, in reality, is theirs? What aspect of matter can they actually claim as their own? Nothing belongs to them. Everything is only lent to them in a sacred trust. Though they pay money and put their name upon some material object, that object is still not theirs. It can be taken from them whenever the Creator of all Life so wills it. Moreover, all physical matter is in a state of degeneration. All of your physical belongings are in a process of decay. Nothing endures forever. The material world is temporal, illusory and changeable; the spiritual world is fixed, immutable and eternal. So on what values are you going to base your life? What are you going to quest for in this life? That which is eternal, or that which could be gone tomorrow?

Surely you can see that there has to be a fundamental change in human consciousness if the Human Race is to survive. Humanity cannot keep on walking along its present path of self-aggrandisement and division, of separation between God and itself. A new understanding of life has to be grounded on the Earth, an understanding based on the principles of wholeness or holiness, of co-operation, sharing and service. This is the choice that now lies before every human being. As each human being chooses so they transform all human consciousness. Every little sacrifice that you make, every act of service that you render, either to the Human Kingdom or the three other Kingdoms of Matter, uplifts the consciousness of Humanity, affects its genetic heritage, and so helps to create the New Age. But the choice is yours. No one can make it but you.

You all have innate soul wisdom. Use it. You have the divine guidance which has been with you since you took your first breath in this incarnation. Use it. Do not be seduced by the material world. Recognise its finiteness and its temporality. Learn to place a ceiling on your desires and to recognise that you are not your body. Choose your lifestyle with care, for upon your choice depends not just your destiny

252

but the destiny of the whole Human Race. Are you finite, mortal, material beings, or are you eternal, divine, cosmic spirits? That is the basic choice that you have to make. When you have made that choice, then you will have recognised your true divinity, you will know that you truly are a son or daughter of the One God.

QUESTIONS AND ANSWERS

Q: We all obviously own various possessions and, as the Master has just said, probably far too many. Will you please tell us how we should handle the possessions that we have?

ZT: The Master also said that you do not own anything. You might think that you do, but you don't really, because everything in the world belongs to your Creator. All that happens is that what you call 'possessions' come into your aura, either you buy them or they are given to you, and you then become responsible for handling, for being the steward of, those possessions correctly. You are, of course, karmically responsible for everything that comes into your aura. So, for example, if you buy a car but fail to service it and look after it, and it literally falls to pieces, then you are responsible for that situation. You are responsible not just because you have lost the usage and therefore the value of that car, but because you have abused your divine stewardship, because you have not acted rightly with regard to that car. So you will have to pay the karma for that misuse.

The Master Jesus warned of this situation when he said how difficult it was for a rich man to enter the Kingdom of Heaven. By this he meant that both rich and poor people have the same opportunity for entering the Kingdom of Heaven but that a rich person has so much more opportunity for creating karma through the misuse of their wealth, through wrong stewardship of their many possessions, that they could be delayed from entering the Kingdom of Heaven by the need to return and pay off their karma. So be aware that more and more possessions represents more and more burdens to bear, because you are karmically responsible for every one of your possessions until you part with them. If you abuse, or do not use any possession, then you are karmically responsible for that and you don't get rid of the responsibility just by giving it away to anyone who is passing by or by throwing it on the rubbish dump. It is your responsibility to pass on that possession to someone who needs it and who will take care of it.

So can you now see why it is best to have few possessions, to walk lightly through life? It is not just because there is a danger of those possessions possessing you. It is because you have to spend so much of your time being responsible for those possessions that you have no time for your own spiritual investigations, to quest after divine consciousness, to be of service to your fellow human beings. Recognise the example of all the great Masters in this respect. They all led simple lives. Finally, remember that what the Lord gives, the Lord can take away. You might spend many days working hard to earn the money to pay for the car of your dreams, but if you have acted wrongly in this respect then someone may come along and steal it from you. So, truly, you possess nothing. All you have is a temporary loan of anything from your Creator whilst you are in physical incarnation.

Q: Everything is only on loan to us?
ZT: Yes, absolutely, on a spiritual loan.

Q: Can this principle be applied to people, to your children for example? Are they just 'on loan'. Can they be taken away from us if we abuse them?
ZT: No, not in the same sense that we have just talked about material possessions. No soul is loaned to anyone.

Q: How about all the pets that we have? Are they possessions too?
ZT: For many people in your world today, pets are regarded and treated as possessions. They see, they desire, they buy, they enjoy for a short time, and then they tire of their pet. They may not physically abuse their pet, they just live in the same house as it, without really being aware of its presence or its needs on any level. As I have said before, if you take a pet into your aura, then, just like a human being, you are totally responsible for that pet and by that I mean not just physically responsible, in the sense of its food and water, but also in the sense of its emotional and animal lifestyle, its need to be in relationship. All animals are ensouled and are, therefore, on an evolutionary path. You must treat them as you would any less evolved soul, that is to say at all times being aware of their needs, of their point of consciousness and learning. If you remove them from their natural state and control them as a pet, then you are totally and karmically responsible for them, a not insignificant burden.

254

So many in your world today regard pets as inanimate toys, as being devoid of feelings. They buy a pet to fulfil their needs but are not in the least bit interested in the animal's needs. In fact they treat them as slaves. Recognise that animals cannot be bartered, put down if they are not considered 'economic', or abandoned if they are not wanted. Like any other possessions that you have, you are totally responsible for your pet's well being and life. Now this is not to say that humans and animals cannot have worthwhile relationships. They can, and do, with both humans and animals being uplifted by a balanced and caring relationship. Nevertheless, I would say that if you cannot devote one tenth of your day to your pet, at the very least, then you should not have one.

Q: I have a strong desire to simplify my life and to spend more time on my spiritual questing. How can I get rid of my large financial empire, which I know attracts great karma, without attracting even further karma?

ZT: Obviously, one would first have to examine the nature of your 'financial empire'. However, what I will say, is that it is wrong to suddenly knock down or end any relationship. You must dismantle such an empire with as much care as you built it up in the first place. You must ensure that no harm is done either to those who work for you or to those who work with you. I find that the best way to handle such a situation is to clearly state your aims to the Universe, on all levels, to fix no time schedule for achieving those aims, and then to hand the whole process over to your Creator, asking that your present situation be resolved for the highest good of all concerned. Once you have clearly stated your aims to your Creator, if your motivation is pure and of the highest, then you will be helped to achieve those aims. You must always act with great responsibility where other people's welfare and destiny are concerned. You do not get rid of something simply by walking away from it or washing your hands of it, because although you might reject something on the physical level, it is still with you on the higher levels of life.

Q: Many people in the world today have this desire to get away from the pressures of modern life, to return to a more simple lifestyle, but we all have financial responsibilities of one kind or another, like earning a living to provide food and shelter for our families. We cannot walk away from these, can we?

ZT: I am not saying that you should. I am simply asking you to consider the level of your financial and material needs and the cost to you of sustaining them. I don't have to tell you that some families have a very high standard of living, whilst other families live very close to penury. Now is the family that lives to a high standard of living any happier, any closer to their Creator, than the family that lives very simply? Is the family that eats caviar and drinks champagne any healthier than the family which eats raw carrots picked from a field and drinks from a spring? What I am talking about is a standard of life rather than a standard of living. I want you to examine how you are living and to see if you can reduce your standard of living and, therefore, the financial commitment needed to support that standard of living. See if you can improve the quality of your life rather than improve the standard of your living.

Q: So are you saying that to live to a high standard of living is not good either for us or for the planet?
ZT: It does not need a wise person to see that in your world today consumerism is rampant and that people are buying things whether they need them or not. For example, people are buying cars, not because their car needs replacing but just because a newer model has come out. Few people seem to realise that the Earth's precious resources have to be used to produce everything and that the industrial processes to produce all these consumer goods require large energy sources which create much of the world's pollution. Even fewer people seem to understand what is the reality of pursuing such policies. What is the reality of producing more and more cars: it is more and more pollution. What is the reality of using more and more of the Earth's resources: they are rapidly becoming exhausted. What is the reality of practising factory farming and the chemical fertilisation of the land: the whole planet's ecology is being threatened. What is the reality of using water as an unlimited supply of energy: there are severe shortages all over the world.

So each of you should examine your lifestyle to see where you can be more sparing of the environment, more sparing of the Earth's precious resources. Be aware of the reality of what you are actually doing. For example, you go to your local supermarket and you buy a small packet of hamburgers. How convenient that is. Most people don't even stop to think that such a product comes from animals! They are not aware of the animal sacrifice that went to give them that meat. They are not

256

aware of the environmental sacrifice that went to support the animal that was eventually slaughtered. They are not aware that the feed for the animal, or perhaps even the animal itself, was raised in some Third World country, where many are faced with starvation and which would not normally be exporting food but for First World financial pressures. Today the whole world is connected not by a sense of mutual support and understanding but rather by the need for financial profit and political manipulation. So be aware of how you are the world and the world is you. You can never act in isolation. You only act in relationship. Examine closely the true nature of every relationship. That is what I am saying.

Q: We are constantly encountering situations where people are destroying the environment, causing pollution and so on. To what degree should we intervene and oppose them?

ZT: In all such situations you should always stand for that which you know to be right rather than oppose that which you know to be wrong. Always be constructive in all conflicts rather than destructive, positive rather than negative. By this I mean that you should not go around attacking people, either mentally, verbally or physically. You should not fight them on a political or financial level. All that you can do is to stand and demonstrate what you believe to be right, and in this case it would be right relationship with the planet. Do not send negative thoughts, thoughts of hatred and criticism, against other people. Just uphold and propound what you know to be right. Allow the Divine Plan to unfold and let your Creator be the judge of all human actions.

Q: When you die, do you automatically forget about all your earthly attachments because you are so busy living life on other levels?

ZT: No. Far from it. If, for example, when you die, you are deeply attached to someone, then, in all probability, you will choose to stay in the aura of the Earth in order to watch over, to help and to protect the loved one you have left behind. Indeed, you may wait in the aura of the Earth until that person dies and joins you. This is the choice of every soul. It is part of the learning experience. You choose the nature of how you want to live and how you want to be of service. At another time we have talked about the dangers of becoming too attached, either to another person or to material possessions, because when you die you can take those attachments with you on a soul level. For example, people that have created a great deal of money and who are attached to

257

that money will stay in the aura of the Earth long after death worrying about how 'their' money is being used, and who is wasting it! It can be a very painful lesson watching someone fritter away your hard earned money and being able to do nothing about it!

So it is important that you learn to release every aspect of life, to live in the moment and not to become attached to anyone or to anything. Death is a moment of joyous release. For many people it is something that they are actually looking forward to. It is the time when they graduate from the school of life and pass on to other, higher things. They have no desire whatsoever to stay behind in the aura of the Earth. Of course, this also works both ways. A person who is still in the school of life should not hang on to someone who has died, because such thought-forms can force the person who has died to remain in the aura of the Earth even though they would want to move on.

Q: But, surely, only old people want to die? Young people with a disease like AIDS fight for life right up to the very end. Is this wrong?
ZT: It really doesn't matter how old you are. Almost everyone that is dying accepts the death experience. It is the people who are left behind, who are observing the death, that fight it. Obviously, the quality of the soul, the nature of its point of consciousness, is the determining factor in any death experience. Often people who die at a very young age exhibit an immense soul quality. This is because, as the saying goes, only the good die young. It is souls who have nothing more to learn, souls who are dying as a sacrifice for other people's learning experiences, souls who only need to touch into the Earth but briefly, who die young.

Q: What happens if the person who dies is rather evolved but the person who is left behind is not? Can such a person hold back the more evolved soul?
ZT: Yes. A strong thought-form can hold anyone to the aura of the Earth, either knowingly or unknowingly. That is why it is so important to learn to release every attachment in life and to do it whilst one is still alive.

Q: We must not grieve over someone for too long then?
ZT: That is correct. I always say that you are only allowed to grieve for seven days. After that, if you keep on grieving it is because you are enjoying the process of grief too much.

Q: What happens to people who die a sudden death, like in a car or an aeroplane accident, people who are killed in war?

ZT: A soldier is obviously aware of the consequences of war and so prepares himself for death, if not for the actual moment of death. So if they are suddenly blown apart by a bomb, on another level of life they know what has happened. They are in a sense daily living with death and so are prepared for it. This is not the case with the person who dies a sudden, violent death in a car or plane accident. They are very often quite unprepared for it and that is why there are quite a few, what I call, lost souls on the other side of life who are still not prepared to accept that they are dead and to move on!

Have you ever thought how you know that you are dead? You are still in an apparently physical body on the astral plane of life. You see life just as it is happening for those who are alive, only you can't communicate with anybody. Your friends are there all around you, only they don't know that you are there, so to speak! This can be the cause of much confusion, as you can imagine, for life appears to be the same and yet it isn't the same. That is why there are spiritual beings who work on that plane 'rescuing' lost souls, but such souls can only be rescued when they have come to an understanding of their position. Some souls, who are very cross about being dead, react with great bitterness and resentment, and take some time to accept what has happened. This is, of course, a learning experience for them on many levels of life.

Q: You constantly use the terminology of 'evolved' and 'unevolved' souls. Would you define these terms for me?

ZT: An evolved soul is a soul of aged evolution, one who has lived and learned from many incarnations on the Earth. It has got nothing to do with age in physical years. An aged soul can be in a baby's body and a young soul can be in an aged person's body. An evolved soul, by definition, will have experienced many cycles of earthly progression and will, through sacrifice and service, have pulled itself up the evolutionary ladder of spiritual consciousness to the point when it is capable of understanding the nature of divinity and the purpose of physical life. As such, it is capable of sacrificing to the whole, of taking responsibility for the world, whereas an unevolved soul, one which is experiencing its first few incarnations on the Earth, lives totally for itself and is barely aware of the presence of the Divine in every aspect of life.

259

You must also recognise that earthly status does not necessarily reflect soul status. The leader of a country, or of a government, is not necessarily a great soul. You should realise that a country gets the leader that its consciousness deserves. If a leader is too evolved for his or her country, if his or her policies are too spiritual, then they will be rejected by the electorate or else suffer the fate of the Master Jesus. Too much soul, too much spiritual consciousness, can be very threatening to an unevolved soul who is, of course, the antithesis of an evolved soul.

Q: On many occasions both you and the Masters talk about 'The Truth'. Would you care to define exactly what it is that you mean by this?
ZT: Yes, but recognise that I am going to have to give you a very simplistic answer. Firstly, be aware that when I talk of God, I talk of our God, the God that created us, the God of our solar system, not the Being that I call Infinite Spirit, the God of the Universe, Which is a Being beyond our comprehension. Our Creator, Whose spirit dwells in the sun, absorbs energy from Infinite Spirit, just as we, in turn, absorb energy from our Creator. I call that energy divine love, the impulse of Divinity, which is, of course, very different from human love. So our Creator absorbs the impulse of Divinity from the Source of all Creation and reflects that Divinity through Its own creations. It is this reflection which we call, which we know as, Truth.

Now this Truth is not infinite, is not absolute. It has its limitations because it is a reflection of the Source, it is not the Source. In a similar fashion, you who receive and recognise the impulse of your Creator, can only understand and demonstrate a reflection of Its Truth. Therefore you can only ever see an aspect of Truth, never the majesty of Infinite Truth. So each of you, as individuals, absorbs the divine energy of your Creator and, according to your soul note, your soul purity, grounds and manifests a point of consciousness, an aspect of Truth. Therefore, although there is only one Truth, there are as many aspects of it as there are people, for you are all unique beings, having walked different paths to arrive at this moment in time or, perhaps I should say, at this moment in consciousness. That is why we are always saying that what is truth for one person is not necessarily truth for another.

Now the Truth of Infinite Spirit manifests through Its Laws, sometimes known as the Cosmic Laws or the Natural Laws. These Laws touch and control every aspect of life on every plane of existence, from the great solar lords right down to the least evolved soul. So the degree to which you both accept and reflect these great Cosmic Laws directly affects your understanding of what is Truth. Let us recognise, therefore, that at your present point of consciousness you can only understand or come to terms with an aspect of Truth. Now for some it may be a high or pure aspect of Truth, for others it may be a low or adulterated aspect of Truth. Nevertheless, you are all on the road to discover Infinite Truth through the aspect of truth of your Creator. Each day, as you encounter the world in which you live, as you experience the drama of life, you are being offered the opportunity to discover what is truth for you, and this truth will eventually lead you to the Truth of the Infinite, to the impulse of all life, Infinite Spirit.

A CHRIST-MASS MESSAGE

It is the time of the Christ-Mass and I choose to celebrate it with you today, rather than on December 25th, because this is the day of the winter solstice and is, therefore, a far more universal day. Why should this be so? It is because today is the day when the whole Earth is touched by the grounding of the Christ Energy. As such, it is a day that does not belong to any one religion or creed. It is that moment in time when the cosmic forces flow down onto the Earth to commemorate the birth of the Christ Energy aeons of time ago. Over successive years I have spoken to you about the true meaning and significance of the Christ-Mass story. I have said that the story should be regarded as a parable and have explained that the Nativity Story, as it is described in the Bible, refers to events that happened long before the birth of the Master Jesus almost two thousand years ago. Furthermore, I have pointed out that the Christ Energy touches every single human being regardless of race, colour, religion or creed.

In your world today the Christian celebration of the birth of the Christ-Mass has, for the most part, become irreligious, yet the anniversary of the birth of the Christ should be one of the holiest days in the Christian calendar. But look at how Christians today have turned this holy day into a holiday. The essence of any holy day is that it is a day that belongs to and is devoted to the Godhead. It is a day in which every human being should make special effort both to contact and to align themselves with the Source of all Life. It is a day in which every man and woman should seek to fulfil the will of that Source. The essence of a holiday, on the other hand, is that it is a day devoted to the self, to the pursuit of pleasure, even if that pleasure is obtained by giving pleasure to others. So recognise that the way in which many people choose to celebrate the Christ-Mass today is simply a reflection of the materialistic thinking that is present in the World at this time. So I want to talk to you about the nature of holiness, of that which is whole or holy, and to lead you all into an understanding of the wholeness or holiness of the Christ Energy and of how It touches every single human being.

If one studies Christian theology, one cannot but help form the impression that Christians believe that Humanity did not deserve to have God send down His only begotten son in order to save Humanity from its self-destructiveness and to point the way to its path of redemption. Christians generally believe that Humanity was not worthy of that great sacrifice and that they should go down on their knees and give thanks for the sacrifice that God made. However we, from our side of life, can see nothing more natural than that the Christ Consciousness should descend into physical incarnation on the Earth. For whereas Humanity has created separation between itself and the Godhead, we see no such separation.

So to us, therefore, it was almost inevitable that the Godhead would send down a part of Itself to redeem another part of Itself that had gone astray or, to put it another way, that one part of the Body of God would try to heal another part of the Body of God. For we are all living organisms in the Body of the one God in Whom we all live, move and have our being. Although we are all unique, individualised cells of divine consciousness, yet we are still part of that one Body and, above all, are all bound by the limitations, by the laws, of that Body. So we, from our viewpoint, can see very clearly that the essence of wholeness, or holiness, is that which represents and looks to the whole in every aspect of life, which sees no separation between Humanity and God and, likewise, in every action that Humanity and God makes. For since we are living with and dwelling in God, everything is a part of that God. As such, all actions should be motivated and empowered by God and the fruits of those actions dedicated back to God.

If you look more closely at the celebration of Christ-Mass today, you will see just how the original Christian traditions have become distorted. How the giving of gifts was originally the sharing of wisdom with those who desired and sought it and how, even on the physical level, gifts were only given, as symbols, to the poor who needed them. Christ-Mass was never intended to be a reason for people giving to those who already had more than enough, to add to their material and karmic burdens. It is just the same with all the food and the drink which today are consumed in such abundance. In the days of old food and drink were given only to the poor, to those people who did not have the money to buy food and drink. Those people who normally had an adequate supply of food and drink usually fasted and took no nourishment at all. The essence of the Christ-Mass ceremony was the humble offering of that which an individual possessed to the other parts of the Body that were in need. It was an example of the living sacrifice, to celebrate the wholeness, in the knowledge that the One God gave to all.

Today the Christ-Mass celebration has become distorted beyond belief. Today the giving is more important than the reason for the giving. The celebration has become more important than the reason for the celebration. Humanity has lost track of its origins, of its roots. It has forgotten from whence it came. It has lost its sense of wholeness. Humanity has created a separation between itself and its Creator and, now, it celebrates that separation! So let us understand that the Christ Energy is in all of us and that we are all touched by that Energy regardless of where we live, what religion we follow, whether we be black or white, rich or poor, in ill health or good health. We separate ourselves from the Godhead only if we choose to do so. It is we who decide to separate ourselves from the Godhead and it is through that separation that we lose our wholeness and become unholy.

Let us see clearly that the universal quality of a holy person, of one who recognises the whole, is that they have not separated themselves from the Godhead and, as such, all power flows to them from that Source. The great Masters that have descended into physical incarnation on the Earth have always possessed and demonstrated cosmic powers which Humanity, in its ignorance, calls miracles. Yet they are no different from you. You possess the same gifts, the same powers, that they possess. The only difference is that they can manifest those powers because they recognise both the nature and the Source of their gifts. They recognise that they are simply channels for the divine energy that flows through them and so they always dedicate the fruits of that energy back to the Source. They see themselves simply as instruments of the divine energy that flows through them. There is, truly, no self present in their beings, only the force of the one God flowing through them.

So I would ask you to understand, especially at this time of the year, that the Christ-Mass celebration is, above all, a celebration of the wholeness of life. It is a celebration that should be shared with all the other Kingdoms of this Earth. Recognise that Humanity is one with the Animal, the Vegetable and the Mineral Kingdoms in its roots, in its energy and in its destiny of service. There truly is no separation between you and your fellow human beings of whom you so often hold evil thoughts, between you and the animals which you so freely slaughter for food, between you and the very soil and water which form and replenish your physical body and which you so unthinkingly abuse. You are truly one with all life. The great Masters have always recognised, demonstrated and celebrated this fact. The essence of any celebration can be simply expressed as the desire to celebrate the oneness of all life. So the purpose of any celebration is to place oneself in the divine flow on the particular holy day, to become empowered by that divine flow and to offer oneself as an instrument of service to the Source of that flow.

It is a fact that many people in your world today dread the approach of the Christ-Mass holiday. For some people the holiday will be a time of great stress and conflict, whilst for others it will be a time when the lower aspects of their nature are brought forth rather than the higher. Many people feel trapped by the ritual of Christ-Mass and resent the fact that they are forced to celebrate Christ-Mass in the traditional manner rather than according to their own personal inspiration. So I would ask you to recognise that you have the God-given right to choose how you wish to celebrate the Christ-Mass and to choose your own particular act of service, your own act of sacrifice, your own act of giving to the whole, as you are inspired by the whole, as an instrument of the Creator. For it is only when you serve the whole that the self begins to slip away, that the need to serve the self no longer becomes so important. It is from serving others that you will discover the root causes of desire and the circle of pain and suffering that desire creates in life after life after life.

In the light of your own understanding, ask yourself this question – 'Is the child that is given only one toy for the Christ-Mass any less happy than the child that is given twenty? Or is it not the case that the child that is only given one toy appreciates it far more, plays with it much more consciously, and gets much more enjoyment and satisfaction from it than the child that is saturated with twenty?'. Understand that it is in the simplicity of life that you will advance, that you will advance not financially, not materially, but spiritually and that, after all, is the essence and purpose of physical life. The person who walks with the fewest physical burdens usually walks the fastest and the farthest. The great curse of Humanity today is its materialistic concepts of life. The people who live in the Western World, in particular, are always desirous of the newest, the fastest, the biggest, the most expensive, without a thought for all the energy that has to be expended in order to produce all their consumer items, without a thought for the many sacrifices of the Vegetable and the Mineral Kingdoms. Above all, they fail to recognise the great distraction that this materialism presents, how it obscures the very purpose and meaning of life.

So at this time I would ask you to consider very carefully just what material possessions you really need for your life. Be aware of how simply you can live, and of how simple are your needs as opposed to your greeds. Remember also, at this time of the Christ-Mass, when you in the Western World, who already have so much, acquire even more, that there are so many people on the planet who have so very little and that they have so very little often because you have so very much. Are you aware just how much of the precious mineral resources of this Earth are directed into armaments, into both individual and national violence, into the protection of vested interests, into the suppressing rather than the granting of the basic rights and freedoms which are the birthright of every human being? So think carefully about how you use the energy of this planet. It is not limitless. I would also ask you to remember the spirit in which the Christ Energy was sent down to Earth, one of sacrificial service, in order to heal and transform this planet which is in such disharmony because of Humanity's erroneous behaviour.

I wonder if you realise the implication behind the simple statement that this Earth is an actual part, an organ, of the Body of our Creator. So everything within that Body, our Solar System, both on the physical and the higher levels of life, is part of our God and is, therefore, imbued with Its Divinity. This means that all things, all beings, are as one in that Body. Therefore recognise that you are as one with every other human being, as one with the Kingdoms of this Earth, as one with the Kingdoms that surround this Earth on the higher planes of life. If you recognise that fact then you will truly understand the nature and purpose of sacrificial service.

So let your Christ-Mass celebration be a celebration of that oneness. Begin by releasing your greeds and by living within your needs. Remember the example of the great Masters who have made their physical incarnations a living sacrifice. They have always led and advocated the most simple of lives. Even though they possessed powers of manifestation beyond human understanding today and could create for themselves whatever they desired on the physical plane of life, yet they chose not to do so. Their powers, when used, were always for the service of others, never for themselves. That is the true nature of

266

service. Similarly, the powers that even now flow through you as individuals should not be used for your own benefit. They are given to you in a sacred trust for the service of all Humanity. You are simply instruments that channel divine energy. Your powers should not be used for self-aggrandisement and the accumulation of material possessions. They should be shared with the whole body of God manifest.

So now is the time to take a serious look at the traditions and customs that have been established around the celebration of the Christ-Mass. Resolve in your own hearts to make it a holy day, not a holiday, a day that is dedicated and devoted to God, not to the pursuit of pleasure, and to let your thoughts, words and deeds demonstrate that dedication, not just for the day but for the days and months to come. If you can do that, then, truly, you will become Christed. You will become one with the Source of all Life.

It is difficult, I know, in your world today, to lead a life based on the principle of sacrificial service, for it would appear that money and possessions are synonymous with power and security and that those who live in the affluent Western World have a happier life than those who live in many of the Third World countries. But I would ask you to remember that a high standard of living is not the same thing as a high standard of life, a life based on spiritual values. Of course there is a high standard of living here in the Western World, but a high standard of living is merely an opportunity for a high standard of service. To whom God has given much, much is expected – and of the Western World, in particular, much is expected in service to the rest of the World. Your talents are not given to you by God just to further your own country, your own race. They are given for service to the whole planet. That was the message of the Christ – service to the One God, regardless of the cost. That was the demonstration of the Master Jesus and the reason why he said 'I and my Father are One'.

At this time there is a great darkness on the face of the Earth, a darkness that touches many people, but, as always, I would ask you to remember that light will always banish the darkness. It will banish the darkness in your own being and, above all, it will banish the darkness in all those with whom you come in contact. When you sit and listen to the wisdom of a great Master you can feel the light of their being. You are touched by their vibration and so are inspired to go forth and to shine your own light, to sound your own note. This, above all else, is what is needed on the Earth at this time. The people of consciousness and spiritual understanding must become light bearers. They must shine their light so as to banish the darkness.

This stage in the cycle of human evolution represents a time of great testing, a time of great challenge. Unless you trust in a Divine Source, unless you trust that there is both plan and purpose in all this darkness, then you will not be able to serve, you will not be able to shine your light. It requires great faith to accept that everything, even the human degradation and bestiality manifesting on the planet at this time, has both meaning and purpose, even if you as an individual cannot understand the reason for it, and that by standing forth and shining your light you are indeed uplifting the whole human race.

So faced with this darkness, darkness of season as well as darkness of human behaviour – and I must warn you that there is even greater darkness still to come – you are being called upon to invoke the cosmic forces flooding down onto the Earth at this time of the Christ-Mass and to be born again. You are being asked to become one with your Creator again, to release the self image, the self of tradition and social conditioning, of what is expected of you by your family and your friends, to release all of that and to literally submerge yourself into the oneness of the Divine Consciousness within you. You are being asked to become an instrument of service as was the Christ. That is the greatest service which you can perform this Christ-Mass. Forget your presents, forget your dinners, forget your parties, just serve the Source and through that service you will be serving not just the Source but the whole human race.

So resolve, therefore, at this very special time, to take advantage of the cosmic forces now grounding themselves upon this planet and to revitalise yourselves for the critical years that are to come. The next few years will prove to be a turning point for many of you, for you will have to choose between self and service, between self-consciousness and Christ-Consciousness, between Mammon and God. Recognise that it is in the simplicity of life, in the release of material desires and possessions, that you will come to terms with the deep spiritual reservoir of your divine being. It is a pool in which once you have bathed, you will always want to return. It is the source of power and understanding that the great Masters possessed. It is the source of cosmic energy that will give you the strength to face any adversity, that will give you the wisdom to handle any test. Use this energy. Go deeply into your being. See the nature of your true self. Understand your unity with the one God. Celebrate Christ-Mass in a holy fashion – by serving the whole and by seeing the whole in every aspect of life.

QUESTIONS AND ANSWERS

Q: I am aware that there are a number of very old souls being born into the diseases of alcoholism and drug addiction at this time and also that some of them are choosing to recover from this illness by a spiritual pathway. I was wondering if you could tell me what part this plays in the upliftment of planetary rather than individual consciousness.

ZT: I would not agree with your statement. An old soul does not descend into addiction of any form whatsoever unless, and this happens only on rare occasions, it chooses to do so for a very particular purpose, usually to help others. An evolved soul would never pollute its body in such a way, indeed, the very vibratory note of its being would prevent it from so doing. The souls that are getting into such forms of addiction today are not evolved souls in the sense that we are using. Rather, they are souls who choose to enter into this field of stimulation because they cannot find the spiritual sustenance that they seek in other fields. They have usually tried many other fields in the past, and in the same way that they are trying this one, so they will try other fields in the future. It is a phase in their evolutionary path that they are going through, a phase that I refer to as the externalisation of their being. They have tried this path in past lives and they will doubtless try it again until they realise that the consciousness that they seek does not lie without but is, rather, within.

For many people the escape into drugs is but an escape from the gross materialism of the world in which they find themselves. It represents an attempt to find cosmic consciousness by the back door, by an artificial way, by a short cut. It cannot be denied that they can reach the higher planes of life through the use of certain drugs but, and this is the big but, they have no control or understanding of their experiences on those planes. This can lead to serious dysfunctions, even to madness and suicide. So it is a very dangerous path to tread, and certainly not the path that an evolved soul would walk. An evolved soul is a relatively pure soul, untainted by the world to a large degree, whose life is God-centered, who does not need to search in this way because it has already discovered the reality of God.

Q: You are constantly talking about the need for purity of thought, word and deed. However I find it very difficult to be pure for any length of time. I can achieve it for short periods of time, when I am in prayer or meditation, but when I return to the world I seem to fall down again. Can you explain why this should be so?

ZT: What you are saying is that when you step out of the world you are pure, to a degree, but that when you are in the world you find it difficult to be pure. I think that most people would empathise with your predicament! It is difficult to be pure in the world in which you live today. Be aware that true purity cannot be imposed by discipline. Many people have tried different spiritual disciplines in order to make themselves pure. Although such disciplines might appear to work in the short term, however, because the people have only temporarily suppressed their desires, once they stop the disciplines they find that they revert to their former behavioural patterns, especially when they are tempted! Moreover it is often the case that when they suppress one form of impurity they find that another form begins to manifest. Now the essence of any form of purity is the motivation behind it. Why does one want to become pure? Is it because you see someone else's purity and you think it would be a good idea to be like them, or is it in response to a deep soul impulse within one? Above all, though, one has to understand the purpose of purity.

Now let us remember that in an impure world, everyone is going to be affected. Even the Master Jesus, upon descending into the physical plane of matter, became impure to a degree. Even a Master like Sai Baba falls and breaks his hip. That is the nature of the world in which you live. Everyone suffers to a degree because of the state of impurity that exists on the Earth. Nevertheless, in that your Creator is the ultimate in Purity for you, if you try to align your being with your Creator at all times, if you try to make yourself a channel for the energy of your Creator to flow through you, the more you pursue these aims with consciousness and devotion, the more you will find yourself becoming purer in every aspect of your being. It will not be a case of imposing purity by discipline, rather that all your impurities will begin to drop away of their own accord. The more one becomes a channel for divine energy, the more one allows the force of God to flow through one, the less there is room for the desires of the self. So it is union with the Source of all Life that truly purifies one's being.

Q: The thing that I am most concerned about at present is the young children who are incarnating into this impure world. How can we best help them in these troubled times?

ZT: The important thing you have to realise with all children is, firstly, that they have chosen to incarnate on the Earth at this time and so, on an inner level anyway, they know what they are getting themselves into, so to speak. Secondly, you must always remember that within that child's body there beats a soul, a soul which could be more evolved and have greater divine potential than yourself. So you must never judge a child's understanding by its outer appearance. Now, obviously, a child that is young in physical years is still coming to terms with the reality of physical life, is still struggling to understand the nature of the society into which it has incarnated. Nevertheless, that child is fresh from the higher planes of life and has great insight and awareness of many human problems. It has a clarity of vision denied to an adult, conditioned by many years of human experience.

So what is important, especially at this time in the evolutionary cycle, is that a child be encouraged to draw upon its own intuitive being and to seek out solutions for itself. It will learn, only too soon, of the trials and tribulations of physical life, of human prejudices and emotions, but it must be encouraged to face them in its own unique way. Obviously a parent will share of their own experiences of life with their child, that is why the child chose them even before birth. No opportunity should be passed by for teaching a child of the Laws of the Universe, like the great Law of Karma, but a child should at all times be taught to learn of life from its own observations. Let the child learn from its own experiences, from its own insights. There is no point in saying to a child 'Don't do that!' unless you say why it shouldn't do that. There is no point in saying to a child 'That's wrong' unless you say why it is wrong. There is no point in teaching a child anything unless you practise that thing yourself, because a child learns most by example.

So it is important that the parents demonstrate their oneness with the Source of all Life, that they exemplify the highest of their spiritual consciousness at all times. In other words they should practise what they preach. They should live their spiritual beliefs and prove to their children that their trust in God is a reality, that their worship is sincere, that divine guidance is their birthright. They must live and teach a God-centred life and invite, not coerce, their children to follow. They must introduce their children to the concept of service, of service to the family, of service to the society in which they live, of service to the

271

planet. They must teach them the great Cosmic Law, that as they give, so shall they receive.

Now it is very easy for a child to become self-centred and selfish, because during the first two cycles of its life, not only is everyone serving it because it cannot fend for itself but its teachers are always encouraging it to develop its own character and to stand on its own two feet. As a result of this, in some children, the ego can become over developed. It is therefore important that all children be taught about the purpose and meaning of sacrifice, that they learn to serve as they have been served. Finally, children must be taught that they choose their lives, they choose their lifestyles, they choose their purpose in life. They must learn that as they sow, so shall they reap. There are no victims, just causes. The Law of Cause and Effect determines all things. So the greatest gift that a parent can give their child is an understanding of this Law, for therein lies the key to the understanding of the world in which they have chosen to live. Learn to accept God's will, and where is the suffering?

Q: On several occasions you have referred to these times as being what the Bible calls Armageddon. Are we actually in Armageddon now or is it still to come?

ZT: Armageddon is not an historical event like the Battle of Hastings in 1066. It cannot even be defined like the Second World War with beginning and ending dates, 1939–1945, although, in truth, that war was set in motion long before 1939 and the fighting was just a period of resolution. Armageddon is an indefinable period stretching over many years, which will, however, culminate in a very short time of extreme change. At present you are in the period leading up to that short period of extreme change. You are in the period where the seeds are being cultivated which will bring about Armageddon, seeds that were sown a long time ago. It would be wrong, indeed stupid, of me to give dates because Humanity will influence the course of events by its own actions. However I would stress that you have no need to worry about such things. All that you can, and should do is live each day as it comes to the highest of your soul consciousness. No more is required of you.

Q: I have two children, aged nineteen and twenty five, who both claim to be very old souls and yet their behaviour in this life has been, in my view, quite self destructive. They have caused me much pain and suffering and I now want to release them from my being and to allow them to live in any way that they so desire. Is it permissible to do this?

ZT: I think we should begin by understanding that simply by stating that you are an old soul, does not make you one! Old souls do not have to state that they are old souls. Old souls demonstrate the fact of their being by their example and by their wisdom. Many people claim to be many things, but be aware that the claim does not prove the fact. Only right demonstration proves the fact. Let us also understand that your children come through you but are not of you. You, as a parent, make the sacrifice of devoting a large part of your life to bringing these souls into physical incarnation. You are responsible for what you have created until that child reaches the age of maturity, twenty one, but from then onwards that child is regarded by the cosmos as being an adult and is karmically responsible for everything that it does in thought, word and deed, for every choice that it makes, for every step that it takes along its evolutionary path. As a parent you will, of course, still be available for help and advice, but too much of that creates a dependence and can inhibit the growth of that being as a mature spiritual being.

It is always difficult for a parent to release their child, to release their child on all levels – physically, mentally and emotionally. But you should recognise that your children's lessons are not your lessons, and should not be, unless you become attached to them. So be strong in your own being and do not let yourself be dragged down by the behaviour of your children. If you have fulfilled all your obligations towards your children, then, at twenty one, you are released to walk your own path in life again. Sometimes, of course, a parent does not want to do this because they still feel the need to control or influence their children. This can be for many reasons, often because the children have become their life, they feel lost without them, and so further periods of adjustment become necessary. Finally, it must also be said that if the children have inherited the faults or personality weaknesses of their parents, then, that, too, will demand karmic settlement and will require that the parents devote more time and energy to their children.

Ultimately, the lesson of children is the lesson of life. You can only do what you feel is best for any given situation. All that you can do is to attune daily to your Creator's will for you and to act from the highest of your being at all times. In any situation of conflict or stress, always invoke what is for the highest good of all concerned. Remember the example of Nature, which can provide so much insight into life. The mother bird devotes herself to raising her brood, but when she feels that they are mature and ready to fly, she pushes them out of the nest, she forces them to learn to fly, and once they can fly they are not allowed back into the nest. The same is true of human evolution as well. There comes a time when we must all stand on our own two feet and fly, fly so that we can discover our own potential and divinity.

Q: Will you please tell us about the spiritual significance of AIDS. What is the purpose of such a disease?

ZT: The purpose of any disease, especially one which can lead to death, is to teach the soul being some important lesson and to transmute karma. Be aware that, basically, all illness is nothing more than karmic settlement. The purpose of diseases such as AIDS and cancer is to get the being who is ill to bring about a transformation of their being in thought, word and deed. If they do not transform themselves then, in all probability, they will die. Either path will prove to be a meaningful learning experience and much karma will have been transmuted as well. So the bottom line of AIDS, as they say, is to transform yourself or to die. Overcome a blockage in yourself by purifying your being or else sacrifice yourself to the illness. Either way you will transmute the karma that created your illness.

Now many people think that they cannot cure themselves of AIDS or cancer. This is not so. Any disease can be cured if the person has the consciousness to do it, if they can remove the psychological blockage that is causing the disease. So at this time, the ending of the cycle, when Humanity is called upon to transmute its karma before the new cycle begins, there is an increase in the numbers catching such diseases. I have to tell you, as well, that there is another disease coming, one more virulent than AIDS, that will rapidly increase the number of people facing such tests.

Q: One of the things which I find so terribly difficult to understand is why all these terrible things are happening today, why all the horrible murders, the child abuse and the rapes, why they are happening to apparently innocent people, and yet you say that no-one is innocent, that everything has a reason for happening, don't you?

ZT: If you accept the principle of karma, then you must also accept the fact that you carry your karma forward to future lives if you do not settle your account, if you do not balance out the energy created by your actions in this life. So in any life you are transmuting the karma of your actions in this life and, when the opportunity presents itself, the karma of your actions in past lives as well. Every action sets in motion a reaction. That is the Law. Now it is stupid to generalise but, very roughly, in these times in which you live, I would say that as much as 75% of the significant events that take place in your life are the result of the need for karmic settlement of actions in past lives. The remaining 25% is due to what has been created in this life.

Q: But does this apply to some poor young girl who is raped? Is she settling karma as well?

ZT: Yes. It is difficult to accept, I know, but you are all magnetic, karmic beings. You attract aspects of life unto yourselves by the very nature of your being on an inner and an outer level, for the outer but reflects the inner. You attract unto yourselves the lessons that you want to learn, the karma that you want to repay. Nothing, no person, no thing, can come into your aura if you are strong, and by that I mean strong spiritually not physically. Both things and people can only get into your aura if you are weak or you allow them to. So do you understand that the person who is raped is only being raped because of some aspect of their being that is attracting that lesson to them. They are attracting the rape to them, not by being deliberately provocative but by their inner energies. No matter what anyone may say outwardly, remember that you are magnetic beings. You attract the nature of your being unto yourselves. Someone who is strong in their spiritual or inner knowingness can pass through the greatest evil and will not be touched by it.

Q: So if we have done something in the past that we are ashamed of, something that we feel guilty about, but something for which we feel genuinely sorry, is there anyway that we can eradicate our karma whilst we are living now?

ZT: Shame and guilt are wasted emotions and do nothing but drag the soul down. Accept what you have done and learn from the experience and awareness of it. Recognise that your Creator will always forgive you for what you have done. In fact God has already forgiven you, before you even repent. What is not taking place is that you have not forgiven yourselves. So it is in the forgiveness of yourselves for what you have done that there comes karmic settlement. You can and will transmute the karma for anything that you have done, at any time, in any life. The greatest transmuter of karma is service. An act of great

275

service can transmute even the greatest evil. Once you acknowledge what you have done, once you ask your Creator for forgiveness, once you consciously offer your being in sacrificial service to atone for your actions, then the slate is wiped clean. Never be ashamed of yourselves, for you are children of God and should walk through life proudly, and very often the greatest sinner will become the greatest servant of the Lord.

THE REALITY OF LOVE

Words can be the cause of much misunderstanding. Now this is not because words do not have exact definition and meaning but because individuals often put their own connotation on them or draw their own inference from them. Even though a word may be precisely defined and illustrated in a dictionary, all of you use words according to your own personal inclination and to your educational conditioning. So when one considers a word such as 'love' one can truly find many interpretations of that word. Everyone of you has your own understanding of love, which is based not only on your own individual experience but also on your unique soul note. Nevertheless, I am going to suggest to you that there is only one root meaning of the word 'love' and that if you understand that root meaning then you are beginning to comprehend the true nature and the reality of love and of how it affects your lives. I am also going to ask you to consider the condition of the absence of love, which is suffering, and to show you why your world is indeed suffering at this time.

Now you are all aware of the many ways in which Humanity uses the term love, not just in the sense of 'falling in love' emotionally but also of love of one's family, love of one's country, and in the greater sense of one's love for life. However, would it not be true to say that that form of love is very selective and divisive and not very universal? Do you not find it difficult to love everything and everybody rather than just the aspects of life, the people, the things, the places, to which you are somehow attracted? Is it not difficult to love someone who hurts you or who thinks badly of you? Do you not find it almost impossible to follow the teachings of the great Masters when they say that you should love every human being regardless of race, colour or creed because they are all aspects of the Divine? It is easy to feel love for one's own family but much more difficult to feel love for a family that is culturally or sociologically very different from you. In just the same way it is easy to feel love for one's country, but much more difficult to feel love for a country that is ideologically or politically opposed to you.

As you begin to investigate the reality of love you will discover that the essence of love is universal rather than individual, that it is an energy that includes rather than excludes, that embraces all forms of life, that links you to the Creator of all Life. Love, therefore, can best be defined as the power of your Creator in physical manifestation and in as much as you align yourself with that power, or energy, then you are 'in love'. Now, of course, aspects of that energy do manifest in individual relationships such as those that exist between a man and a woman, a man and an animal, a woman and a garden, a child and its toy, and so on, but in essence they are all one and the same thing, namely, the divine energy of your Creator flowing through Its creations. So love can be seen as a universal force which touches, empowers and unites every aspect of Creation.

How, therefore, is it possible to become separated from this universal energy of love that flows to everything and everybody from the Source of all Life? Only by placing one's self above the Source, by following a path of self-interest, of self-seeking. When love becomes personal rather than universal then it becomes selfish, it becomes self-centred, and ceases to be love. You can see very clearly in your world today how self-centred love leads to suffering. If you love your husband or your wife because of what they do for *you*, because of what they mean to *you*, if they then stop doing or meaning what you want, what happens to that love? If you love your children because of the needs that they fulfil in *you*, when those children grow up and leave you, do you not feel that you have lost their love, whereas the truth of the matter is probably that they are no longer fulfilling *your* needs. Be aware that love is best expressed through service to the Source of all Love, your Creator and Its creations, and that it is when you are serving the world, no matter what the aspect may be, your family, your country or the planet as a whole, as opposed to serving your self, that you truly experience love.

Now you will have noticed that the love about which I have been talking has nothing whatsoever to do with the sexual love which has become such an obsession in your world today. Sexual love is, for the most part, selfish, self-seeking and self-centred. You love someone on a sexual level because of what that person gives to you, because of what that person means to you, rather than for what you can give to that person. As I said earlier, do you not find it difficult to love someone who dislikes you and yet to whom, perhaps, you can be most of service? Why should I say this? Because in that a person dislikes you, what they are disliking in you are the flaws in their own being, the lessons which they have still to learn and which you, by your loving demonstration and energy, can bring forward into their physical consciousness.

I want you to see very clearly, therefore, that the true nature of love is demonstrated only when there is no self-interest. It is only when you are serving others that you can truly be said to be 'in love' and the very nature of that love is that it expects no reward. When great Masters, such as the Master Jesus, incarnate on the Earth, they are not in the least concerned about whether Humanity accepts or rejects them, about whether Humanity worships or ignores them. They are simply not concerned with either the individual or the collective response of Humanity. They come only to fulfil the Will of their Creator and it is because they fulfil that Will to the highest of their physical and spiritual beings that they are able to manifest such a powerful and universal form of love. The being that serves the Source regardless of personal cost, regardless of the reward, is the being that is truly empowered by love for they are in love with the Source of all Life.

Now you may think that I am talking of a very idealistic form of love. I am indeed talking of what is, for you, the supreme form of love, but recognise that there can be many reflections or facets of it. Every human being manifests the power of love according to his or her point of consciousness and this love will be a reflection, a unique reflection, of that greater love. As your consciousness grows, so does your awareness of the true nature of love. My purpose in talking to you, therefore, is to ask you to look more closely at the nature of your own love through your relationships with your husband or wife, your family or your children, and to compare that love with the ideal of love that I have just talked about.

So examine your love to discover if it is self-centred and based on self-interest, to see if it grows out of your needs rather than universal needs. If you do this, then, gradually, you will begin to develop a far deeper and richer understanding of love. You will understand the love that can lead a man or a woman to lay down their life for another because of the love that they feel for that being. You will understand that they sacrifice their life not for some mental ideal but because of their love for the Source of all Life that is manifesting in that person. Slowly you will become aware of the fact that what you actually love in a person is not the person but the manifestation of God that is being grounded upon the Earth through them.

Some of you have been privileged, in this incarnation, to come into physical contact with a true Master, a pure channel of love, and some of you have found it difficult to understand why you are so attracted to such a being. This is because when you come into the presence of a true Master you become devoted to the form, to the channel that stands before you, rather than to the energy that flows through that channel and which touches you in the innermost part of your being. You feel that you would happily lay down your life for that Master, but such devotion is aroused not by the Master but by the pure energy of love flowing through that being from the Source of all Life. It is this energy, God's love, that inspires you to sacrifice, to seek greater purpose and meaning in your life.

Recognise that one of the essential qualities of divine love is compassion, that is a feeling of oneness with the world around you, of seeing both the planet and Humanity as a whole, rather than from the individual viewpoint of self-centredness and divisiveness. If you are a compassionate being then you serve every single aspect of matter that comes into your aura each day, neither giving suffering nor accepting suffering, giving of your divine energy regardless of your own personal inclinations and feelings. This means that you help those whom you like as well as those whom you dislike on a personality level. Are you able to lay down your ego love and to recognize the greater love, the universal love, God's Love, that flows through every human being? Can you be of service to the whole rather than to a selected individual? For that is the true expression and meaning of love.

It is difficult, especially in your world at this time, where there is so much individual and collective violence, so much human degradation, to love all people equally, but is this not what the great Masters have always taught and demonstrated? You should love the murderer, the rapist, the child abuser, those who abuse the Animal, the Vegetable and the Mineral Kingdoms, not hate and despise them. Have you ever thought that if you are indeed to transform such people, if you are indeed going to help them to rise onto a higher level of consciousness, that this can only be done through love, through bringing out God's love in them? People only behave in a degrading and ungodly way because they have become separated from the vital flow of God's Love. For if they truly loved their God, if they were truly as one with the Source of all Life, how could they behave in such a manner? Remember the times in your own life when you were suffering and recognise that you were only suffering because you had chosen to separate yourself from the flow of God's Love. The root cause of all your suffering is that you have chosen to shut yourself off from God's Love. You have erected a barrier of your own thought, of your own conditioned being, and have chosen to live in that reality rather than in God's reality.

I would like you to see clearly that the moment you open your heart to God's Love all suffering ends and that this decision lies entirely within your own hands, both for you as an individual and for Humanity as a whole. If you would all open your heart-centres and allow the flow of God's Love to enter and touch you, then Humanity would cease to sorrow. Realise that in the world today self-interest is the major factor in the creation of all division and hatred, for where you are concerned only with the self, where you place the love of the self before the love of the whole, then you are sowing the seeds of competition, envy, greed and possessiveness. But where you place the whole before the self, where you serve the whole before the self, then there is the energy of the Creator flowing through you and empowering you. You become, as the Christians say, a Christed being, one who knows and is at one with all things.

In as much as you love any individual – your child, your husband, your wife, your parents, your friends – recognise that it is not the personality aspect that you love and see in them but the force of God flowing through them. It is the living aspect of divinity in manifestation that attracts you to them. Even if their outer personality were to change, you would still love them. Even if they were to hurt you in some way, through wrong action or wrong speech, you would still make sacrifices for them because you have recognised the divinity within them. On the other hand, though, there is the paradox of a man and a woman living together as husband and wife, who have truly never experienced the emotion of genuine love, even though they did 'fall in love' and get married. Yet either one of them could witness, perhaps for only a few hours, a complete stranger performing an act of service to someone in need and truly love that person with a depth of feeling they have never experienced before, in spite of the fact that they have never met that person on a personality level. What arouses that emotion of love within them is the energy created by sacrificial service to the Godhead. For all those who serve the Godhead are truly in love with each other. They are linked and empowered by the force of God which moves all things.

281

I would like you to see clearly that the suffering that exists in the world at this time is entirely due to a lack of love by Humanity both for the Creator of all Life and for the Creator's manifestations. Humanity cannot see the Godhead in all things and, therefore, finds it impossible to love all things. This is because Humanity's love, for the most part, is self-centred. Most people only love those who love them, only love those who give them what they want on either the physical, the emotional or the mental levels. But genuine love does not need or demand a response. Genuine love seeks no reward, save that of knowing that it serves the Source of all Life. So look at the sorrow in your own life, look at the relationships which are giving you sorrow and see clearly that that sorrow exists only because you have stopped the flow of Universal Love. If you become once more an instrument of true service to the people in those relationships, if you give of yourself regardless of the cost, regardless of the reward, then you will begin to feel real love for them once more and that will signify the ending of sorrow.

Can you not recognise that when you serve other people you are serving the Creator of all Life, for you are all aspects of God in physical manifestation? So if you cannot love and serve your fellow human beings you truly do not, and cannot, love and serve God. Now there are many in your world today who say that they love God, who spend hours worshipping and proselytising their God, but who also persecute and think evilly of those who are different from them in race, caste or creed. Such a God is not the true God of this Solar System but a God that they have created in their minds to support their own concepts of life. The one true God enfolds all Humanity, sees no division between the races, no separation into caste and creed, and embraces every level of Humanity with the same love. Above all, the one true God allows each and every one of you the total freedom to express your self according to your own unique note of consciousness, to create according to your own will, no matter what the mistakes you make and, indeed, loves you for those mistakes.

Have you ever considered the nature of a mother's and a father's love for their child, which is simply a reflection of God's love for Humanity only on a lower level? A mother and a father understand that within that small child there is a soul coming into incarnation which has yet to grow into the full awareness of its potential, which has yet to be the master of its physical surroundings. Therefore they nurture that small seed of Humanity until it can begin to take responsibility for its own creativity. They give to it regardless of its wrong doing, regardless of whether it thanks them or not, regardless of whether it returns their love or not. They give to their child because, for them, it represents divine creation in motion. It is the promise of life to come, the continuation of the cycle of human evolution. A parent's love, therefore, is not restricted by judgement or opinion, by self-interest or self-seeking. A parent's love is unconditional, because it represents a surrender to the Divine.

So the true expression of love is to be found when the energy of the Divine flows through you unchecked, untainted. The purer is your channel, the greater is the expression of God's love. It is easiest found and best expressed in service, in service to the planet, in service to Humanity and in service to the three other Kingdoms over which you have been given dominion. A person who truly serves from the heart can be said to be in love, even though they are often unaware of that fact, because the very act of uniting with the divine flow of your Creator's energy removes one's self-identity, one's feelings of separation from the Source. If you have to ask yourself if you are in love, if the emotions that you are feeling are genuine, then the answer is 'No', for the state of love is a state of oneness with the Will of your Creator which does not have to ask questions. For those who live at one with the Source, who have experienced the reality of Divine Love, there is the peace that passes all understanding.

If you are in love with the world, then the world is in love with you. In that you give freely to the world, of the divine energy that is freely given to you, then you are helping to increase the flow of God's love, of God's energy, around the world. How do you learn to love? Begin to sacrifice your self-interest. Begin to release the desires and the expectations that you have for love. Give up your opinions of what love is or of what love should be. Do not feel that you have to seek love. Realise that love is already within you and that the very thing that you seek the most in the whole world can become yours in the twinkling of an eye simply by the expression of outward service. You truly are beings of love, empowered by love, designed to love. Love is the true nature of your being. Love is the true nature of human expression. Understand that love and truly you will understand the nature and the purpose of your Creator.

QUESTIONS AND ANSWERS

Q: I work with a very intellectual person, who laughs at my spiritual beliefs. Sometimes he says terrible things to me. He believes that we are no different from the animals, just a little more evolved, and that when we die, we die for ever. Is it wrong to discuss spiritual matters with him, Zen Tao? Or should I just send loving thoughts to him? Or is it none of my business? What advice could you give me, especially since I have to work with him every day?

ZT: It is difficult, I know, but you should never allow the thoughts and the opinions of other people to affect you. Now in your present situation it is doubly difficult because the individual concerned is obviously trying to put down your understanding of life and to denigrate your spiritual values. Why should he choose to do this? Because in some way, in some small aspect, your understanding of life, your soul point of consciousness, is touching him and is creating conflict in his mind. If something does not touch you or interest you then you ignore it. It is of no significance. So in this situation all that you can do is to be true to yourself, and by this I mean that you do not set out either to sell your spiritual beliefs like a vendor on the street corner or to deliberately seek conflict, but that you simply lead your life each day based on your understanding of what is right living.

Do not feel that you are responsible for converting anyone and that if you fail 'to save someone's soul' that they will be condemned to eternal damnation! That is never your path. You are simply called upon to be examples of the Living God and to demonstrate right living to the world around you. If you live your life to the highest of your spiritual consciousness then you will sow seeds that will slowly, so very slowly, grow to fruition. Remember that the words that people speak do not necessarily reflect their soul being. Often it is the little ego that speaks out of self interest in order to protect itself. So always be aware of the spiritual being that resides within every human being and in your thoughts and prayers and in your meditations seek to contact that presence. Perhaps the greatest test that exists in this world, and one which you will all have to face at some time, as did the Master Jesus, is to love those who are persecuting you, who are even trying to kill you, because of the aspect of Truth that you are grounding and demonstrating. Will you then be able to say: Father forgive them, for they know not what they do?

Q: Zen Tao, I have a big problem. I doubt too much. One week I am completely in tune with everything and the next week I am completely out of tune. I have real atheistic feelings. What should I do to resolve this situation?

ZT: How do you know when you are in tune and how do you know when you are out of tune? Who is making this judgement?

Q: I have a very analytical mind. When I turn off the analysis, stop philosophising and just be, then I feel in tune, but as soon as I start to analyse and to look at both sides and let my mind get in the way, then I feel out of tune.

ZT: You have just answered your own question! When you live only in your mind you feel out of tune, but when you lead your life more from your heart centre, then you feel more in tune with life. So you obviously have to learn to approach life more from your heart centre and to recognise the games that the mind can play. The mind will seek to justify any action and will contort itself in its attempts to justify that action as the truth. The mind can always justify taking action against anything that threatens either it or its concepts of life, even to the point of taking another person's life. So remember that the mind is but the tool of the spiritual impulse that lies in your heart. The mind is the servant not the master and you will lead a more balanced life by feeling as well as thinking.

It is often the case with intellectual people that the games that the intellect plays become more important than the reality of life itself. That is often the reason why so many intellectual people assert that they are atheists. If you, for example, use your superior intellect to win an argument and to crush some poor individual who has dared to challenge your understanding of life, do you not then feel that you must be right, that your idea of the universe is correct and that theirs must be wrong, whereas in actual fact the reverse could be true. So let us see clearly that the intellect alone will never discover God. The only God that your intellect knows is the God that you have discovered in this life so far. The only knowledge that your intellect possesses is the conditioning of this life, all the books you have read, all the religions and philosophies to which you have been exposed. But there is the other side of your being, the intuitive side, the inspirational side, which is receptive to the force of God in motion through the reality of the world in which you are living. God is not in your head. God is in your heart. That is the reality that you have to come to terms with. Love the world around you and

285

you love God. It is foolish to create an image of God in your head and to love that, for that is a false idol which will soon come crashing down.

Q: But is not knowledge a very useful and powerful tool in our everyday lives?

ZT: Knowledge is a useful tool, but you must always remember the limitations of knowledge. For example, you can have a doctor who has been trained in a certain way, who has been given the knowledge that the only way to get rid of cancer is to cut it out through surgery. So whenever that doctor is faced with a person who has cancer he will use that knowledge to justify the need for surgery because that is how he has been taught to cure cancer. But that does not mean that that form of treatment is correct either for that patient in particular or for the cure of cancer in general. Indeed, people are just discovering that there are many ways of curing cancer that do not involve surgery. So you should always be open to each new situation in life. Look at each patient or situation in life with a fresh vision. Seek the vibration of the moment through your collective senses. Finally, remember that knowledge is only a tool, it is not the source. Knowledge can only create from existing information. Creation requires inspiration, the love impulse of your God.

Q: Is it wrong to save a life through an operation such as a heart or kidney transplant? Is it possible to prolong a person's life beyond the time when they should have died?

ZT: When a person is seriously ill, let us say with a heart disease, they are suddenly faced with choices which strike at their very understanding of the purpose of life and death. Some people, when faced with the choice of whether or not to undergo major surgery, perhaps involving a heart transplant, would choose to let the body decide its own course of action and to die when their body died. They would have no fear of death and would see the 'death' of their body as a signal to return home. Equally so, many other people would choose to prolong their physical lives by any means possible, including the insertion of mechanical valves or even a heart transplant itself. Therefore they would willingly undergo surgery and would, perhaps, live for several more years. Now obviously this is not a question of right or wrong. It is a question of consciousness. The decision that is made will be based on how the individual concerned views life and on the quality of life that it expects and needs. What is important, at such a time, is not that the body is allowed to continue to function for a few more years but that the consciousness of the individual concerned undergoes a dramatic change.

I can tell you, however, that everyone has an appointed time to die and that no one can stay alive for long after their appointed time. There are, of course, some instances when people do choose to prolong their lives beyond the point when they should have died, but that in itself is also a great learning lesson. On another occasion I have asked you: 'Do you know what Hell is on Earth?'. My answer has been 'Not being allowed to die'! If you truly were condemned to eternal physical life, you would go mad. You would soon go down on your knees and would pray for death. For death is the great saviour. Death is the great transmuter. Death is a time of reunification with your Creator. It is a time of returning to your true home. Death marks the end of the nightmare, the ending of the drama. It is a time when you will experience peace beyond your comprehension, when you will feel the true nature of God's Love. It is a time when you will truly know yourself as you really are, as a cosmic being not limited by form.

Q: I actually underwent a coronary bypass operation some years ago. Before the operation I seemed to be an absolutely closed book, but since the operation I seemed to have opened up and gained a lot in soul consciousness. So do you feel that it was in my destiny that this should happen?
ZT: Because of the way that so many of you abuse your physical bodies today it is obvious that people will die before their appointed time and, as such, they are not fulfilling their full destinies. Some people also commit suicide and end their lives prematurely. No matter what the reason for the death, one has to pay the karma for such actions. Nevertheless, due to the skills of medical science today, it is sometimes possible to repair the damage caused by years of erroneous living and so allow people to carry on with their destined lives. However, you must recognise that that too is all part of God's plan. No-one gets a second chance by luck! You have every right to be here today because of the way in which you have changed and developed your point of consciousness. If you had not done so, then you would probably have died by now.

Q: I cannot understand why so many Jewish people have been massacred over the centuries. Was it really their appointed time to go,

287

as you have just said, when they all died in their thousands in the concentration camps of Nazi Germany?

ZT: If you view situations such as this from the point of understanding that death is the extinction of human reality and that you only have one life to live and that that life ends at death, then such a thing as the Holocaust appears inexplicable. Furthermore, if you then say that this is all part of God's Plan, that God deliberately allows such things to happen, the question inevitably must be asked: 'Is our God really a God of Love?'.

Now a young soul will never understand or see purpose in tragedy, and I say this meaning no disrespect to all those who hold to the point of view that I have just expressed. But for those who have walked a little further along the spiritual path an understanding is, perhaps, just beginning to dawn that there is always a reason and a purpose behind every tragedy and that God is only the observer of the karmic transmutation that the people themselves have sown. So even if you do not understand the reason why such deaths are necessary on a karmic level, you do believe that there is a reason and a purpose behind every death, behind every tragic situation, and that no-one ever dies in vain. You know that the Lord, your God, is a just and loving God and that the great cosmic Law of Karma is a just Law that is always administered with total impartiality.

Now on another occasion I have been asked a similar question about why the Black Race, in particular, is subject to so much racial prejudice today, why it is persecuted in so many countries simply because of the colour of its skin. The reason is because the black people are still transmuting the karma created by their past actions. I wonder if you know, and you can find mention of this fact in the history books, that even within living memory the black people were the worst slavers in the whole world, for they sold not only their enemies but even their own people into slavery for financial gain. For many thousands of years they have practised slavery and now they are reaping the final karmic reactions to those actions.

Now the seeds of the karma of the Jews were sown in prehistory and can only be discovered by reading the great Akashic Record of this World, yet even amongst the Jews in Israel today you can discern traces of the former patterns that have brought about the need for karmic settlement – the sense of racial isolationism, the concept of the chosen race, the actions of placing and helping their race before all others. Now it is a fact that among the Jewish race are many of the most evolved human beings on this Earth. This is because they come from a planetary source very different from the rest of Humanity. Nevertheless, they have been placed on this Earth in order to learn one lesson and that is the lesson of ONENESS. They have come to learn to be part of the Human race as opposed to just the Jewish race.

As you look back through even recent Jewish history you will find that the Jews nearly always choose to live in racial isolation. They create their own enclaves where they live according to their own rules, following their own understanding of life. They live in separation from the other people of the country in which they live. Even now with the creation of the state of Israel there is the desire to re-establish these old patterns. But the lesson of the Jewish race is to integrate with the rest of the Human Race and therefore any act which promotes racial isolationism will attract karmic settlement. Out of all the suffering of the Jews that took place in the last World War there was one great positive advance, namely, the breaking up of the Jewish enclaves in Europe and the emigration of millions of souls all over the world to begin a new life with new roots. So I would ask you not to dwell on all the bestiality and the human degradation of the Nazi concentration camps but rather to remember that all those souls are now back in physical bodies again and are once more living and learning their karmic lessons.

Q: I have recently stopped associating with some friends of mine who I have known for many years for reasons which I can't really explain. However I know that they are still very keen to see me. At times I feel very guilty about this situation because I feel that I am withholding something from them. Do you think this is a genuine feeling or is it just an ego trip?

ZT: Obviously there can be many reasons why you feel this way and without knowing all the souls concerned I cannot make any specific comments. However, speaking in more general terms, I can say that if your friends have need of you, and you can be of service to them in some way, then you should be of service to them. The very essence of human life is service. Now you may think that it is very inconvenient to have to serve in this way and that you don't particularly feel that you want to serve them, but that very act of service could, perhaps, help you to remove some karmic blockage in your own being. Be aware that if you restrict the flow of divine energy through you to them that you are also restricting the flow to yourself.

I would also advise that before you meet these friends again that you need to resolve the aspect in your own being that feels resistance to being of service. Remember that the sooner you fulfil this service to them to the highest of your ability, and discharge your karmic debt, the sooner you will be released to move on to other things. Until you can complete the little tasks that your Creator asks you to perform you cannot expect to be given bigger ones. Finally, is it not often the case that the tasks that you put off, because you hate doing them, when you actually do them, to the highest of your abilities, can produce an unexpected reward!

Q: On several occasions the Masters have said that we are gods in the making and that, by implication, the Earth is a school or training ground for gods. Can you tell me, if you know, what, exactly, we will be gods of?
ZT: Why does it matter?

Q: Just curiosity! I would like to know what job I am trained for when I leave this school of life, that's all.
ZT: The question that you are really asking is 'What is the purpose of Creation?', but how can any of us, with our limited points of consciousness, even begin to understand the nature and the purpose of Divinity. So my answer, inevitably, will only reflect my understanding and what I have been told by souls who have walked further along the path than myself.

In essence, Infinite Spirit created the Universe in physical form so that It might know of Itself. Now this might seem a strange thing to say of a Being Who is both omnipotent, omniscient and omnipresent, but remember that the inherent nature of Creation is to express Itself. Similarly, your God, the Lord of this Solar System, created the Race of Humanity, in His own image, because of the innermost urging of His Divine Being to express Himself, just as Humanity, in turn, creates or reproduces itself. The inherent nature of the Human Race is to express its creativity in thought, word and deed, just as its Creator has done. Why should this be so? Why does a flower grow and reproduce itself. Because that process is inherent in the seed of the flower. The force of God in motion compels it to fulfil its evolutionary cycle and to manifest the nature of its flower being when all the environmental conditions are appropriate. It is just the same with Humanity. You are impelled to follow your own evolutionary cycle although, of course, it is a cycle that is very different to the flower's.

Now it is not for you to know of that evolutionary cycle. Even though I, on my plane of life, may witness and understand aspects of the cycle which you do not, nevertheless, I too do not know of the design or purpose of our Creator's Plan. I can only describe the purpose of your being by way of an analogy. The totality of Humanity can be compared to a great being of light and power, rather like your Sun. But that being has dissolved itself into millions and millions of individualised atoms, or spiritual microcosms, which have been released to experience the different planes of life in the universe in order to learn and grow in consciousness. These individualised atoms possess in their seeds all the inherent qualities of the great being from which they came. Their aim, therefore, is to discover the reality of the seed in them, which is their own divinity, and to journey back to the Source of all Life from whence they came and to merge with it.

THE NEED FOR WHOLENESS

As I talk to you at this time, it is important that you understand that I am communicating with you on several levels. I am communicating with you not just on the physical level, through your sense of hearing, but also on the more subtle levels, through the senses of your higher bodies. So recognise that you are receiving my message not just on the physical level but also on the higher levels of life and, as such, do not feel that it is necessary for you either to accept or to reject what I say. I would ask only that you listen to me with an open heart and with an open mind and that you try, as much as it is humanly possible, to really be present in and to live this moment in time.

For what is important, after all, is not the source, is not this channel, who simply acts as a funnel, but the energy that flows through the funnel. When you are faced with the need to pour water from a large container into a small bottle you use a funnel, but what you are concerned about is not the funnel but is the pouring of the water into the bottle without spilling or wasting a single drop. When the water is safely in the bottle, then the funnel can be discarded, for it has served its purpose. In a similar fashion, therefore, you too should discard both this instrument and I who speak to you. We should be regarded as being without form or personality, for what is important is not the means but the energy that is imparted to you through the vibration of my words.

Over the past few days I have been listening to you all, as you have talked about the problems and the tests that you are facing in your physical lives. This should be of interest to you, because it should help you to understand that you are truly never alone and that although the world visible and the world invisible is separated by a veil, nevertheless, every thought, word and deed that you express is noted and observed by millions upon millions of beings of consciousness. So, although you consider yourselves to be alone, to be separate individuals, living in a unique world of physical matter, in reality you are but one small aspect of a universe that is beyond your

292

comprehension, a universe which interlinks on the levels of what I will call Cosmic Consciousness.

I wonder if you have noticed that you have all been asking questions that have begun with the word 'why', questions such as 'Why am I here?', 'Why is the world in the state that it is today?', 'Why can I not understand the true nature of my being?' and 'Why do I not know of my future?'. It is important, therefore, that you understand both the nature of that 'why' and, above all, the source that is asking that 'why'. You are, in essence, a duality, consisting of body and spirit, meeting and creating in the vacuum of mind. Your body is controlled by your brain which, from the moment of its birth, creates a record of all the happenings in your present life. That record, which you call your memory, is filled with all your individual thoughts, opinions and judgments. It is filled with all the knowledge and the perceptions of the race into which you have incarnated. So your memory is both highly subjective and very limited, for it knows only of the world that it has experienced either through its own observations or else through the observations of other people, shared through the medium of books, television, films and conversations. It therefore reflects a very narrow viewpoint of life. It is this memory that is asking 'Why?'. It is this memory that is the source of all your questioning, for it is always seeking to create order and stability in a world of great disorder and instability.

When you ask questions such as these you are, in effect, asking 'What is the purpose of human existence?', 'What is the nature of Creation?'. Such questions the brain can not and will not ever understand, because it is not capable of understanding such things. Your brain can be compared to a complex computer and, as such, it only stores and reproduces the experiences of your present life, the earthly knowledge that you have accrued so far. That is the nature of its input and so it cannot be creative, or innovative, except in the sense that it creates from the information that it has already stored. If you acknowledge this simple fact then you must also acknowledge that the source that can answer these questions cannot be in the physical world. Therefore recognise your divine birthright and the fact that you are spiritual beings, linked eternally to the Godhead. Be aware that through your minds, which are universal not individual, for each individual aspect of mind is part of Universal Mind, you are linked to the Source of all Life and, therefore, that it is your birthright to know all things pertaining to that Source's point of consciousness and vibratory note.

I would like you to understand that Creation is not the material form that you believe it to be, for the very essence of Creation is energy not form. Furthermore, if you take your concept of God's power and multiply it by a factor of one million, then you are only just beginning to approach an understanding of the true nature of that divine energy. For at the centre of Creation is peace and quietness. I can only compare it to you going into space where there is no sound, only total stillness, and yet inherent in that stillness is an incredible energy, is an energy that creates and impels all things, that inspires total devotion and love, that embraces and knows every aspect of Its creations.

So the centre of Creation is actually a place of complete tranquillity. Compare this with your own lives. How hard it is for you to be still. Even now your physical bodies are restless and are shuffling around in response to your brains as they dart hither and thither directed by some impulse, by some thought form. How rarely do you yourselves know inner peace and tranquillity. How rarely do you yourselves make contact with the centre of your own being, that point of stillness which knows all things and can answer all questions. You have all forgotten your divine heritage, the fact that when you were placed upon this plane of Earth you were given that divine link to your Creator, of mind to Universal Mind and of spirit to Universal Spirit.

Now many people have attempted to define the nature of God and Its creations, but I would like you to see clearly that all the attempts by the religions of the world, by the gurus and by the priests, are but human attempts, founded on intellect and reasoning, to explain a cosmic reality. So why do they all feel the need to do it? Because Humanity, both individually and collectively, needs a point of reference to which to relate outside of its own being. Since birth you have been taught by your parents and by your teachers always to seek outwardly in order to obtain an understanding of life. So if you want to know about God and Its purpose you feel that it is only right and proper that you should go to your priest or to your guru and that they will reveal the answer to you. But I would like you to understand that this belief is illusory, for knowledge such as this is not held by any one person, no matter what they might claim.

So to whom can you turn in order to find the answers to your questions? There can only be one answer – to the God force that lies within each and every one of you, to the divine force of spirit which links you both one to another and to the great Infinite Spirit. Have you not yet recognised that the Human Race is one race, is one body, is one mind and is one spirit? You are all linked together and what one person knows is automatically known to the rest of Humanity, what one person grounds and manifests in spiritual consciousness automatically becomes part of all human consciousness. You are all linked through a great universal consciousness. So here is the true nature of wholeness, or holiness, which can be defined as the universal consciousness that knows and embraces all things, all beings. Recognise that it is not this universal consciousness that compares and judges, that creates division between race, colour, creed and form, but your conditioned brains, your little egos. So I would like you to recognise that they cannot possibly lead you into an understanding of wholeness, for you cannot know of wholeness from a point of separation from the whole. You can only know of wholeness, of that which is most holy and most sacred, from that part of your being which is whole or holy, your spirit.

So now we come to the question – how are you to contact this source of wholeness or holiness? How can you become one with this great universal stream of consciousness? The answer is, of course, through the stillness of meditation. Now let us understand clearly that meditation is not an act of thought. If you enter into meditation in order to achieve something, no matter whether it be to seek God, to raise your consciousness or to attain inner peace, if you enter into meditation by following some set form of meditation, either the following of a ritual or the chanting of a mantra, then see clearly that that is the creation of your brain, that that is the same source that is leading your physical bodies into activity rather than passivity. Recognise that any response from that source is based on the conditioning of your present life and comes from the fragmented self that knows only of division and separation. Meditation, therefore, is the act of entering into the stillness of your being, into the stillness of the creative Source of all Life. Recognise that it requires no conscious effort. It requires no long periods of ritualistic techniques or chanting. It is an automatic function of your being in the stillness of your being. It can happen to you at any moment of the day. It can happen to you no matter whether you are sitting in a temple or walking in the countryside. It can happen to you any time that you become one with the Source of all Life through that link of mind to Universal Mind.

I would like you to understand that the power to create is a unique power and belongs only to the Source of Creation, to your Creator. Human beings cannot create. They can only create from that which has already been created. Even when they invent something they are only improving or building upon something that has already been invented. They cannot create, except through the creative energy that comes to them from the Source of all Creation. So recognise that if you are to truly create in your own lives, it can only be through the divine energy received from the Source of all Life, otherwise you are merely repeating that which has already been given to you by another human being. So can you now see that all the holy books and scriptures are but a repetition of other people's understandings, no matter what divine source is attributed to them? How can they possibly know what is the source or the purpose of Creation?

Have you ever considered, in your own lives, where you have been truly creative, where you have created through the energy from that point of stillness within your own being rather than in response to the world around you, where you have created from passivity rather than from activity? Have you ever created from that centre of spiritual energy which links you with the world around you rather than from the form which separates you? Have you ever conceived of your mind as being part of a Universal Mind, of all Humanity being empowered by One Being? I therefore invite you to consider the nature of the divine energy which impels and, indeed, controls all things. Recognise the absolute order that is present in the Universe, an order that is beyond your comprehension. Search for the true creativity that exists on the Earth, a creativity that would exist whether the human race was in incarnation upon it or not. Strive to recognise how Humanity is interfering with that creative process and how, even at this very moment, from its position of apparent isolation, is destroying the natural unity of this planet.

Most people on the Earth today regard themselves as being separate from each other and, above all, as being separate from God. They find it difficult to accept that they are really spiritual beings and that they only incarnate into a dense physical body of matter, a body limited in both expression and reception to a narrow band of frequencies, for a relatively short period of time. They do not understand that their physical body is like a garment which they have put on for a very definite purpose and that it is they themselves that have chosen to wear this garment in order to rediscover the reality of their spiritual being. It can be said, therefore, that the purpose of life on the Earth is to overcome the limitations and the restrictions of the physical body and is to rediscover the wholeness or holiness of life, to become one with the Source. Once you are one with the Source then the energy of the Source flows through your physical body like a funnel. But, as I said at the very beginning of my talk, what is important is not the funnel but is the energy that flows through it.

Whether you accept the fact or not, you are all channels of divine energy from the Cosmos into physical manifestation and the only limit on the flow of this divine energy is the size of your funnel, which is the purity and the spiritual capacity of your physical being. The sole purpose of the funnel, the reason for its very existence, is to channel energy, but so many people today are concerned only with the funnel, the physical form, that they forget about the energy that is flowing through it. Moreover, many of you are so concerned with the outer appearance of all the other funnels around you, that you forget about the energy that is flowing through them too. You see only the diversity of the physical form and not the unity of the spiritual energy flowing through it. You forget about the source of the energy flowing through each and every human being. You forget that every funnel has a divine purpose which is, according to its size, its point of consciousness, to manifest Cosmic Consciousness upon the plane of Earth. In this great design you are all inescapably linked together.

I hope that you are all now beginning to recognise the limitations of your physical brains. They are but servants. They are not the masters. They naturally possess only a very limited understanding of the reality of physical life because that understanding can only be based on the experiences of this present life. Yet you have walked this Earth so many times, in so many different bodies. Nevertheless, can you remember any of your previous earthly knowledge, of the times when you lived in Thebes, in Troy or in Babylon? It has all gone. All the things that you created with such great care and love have returned to the dust of this Earth. Humanity only scratches the surface of the planet and even those scratches are soon erased. But what is never erased, what is never lost, is spiritual consciousness.

What the Earth needs at this critical time, therefore, is spiritual consciousness. It needs people who will create on a spiritual level rather than just on a physical level, people who will devote their lives to the grounding of spiritual consciousness. Be aware that the power or the energy that will be responsible for bringing about a significant change in the path of human evolution is divine consciousness, not human creativity. I would like you all to realise that the greatest gift that you can give to help in the transformation of this planet is the grounding of spiritual consciousness. Human creativity has existed for as long as the human race has existed, but it has not brought about an increase in human consciousness. Is your world today any more spiritually aware, any more aware of the God Presence, than it was ten thousand years ago? Are you not probably asking the same questions now that you did when you lived ten thousand years ago? Consider, with care, the import of this. Recognise that there has to be a new form of human creativity, that there has to be wholeness or holiness on the Earth. Though you are individualised cells of a universal brain yet each one of you has a vital aspect of your being to give to the Earth and to the whole of human consciousness.

If I was at this time to give you some of the highest knowledge of the Universe and to describe the nature of cosmic creation, it would be of great interest to you but you would neither believe it nor understand it, and within a few hours you would be adapting it to suit your own understanding of how the world should look through your eyes. Within a day the truth would be lost. Within a week it would be nothing but a memory. For that which is unwhole cannot know of the whole, of that which is holy, just as that which is impure cannot know of purity. It is only when you as individuals purify yourselves in thought, word and deed, become still within and attune to the Source of all Life, that you will know of divine purity, of divine consciousness. When you open your minds to divine consciousness there is no need to study books, to seek out earthly teachers and to question the nature of God, for you are both the question and the answer, you are God.

I would like you to recognise, therefore, that when you talk about God and spirituality, that when you refer to some one as being a Master or even the Son of God, a Saviour, that these are human words, that these are human descriptions. They simply represent a desperate attempt by Humanity to create an understanding of physical life, to give meaning to its apparent separation from God. They are an attempt to form an external link with God. But that is not a link, that is an illusion. The only reality of God lies within you. The only contact with God is through your inner being and that contact can only come about when you place aside the content of your conditioned minds. It is only when you enter into that place of stillness, when you are truly still within your own being, that you will begin to experience that which is divine, that you will truly feel the presence of God. It is at such times that you become God, that you and the Source become one.

So there is no separation from God except where you choose to create that separation. The whole purpose of your physical incarnation is to transmute the karma that you have created by separating yourself from God, is to rediscover the wholeness, the holiness, of all life, is to relearn the great truth that everything is God. You can only do this through observing and knowing yourself. For if you yourself are unwhole, how can you know holiness? If you yourself are fragmented how can you recognise the unity of all life? If you are not at peace with yourself, how can you hope to be at peace with the world? Until you are able to embrace all human beings as being part of the one God, you will never know God. So I would invite you all, at this time, through the process of meditation, to attune to the Source of all Life, to seek that which is whole or holy in life and to understand that Nature, being created by Wholeness, manifests wholeness. There is no need to sit for hours chanting or following some predetermined technique of posture or breathing but, rather, simply by observing life around you, by walking with awareness through the countryside, you can enter into that state of wholeness and truly feel the presence of the Divine without you even consciously seeking It.

So it is essential, therefore, that you learn to be still. You must learn to enter into that point of stillness within your own being. You must learn to recognise the wholeness of all life, to see all creation as divine, to see God's plan and purpose in every being and in every thing. It is not for you to destroy or to change something simply because it does not fit in with your concept of creation, rather it is for you to change your concept of creation and to accept God's creations. It is for you to seek and accept God's Purpose and Plan in all things. If you follow this simple path then every question that you ask will be answered, but it will not be answered by an outside source, it will be answered by a source deep within you. For you are the source of all knowledge. You are the source of all wisdom. You are the source of all power. For you, truly, are God made manifest. Recognise that fact and become God-like, for that is your divine inheritance.

QUESTIONS AND ANSWERS

Q: Over the past eighteen months I seem to have been receiving the same message from many different sources, namely, 'That the purpose of life is simply to be'. Do you feel this is a valid message for me?
ZT: What other option have you got?

Q: I am usually a do-er rather than a be-er.

ZT: Oh, I see. I understand your question now. We are back to the age old conflict between be-ers and do-ers! Is the purpose of life simply to be or to do? For me the answer has always lain in establishing a correct balance between these two aspects of your self. There is obviously a time for be-ing and a time for do-ing. The be-er has to learn to translate their state of be-ing into physical manifestation and the do-er has to learn that it is first necessary to be in order to see if their do-ing is appropriate to the situation in which they find themselves. It is surely obvious that both are necessary states of life. Nevertheless, you must also understand that the importance of any thought, word or deed is the motivation that lies behind it. What is the source or the energy that is empowering your actions?

Now if you spend all your waking time living and operating in your head, just thinking, then your lifestyle simply becomes repetitive. You have no time to be truly creative because you are continually reproducing old patterns. Of course, for some people, who do not want to face the reality of life, this is a great escape, and much of the Western World today is indeed doing just that. There is no true creativity in its actions, just the constant repetition of old patterns. So if you are to be truly creative you must centre yourself before you act, you must consciously attune throughout the day to the Source of all Life. Now at first this becomes almost a matter of mechanical repetition. At three or four set times during the day you stop whatever you are doing and just become still. You try to still that bumblebee of a brain and to enter into the stillness of your being, and it is in that stillness that what I will call inspiration comes.

I wonder if you can appreciate the truth behind that wonderful aphorism – an ounce of inspiration is worth a ton of perspiration! It is so easy just to go at something full pelt and to try to handle a certain situation or relationship with a great deal of energy and application, but if you are doing it in an inappropriate way, a way that is not going to succeed, then you are simply wasting all that energy and application. However, if you were to approach that problem after a period of meditation, perhaps with fresh inspiration, then what was previously an apparently insoluble situation could, perhaps, be solved in the twinkling of an eye.

So before you act you must always try to be aware of what lies behind all your actions. What is your motivation for those actions? If your motivation is coming from a point of self-aggrandisement and self-

300

satisfaction, from a desire to forward yourself at the expense of somebody else, then it is coming from a point of separation and division which will, almost inevitably, lead to conflict. But if your motivation is coming from a point of wholeness, from a sense of being at one with the Source of all Life, then every action becomes a source of healing, a contribution to human unification rather than to human separation. How rarely does Humanity ever examine the real motivations for its actions. For the most part it acts automatically, out of past conditioning, because that is the way that it has always been done. But you do have a choice. You can be creative and just for once act out of inspiration. It just needs a little bit of courage and resolution in order to venture where you have never been before, but it could change your whole life and, therefore, the whole world.

Q: To what extent does non-violence involve submission to outside influences and is it justifiable to use one's own power in order to free oneself from that kind of situation?

ZT: I would like you to understand that the true demonstration of non-violence is born out of a great strength, out of a great spiritual understanding. Let us take the example of the Master Jesus, and I use this example simply because you are all aware of his life because of your Christian upbringing, for there you can see a true demonstration of non-violence. The Master Jesus was a man who, although innocent, consciously allowed himself to be arrested, tried, convicted and then crucified, when at any time he could have avoided those situations by using his great cosmic powers. Moreover, he allowed the people who did those things to him to think that they had won, that their understanding of life had triumphed, and yet today we know the reality of that act of non-violence and can see what it has grounded in the world. Nevertheless, we can also see that in spite of that great sacrifice and act of karmic settlement, because any sacrifice is also an act of karmic settlement, both for the individual concerned and for Humanity as a whole, that the world has not become any less violent. However what is important with any such demonstration of non-violence is that it becomes part of the eternal stream of Human Consciousness and is there waiting for all like-minded people to tap into and to manifest.

So recognise that non-violence can only come from a point of spiritual power. It is not a philosophy, an ideal, a way of life, to which you subscribe in some aspects but not in others. It is no good just being non-violent in the sense that you are not prepared to kill your fellow human beings, no matter what the provocation, but then being violent either in thought, word or deed towards your wife, your children and your neighbours. If you do this, then you are just playing an intellectual game. The true exemplar of non-violence is the person who is allowing the energy from the Source of all Life to flow through them. So it is not a question of any particular individual being non-violent simply because they have attained a certain point of spiritual consciousness. They are non-violent because the very nature of the energy from the Source of all Life which is flowing through them is non-violent. Non-violence is not like a religious coat that you put on and off as and when it is convenient to you. True non-violence comes from the state of being at one with the energy of the Source, the love of your Creator. Recognise, therefore, that any spiritual discipline or practice that is carried out simply on a mental level will not last and will, in fact, be of little value either to you or to the world around you. It is very often the case that those who spend all their time preaching non-violence are merely doing so in order to cover up their own dysfunctional behaviour in other fields.

However, do not think that what I have said means that you yourself should not practise at being non-violent, that there is no point in you even trying to be non-violent until you have become one with your Creator, for that could be some time away! You can begin *now* by trying to be non-violent in thought, word and deed towards everyone that you meet each day. If someone does or says something which aggravates and upsets you, then don't feel that you have to respond and try to get even with them. Just because someone threatens you, either physically or verbally, that does not mean that you have the right to strike back. Just because someone says evil things about you, that does not mean that you have the right to denigrate them in return. No, rather, visualise a circle of white light around yourself and see all that negative energy just flowing around you and not entering into your being. Then try to recognise the source of the energy that is attacking you. It does not come from a person's spirit, only from their personality being, and that for a person to act in this way is only because they have become separated from their source, they have lost touch with the God in them. Then consider how you would like to be helped and treated if you were in the same situation as them, and so give of the highest of yourself. Finally, remember that the truly non-violent person is the person who sees themselves as being part of the whole, the Race of Humanity, who sees no separation between themselves and every person that they meet, who truly knows that by hurting another human being they are truly hurting themselves. It is the whole or holy person that is truly non-violent.

Q: If we really have a source inside us that can give us the answers to all our spiritual questions, then why do we need all these different gurus and teachers? Is it wrong to follow someone else?

ZT: Humanity only follows all these gurus and teachers because it has not yet recognised the God within itself. Humanity believes that God is an external force. It really does not believe that God is within each and every human being. Whilst many believe in the concept of the eternal spirit and of the existence of the spirit after death, they see this as being a return to God after a period of separation. They simply cannot believe that God is in them now, as it is in every other aspect of life around them. That is why some people behave in the way that they do, that is why there is so much conflict and disharmony in the world. The greatest discovery in life that you can make is to realise that you are God.

Having said that, of course, there is a stage in everyone's evolutionary pattern when a guru or a teacher can be of great value, if only to teach someone that they don't need a guru or a teacher! I have said before that your recognition of God falls into three phases. The first phase is when you feel that God is the master and that you are the servant. The second phase occurs when you grow closer to God and begin to see yourself as a son or daughter of God, as being related to God and having a divine heritage. The third phase occurs when you discover that you are one with God, that you are God. So it is primarily in the first phase that you feel the need for an outer guru, a teacher, to take the place of the God you have yet to discover within you.

Now please do not think that I am trying to denigrate all the many gurus and teachers, I am not. As I have just said, there is a time in everyone's life when there is a need to follow a guru, to have a religion, to follow some form of spiritual discipline. This is all part of being human and of being 'separated' from God. This process can go on for many lives. You will incarnate for life after life following this and that path, but then, gradually, through the observation and the living of those paths, you will come to the realisation that God is greater than any one path, than any one religion, than any one guru, and that they are only manifesting one aspect of the Truth, not the whole Truth, and so you will grow beyond your religion and your guru. You will have discovered that there is a Truth which embraces all gurus, all religions, all spiritual disciplines and paths, a Truth that is truly whole or holy, which can embrace the whole human race.

Q: I have read in the Ramala Teachings that the Animal and the Human Kingdoms are separate streams of soul consciousness with separate destinies to fulfil. Other philosophies, however, talk of animals evolving to incarnate as humans and of humans incarnating in animal bodies. I would like to know, therefore, what you feel about all of this and, in particular, can you tell me what happens to an animal species that becomes extinct? Is it lost forever or can it incarnate in another form?

ZT: You must first understand that the Earth had been in existence for aeons of time before Humanity first incarnated on its surface. So Humanity's relationship with the Earth is of a relatively short duration. The Animal Kingdom, along with the other Kingdoms which you call the Vegetable and the Mineral, was created by the energy of the Lord of the Earth, that being whom you sometimes call the Goddess or Mother Earth, uniting with the energy of the God of this Solar System, Whose Spirit dwells in the Sun. These three Kingdoms, therefore, are all part of her expression, her divine manifestation. So when Humanity was placed upon the Earth, an animal form was used to create the physical vehicle best suited for manifesting human consciousness and creativity. However, it has always been the case that the animal group souls are linked to the Goddess of the Earth, whereas human individual souls are linked to a source that dwells far beyond this planet.

Now the Goddess of the Earth, if she had so chosen, could have controlled the path of human evolution, as she controlled the three Kingdoms of Matter. However, because of Humanity's divine link and its unique cosmic destiny, because of the fact that Humanity had been given the divine gift of free choice, so the Goddess temporarily renounced her authority and allowed the Race of Humanity to control her Kingdoms. Therefore, as it says in the Bible, Humanity was given dominion over the Animal, the Vegetable and the Mineral Kingdoms. So Humanity can either uplift or destroy these Kingdoms, as it so chooses. That is the nature of its karmic responsibility. Let us, however, also remember that nothing dies for ever. Though your physical body decays and eventually dies, your spirit still lives on other levels of life. Though Humanity exterminates a particular animal species and it disappears from physical manifestation, the etheric seed still remains. Even if every human being living on the Earth were to be

304

exterminated too, the human race would incarnate again because the etheric seed is still there. Nothing is ever lost even though it disappears from physical manifestation on the surface of the planet.

So what you are witnessing on the Earth at this time is the degradation of the Animal, the Vegetable and the Mineral Kingdoms, the breakdown of the natural ecological relationships that have existed for millennia, all caused by Humanity's own degraded behaviour in thought, word and deed. As Humanity treats its fellow human beings, so it is treating the Kingdoms of this Earth. The further that Humanity separates itself from its God, the further that it acts out of a sense of self-centredness rather than wholeness or holiness, the further will be the downfall of this planet and of all the Kingdoms living on it. Remember, also, that Humanity will have to pay the karma for its actions. That is why you are all here, why you are all in physical incarnation on this planet – to experience the great moment of cataclysmic rebirth that is soon to come. Above all, be aware that the events now unfolding upon the Earth are all of Humanity's creation and that Humanity is simply reaping what it has sowed. They are not the actions of a vengeful God on an innocent people.

In conclusion, therefore, I would ask you to remember that animals are ensouled. They do have consciousness and they are walking along their own evolutionary path. You have dominion over them because of your greater point of consciousness, and any relationship with them must be based on that understanding. You should treat an animal just as you would treat your own child, just as you would want to be treated if you were that child. Now there are instances when human spirits do choose to incarnate in animal form for very specific karmic lessons but, for the most part, the kingdoms remain separate, since they do come from entirely different streams of cosmic consciousness and are here to learn very different lessons, to serve in very different ways. The problems in relationship which exist today between Humanity and the Animal Kingdom are caused entirely by Humanity's possessiveness, by its desires to enslave and to subject everything to its will. Instead of feeling the need to be of service to life, Humanity expects life to serve it. Humanity has only recently abolished human slavery. It will need a little more time before it abolishes animal slavery. Only then will Humanity really learn to co-create with the Animal Kingdom, to respect its role in life and to give it its birthright, the right to walk its own divine evolutionary path. Only then will peace and harmony return to this planet.

THE LAW OF KARMA

On many occasions when we have spoken to you in the past we have said that the purpose of incarnating into this school of life called Earth is simply to rediscover God. Humanity has been given apparent separation from the Godhead – and note that I use the word apparent – and the purpose of this separation is to enable Humanity to rediscover the attributes of the Divine, attributes which, incidentally, dwell within each and every human being. It is through the discovery of this knowledge, over many aeons of time, that Humanity itself slowly grows to become divine and to exhibit the powers of the Godhead. In order to do this Humanity has been given self-identity, an identity separate from the Godhead, and it is through this self-identity, which you call the personality manifestation, that Humanity learns the lessons of life.

However, Humanity, using the divine gift of free choice, has chosen to develop rather than to renounce its sense of self-identity. Using its powers of rational thought Humanity has created even further separation between itself and its Creator and has isolated itself not just from its Creator but also from the physical world around it. There is, therefore, an increasing sense of separation between the world created by God and the world created by Humanity and at this moment in time you can see very clearly where this separation is leading and what, inevitably, lies in the future for Humanity if it continues on this path.

So in your world today a belief in human isolationism is growing, and it is growing not just between individuals but also between Humanity and the planet as a whole. Yet it is amazing to us that Humanity could ever entertain such a belief, for if you look up at your sky on a clear night you can see, even with the naked eye, a vast and complex universe which, in itself, is small when compared to the great invisible universe. An aware observer cannot but fail to be impressed both by the order and balance that is present in this universe, by the sense of unity and wholeness that prevails in it, and by the nature of the power that is

306

capable of linking and balancing the many thousands of suns present even in the visible sky with the little sun which is the centre of your solar system. There has to be a Supreme Power or a Supreme Being that both created and controls this complex universe.

This Supreme Being manifests Itself and maintains order and balance in Its creations through what are sometimes known as the great Natural Laws of the Cosmos. These Natural Laws are comparable to your earthly scientific laws and define the relationship between all created things both on the physical plane and on the planes above and below the physical. They control and hold in perfect balance every divine manifestation of Infinite Spirit, every degree of spiritual consciousness, every molecule of matter. They control the lives not only of each and every human being, but of your Creator, the Solar Lord within Whom you live, move and have your being, and also of the Great God within Whom your Creator lives, moves and has Its being. All levels and degrees of consciousness are bound by these great Natural Laws, one of which is sometimes known as the Law of Karma.

Now I know that many of you have a wrong understanding about the meaning of the word karma. The fact that the word comes from the ancient Sanskrit language has led to much misinterpretation. Here in the Western World the Law of Karma is known under another name, namely, Newton's Third Law, which states that every force has associated with it an equal and opposite force. So the Law becomes known as the Law of Action and Reaction. For every action there is an equal and opposite reaction. That, put in a human scientific way, is the basis of the Law of Karma. Everything that you do in thought, word and deed creates a ripple in the cosmic energy field and will, therefore, affect you who are a part of that energy field.

So it is wrong to think of karma as a being a form of punishment, either by God or by any other Force, as I know that many of you do. Karma is not something which is meted out to you by a Divine Being because of something that you have done. Karma is simply the reaction to an action that you yourselves have performed. You act and, therefore, you create a reaction. You are the cause of every action that happens to you and, as such, you can see very clearly that the nature of your actions determines the nature of your reactions. In the Christian religion the Law of Karma is to be found in that great Christian teaching – 'Do unto others as you would have others do unto you'. This simply means that the thoughts, the words and the deeds which you send out to others, how you treat others, will attract back to you similar treatment or similar energies. Therefore as you would wish that only the highest and the purest energies should come to you, so you should send out only the highest and the purest energies, for what you send out you will receive back.

Now you will notice that I have very carefully left any reference to God out of the Law of Karma. This is because the Law of Karma, the Law of Action and Reaction, stands above, is more omnipotent than, even your Creator, your own Solar Lord. The Natural Laws stand above all the Solar Lords. They govern the existence and the creativity not only of the many thousands of Solar Lords or Gods that exist within your visible universe but also of Those that dwell on the other levels of creation. So your God, Whose spirit dwells in the sun, is subject to the Law of Karma just as much as you are, even if the nature of Its Karma is very different to yours.

Once you have understood that the basis of the Law of Karma is action and reaction, then you will begin to appreciate that every time you create a ripple in the cosmic energy pool or, as you call it, the universe, that that ripple will then automatically affect every other vibration in the cosmic energy pool and, consequently, will also affect you yourself, for you, too, are part of that pool. Many people, of course, choose to believe that they are living in isolation from each other, that they are separate from the Godhead and from the physical world around them. It is the wise soul who recognises that all Humanity is indeed part of the one great whole, that every human being can be considered as an individual cell in the cosmic brain of your Creator. There is, truly, no separation except where Humanity chooses to create it, except where Humanity chooses to live it. So one of the great lessons of physical life is to rise above this apparent separation, to see that it is apparent and to learn that truly you are one with your Creator, not just in your physical but also in your spiritual being. There is no separation in this physical world between you and your God. This world is your God. Your God is this world. You are living in and are an actual part of your God just as an aspect of your God is living in and is an actual part of you. So the greater is to be found within the smaller which is contained within the greater.

I hope that you are now beginning to see that the Law of Karma transcends all human affairs. It controls everything that manifests not only on the physical but also on the other planes of life. However, what is of particular significance to you who dwell on the physical plane of life, this unique school of learning established for you by your Creator, is the fact that everything that manifests on this planet is simply the creation of the Law of Karma in physical manifestation, as opposed to spiritual manifestation. Your physical world, therefore, is karma made manifest. You, not the spiritual you but the physical you, are a creation of karma. Your body is your karma. Your life is your karma. Your death is your karma. Everything that exists on the physical plane of life is a result of the Law of Karma made manifest. Every happening that occurs to you is as a result of the Law of Karma seeking to balance out either your actions in this life or your actions in past lives. Karma creates your physical body. Karma creates your destiny. Karma creates your death.

I hope you now understand that everything, and I mean everything, that is created on this Earth is as a direct result of human karma, both individual and collective. You created the physical body in which you now live. You, and the rest of Humanity, helped to create the nature of the world in which you are now living. If you are able to understand that fact, and to see clearly that the nature of your actions determines the nature of the Universe's reactions, then you will also see that there is no such thing as divine punishment. For your Creator is subject to the same Laws that you are. Worldly reactions, therefore, do not originate with your Creator. Your destiny is entirely independent of your Creator, except in the one case when your Creator chooses to intervene and to moderate your karma by taking on your karmic account Itself. But, for the most part, God is the observer of your karmic patterns. God does not intervene or interfere. God allows you to sow and to reap through both your past and present actions, to observe and to experience the reactions they attract and from that point of understanding to grow in spiritual knowledge of the oneness of all life.

The more you respond to the Will of God and create in Its image the more you create what I will call positive karma. Conversely, the more you oppose the Will of God and create in your own image the more you create what I will call negative karma. Throughout your many lives, therefore, rather like when you save or withdraw money from a bank account, you build up a bank account of either positive or negative karma depending on the nature of your past actions. This account can be used and can be drawn upon both in your present life and in your lives to come. So if you come back into physical incarnation with a bank account full of good karma, this will entitle you to a relatively smooth and happy life in circumstances which will provide few tests. However, ultimately, when you have used up the positive balance in your account you will once more have to face the challenges and tests of this school of life called Earth, and will have to handle new situations which will promote growth and learning. Your karmic bank account will then either go into a surplus or a deficit.

Recognise that you cannot avoid the Law of Karma just as your Creator cannot avoid the Law of Karma. Everything that you do creates a karmic response. Therefore you must accept responsibility for everything that happens to you for you have created it. Realise that God plays no part in this karmic account, that the Law of Karma stands above even your Creator, and is a universal, a cosmic Law that touches and controls all things. Now as you get wiser, as you evolve your soul note and raise your point of consciousness, so you gain the ability to take on other people's karma, to accept the responsibility for their actions, and to transmute their karma through your own actions and so reduce their karmic debts. Great souls such as the Master Jesus are very capable of doing this. Recognise, however, that all karma has to be faced and transmuted and accounted for. It cannot be dissolved or placed aside and ignored. For every action there will always be a reaction. The Law of Karma demands that someone has to be responsible for maintaining and restoring balance in the Universe. Beings such as the great Masters do incarnate onto the physical plane of Earth in order to transmute and remove some of the karma that Humanity has created. They do this in order to help Humanity to progress further along its spiritual path by reducing Humanity's karmic burden. They make that sacrifice out of love for Humanity even though they know that Humanity will create new karma and will in time restore the burden which they have removed by their sacrifice.

It is a wise person who recognises that Science and Religion are both seeking the same thing no matter whether it be called Truth, the Knowledge of the Universe, or God. The Natural Laws of the Universe are the same as Humanity's Laws of Science only expressed on a higher, more holistic level. Let me give you a simple analogy. A farmer has a field in which he grows vegetables year after year without nourishing the soil with compost. If he does not replace that which he takes out of the soil each year, gradually his crop will become less and less as the soil becomes more and more barren. After five years his field will produce very little. Then what does the farmer say? Does he say that the fact that his field has become barren is the punishment of God for his sins or does he recognise that he is to blame? Only the ignorant blame God, or rather their concept of God, for the adversities of life. Those who are wise know full well that it is their actions, in this case the use of the field, that brings about the karmic reactions. It was the farmer not God that created the barrenness, that destroyed the fertility of the soil. It was neither a divine punishment nor an act of blind fate that was visited upon him.

It is a hard fact to accept but ignorance of the Law is no excuse for breaking the Law of Karma and for avoiding the karmic reaction to one's actions. You will reap what you have sown even if you are ignorant of the reality of what you have done, as was the farmer. So it is the unevolved soul, out of ignorance, that always blames outside forces for all the misfortunes of life, that does not consider the possibility that they alone are the cause of all their misfortunes. Such people attribute all trials and tribulations either to other people or else to beings on other levels of life, even to God Itself. It is the unevolved soul who accuses either God or life of being unfair and unjust. It is the evolved soul who recognises that the Law of Karma cannot be anything but fair and just and is responsible for holding all creation in perfect balance.

I hope that you are now beginning to understand that you create the nature of your physical life, which is based solely on your karmic account. Recognise that everything in your life is attributable either to what you have earned or to what you have to pay back in order to balance your karmic account. You create your physical body according to your karmic account. You enter into your human relationships, your family, your marriage, your children, your work, your creativity, even your spirituality, according to your karmic account. Your physical life is nothing but the Law of Karma made manifest. Karma determines the lessons you have to learn. So it can be seen that you, through both your past and your present actions, create your own lessons. In this school of life called Earth you are your own teachers.

If you truly understand the Law of Karma then you must recognise that you are responsible for the state of the world in which you now live. You cannot blame anyone else for the situation in which you now find yourselves. You cannot blame anyone else for the tests that you are now having to face in this life. You should therefore face all the challenges and the tests of life with equanimity. Instead of saying that you are suffering unjustly, that you don't deserve to be in this situation, say rather that this is the situation that you have consciously chosen to be in, because it presents you with the best learning experience and with the best opportunity of settling your karmic account.

311

The Law of Karma dictates that if you have created positive karma, then positive karma will come back to you, and that if you have created negative karma, then negative karma will come back to you. So you must learn to accept both the positive and the negative with equal equanimity, for you have created them both. When you can recognise and accept this great Law it will transform your attitude towards physical life, for you will understand that life is not a series of random acts of fate, where some people live in great hardship and others in a land of plenty, where some people experience horrible accidents and others lead lives of great happiness. You will understand that underneath the physical form there always lies the soul which has demanded and, indeed, has chosen that very situation.

Once you understand that the Law of Karma governs your every action, once you become aware of the fact that as you create now, so you will experience the seeds of those creations at some time in the future, then you begin to pay attention to and observe your every action. You become very conscious of the need to motivate your actions according to Divine Will, to follow the commandments of your Creator so that you create only positive karma. For it is when you act against God's Will, when you create according to your own little wills rather than God's Will, that you create negative karma. Therefore you should pay constant attention to your thoughts, your words and your deeds and carefully examine the motivation behind them. Anything which does not contribute to your spiritual, to your inner growth, which does not lead you back towards the Godhead, should be seen only as an opportunity for creating negative karma. Remember that the material possessions which so many people strive to accumulate, usually at the expense of their fellow human beings, carry with their use great karmic responsibility. Though you be a millionaire, with great monetary wealth and many material possessions, yet you still may be falling heavily into debt where your karmic account is concerned and may be creating the need to return in many more lives in order to transmute the karma for the misuse of that wealth and those possessions.

I would like you to understand clearly that when you dedicate both your work and the fruits of your work to your Creator that you are practising what is known in Sanskrit as Karma Yoga. This means that you are creating only positive karma because of your union with God. Actions based only on the little self, the ego, will always be narrow and harmful and will attract negative karma, whereas actions which you dedicate to your Creator, expecting no reward or pleasure for yourself

312

but, rather, dedicating both the reward and the pleasure to your Creator, create much positive karma. By dedicating all your actions to your Creator, so your life becomes a holy sacrifice. It is through Karma Yoga that you will be able to transmute much past karma, not only for yourself but for the whole human race.

Such dedication, however, can only come about through a recognition of the omnipresence of God. You must be prepared to work with everything that comes into your aura each day, to serve every human being that you meet to the highest of your physical and spiritual consciousness, knowing that when you serve another human being you are, in fact, serving your Creator. Though you meet and serve a complete stranger, yet you are serving your Creator. Though you help to nurture an animal or a piece of land that does not 'belong' to you, yet you are serving your Creator. Your motivation for all these actions should be based on the precept that you are giving back to the Source of all Life just as the Source of all Life has given to you and, as such, no praise or thanks is expected. Your Creator has given you the divine gift of self-identity, and in recognition of that great gift you should give back freely to your Creator.

I know that many of you are aware of the esoteric concept of the so-called Wheel of Life, the continuing circle or cycle of birth, death and rebirth, brought about by the need to settle one's karmic account. It does not need me to say that the act of incarnation, of going through the physical process of birth and death, can be very demanding. It takes a long time, thirty years, for a human being to reach adulthood; thirty years before a human being is acknowledged as being mature. So the continuing cycles of life and death make the lessons of physical life very disconnected. Having to come back each incarnation in different bodies and in different karmic situations makes the lessons of life much harder to learn. So the need to incarnate frequently should be avoided at all costs. The cycle should be adjusted so that you spend as little, but as valuable a time as possible on the physical plane and as much time as possible on the higher planes. So the less you have to settle in your karmic account, the less your need to incarnate on the Earth. The more you recognise this continuing cycle of birth, death and rebirth and choose to avoid it, the more you base your life on the need to avoid increasing your karmic liabilities and to realise your true spiritual being so that you can progress beyond this school of life called Earth. You then reach that point in time when you can choose when you want to incarnate because your karmic account is in balance and you are then in the position of being able to give fully to the world because you are one with God and create no karma. You are truly a living Master, living on the Earth.

In conclusion, therefore, I would ask you to remember that karma is never punishment, that there is no such thing as blind fate, that nothing ever happens to you by chance. The Law of Karma is always just. You are always treated fairly. You never suffer unnecessarily, for the great Lords of Karma who balance your karmic account are totally impartial. They are true judges. They know your soul note and your soul quality and they balance your karmic account according to your unique needs. You are never placed in a situation which you cannot handle, from which you cannot learn some aspect of cosmic consciousness. Every test that you meet in life is designed specifically for your needs. Therefore the wisest thing that you can do is to accept the world in which you live and to recognise that you have created that world. The world is just perfect for you at this time to teach you the lessons that you have come to learn and to provide you with an opportunity for service. Recognise that the easiest way of transmuting karma and of redressing your karmic balance is through service to the Source of all Life and by that I mean serving the Source that is present in every aspect of life, not just your fellow human beings but the Animal, the Vegetable and the Mineral Kingdoms as well. You serve the Source by serving the World, which is the Source made manifest.

Recognise that karma is the reason why you come into physical incarnation and, as such, it defines both the nature of your body, the nature of your destiny and the nature of your death. The purpose or design of karma is to teach you what you have yet to learn, to bring out the highest potential in you and to help you to come to that moment in time when there truly is no separation between you and your Creator. You will then have no karmic account to settle because you will have become one with the Source of all Life. At that moment you will be able to look back and to see very clearly how the Law of Karma has strengthened and purified your soul, how it has led you back to become one with the God from Whom at present you believe you are separated. You will then appreciate the justness of the great Law of Karma and will marvel at the power that holds the whole Universe in balance and controls organisms that range from the simple human form to constellations and galaxies a thousand times larger than yours.

Recognise that the Law of Karma is an all-embracing, all-powerful Law, which touches every aspect of your physical life. Always be conscious of the need to serve and to give back to the Source and to transmute not just your own karma but the karma of the world in which you live. Remember that just as there is individual, national and racial karma so too there is planetary and solar karma. The nature of life is service. One is always giving to the Source. One is always surrendering to the supreme Being that controls and defines all things. It is the wise soul who releases the feelings of self-identity, of egoism, of separation from the whole, who recognises that with the sacrifice of one's personality one has truly sacrificed nothing but one's karmic debt.

QUESTIONS AND ANSWERS

Q: I would like to ask a question about the disability of autism that occurs in children. What on earth is the purpose of a soul coming into an autistic body? Is it really just karmic settlement or is there some other reason?

ZT: Firstly, you must always remember that within every deformed body there is always a perfect soul. The outer body does not reflect the perfection of the inner spiritual being. As the Master has just said, your physical body is created by your karma. For reasons known only to the Lords of Karma the being that is in that deformed body has chosen to incarnate in that body in order to settle his or her karmic account. It is not for us either to question those reasons or to delve into the causes of that karmic debt. The great Masters, of course, do have the power to look into an individual's akashic record and to see clearly the nature of the deeds that created the necessity for such a lesson, but they do so not out of idle curiosity but to see if they can help the individual concerned to more speedily learn his or her lesson and to be released from their karmic debt.

It should also be remembered that the lesson of a physical deformity is not just for the soul incarnating in that body but for all those who come in contact with that soul and who have to serve it, people such as parents and relations, doctors and nurses, teachers and fellow pupils. It is often the case that a great soul will take on some physical impediment, not because it needs to settle its own karmic account but because it has offered to be of service to those around it. So the lesson of autism is as much for the parents as it is for the child and, of course, for everyone who witnesses that physical impediment. Remember, however, that such an impediment is only temporary. It is only of this life and, as such, is illusory.

Q: I am learning to be a teacher but sometimes I doubt whether I am suited to the job. Can you tell me anything which would help me to make a correct decision?

ZT: Teaching is a calling, never a job. It is something which you feel deep within your being that you have to do. Teachers are born rather than made. So your motivation for becoming a teacher should not be born out of the egotistical feeling that you want to have control and power over other people because you know more about a certain subject than they do but, rather, that you are truly devoted to the spiritual, as well as the intellectual upliftment of all the people that you teach. You should teach not for your own satisfaction but for the good of the whole human race. You must recognise that by inspiring and teaching even the least soul in your class you are, indeed, uplifting the whole human race. No sacrifice should be too great for your pupils. Teaching is a job for life although, of course, you will be entitled to your holidays in order to replenish and revitalise your physical beings!

What is the reward for such service and dedication? The fact that those whom you teach, teach you. As with every other aspect of human relationships you learn as much as you give: the more you give in your teaching, the more you will receive. That is the Law of Karma in action. Now I know that you are young in physical years and uncertain as to your vocation in life, but if you truly surrender your mind and your will to your Creator and allow life to come to you, a pattern will begin to emerge which will show you what you should do. Do not feel the need to force the future! Just let the future unfold before you. There is, however, one fact of which I am certain, namely, that if it is in your destiny to be a teacher you will not escape it!

Q: I am concerned about my son, even though he is now an adult and has left home. His lifestyle is very bad and he must be far removed from his destiny path. What can I do about this?

ZT: It is interesting to note that I usually get asked such a question by a lady rather than by a man, because ladies find it so difficult to release their attachments to their children. Men have to conquer their egos but ladies their attachments. What you are really saying to me, my lady, is that you do not feel that the good Lord is taking care of him, and that you alone are responsible for him! It is, indeed, a most difficult thing for a mother to truly release her child when it becomes an adult.

It is a fact that a man or a woman does not reach full maturity until the age of 30, by which time they should have opened and developed their physical, emotional and mental chakras or energy centres. Nevertheless, remember that the soul is fully in the body by the age of 12 and is irrevocably committed to its destiny at that time. It is linked to its Creator and has a definite sense of right and wrong even if it is not karmically accountable for its actions until the age of 21. As such, your Creator is fully responsible for that child. Therefore the path which a soul walks is of its own choosing and, after 21, it alone is responsible for its karmic account.

Now, as I have said on many other occasions, if you do not establish a correct relationship with your child during the first twenty years of its life, it will not be possible, or even desirable, after that time for you to influence the path along which your child walks. Even then, to use the analogy of a boat, all that you can do is to very gently nudge the tiller and to point him or her in what you feel, or think, is the appropriate direction. You must accept the fact that your son is steering his own boat. You must accept the fact that he has his own destiny to follow. You must accept the fact that he has his own lessons to learn and that you should not make his karma your karma.

One of the great lessons that a parent has to learn is to be detached from their children's suffering. They can give them all the love and the compassion that they possess, but they must not take on their children's lessons. Do not let your children drag you down. Rather it is by your example that you will uplift your children. It is by standing up for what you believe and what you hold to be truth that you can be the greatest help to your children. Your children are through you, but not of you. They are part of the Godhead, protected by the Godhead, nurtured by the Godhead. You have nothing to fear for them. What they attract unto themselves is their karmic pattern. The life which they choose is of their own making. You should be a mirror, but not a judge. You can be their parent, but not their God. Through the great Law of Karma they will experience the reactions to their actions. That is their learning experience.

Q: Many people today regard Sathya Sai Baba as an Avatar of our Age. Will you please explain to me what an Avatar is, where do they come from and what is their purpose?

ZT: Avatars are aspects of your Solar Lord or God that have descended into physical manifestation. An Avatar is a perfect aspect of your Creator incarnating on the physical plane of Earth so that Humanity can actually witness divine perfection and can begin to understand a little of the true nature and power of its Creator. In one sense an Avatar can be regarded as an attempt to do the impossible, namely, to manifest the formlessness of God into form. An Avatar usually incarnates on the Earth for a very specific purpose and very often does not appear in the public eye at all.

The role of an Avatar is twofold. Firstly, to restore divine qualities amongst Humanity and to redefine the codes of morality, righteousness and justice, usually after a period of great human degradation. Secondly, to bring about a sudden transformation in human understanding and consciousness and to prepare Humanity for changes on the material or psychological planes of Earth that are about to manifest. Avatars serve as safe harbours in a world threatened by storms. They are a point of permanence in a world of continual impermanence. They normally reside on the divine plane itself and their physical incarnation on the plane of Earth can only be regarded as an act of great sacrifice.

Q: It would seem that many channels are receiving messages from beings that say they come from the constellation of the Pleiades. Is this the case and, if so, of what significance are their messages?

ZT: As has been said on several occasions the Human Race does not belong to this planetary system. It originally came from Sirius in the constellation that you call Canis Major. In its innumerable incarnations on that planet – and we are now going back beyond physical time as you know it – it shared its evolutionary path with the beings who now inhabit the Pleiades. They were, so to speak, Humanity's spiritual brothers and sisters. However, with the changing of the zodiacal cycle on Sirius, aeons of time ago, because they had reached a higher point of consciousness than Humanity, so they transferred their evolutionary path to the Pleiades, whereas Humanity, with cosmic lessons still to learn, was directed to this very special school of life called Earth, to learn the lesson of self-sacrifice, the lesson that it had failed to learn on Sirius.

So nothing would be more natural than that your spiritual brothers and sisters should continue to take an interest in your evolutionary progress and that they would want to assist you at this most critical time in your evolutionary cycle. So they share of their wisdom and knowledge in many ways, always, of course, being mindful of the necessity not to interfere with your evolutionary pattern and not to transgress against the Law of Karma. I should also say that at this time many other planetary beings are drawing close to the Earth to aid in its great moment of transformation and transmutation. The present situation can be compared to one branch of the family offering their help to another branch of the family in a time of crisis.

Now some psychic people are feeling the presence of these planetary beings on the higher levels of life as they send their thought impulses down to Humanity, and this is probably the source of the messages that are being received by various channels. However, I should make it very clear that their purpose in any such action is not to take away Humanity's free choice but is, rather, to help Humanity to make the right choice. Nevertheless, having said all of that, I would advise you always to exercise discretion and discrimination when confronted by such 'channellings', for not all of the sources are what they profess to be. We do have mischievous spirits on our side of life too, who will happily assume a false identity in order to get attraction and recognition!

THE LAST CHANNELLING

It is not without significance that you are gathered here this morning under the zodiacal sign of Aquarius, symbolised by the Phoenix, and that I am talking to you in the Phoenix Room, so named because of the beautiful stained glass window behind me which depicts that mythical bird. For thousands of years the Phoenix has been a symbol of resurrection. The legend relates that at regular intervals the Phoenix renewed itself by placing itself willingly on a self-made funeral pyre and that out of the ashes emerged a new and more splendid bird. The Phoenix, therefore, not only marks the ending of one life and the beginning of the next, but is also a symbol of transfiguration into a new cycle, into a new point of consciousness. The old has to die so that the new may come forth.

For almost two cycles, twenty years, I and a small band of Masters have used this instrument for the purpose of teaching and disseminating our spiritual wisdom and knowledge to all those who have heard and responded to the note that we have sounded. It can truly be said that through the medium of the books and the audio tapes our words have touched almost every country in the world and have been translated into several languages. Nevertheless, the time has now come to end this process. Why should this be so? I will give you two reasons.

Firstly, because if the teacher is always present then the pupil will never learn to walk alone and to take their own initiative, to truly live by what they have learned. If one knows that one can always return and ask the teacher then, inevitably, one becomes accustomed to relying on this form of support. This, to varying degrees, tends to take away the initiative and free will of the individual concerned. So much wisdom and so much knowledge has come through this instrument and yet so much has been ignored. So now is the time for all those who feel in harmony with our note to listen to it, to absorb it and, above all, to practise it. Now is the time to assimilate everything that has been given to you and for this instrument, in particular, to produce the last book in the trilogy that we wish to be published and to send it forth for all to see and read.

Secondly, for as long as I and this instrument are separate in identity, and for as long as you and I are separate in identity too for that matter, then we cannot become one, and the whole purpose of taking incarnation on the planet is to become one with the Source. So for you and this instrument to become one with me, there must be no separate identity, no division into the speaker and the listener, the physical and the non-physical planes of life. We must both merge with the Source of all Life and so speak with one voice, act as one being, both now and forever. We must all become one with the Godhead and so become the Godhead. We must all lose our sense of individuality in order to achieve totality.

In the more recent teachings that have gone forth we have spoken to you of the great changes that are to come. We have also said that the most precious thing which you have at this moment, and one which you waste so freely, is time. Though you be the greatest king in your world, though you be the richest man in your world, you cannot buy time. Yet time for you is running out. Now on one level, as beings of infinite spirit, for you there is no such thing as time. You all come from timelessness. You all return to timelessness. You are not limited by time. But the Earth and your physical bodies are, and the time of great change both for the Earth and for your physical bodies is fast approaching. You cannot buy extra time. You have to use the time that is available to you with wisdom and understanding. You must begin to practise now the union with God of which we have spoken, so that it becomes a natural part of your being, so that in times of crisis and great need there is no separation between you and the Godhead, so that you act as one with the Source of all Life and automatically fulfil Its Will. No longer is there time available for intellectual discussion and theorizing. Now is the time, above all else, for right action based on right knowledge, which comes from union with the Creator of all Life. You must dedicate your lives to God. You must devote your actions to God. You must at all times seek God. You must at all times promote God. You must become God-centred beings in a God-centred world.

The whole purpose of I and the other Masters sharing our wisdom and knowledge with you has always been to lead you into a greater understanding of yourselves and of your own divine relationship with God. It has always been to show you that what is important in your life is not the world but God, that the world is but a manifestation of God, a drama enacted for you, so that you can discover the reality of yourselves and the reality of God. Yet in your world today so many have been seduced into a belief in the reality of the physical world and the unreality of God! They devote their precious lives and their precious time to the pursuit of pleasure, to the accumulation of material possessions and personal wealth, to the constant search for self-gratification even at the expense of their fellow human beings and the three other Kingdoms of this Earth over whom they have been given temporary dominion.

Can you not see that the physical world, being governed by time, is illusory? Physical matter, no matter what form it takes, always decays and dies and has physical limits. All physical things experience birth and death according to the nature of their evolutionary cycle. All physical things die in the fullness of time and return to the Earth, to the essence of physical matter. You, however, do not do this because you are not of this planet. You can never be born because you have never died. Why, therefore, do you spend so much of your precious time bent on the pursuit of physical matter? Now that is not to say that you should not act with responsibility towards the matter which God has placed in your hands. You cannot ignore the world and simply say that it does not matter, because, of course, karmically, it does. But, on the other hand, you must always keep the matter of this world in correct perspective. You must always remember that you are eternal beings of spirit living for only a short time in matter. You are not of matter. You are simply dwelling in matter in order to learn the lessons of this school of life called Earth and to grow in spiritual consciousness and awareness.

There is a wonderful story about the Buddha, which I would like to relate to you. The Buddha, as I am sure you know, was of royal lineage, yet he renounced all the luxuries and the comforts of palace life and became a sanyasin. His father, the king, was desolated to hear that his son was begging for alms in the streets, having no money and no possessions, and was sleeping on the ground and having to rely on humble people for his daily food. So he sent a messenger to his son and begged him to return to the palace, saying that he could be king in his place if he would renounce the life that he had chosen and would return to his birthright. But the Buddha sent a message back to the king, his father, saying that he would only return and live in the palace, as the king desired, if he could answer these three questions:–

'Do you have the power to save me from death?'

322

'Do you have the power to keep disease away from me and to keep me in sound health?'

'Do you have the power to prevent old age and senility from descending upon me?'.

The Buddha then carried on to say, 'If you can save me from these three evils then I will return to the palace'. The king, of course, could not say 'Yes' to any one of these questions. So the Buddha continued with his life of renunciation, to become eventually a realised being and to ground a point of consciousness on the Earth which, over the years, has touched millions of people all around the world. But what can you say of his father and his grandfather and of the kings that were before him with all of their servants and their palaces. They have all passed into history but the consciousness, the God-centredness, of the Buddha lives even today.

The Buddha saw that birth, life and death were sorrowful and so he replied to his father in the correct way. Having watched so many people suffering throughout his life he could not bear to waste another minute of his life living in a state of ignorance and illusion. He wished to devote the limited time that was given to him to discover the true nature of life and the true nature of his own being. His life should be an object lesson to you. So many of you are attached to the material possessions of life. You are constantly wasting your valuable time searching for better and faster cars, for bigger and grander houses. But what can you say of your chariots, your coaches and your houses in your past lives? Are they really so important to you today? Is the horse and the chariot that you rode down the roads of ancient Greece still to be found in your memory? Do you recall the beautiful villa that you worked so hard to buy in ancient Rome? Or is it not the case that they have returned to the dust of this Earth and are gone forever, that they are no longer of importance to you?

What endures is not physical matter but the consciousness with which you handle it. Always remember, therefore, that you are beings of consciousness. You come into this world with consciousness and you leave this world with consciousness, nothing else. All else is simply matter in your hands, is Maya, or illusion, which you handle and play with in order to gain consciousness. Therefore every second of your life should be devoted to the garnering of consciousness, for that is why you are here, and the garnering of that consciousness can only come about though your uniting with the Source of all Life, the Source of all

Creativity. As you become one with that Source, so you become one with all things. You acquire the powers to understand and to control all things, and to recognise their place and their purpose in the evolutionary scheme. You have dominion over all life. But such an understanding does not come from separation, but from oneness. It does not come from pursuing your own self-centred aims in the physical world but from the sacrifice of those aims to the oneness of all life.

The time is fast approaching when the world as you know it will change. It will change beyond your wildest dreams and those of you that have clung to matter, to Maya, to the illusion of financial security and material possessions, to personal security and unlimited amounts of food and drink, will overnight be placed in a position of helplessness. You will find that life beyond survival becomes quite purposeless and meaningless. So what is vital at this time, therefore, is that you use the limited time that is left to you to the full. Now is the time to practise union with your Creator, to search diligently for an understanding of the purpose of life and to become one with the force of God in motion. If you can do this now, then, in times of need you will have already established that divine link and can rely on it, not just to save, help and uplift yourself but all those people who will be relying on you. It is the people who have established the divine link with their Creator who will automatically become the leaders of the New Age, because in times of great crisis they will be able to say: 'I know. I can explain. Follow me.' But this union will not be thrust upon you. It is something you will have to acquire through right practice now, through discipline in your life now, through establishing your values now, through right relationship with the world around you now.

Do not be seduced by the glamour of the material world around you, for as the Piscean Age draws to its dramatic end so there is great materialism present, which outwardly can appear both glamorous and attractive. The things that most people desire in the world today are largely irrelevant to the purpose and meaning of life. Those that do try to follow a spiritual path are mocked. Television, which could have been a great instrument of communication and education, has instead become a drug, like opium, which enervates the creative energy and distracts millions of people from the true purpose of life. It is, perhaps, the greatest physical time waster that exists in the world today and it is physical time that is so precious to you right now, it is physical time that is so limited, that will soon no longer be available to you.

So recognise that this physical world is really nothing but an illusion. It is simply your modelling clay. In the fullness of time, when its cycle is complete, your world will return to cosmic dust, and who will remember it? When you die, you, too, will soon forget about your physical life, but what you will never forget, and what you will return with in your next life, is your divine consciousness, is the God-centredness that you have established. But to gain this, like the Buddha, you first have to renounce. You have to make the sacrifice. You have to devote both physical time and energy to your quest for the oneness. However, once you have realised that oneness, once you have realised that you *are* God manifest, then, truly you have become a realised Master with the power to help uplift and transmute the evil of this world. What your world needs at this time, and will need even more in the future, is realised Masters, Masters who are one with the Source, who have no separation from the Source, who unquestioningly accept and fulfil the Will of the Source.

Have you ever recognised in your own lives, even if it is on an unconscious level, how often you actually state the fact that you are not your body, even if you are not aware that you are doing it? Do you not always use the possessive pronoun when referring to your body? Do you not always talk about 'my' body, 'my' health, 'my' eyesight, etc, in the same sense as you say 'my' car? Yet it is the use of that very possessiveness that is unwittingly indicating that the source of the comment is separate from your body. For when you are saying 'my body is ill', 'my eyes are weak', you are aware, on another level, that although your body and your eyes belong to you, they are not you. You are not the body, you are not the eyes. You are separate from that body and those eyes. For you are a divine being, an eternal soul, that exists beyond time and matter. Of course you must be responsible for your body at all times and keep it as the temple of the soul. You must respect its needs but, at the same time, you must never be dragged down by its desires and feelings. Recognise that you are the master. You are the driver of the car; you should never let the car drive you. Recognise that your wisdom, your consciousness, is based on eternity, whereas the body knows only the limitations of this world, namely time and decay.

At this time, therefore, the ending of the cycle, the time that has sometimes been described as Kali Yuga, the Iron Age or Armageddon, recognise that great changes are about to manifest. Nevertheless, you have been given the tools, you have been given the wisdom and the understanding, to face these changes. But the events that are to come

325

cannot be faced simply by the reading of spiritual books, by attending so-called 'New Age' lectures, by engaging in deep philosophical discussions, by the putting on or off of any particular religious overcoat. They can only be faced through right practice, through the sounding of your soul note, your point of consciousness, in your everyday living, no matter what the cost.

You must manifest the divinity in you and have it flowing through you every second of the day. This requires both attention, observation and meditation. It requires that you consciously dedicate your life to the Creator of all Life in every thing that you think and do, that you constantly hold a vision of that Being before you. It requires that you dedicate every action that you perform to the glory of your Creator, without being attached to the fruits of those actions, without receiving either pain or pleasure from them, and in that you dedicate all your actions to the one and only God, then your God accepts the karmic responsibility for them. So always dedicate your lives to the Source. Always dedicate your thoughts, your words and your deeds to the Source. Constantly seek to align yourself with the Source until eventually the time will come when you will truly be able to say not that you are a messenger of God, not that you are a son or a daughter of God, but that you are God, that you and God have become one. At such a time, when there is no separation between you and your God, you will have become a realised being, a true Master.

So it is not with sadness that we come to the end of our communication with you through this channel. Much has been given, much has been received. More wisdom and knowledge will be given in the future but in a different form and in a different place. First of all, though, you must digest and use what you have been given. You must devote time and energy to assimilating the teachings that have been received. You must discover the truth in them for you, but this can only be done through right practice, and it will be by that very practice that you will create the funeral pyre on which you will sacrifice the old and so allow the more splendid new to come forth. Remember the legend of the Phoenix, to which I referred at the beginning of my talk. It was out of the ashes of the old that the new and more magnificent bird arose. So too will it be with this channel, for out of that old separation of identity of channel and instrument, of the world visible and the world invisible, of the Masters and interplanetary Masters on one plane and Humanity on another, out of the ending of all of that will come the Oneness of the one and only God Which embraces and is all things, Which empowers and knows all things, Which is truly one with the whole Cosmos.

QUESTIONS AND ANSWERS

Q: We are all a bit stunned because although we knew that this moment was going to happen one day, we hadn't quite expected it to be so soon! Does this mean that your instrument and the Ramala Centre will continue with their work, only in a different way, or will there be a sabbatical period while they both release the old and seek a new direction?

ZT: There will obviously be a period of withdrawal, of rebirth and then coming forth renewed but the dissemination of the knowledge and the wisdom of Ramala will still continue. The books will still be available and will circulate all over the world. However, slowly, a new purpose will emerge as you come to terms with the significance of today's events. What has happened so far can be likened to the foundations of a great building. You have at long last got up to the ground level! Now we can commence building the real edifice.

Q: I would like to ask you about the omnipresence of God. I am sure you are familiar with the philosophy. As one who is trying to come to terms with the illusion of life and the reality of spirit, to renounce the physical desires of life, I am always coming across people who argue that if everything is indeed divine, then everything is just perfect. So why do we need to renounce it? Perhaps you could share with us your understanding and perspective of the concept of omnipresence?

ZT: Let us understand that the Being or the Force which you call God created the physical world of which you are aware, as well as many other worlds of which you are not aware. That Being also created what I will call a spiritual hierarchy to empower and to bring order to these worlds. That is why you have the angelic, the devic and the elemental kingdoms. Even if Humanity did not incarnate on the Earth, as indeed was the case at one time, your God would still manifest Its creativeness and would control Its creations through these kingdoms. So in this sense it can be said that your God is present in and controls every aspect of matter that exists in the physical world.

God's Consciousness permeates throughout every aspect of Its creations and without that Consciousness there would be no life at all.

The same thing, incidentally, is also true of your own human consciousness and of the things that you create. Furthermore, since the planets of your solar system are the actual organs or chakras of your God's physical body, recognise that everything that manifests on them is automatically part of and is imbued with the energies of that divine body. So the Earth and Humanity living on it are an actual part of your God's physical body. You should, however, be aware that there is one great difference between Humanity and the other Kingdoms of Matter. Physical matter, although empowered and suffused by God, is not impregnated with God's Consciousness to the degree that Humanity is and, as such, does not possess Humanity's ability to express divine love and compassion. Every human being has an infinitesimal spark of their Creator's spirit beating within their heart and is, therefore, linked for eternity to their Creator. Every human being, therefore, possesses all the divine potential of that great Being.

Now because of the nature of divine creation on the Earth at this time Humanity has been given the gift of free choice. You can, therefore, attract unto yourself whatever you choose for your life. For example, if you really have your heart set upon making money and you feel that the purpose of your life is simply to create more and more wealth, then you will do just that and your Creator will help you in that objective. You will attract more and more wealth unto yourself. Your Creator will help you to fulfil your desires, because that is part of the physical experience that you have chosen to learn. Now, of course, God is not actually in the money that you attract unto yourself but, ultimately, God is the supplier and the provider of that money and of that test. God therefore empowers your every learning experience. Every aspect of matter on the Earth dances to Its cosmic tune and responds to the note that your Creator sounds. In this way it can be said that God is present in every aspect of matter.

So can we now see clearly that even though the spirit of your Creator is separate from Its creations, in the same way that your spirit is separate from your creations, that when the spirit of your Creator is in Its Solar Body, just as when your spirit is in your physical body, that both those bodies are suffused by those spiritual impulses. The Earth is controlled by the spiritual impulse of your Creator just as your physical body is controlled by your spiritual impulse. So recognise, therefore, that everything that comes into your aura is a part of your Lord's creations and has been placed there by your Lord as part of the learning experience that you have come to learn. If, through your own desires,

328

you choose to create further learning experiences, then you will draw into your aura the material aspects of life appropriate for those learning experiences. Nevertheless, recognise that everything that comes into your aura has been created by God, belongs to God, and is therefore worthy of the respect that one accords to God.

To understand the nature of God you have only to understand yourselves for you are created in the image of your Creator. You are cosmic spirit in physical manifestation. Everything that you do in thought, word and deed reflects that cosmic creativity. Remember, however, that everyone else that you meet is the same as you. You all possess the ability to control and manipulate matter, to be in a sense God-like if not as God. Be aware that all the Kingdoms of the Earth are divine even though you have been given the freedom to do what you like with them, either to abuse them or to uplift them. It is your relationship with those Kingdoms that determines your karma.

Finally, recognise that physical life can be compared to a great drama. Your Creator is both the author and the director of that drama. It has chosen the nature of the drama. It has chosen both the players and their roles. It has placed those players and, some might say, even rehearsed them in the roles that they have to play. You are, therefore, all empowered by your Creator so that you may play your roles. So in this sense too it can be said that God is omnipresent. The role of the so-called evil person is just as important as the role of the so-called good person, for without darkness you would not know light. The tester is just as important as the person that is being tested. Remember that all evil is inherently transitory in nature and that when that great Day of Judgement comes, the day when you pass over from the world of Matter into the world of Spirit, that truly the forgiveness of your Creator, no matter what you have done, always awaits you.

Q: The first speaker said that we should start to put away our involvement with spiritual teachers and with books and should turn to living through right action. If he feels that the time has passed for learning through teachers and books, how are we going to develop ourselves, how are we to learn?

ZT: I do not believe that the Master said that you should put away books but rather that now is the time that you should start practising just a little of the wisdom which you have been so carefully garnering. In the world in which you live today the methods of transmitting and communicating information are evolving very rapidly. Every day brings a new spiritual book or a new spiritual technique into the market place. It would seem that almost everybody is publishing their idea of God, their idea of transformation, their idea of the New Age, which, of course, it is their birthright to do. However, if you feel that the path to God is through reading books and that the more books you read, the more knowledge you will acquire about God and so the more evolved you will become, then you are sadly mistaken. For all that you are acquiring is simply intellectual knowledge and, what is more, other people's intellectual knowledge at that. It is all second-hand, passed down and diluted through many beings. The purpose of reading any book, therefore, is not to take on board all the concepts of truth expressed in it but, rather, to allow the book to stimulate within you your own concepts of truth. For many people a book is rather like a coat which they put on and then say: 'Now I have become that book', and which just as easily they can take off, to replace it with another coat. The purpose of any book is simply to stimulate your own knowledge, to bring forth your own aspect of truth.

In your world today so many, many people are reading and intellectualising about God that they are continually ignoring the observation of their own eyes and the intuitive process of their own being. Life is the teacher, because God is life. You learn about God from life. You learn about God from your relationship with divinity in manifestation, which is both the people and the world in which you live. Now some of you, who have advanced a little way along the path towards Infinite Consciousness, have gained an understanding of right living, but are you prepared to demonstrate it in the world today? Are you prepared to make the necessary sacrifices and to risk the scorn or the persecution of your fellow human beings? How many of you can follow a simple discipline like getting up early each morning to talk to your Creator before you commence your day? How often do you think of your Creator during the day? How many times do you positively attune to the Source of all Life and seek your Creator's help in solving the problems of the day? How many of you, when you clash with someone on the personality level, are able to say: 'There is not someone who I dislike or hate. There is my Creator standing in front of me! How best can I help this person? How best can I help the God presence to manifest in them?'.

What the Master was saying is that you should be striving with all your spiritual determination to establish union with God *now*. To give you an analogy: if a period of drought is coming, unless you prepare now for that drought, take care of your garden and put water in storage, you will find it very difficult to survive when the drought is upon you. It will be too late then to save water. Now the water is but an analogy for spirit, and when the times of great conflict and physical hardship come upon you, unless you have that divine link with your Creator, you will find it difficult to survive. So you should practise your union with God *now* while the times are good, while you still have time to do it. Seize this last opportunity and use it wisely.

Q: Who or what is the Anti-Christ that we hear so many people talking about today?

ZT: The Anti-Christ is the name given in Christian dogma to the energy which will appear to challenge or test the Christ Energy when it next manifests on the Earth at the ending of the present human cycle. We would prefer to describe it as the final saturnic or satanic influence of the Piscean Age, the final test of the Age. It will be embodied in a human being who even now is upon the Earth and who will appear, outwardly anyway, to have all the characteristics and all the attributes of a messiah. This being will possess all the wisdom, all the power, all the knowingness of the Christ, but will be different in one vital aspect. He will use all of his powers not in service to the One God but to serve his own ends. He will use his great charisma to persuade people to worship him rather than to worship God.

Now many people will be deceived by this being for a considerable length of time and it will not be until the very last moment, in fact until the very last second, of the very last hour, of the very last day, when suddenly he will reveal the true nature of his being. Some people will not even recognise the deception and will die believing in that being. The implication of this is that you must always exercise your God-given powers of discrimination with regard to everything that you hear, read and see. Just because a man has great occult powers, and can manipulate physical matter, do not automatically believe what he says and follow him. Rather, look closely at his personal demonstration and his lifestyle. Look at the nature of those that follow him and how they lead their lives. Are both they and their Master true embodiments of service and sacrifice? Above all, always follow your own intuitive channel, always listen to your own inner guidance, your eternal spiritual being.

Q: But surely we must take great care not to become paranoid about every teacher that we meet, just because they do not appear to be perfect in thought, word and deed? That way we could finish up by rejecting everything.

ZT: What I am talking about now is not of normal mortals but is of the Christ and the Anti-Christ. These are not ordinary teachers.

Q: But surely when the Christ returns, or when he begins his public ministry, if he does something which people don't feel is right, at their point of consciousness, then they will say that he is the Anti-Christ and will reject him. So we have to be very careful over this process of discrimination that you are talking about. We could wind up by rejecting everything because we are so paranoid about choosing the wrong being.

ZT: Only a relatively small number of people, at the level about which we are now talking, are even concerned about the Christ, let alone the Anti-Christ. When the Christ Energy last incarnated on the Earth, almost two thousand years ago, how many people in the world actually recognised that impulse? How many people would recognise or, indeed, are recognising the Christ Energy today? But that is another question!

Q: Zen Tao, did I understand you to say that a guide, like yourself, is just another soul being walking an evolutionary path and that we should not therefore assume that a guide is of far greater soul consciousness than ourselves?

ZT: That is correct. A guide, more often than not, is of a comparable soul consciousness to the being that it is watching over. As I am a guide to this instrument now, so he has been a guide to me when I have been in incarnation on the Earth in past lives. We are attracted to each other both by our consciousnesses and by our karma. We learn by watching each other from the different planes of life. We share our lessons, so to speak! It is a two way learning process. You should always recognise, however, that a guide is simply one small aspect of the great Spiritual Hierarchy of divine consciousness that controls and watches over every single aspect of human life. The Source of all Life administers Its Plan and sends help to Humanity through Its Spiritual Hierarchy.

Q: But we should always pray to the Source for help, not to the guide?

ZT: That is correct. Thou shalt have no other gods before me.

332

Q: If that is the case, then why do we need a guide at all?

ZT: Because at certain stages in your evolutionary path you need the help of intermediaries, be it guides on the higher planes of life or teachers on the physical plane of life. Because your God is a formless, nameless Energy, so, sometimes, you have a need to identify with a form and a name. Moreover, in an impure state you cannot know or look at God, just as you cannot look directly at the Sun, Its Spirit, with your physical eyes. You are not able to handle the full power and majesty of your God. You need an intermediary, which is its Spiritual Hierarchy.

Q: But if the whole purpose of life is to become one with the Source of all Life, then we don't want to get too hung up on any intermediary, do we?

ZT: I would agree, but let us keep things in perspective. God works through people and it is the aware soul who thanks God as well as the person that brings the help. You know that the human being that is helping you is not God, but is just an aspect of God. You don't, as you put it, get hung up on them, do you? So don't get hung up on a guide or a Master!

Q: So we should look on the guides and Masters in just the same way as we look on human beings.

ZT: Yes.

Q: They are an aspect of God, but they are not God.

ZT: Yes.

Q: Zen Tao, will you please give us a closing message for this last communication.

ZT: If I could wave a magic wand, like the good fairy in the story of Cinderella, and could give you all one gift, I would give you the ability to recognise that God is real and that physical life is unreal. You would then be able to correctly establish your priorities in life, for you would recognise that you really are God-beings, imbued with God-spirit, created for God-love, in a God-centred world. Anything or anybody which denies that reality is itself not real. So the purpose of your life should be to seek God in all things, to devote your life to God and, above all, to dedicate everything that you do to God. For, in truth, you are all working for God and everything that you do in thought, word and deed is noted, every sacrifice that you make is recorded.

333

Your world today is presenting you with the supreme test of body consciousness as it becomes more and more degraded. Your world today is the great seducer – both technologically, financially and, yes, even religiously. It is so easy to become distracted by the world and to forget that there is only one true God and that it is for you and you alone to use your God-given powers to become one with that great Being. If any technology, any ideology or any religion, as the Buddha said, cannot save you from death, cannot teach you how to avoid disease and physical decay, cannot tell you how to end sorrow, then reject it and concentrate all your energies on the search for Truth. That is your quest in life.

> As I am happy to serve you,
> so may you be happy to serve others.
> As I am happy to serve you, expecting no reward,
> so may you be happy to serve others, expecting no reward.
> May you grow to understand that the path to God lies in
> service and that as you uplift the least one of your brothers
> and sisters you are uplifting God Itself.
> To this end, may your motto each day always be
> 'Service with a smile'!

I thank you for your attention.

THE RAMALA CENTRE

at

CHALICE HILL HOUSE
DOD LANE
GLASTONBURY
SOMERSET BA6 8BZ
ENGLAND

FRIENDS OF RAMALA

If you have found the Ramala Teachings to be meaningful and would like to find out more about the Ramala Centre and its courses and activities, then why not become a Friend of Ramala?

The Friends of Ramala was formed in 1986 in order to facilitate a greater exchange of energy between the Ramala Centre and those who support the work of the Centre. In return for an annual subscription you will be registered as a Friend of Ramala. As a Friend you will be entitled to receive the Ramala Newsletters that are published twice a year, one at the end of July, one at the end of January. You will also be entitled to a 10% discount on all purchases of books, video and audio tape cassettes from the Centre.

In the Newsletters you will find a selection of the latest Ramala teachings, together with reports of all the Centre's activities during the past six months and details of future courses and events, including forthcoming Ramala presentations both at home and abroad. The Newsletters also include interviews with significant spiritual teachers who have passed through the Centre in recent months and reports on conferences or workshops attended by members of the Centre. Finally, in the Newsletters you will find up to date lists of the Ramala Teachings that are available on video and audio cassette.

So why not be a Friend by becoming a Friend and help to support the continuing work of Ramala?

RAMALA PUBLICATIONS
(As of July 1991)

THE REVELATION OF RAMALA –
Published in English, Dutch, German, Spanish and Danish.

THE WISDOM OF RAMALA –
Published in English, Dutch and German.

THE VISION OF RAMALA –
Published in English.